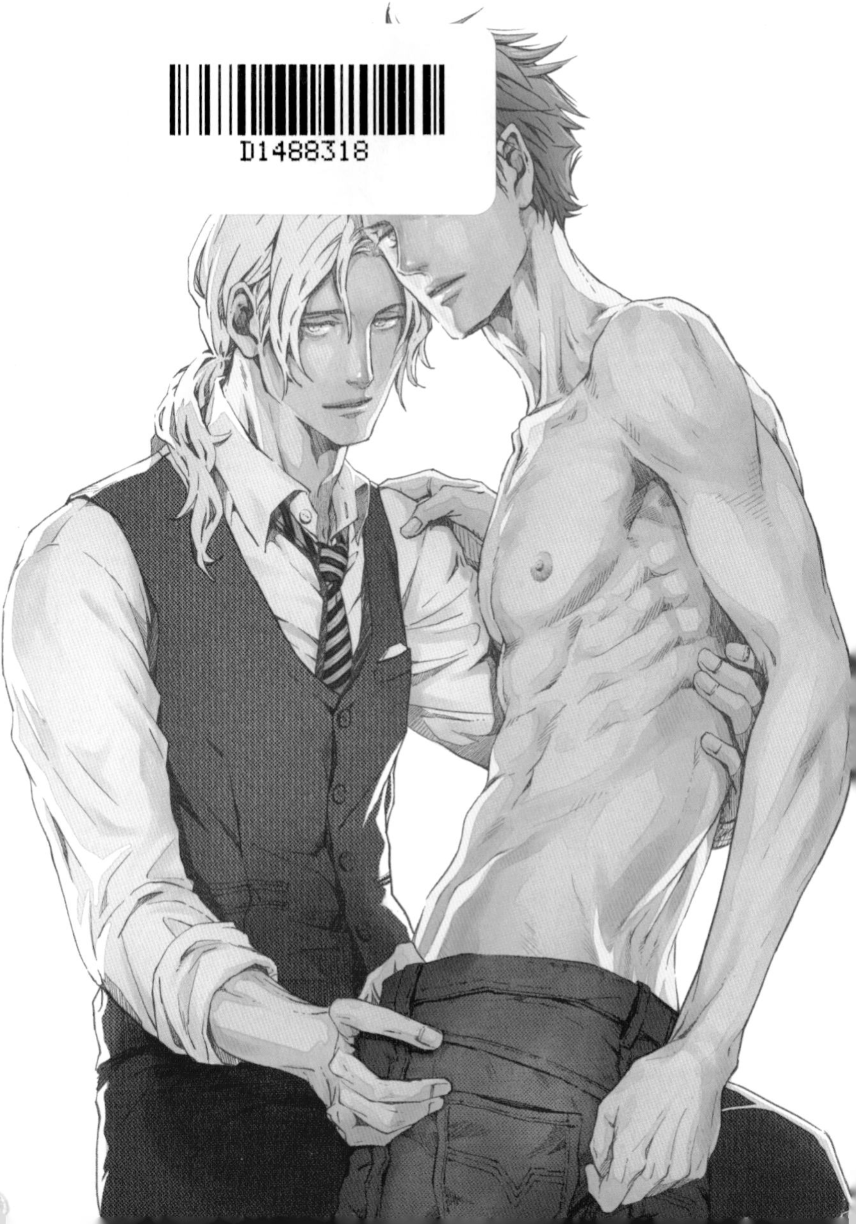

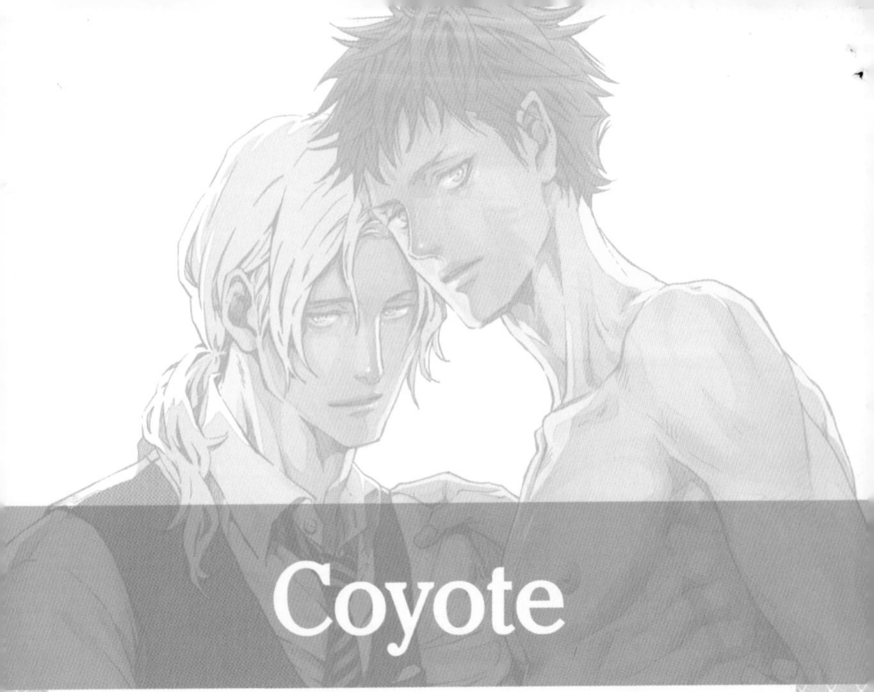

Coyote

Story and Art by RANMARU ZARIYA volume 1

CONTENTS

SUBLIME

SuBLime Manga Edition

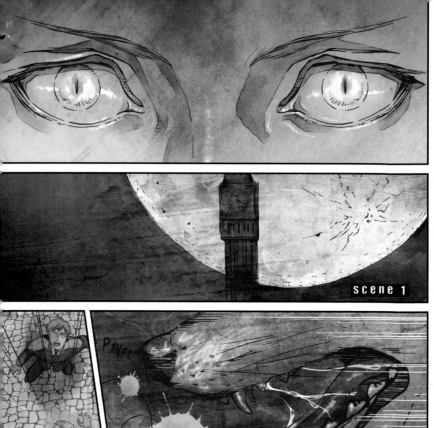

SCENE 1

PANT!

PANT!

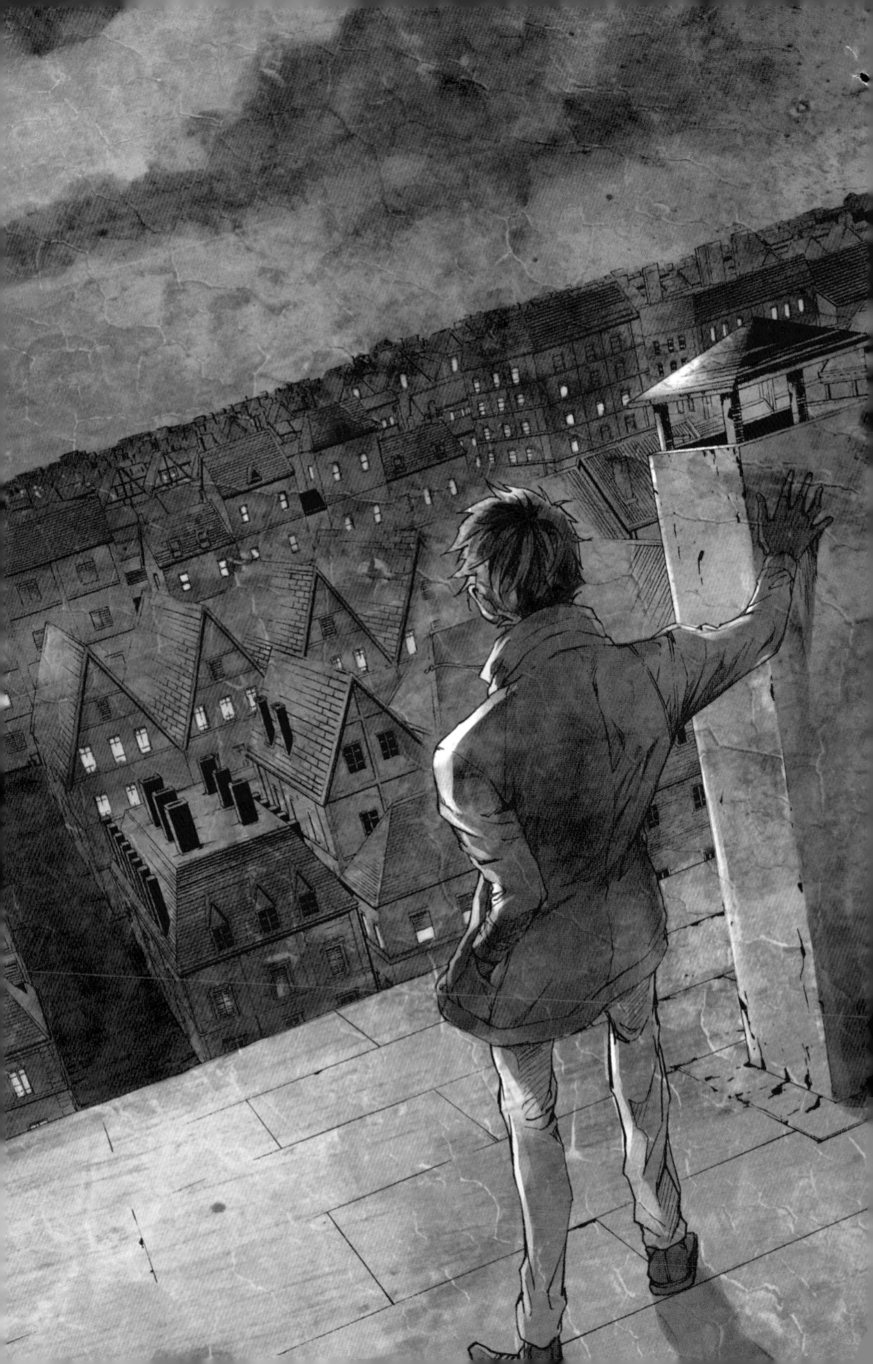

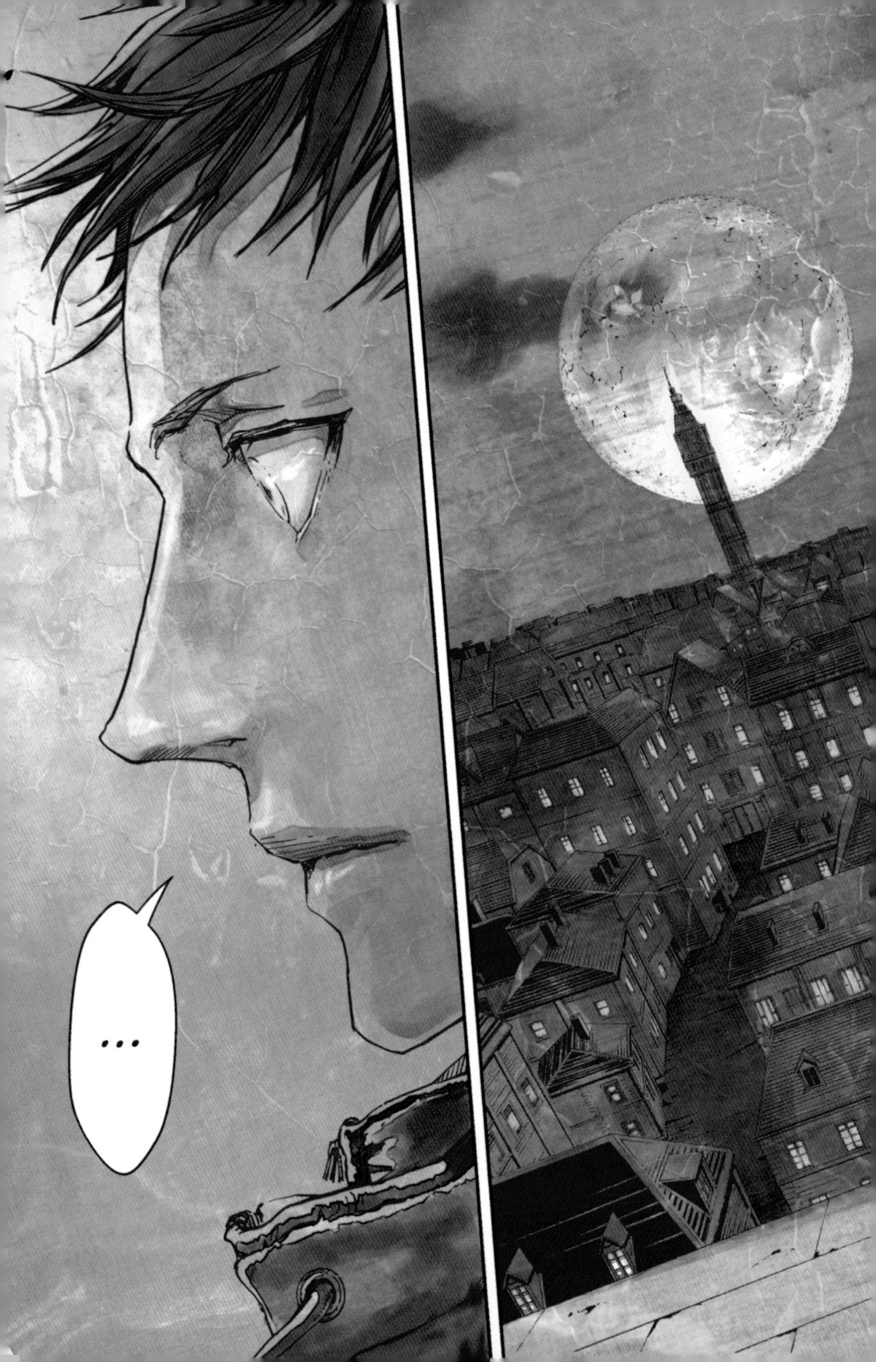
...

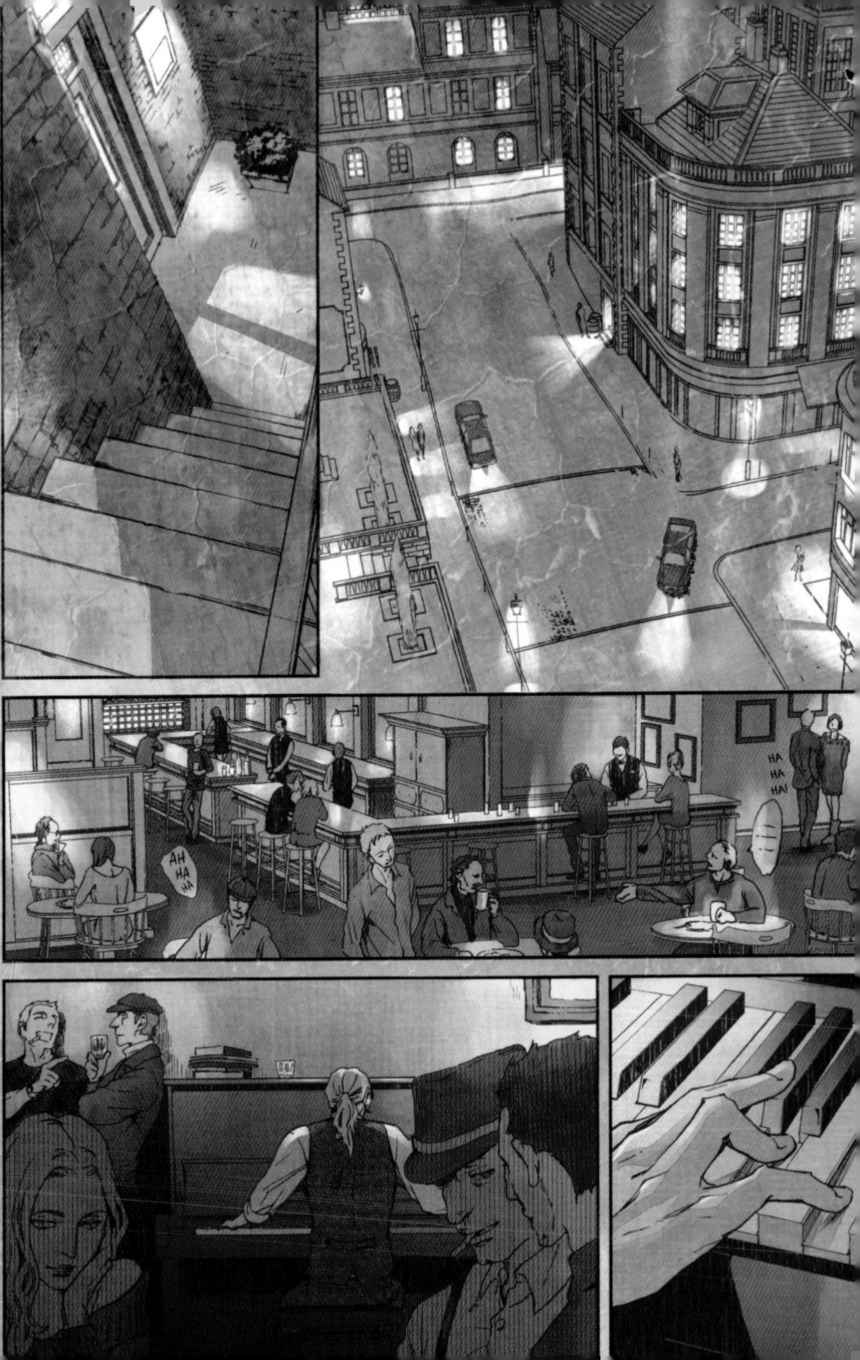
HA HA HA!
AH HA HA

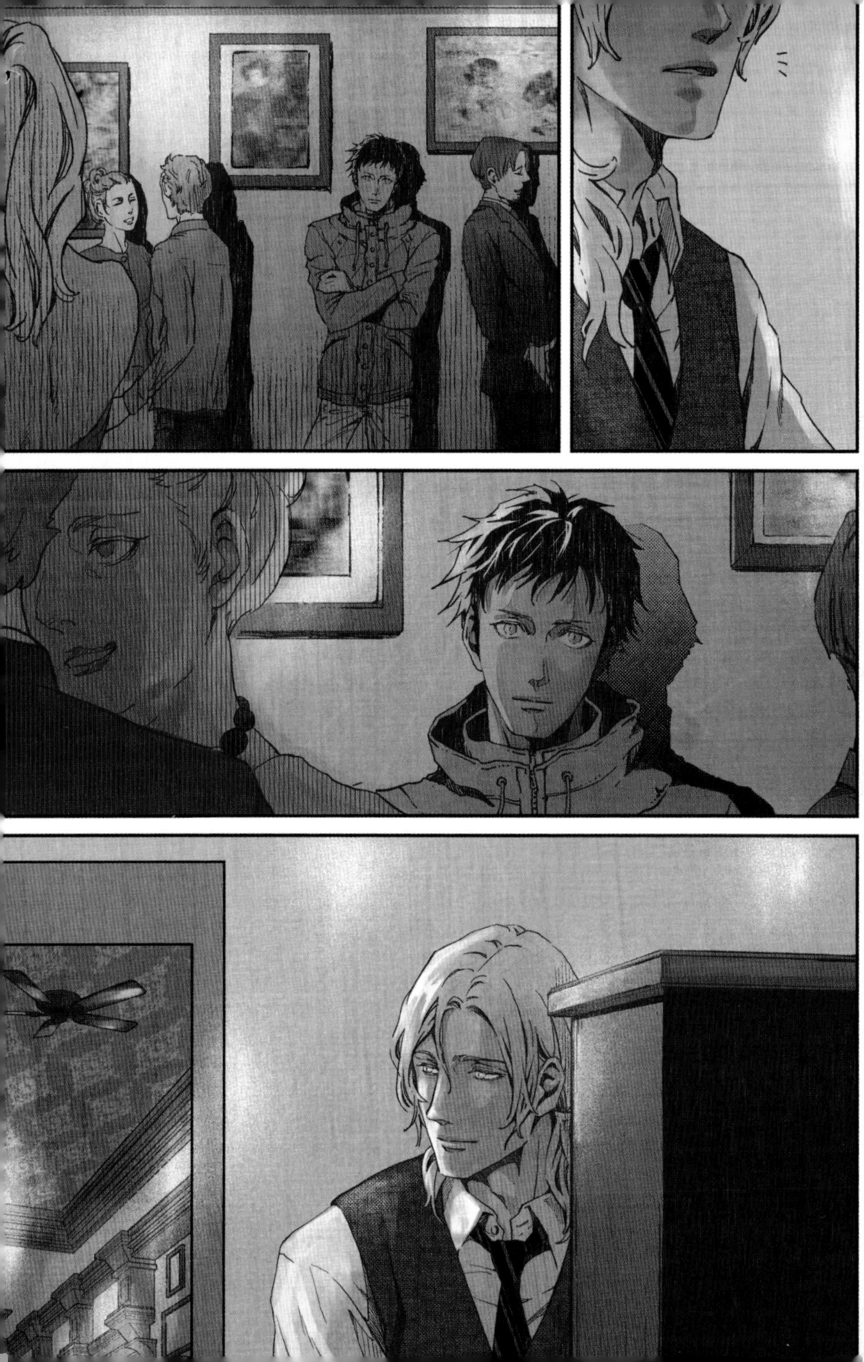

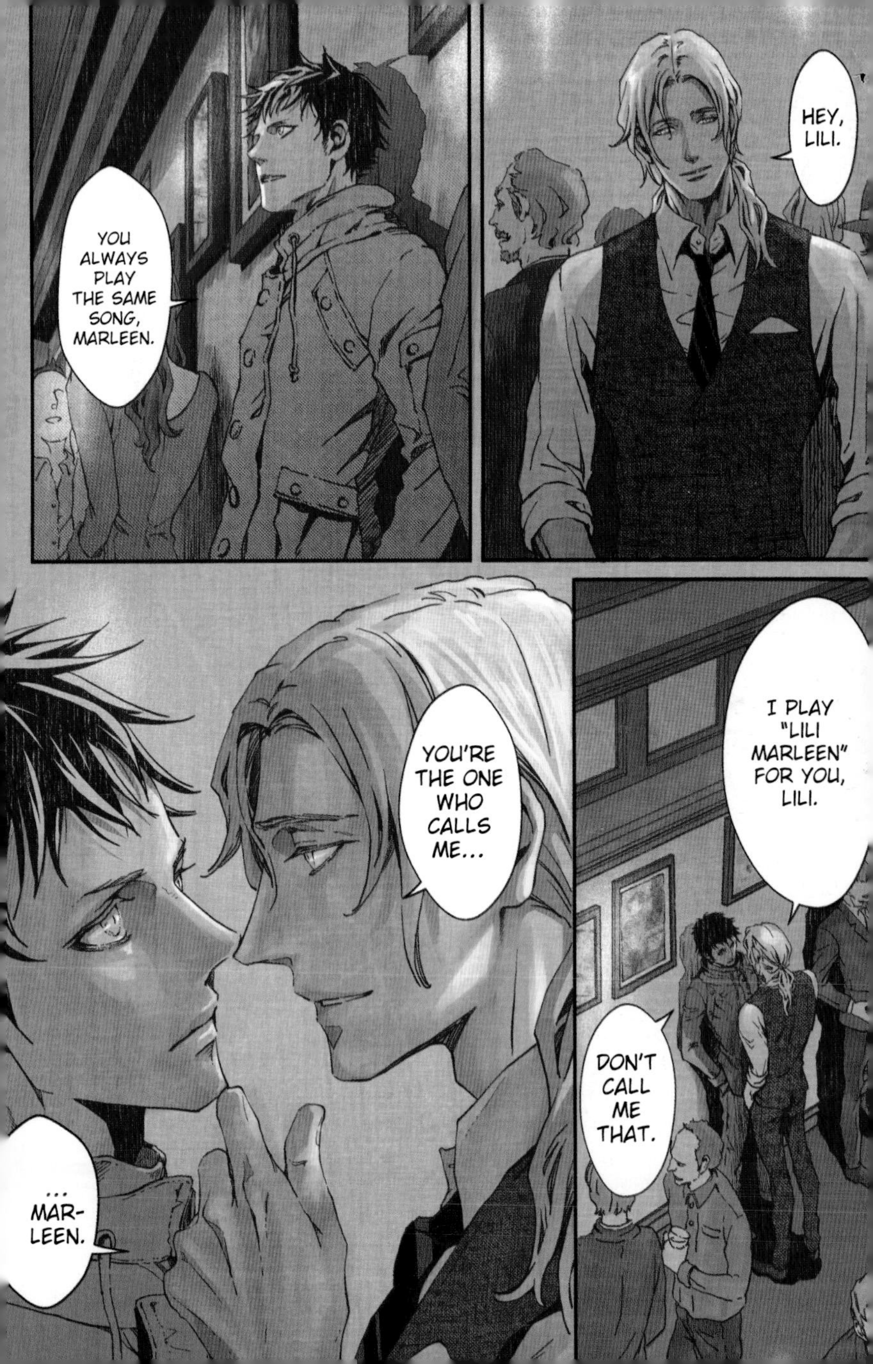
HEY, LILI.
YOU ALWAYS PLAY THE SAME SONG, MARLEEN.
I PLAY "LILI MARLEEN" FOR YOU, LILI.
DON'T CALL ME THAT.
YOU'RE THE ONE WHO CALLS ME...
... MAR-LEEN.

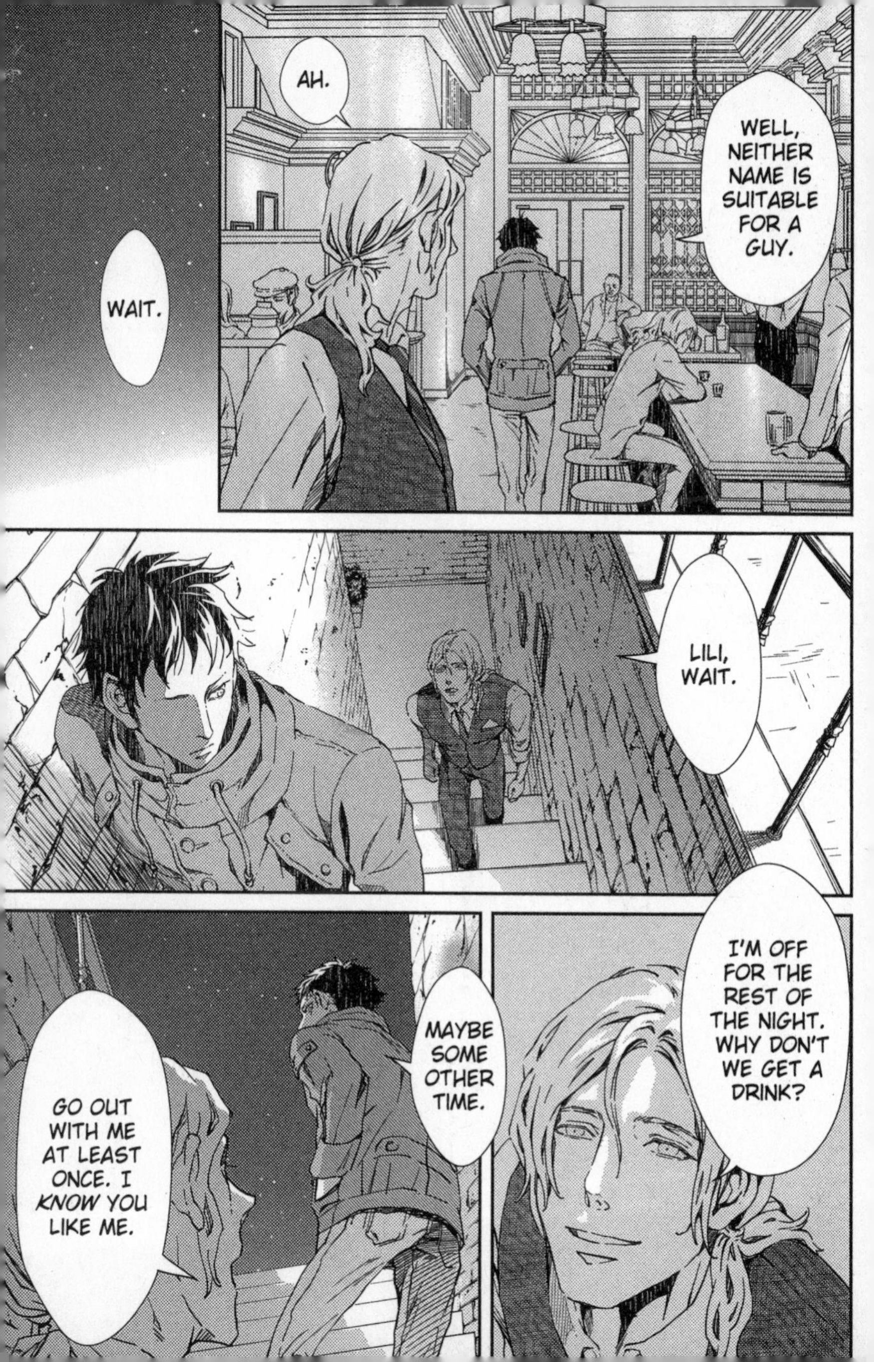
WELL, NEITHER NAME IS SUITABLE FOR A GUY.
AH.
WAIT.
LILI, WAIT.
I'M OFF FOR THE REST OF THE NIGHT. WHY DON'T WE GET A DRINK?
MAYBE SOME OTHER TIME.
GO OUT WITH ME AT LEAST ONCE. I *KNOW* YOU LIKE ME.

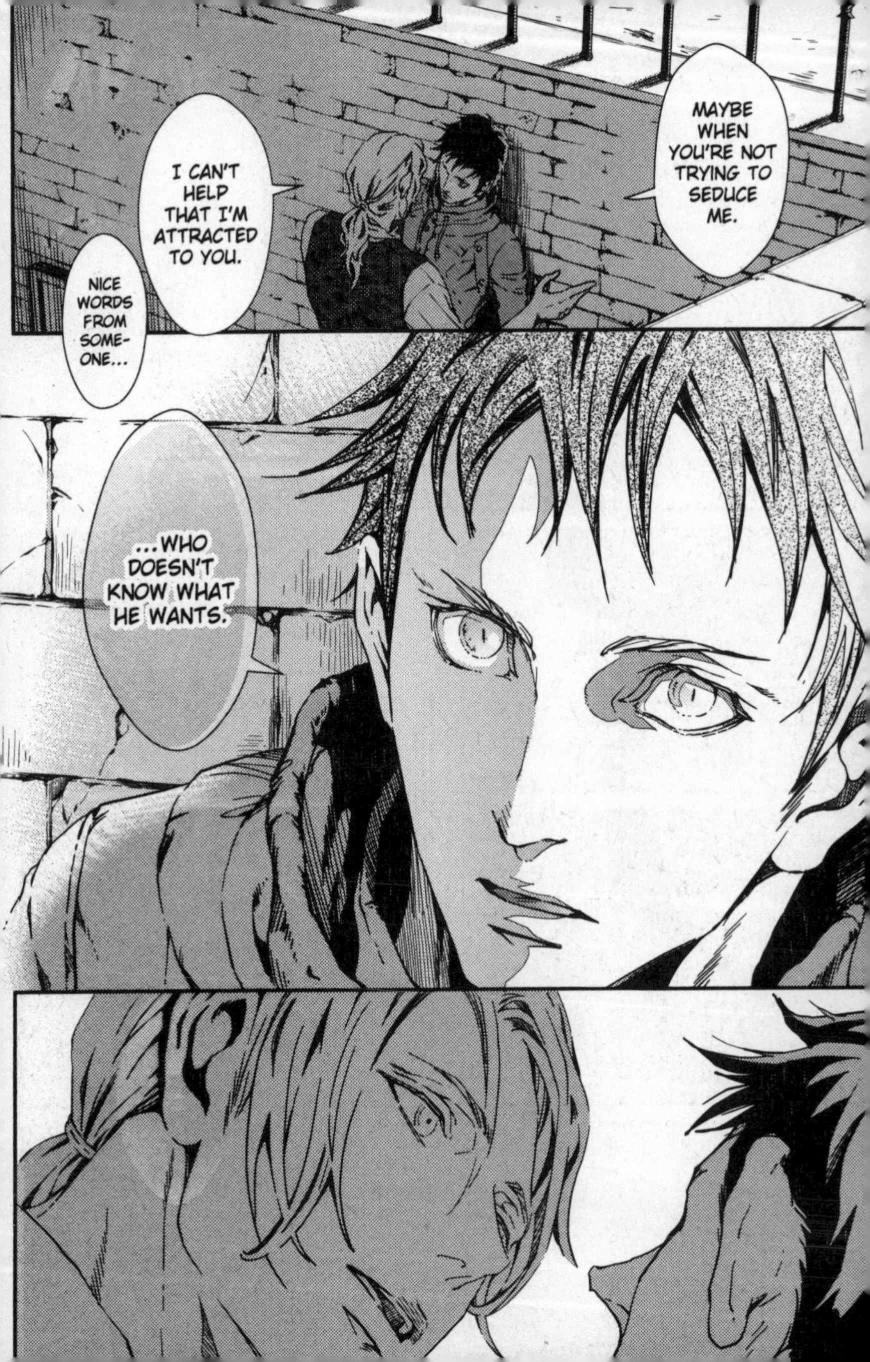
MAYBE WHEN YOU'RE NOT TRYING TO SEDUCE ME.
I CAN'T HELP THAT I'M ATTRACTED TO YOU.
NICE WORDS FROM SOME-ONE...
...WHO DOESN'T KNOW WHAT HE WANTS.

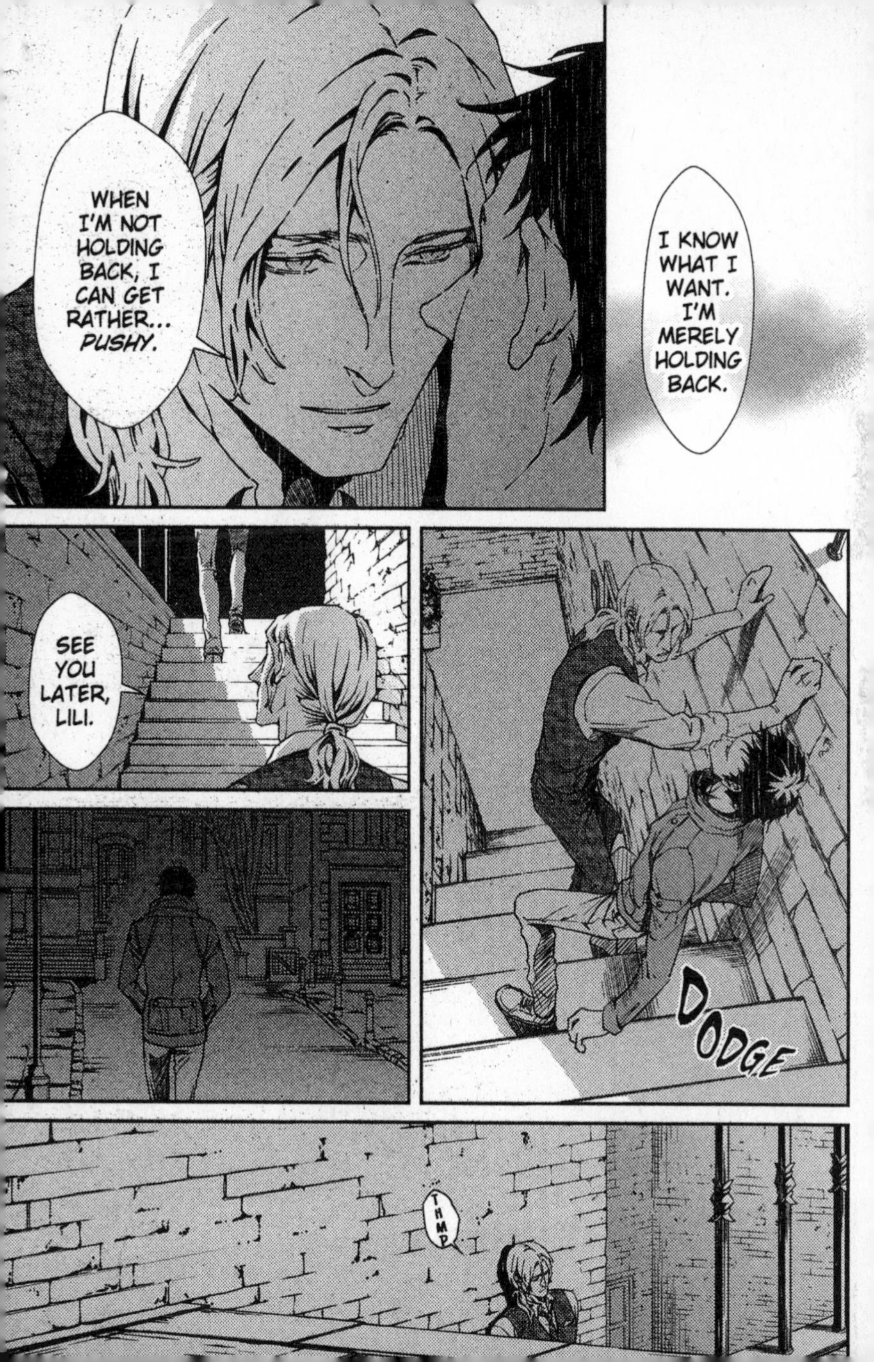
I KNOW WHAT I WANT. I'M MERELY HOLDING BACK.
WHEN I'M NOT HOLDING BACK, I CAN GET RATHER... *PUSHY*.
DODGE
SEE YOU LATER, LILI.
THMP

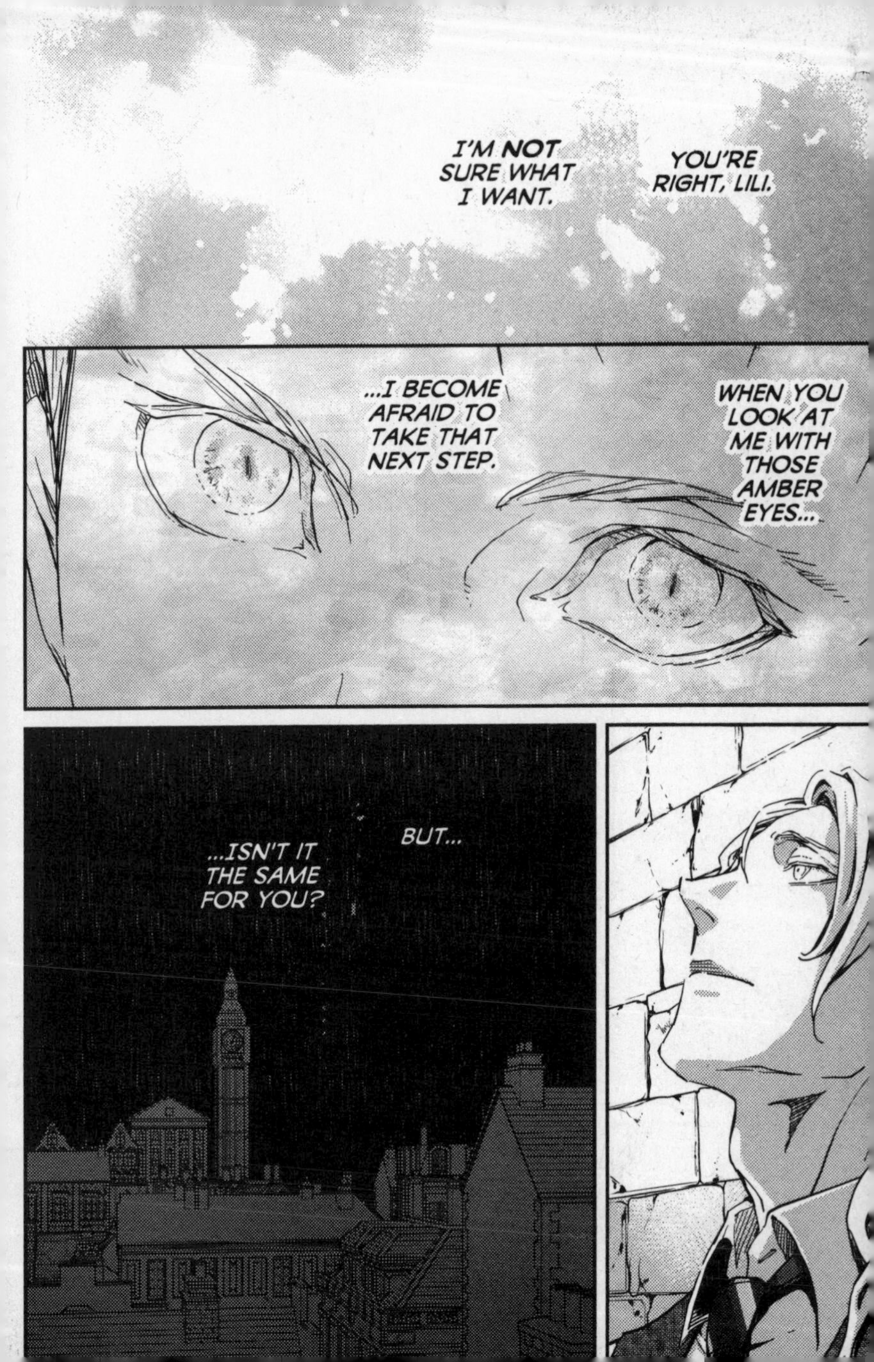
YOU'RE RIGHT, LILI.
I'M **NOT** SURE WHAT I WANT.
WHEN YOU LOOK AT ME WITH THOSE AMBER EYES...
...I BECOME AFRAID TO TAKE THAT NEXT STEP.
BUT...
...ISN'T IT THE SAME FOR YOU?

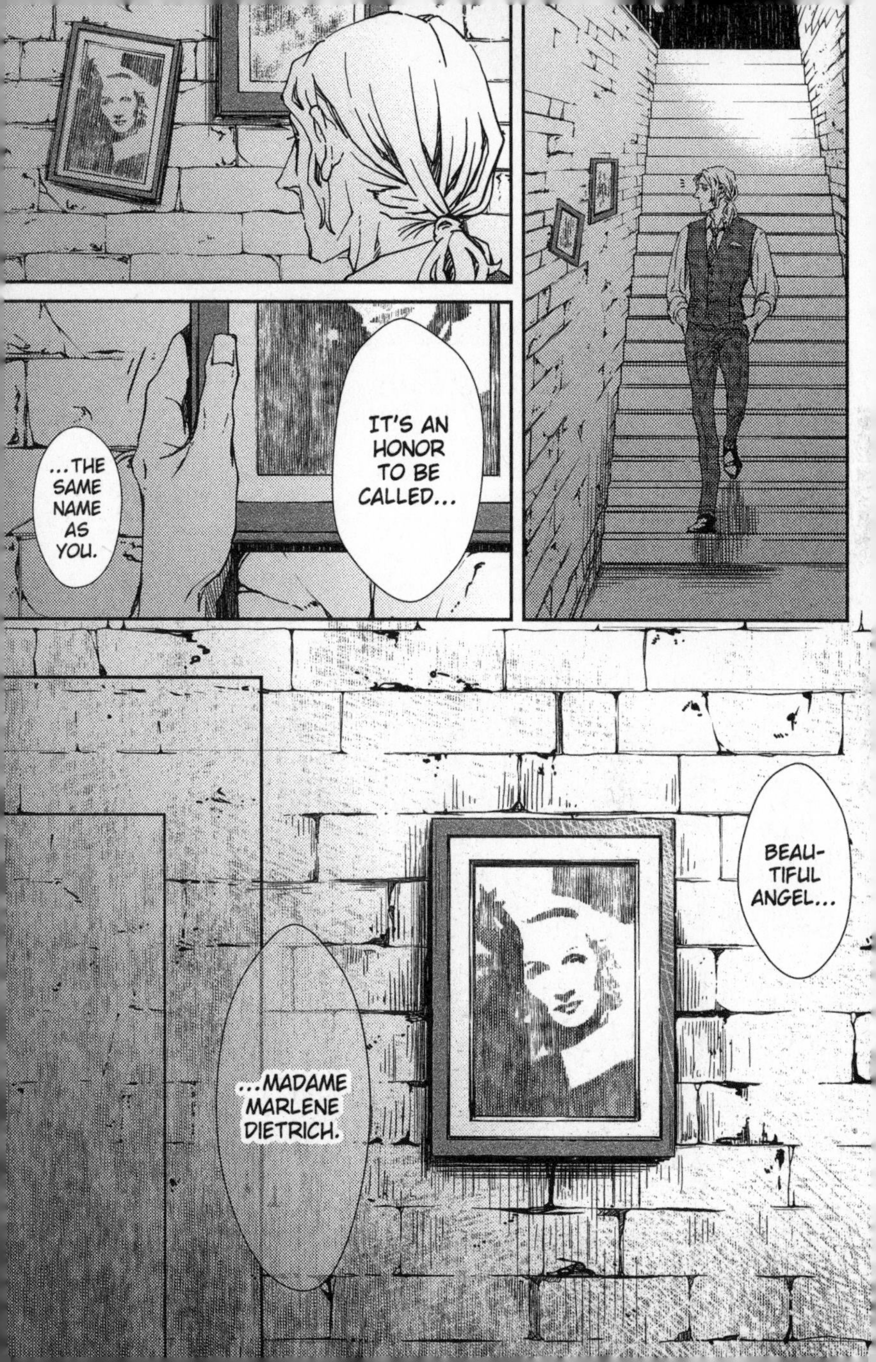
IT'S AN HONOR TO BE CALLED...
...THE SAME NAME AS YOU.
BEAU-TIFUL ANGEL...
...MADAME MARLENE DIETRICH.

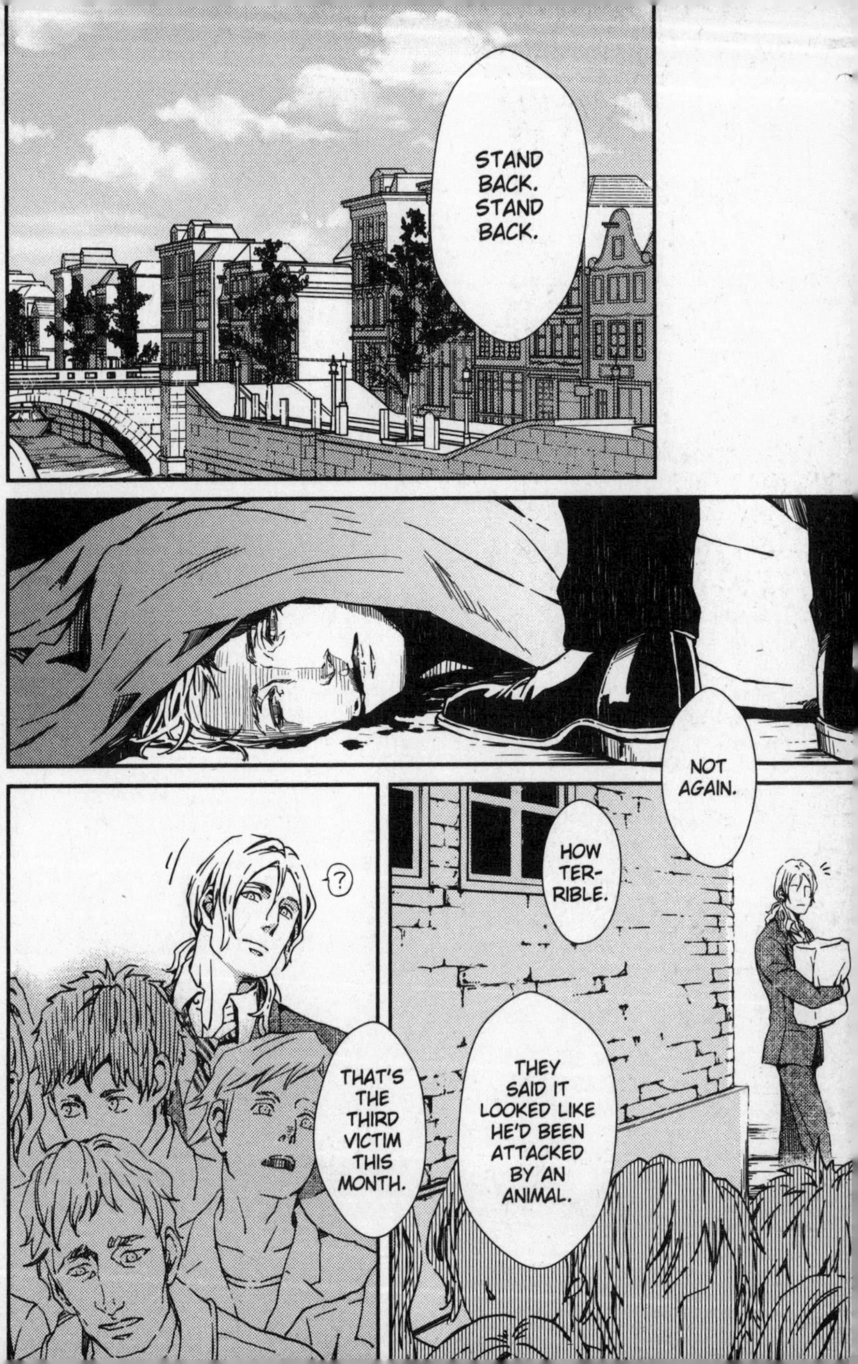
STAND BACK. STAND BACK.
NOT AGAIN.
HOW TER-RIBLE.
THEY SAID IT LOOKED LIKE HE'D BEEN ATTACKED BY AN ANIMAL.
THAT'S THE THIRD VICTIM THIS MONTH.
?

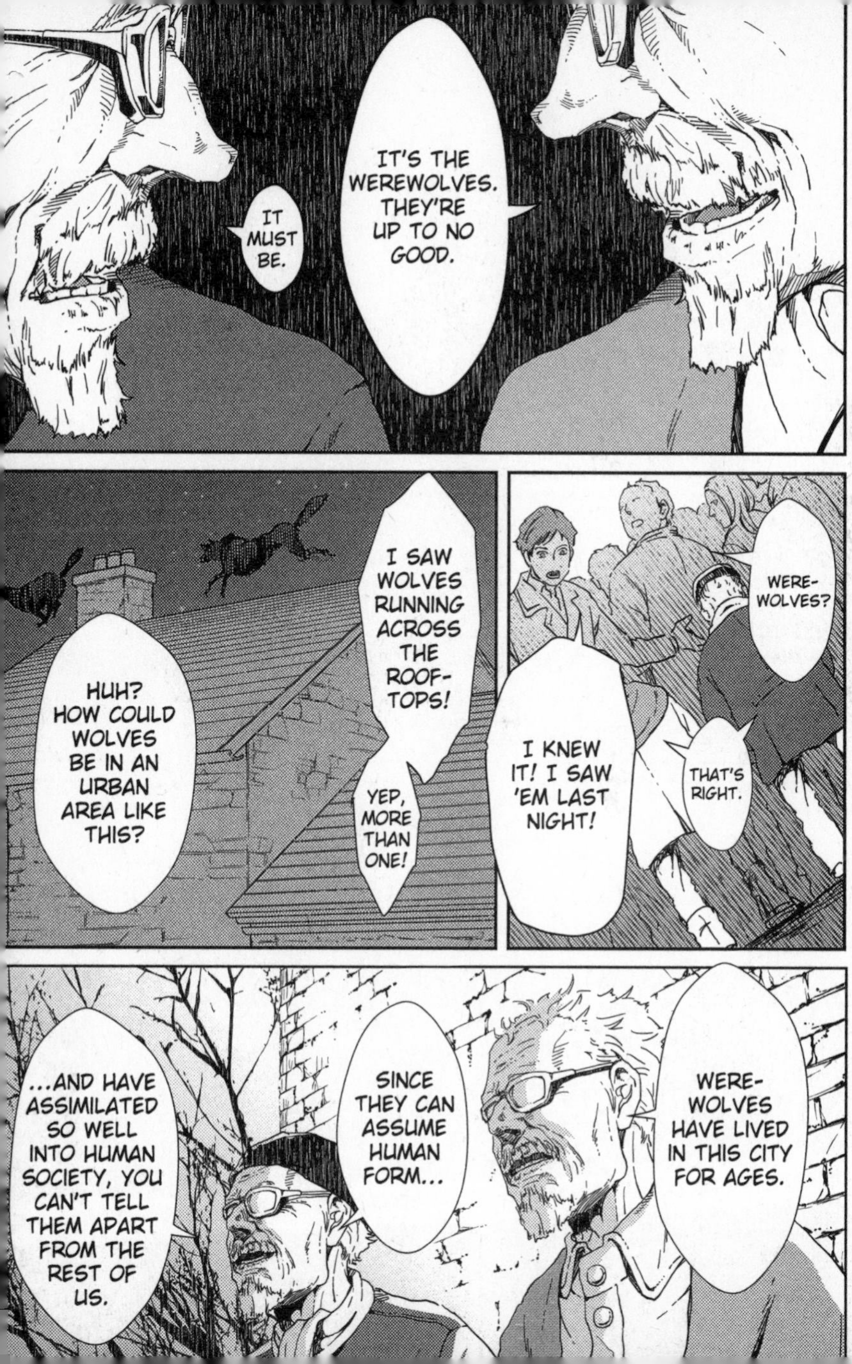
IT'S THE WEREWOLVES. THEY'RE UP TO NO GOOD.
IT MUST BE.
WERE-WOLVES?
THAT'S RIGHT.
I KNEW IT! I SAW 'EM LAST NIGHT!
I SAW WOLVES RUNNING ACROSS THE ROOF-TOPS!
YEP, MORE THAN ONE!
HUH? HOW COULD WOLVES BE IN AN URBAN AREA LIKE THIS?
WERE-WOLVES HAVE LIVED IN THIS CITY FOR AGES.
SINCE THEY CAN ASSUME HUMAN FORM...
...AND HAVE ASSIMILATED SO WELL INTO HUMAN SOCIETY, YOU CAN'T TELL THEM APART FROM THE REST OF US.

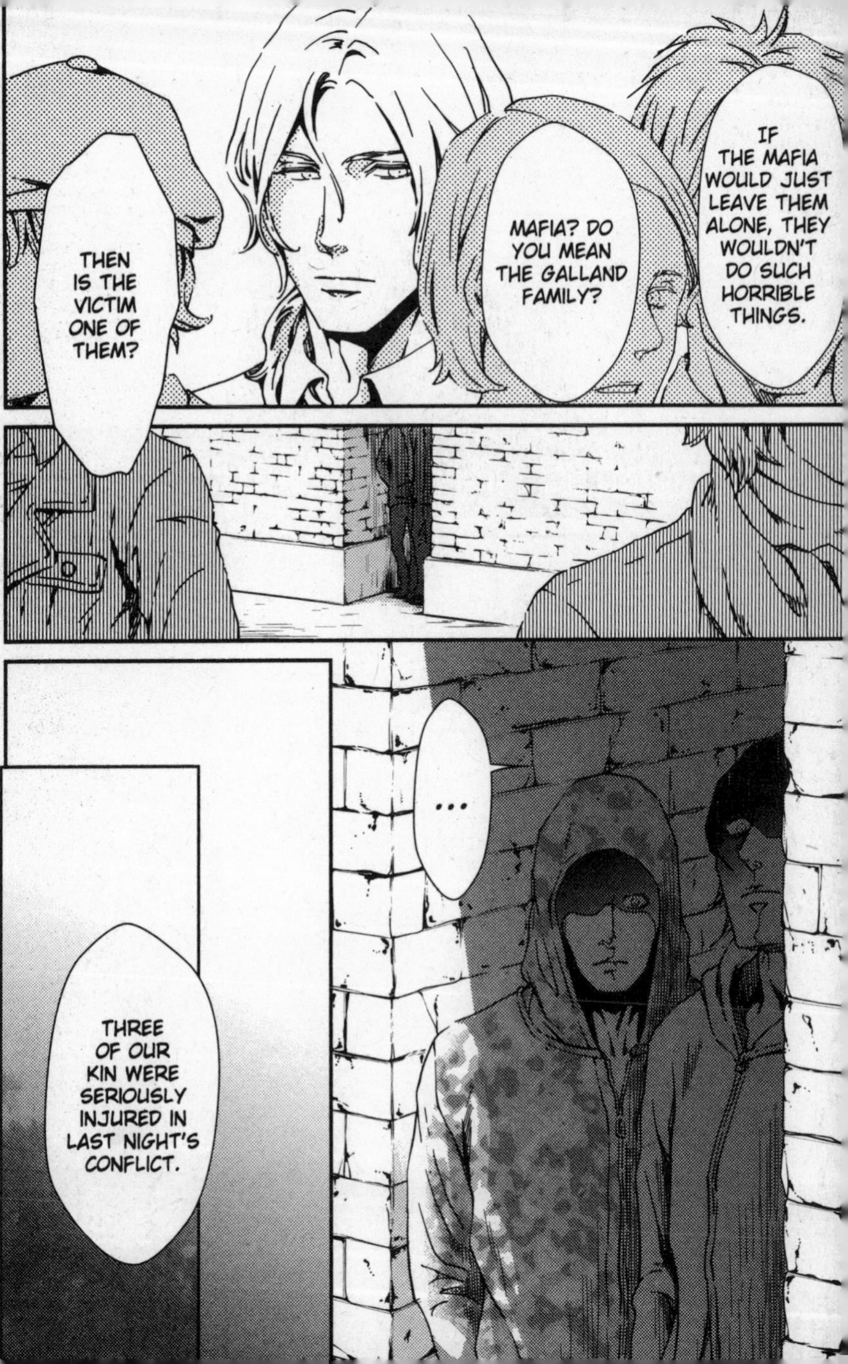
IF THE MAFIA WOULD JUST LEAVE THEM ALONE, THEY WOULDN'T DO SUCH HORRIBLE THINGS.
MAFIA? DO YOU MEAN THE GALLAND FAMILY?
THEN IS THE VICTIM ONE OF THEM?
...
THREE OF OUR KIN WERE SERIOUSLY INJURED IN LAST NIGHT'S CONFLICT.

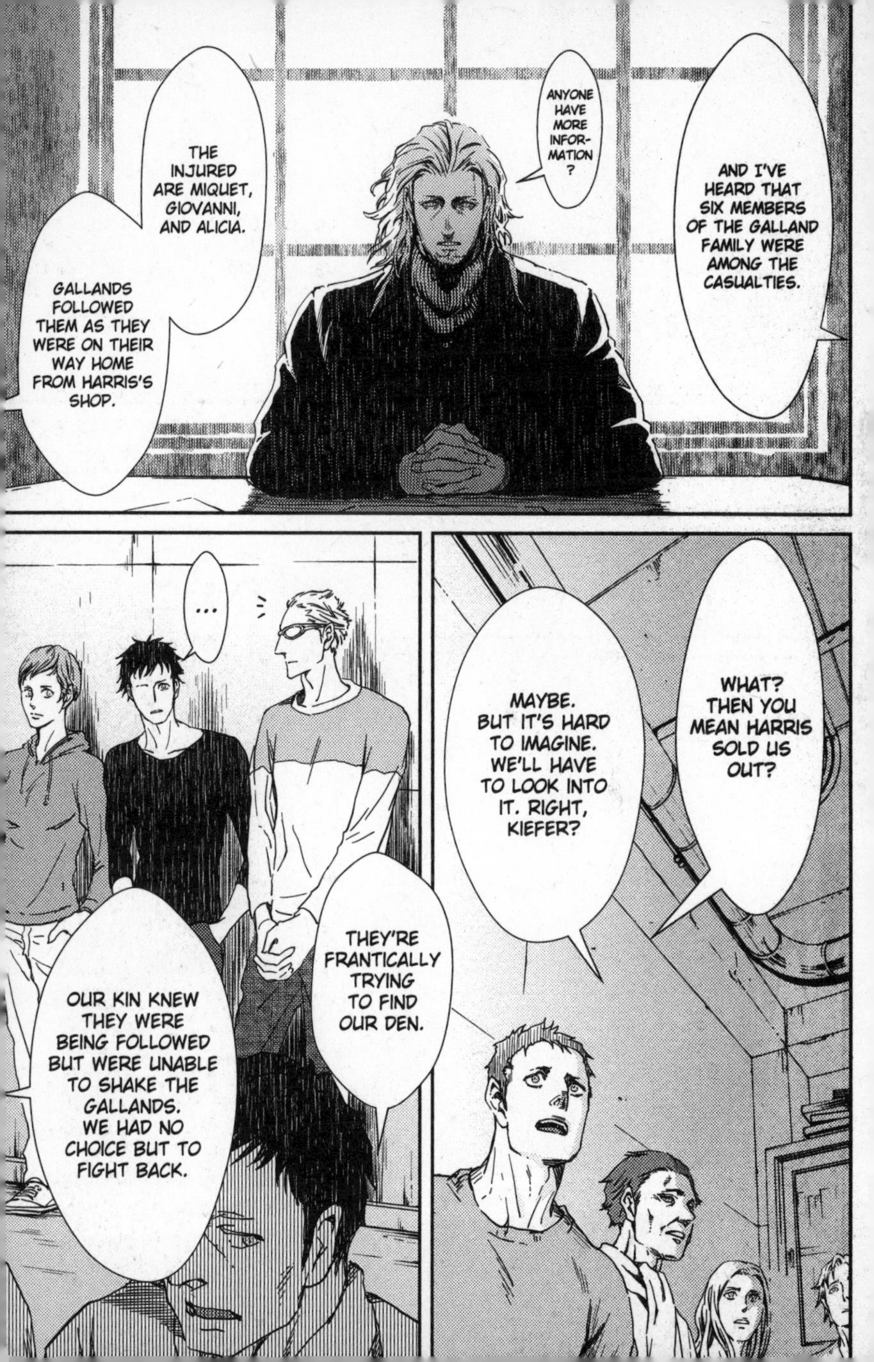
AND I'VE HEARD THAT SIX MEMBERS OF THE GALLAND FAMILY WERE AMONG THE CASUALTIES.
ANYONE HAVE MORE INFOR-MATION ?
THE INJURED ARE MIQUET, GIOVANNI, AND ALICIA.
GALLANDS FOLLOWED THEM AS THEY WERE ON THEIR WAY HOME FROM HARRIS'S SHOP.
WHAT? THEN YOU MEAN HARRIS SOLD US OUT?
MAYBE. BUT IT'S HARD TO IMAGINE. WE'LL HAVE TO LOOK INTO IT. RIGHT, KIEFER?
...
THEY'RE FRANTICALLY TRYING TO FIND OUR DEN.
OUR KIN KNEW THEY WERE BEING FOLLOWED BUT WERE UNABLE TO SHAKE THE GALLANDS. WE HAD NO CHOICE BUT TO FIGHT BACK.

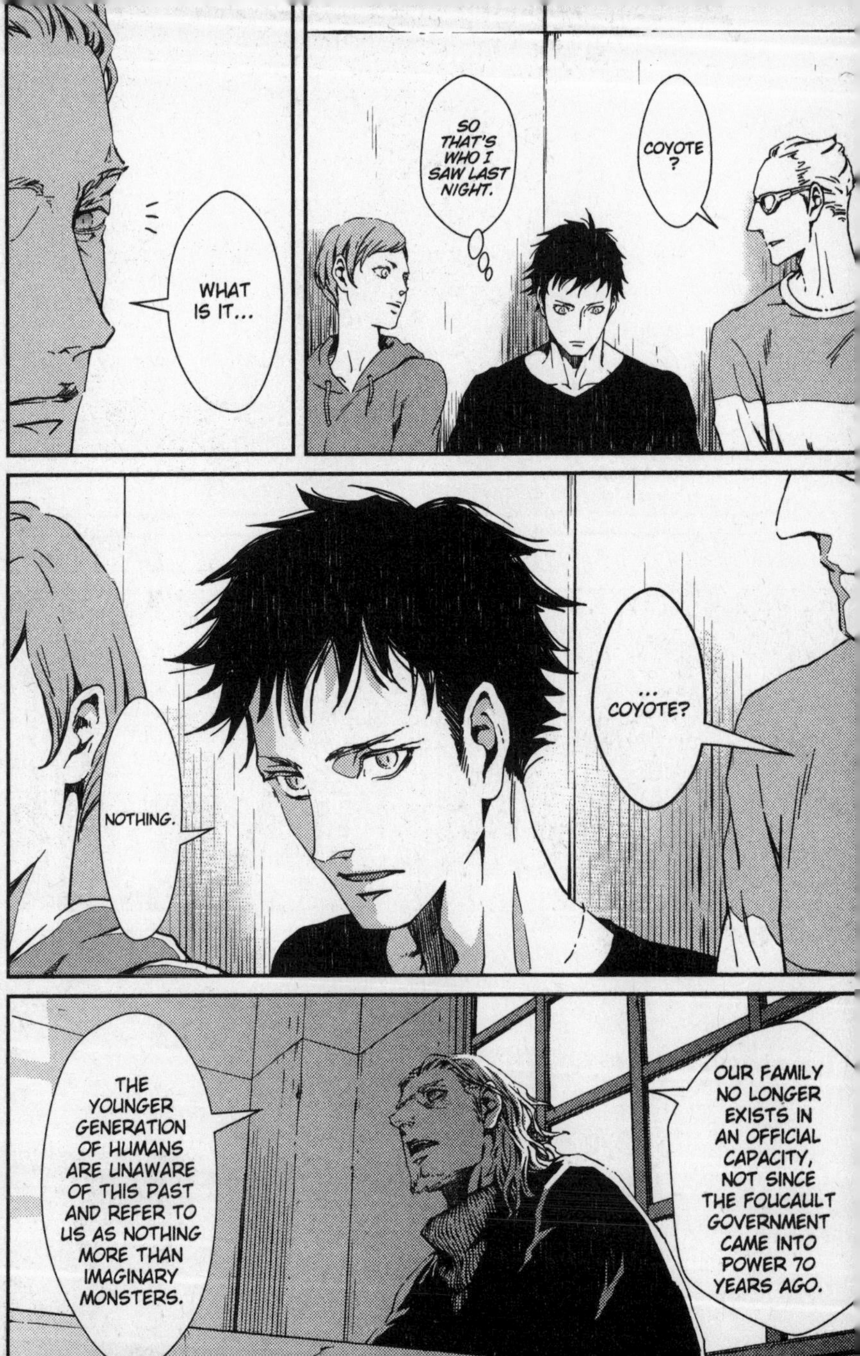
COYOTE?
SO THAT'S WHO I SAW LAST NIGHT.
WHAT IS IT...
...COYOTE?
NOTHING.
OUR FAMILY NO LONGER EXISTS IN AN OFFICIAL CAPACITY, NOT SINCE THE FOUCAULT GOVERNMENT CAME INTO POWER 70 YEARS AGO.
THE YOUNGER GENERATION OF HUMANS ARE UNAWARE OF THIS PAST AND REFER TO US AS NOTHING MORE THAN IMAGINARY MONSTERS.

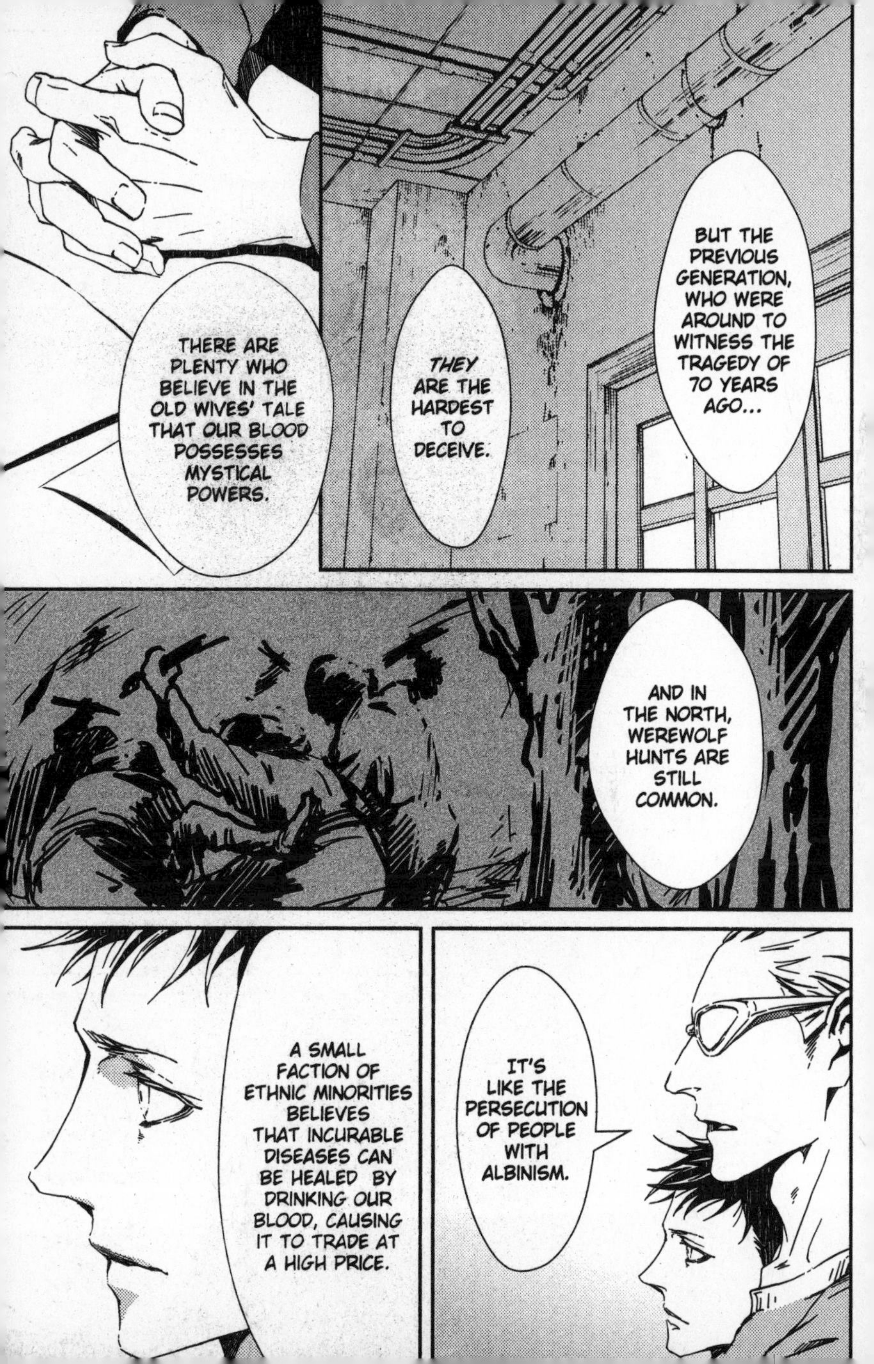
BUT THE PREVIOUS GENERATION, WHO WERE AROUND TO WITNESS THE TRAGEDY OF 70 YEARS AGO...
THEY ARE THE HARDEST TO DECEIVE.
THERE ARE PLENTY WHO BELIEVE IN THE OLD WIVES' TALE THAT OUR BLOOD POSSESSES MYSTICAL POWERS.
AND IN THE NORTH, WEREWOLF HUNTS ARE STILL COMMON.
IT'S LIKE THE PERSECUTION OF PEOPLE WITH ALBINISM.
A SMALL FACTION OF ETHNIC MINORITIES BELIEVES THAT INCURABLE DISEASES CAN BE HEALED BY DRINKING OUR BLOOD, CAUSING IT TO TRADE AT A HIGH PRICE.

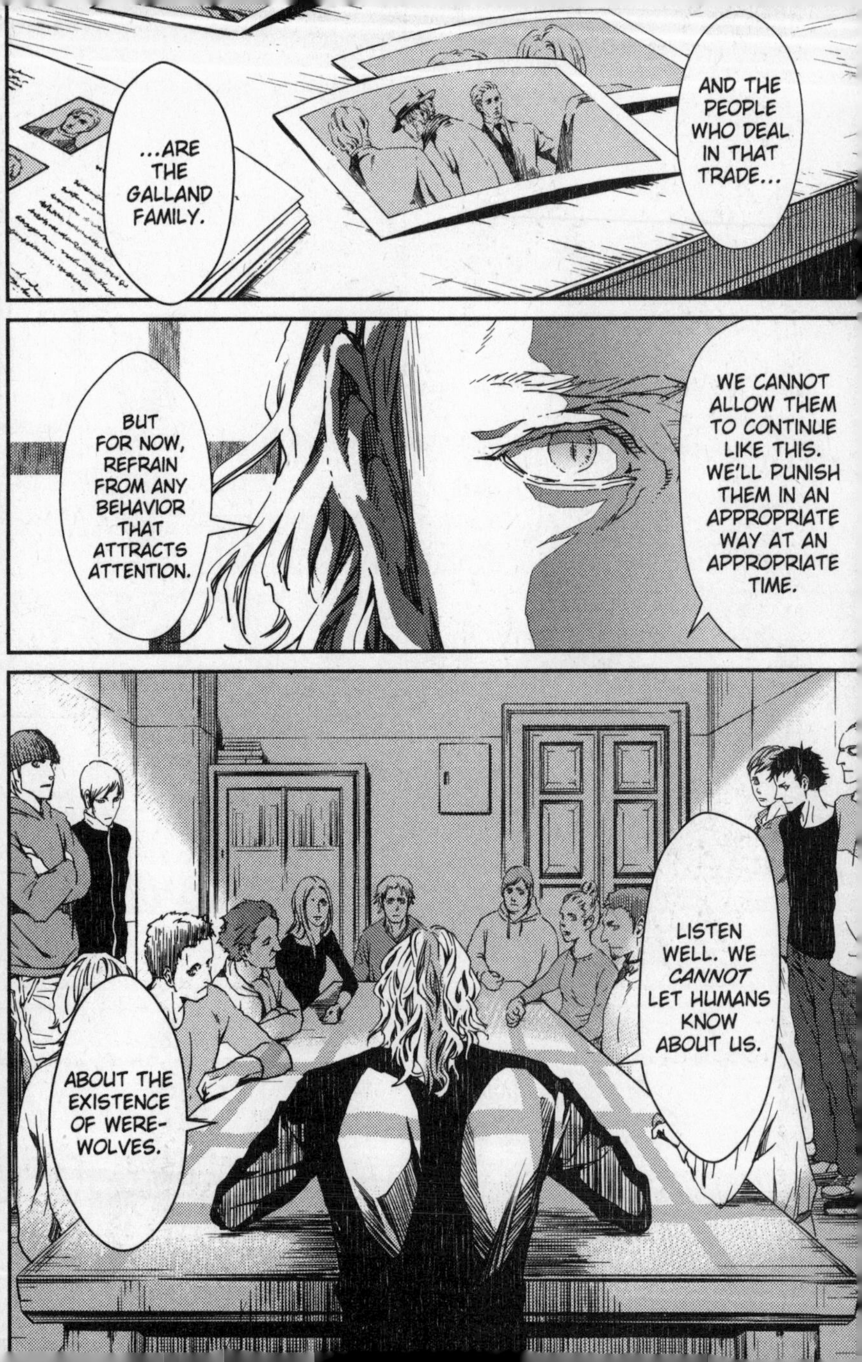
AND THE PEOPLE WHO DEAL IN THAT TRADE...
...ARE THE GALLAND FAMILY.
WE CANNOT ALLOW THEM TO CONTINUE LIKE THIS. WE'LL PUNISH THEM IN AN APPROPRIATE WAY AT AN APPROPRIATE TIME.
BUT FOR NOW, REFRAIN FROM ANY BEHAVIOR THAT ATTRACTS ATTENTION.
LISTEN WELL. WE *CANNOT* LET HUMANS KNOW ABOUT US.
ABOUT THE EXISTENCE OF WERE-WOLVES.

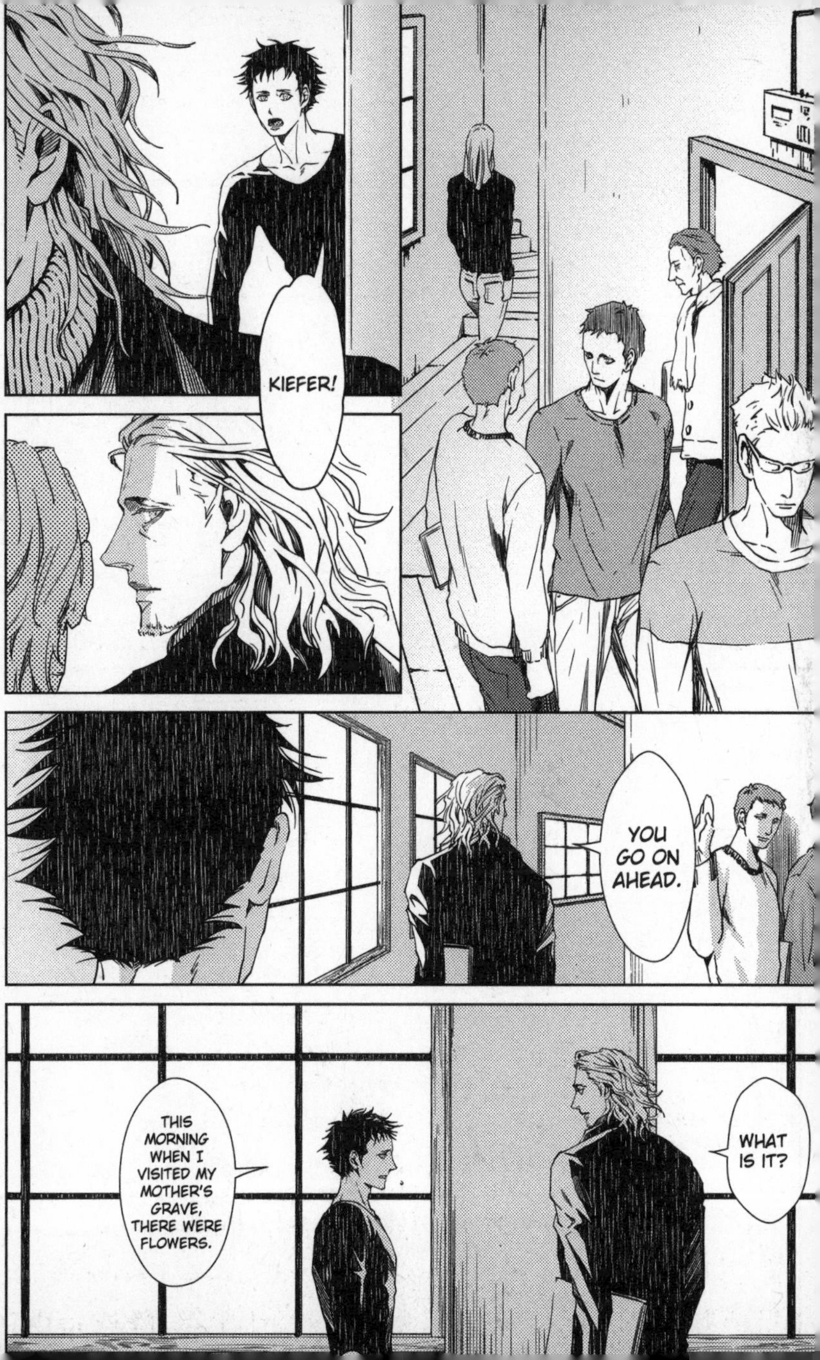
KIEFER!
YOU GO ON AHEAD.
WHAT IS IT?
THIS MORNING WHEN I VISITED MY MOTHER'S GRAVE, THERE WERE FLOWERS.

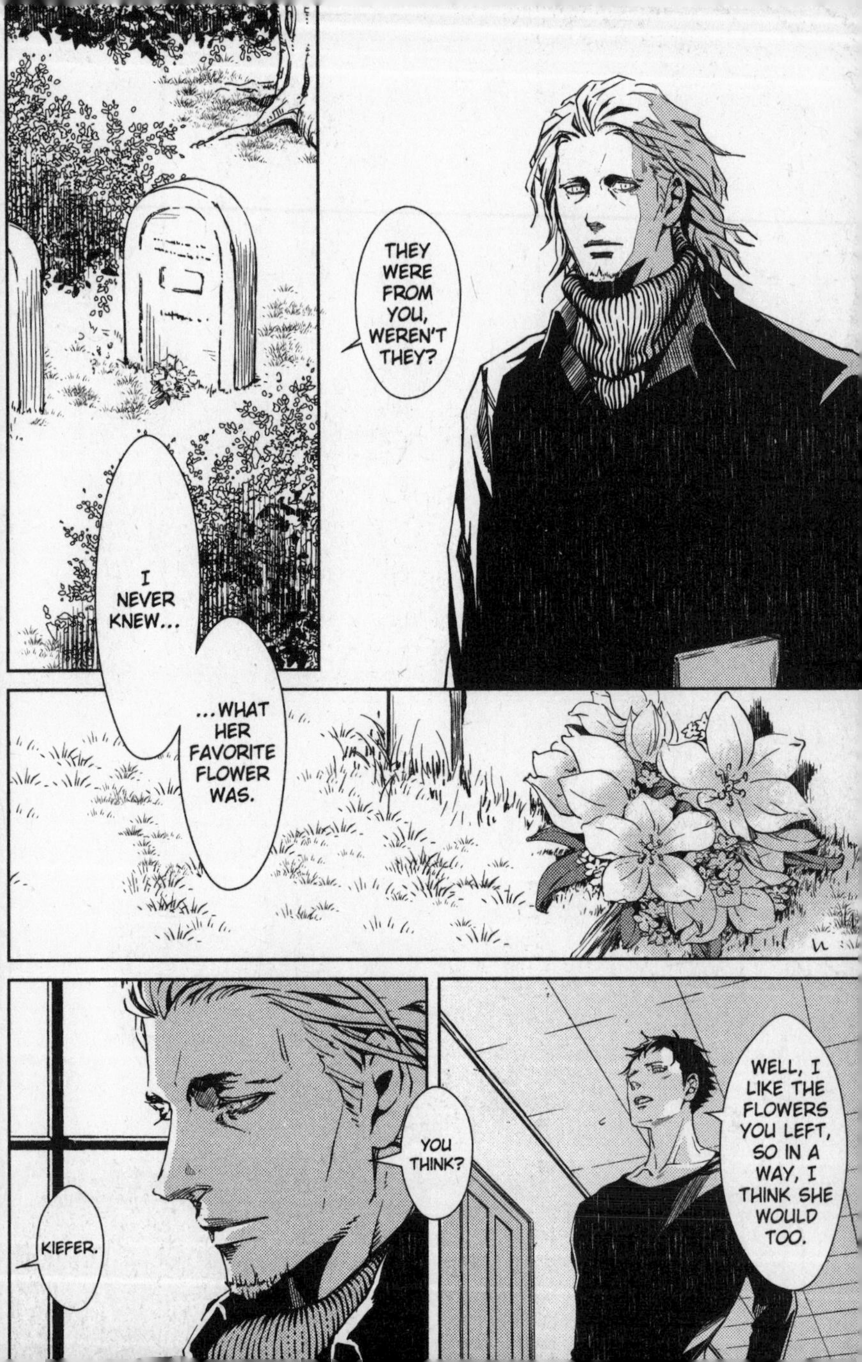
THEY WERE FROM YOU, WEREN'T THEY?
I NEVER KNEW...
...WHAT HER FAVORITE FLOWER WAS.
WELL, I LIKE THE FLOWERS YOU LEFT, SO IN A WAY, I THINK SHE WOULD TOO.
YOU THINK?
KIEFER.

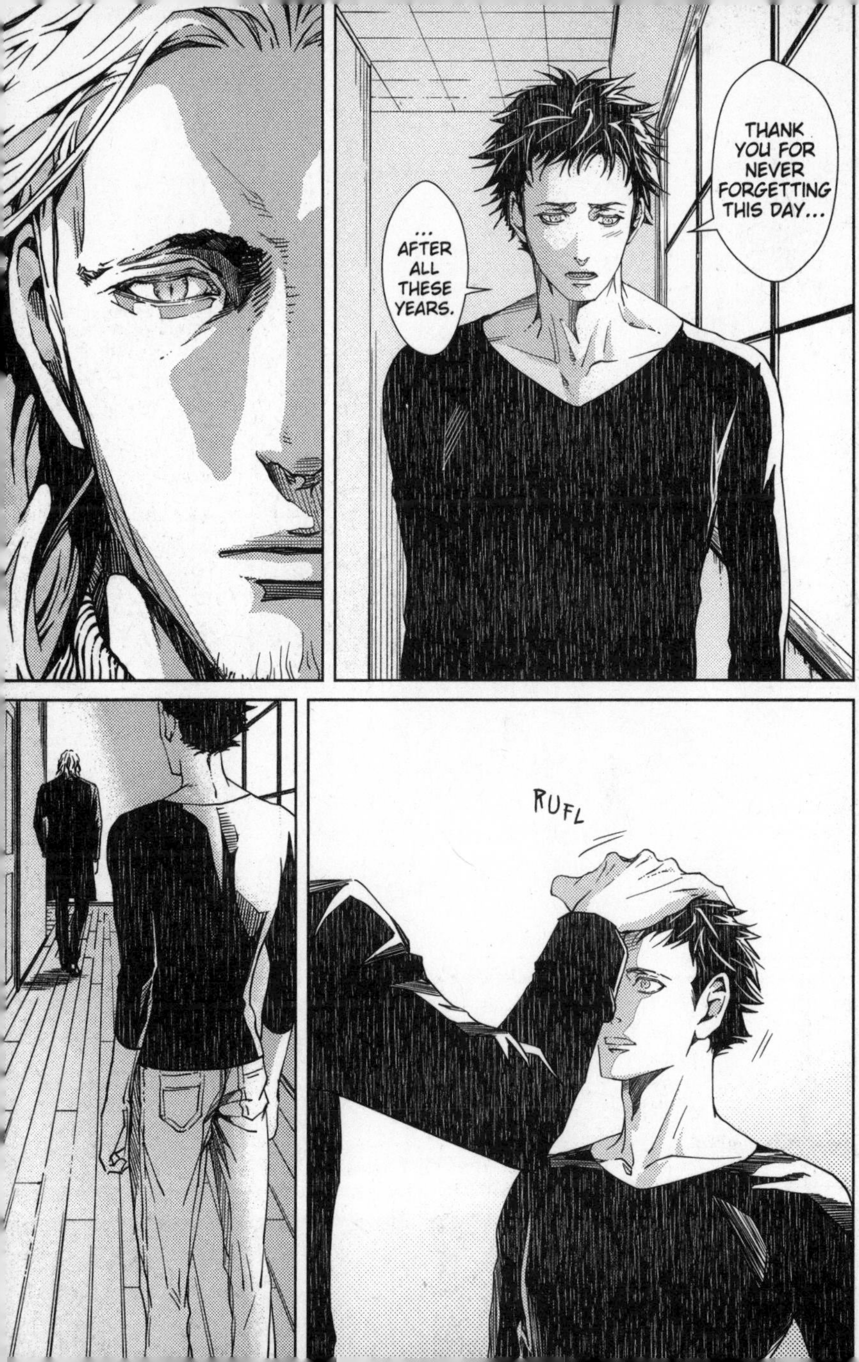
THANK YOU FOR NEVER FORGETTING THIS DAY...
...AFTER ALL THESE YEARS.
RUFL

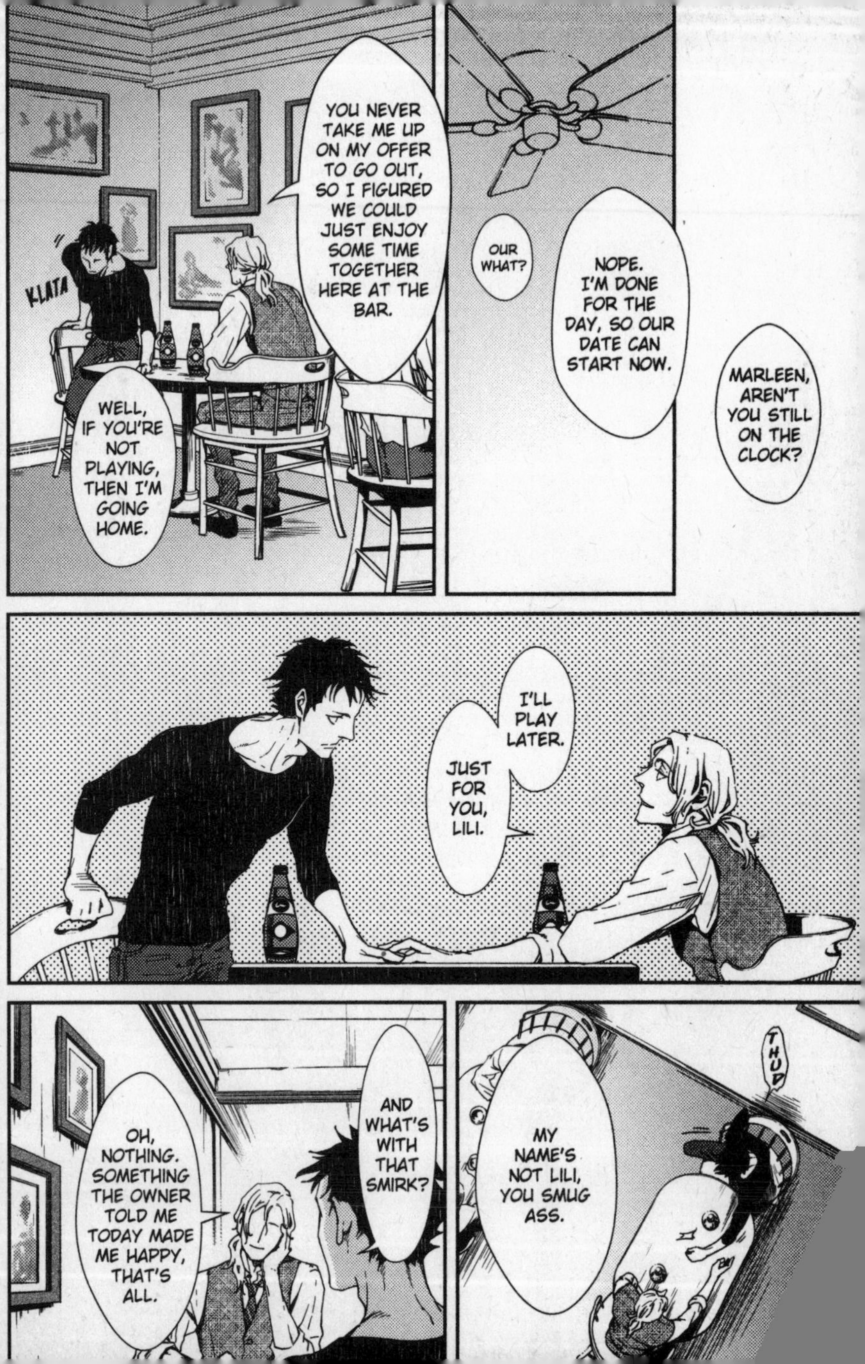

MARLEEN, AREN'T YOU STILL ON THE CLOCK?
NOPE. I'M DONE FOR THE DAY, SO OUR DATE CAN START NOW.
OUR WHAT?
YOU NEVER TAKE ME UP ON MY OFFER TO GO OUT, SO I FIGURED WE COULD JUST ENJOY SOME TIME TOGETHER HERE AT THE BAR.
KLATA
WELL, IF YOU'RE NOT PLAYING, THEN I'M GOING HOME.
I'LL PLAY LATER.
JUST FOR YOU, LILI.
THUD
MY NAME'S NOT LILI, YOU SMUG ASS.
AND WHAT'S WITH THAT SMIRK?
OH, NOTHING. SOMETHING THE OWNER TOLD ME TODAY MADE ME HAPPY, THAT'S ALL.

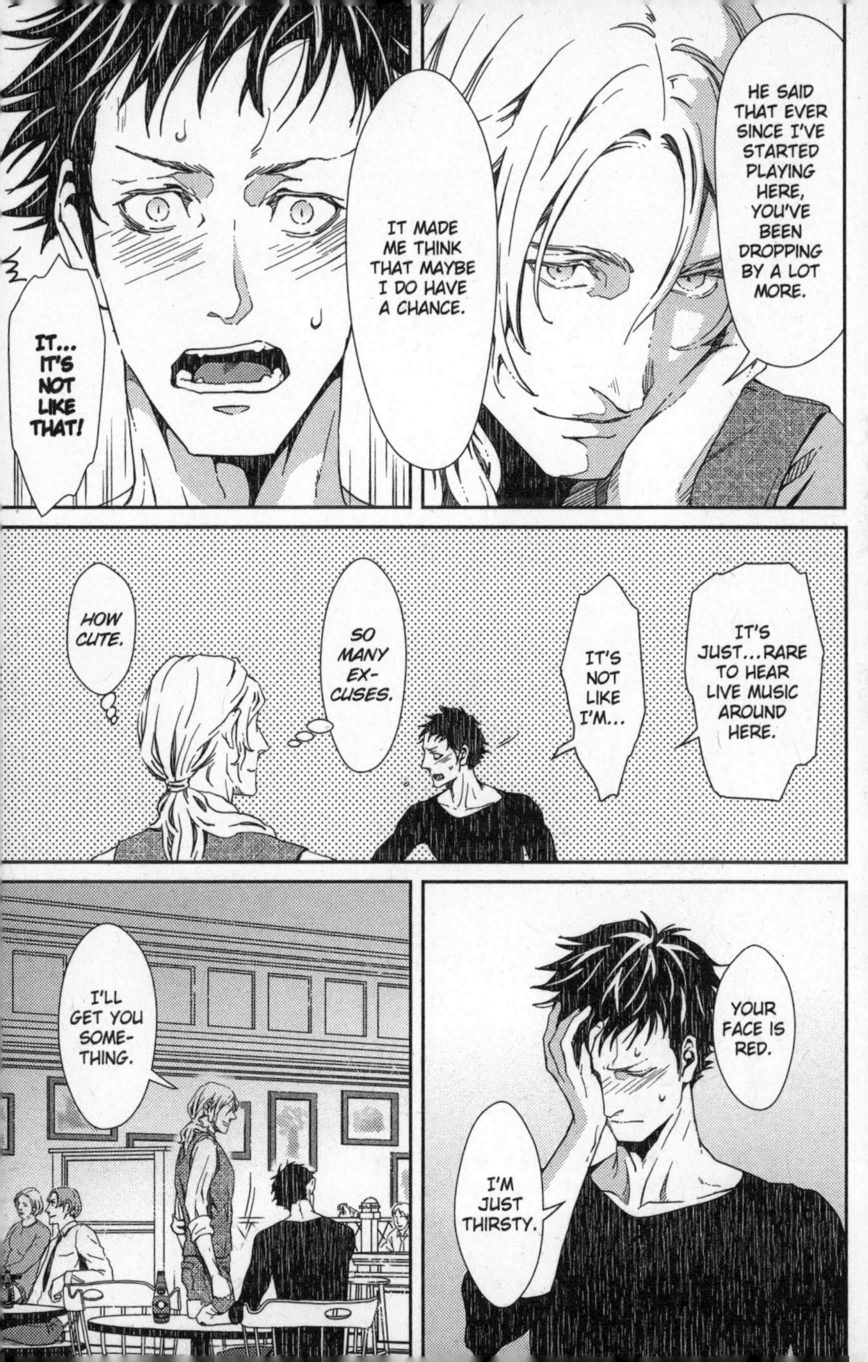
HE SAID THAT EVER SINCE I'VE STARTED PLAYING HERE, YOU'VE BEEN DROPPING BY A LOT MORE.
IT MADE ME THINK THAT MAYBE I DO HAVE A CHANCE.
IT... IT'S NOT LIKE THAT!
IT'S JUST...RARE TO HEAR LIVE MUSIC AROUND HERE.
IT'S NOT LIKE I'M...
SO MANY EX-CUSES.
HOW CUTE.
YOUR FACE IS RED.
I'M JUST THIRSTY.
I'LL GET YOU SOME-THING.

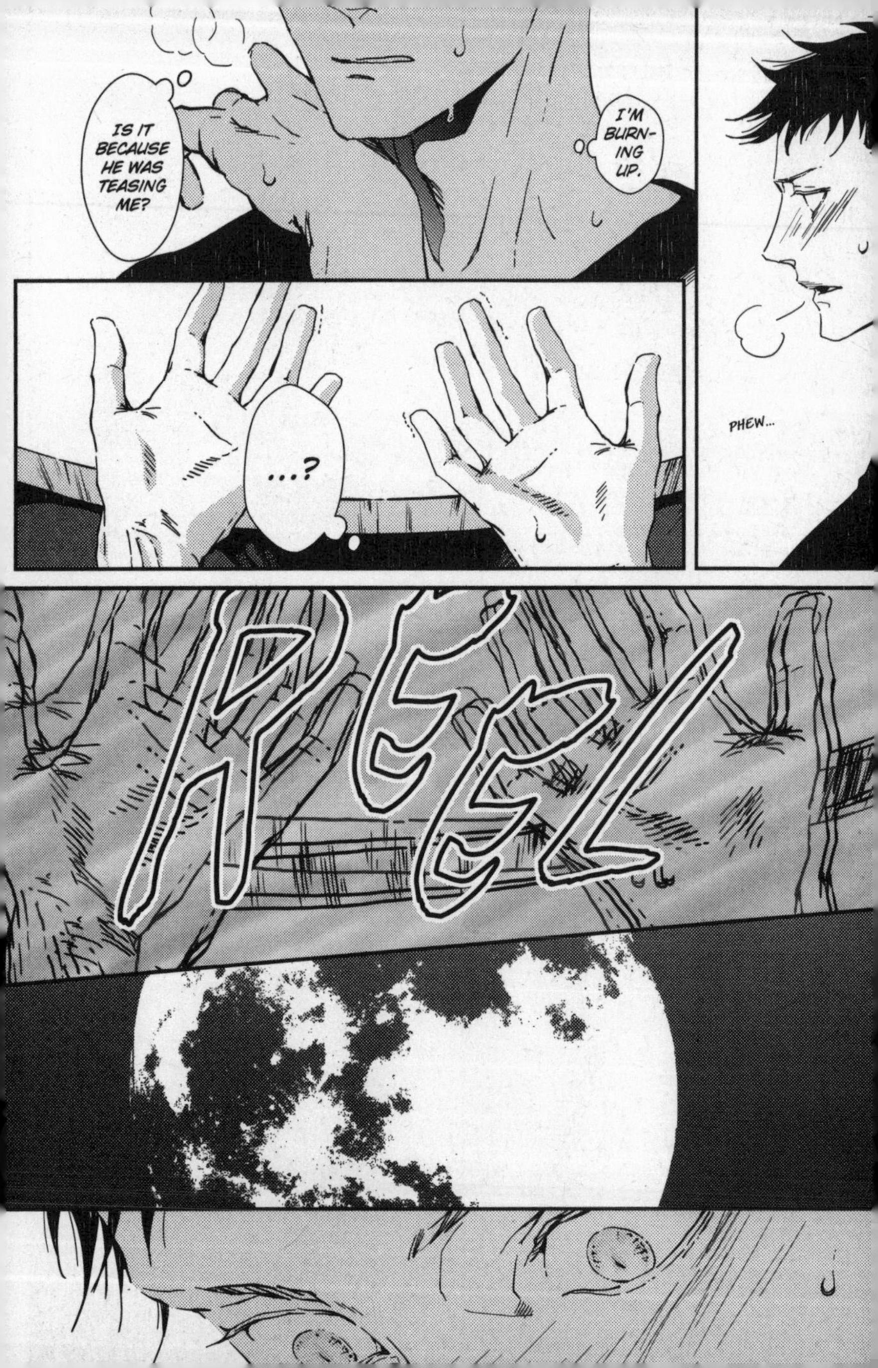
PHEW...
I'M BURN-ING UP.
IS IT BECAUSE HE WAS TEASING ME?
...?
REEL

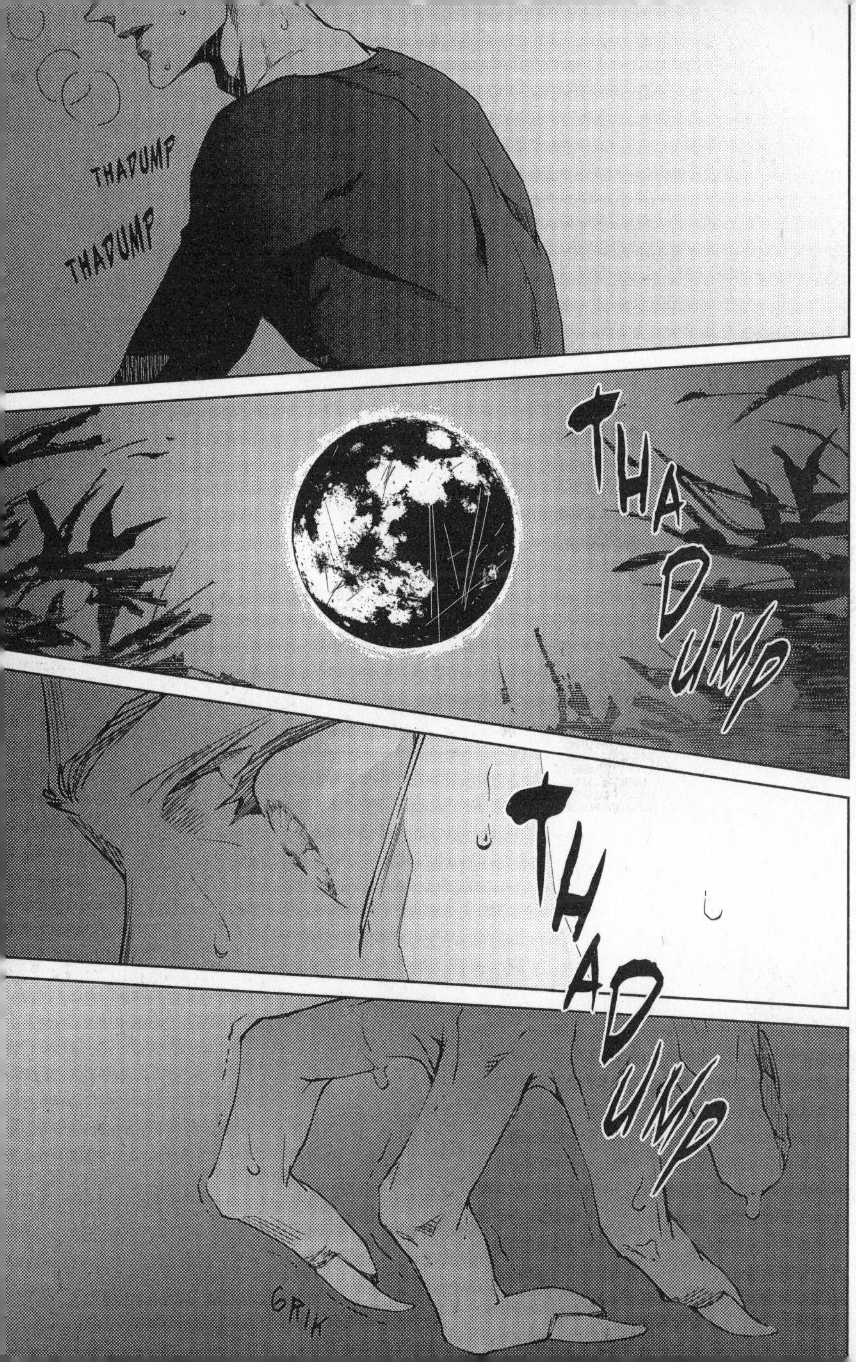
THADUMP
THADUMP
THADUMP
THADUMP
GRIK

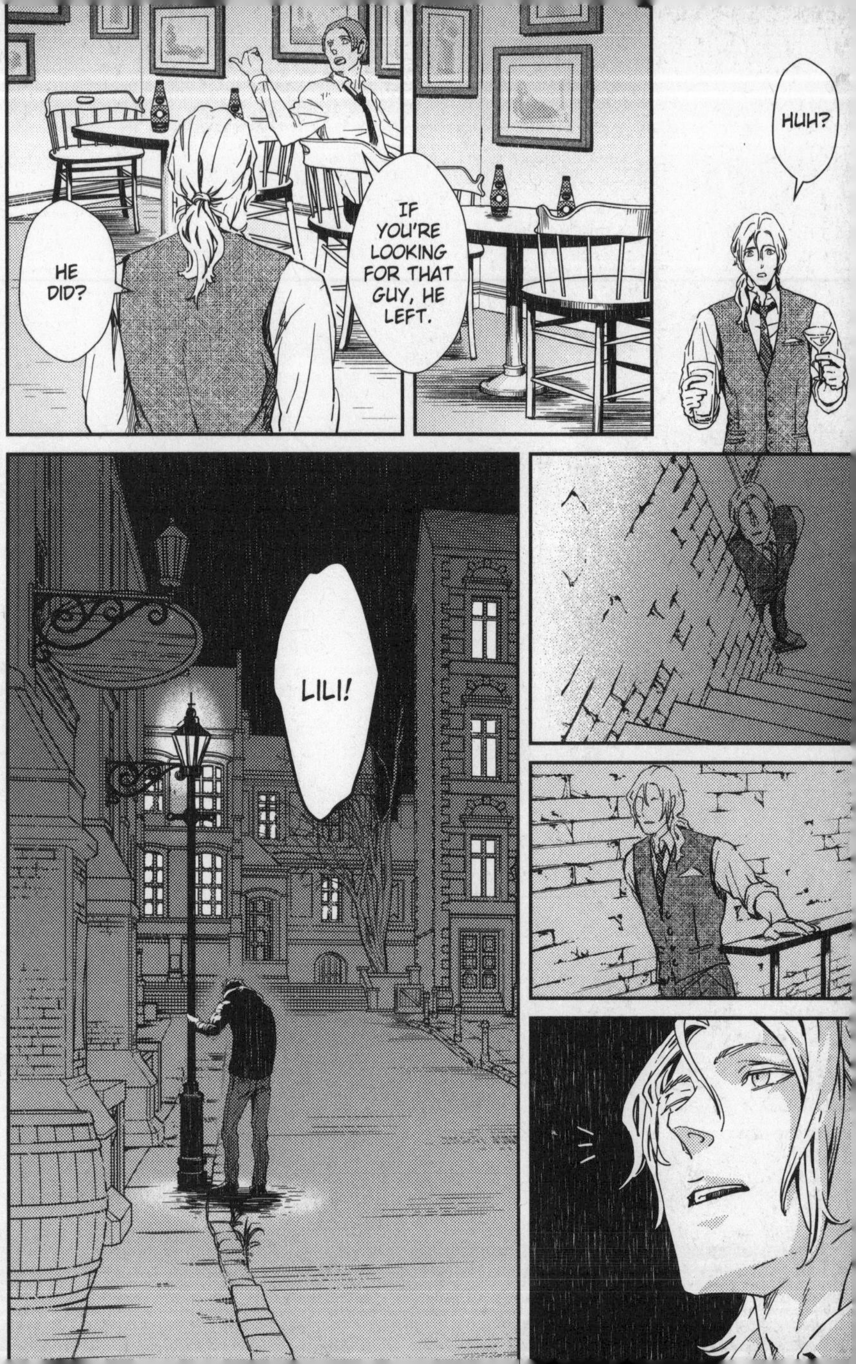
HUH?
IF YOU'RE LOOKING FOR THAT GUY, HE LEFT.
HE DID?
LILI!

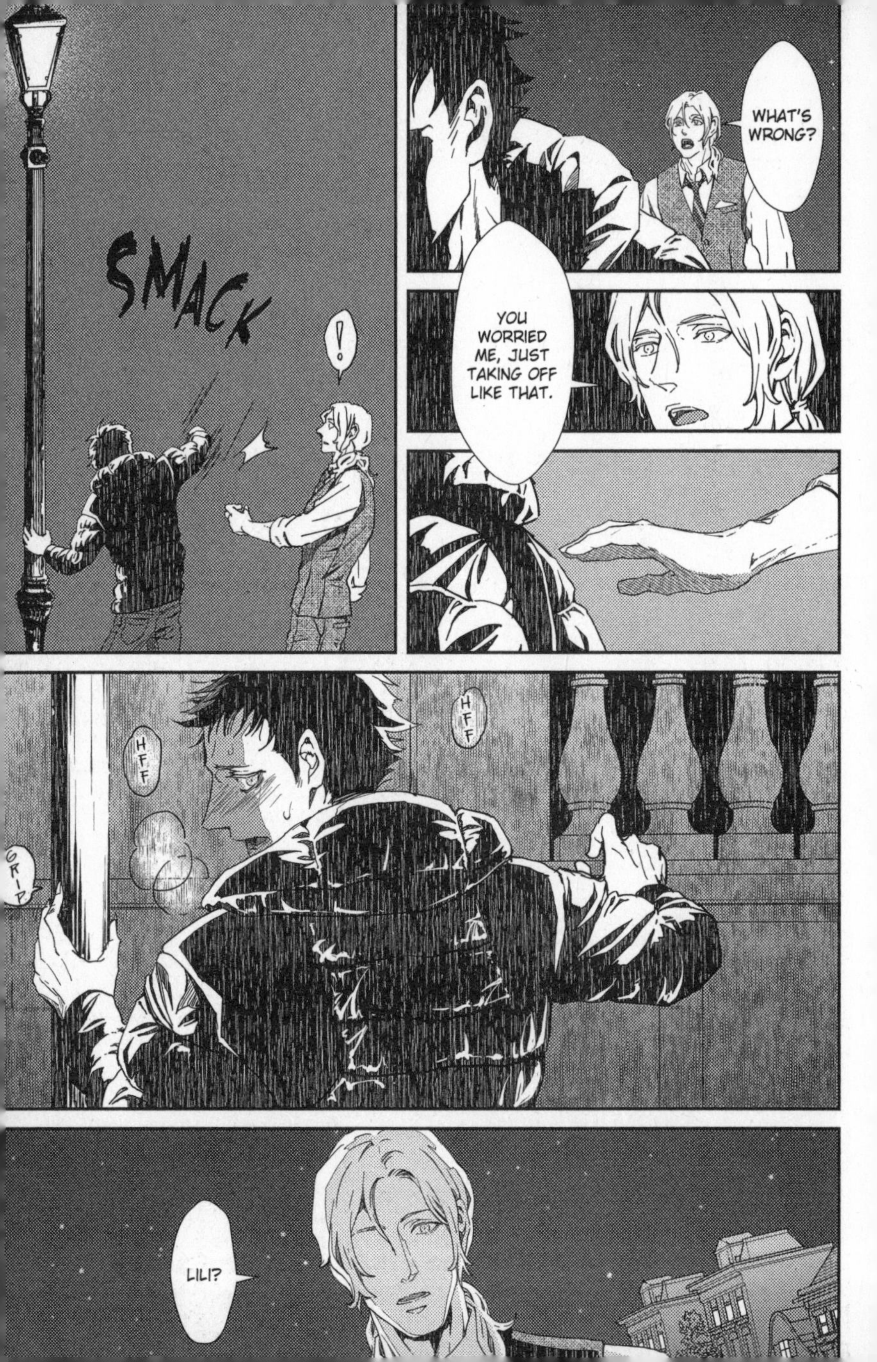
WHAT'S WRONG?
YOU WORRIED ME, JUST TAKING OFF LIKE THAT.
SMACK
!
HFF
HFF
GRIP
LILI?

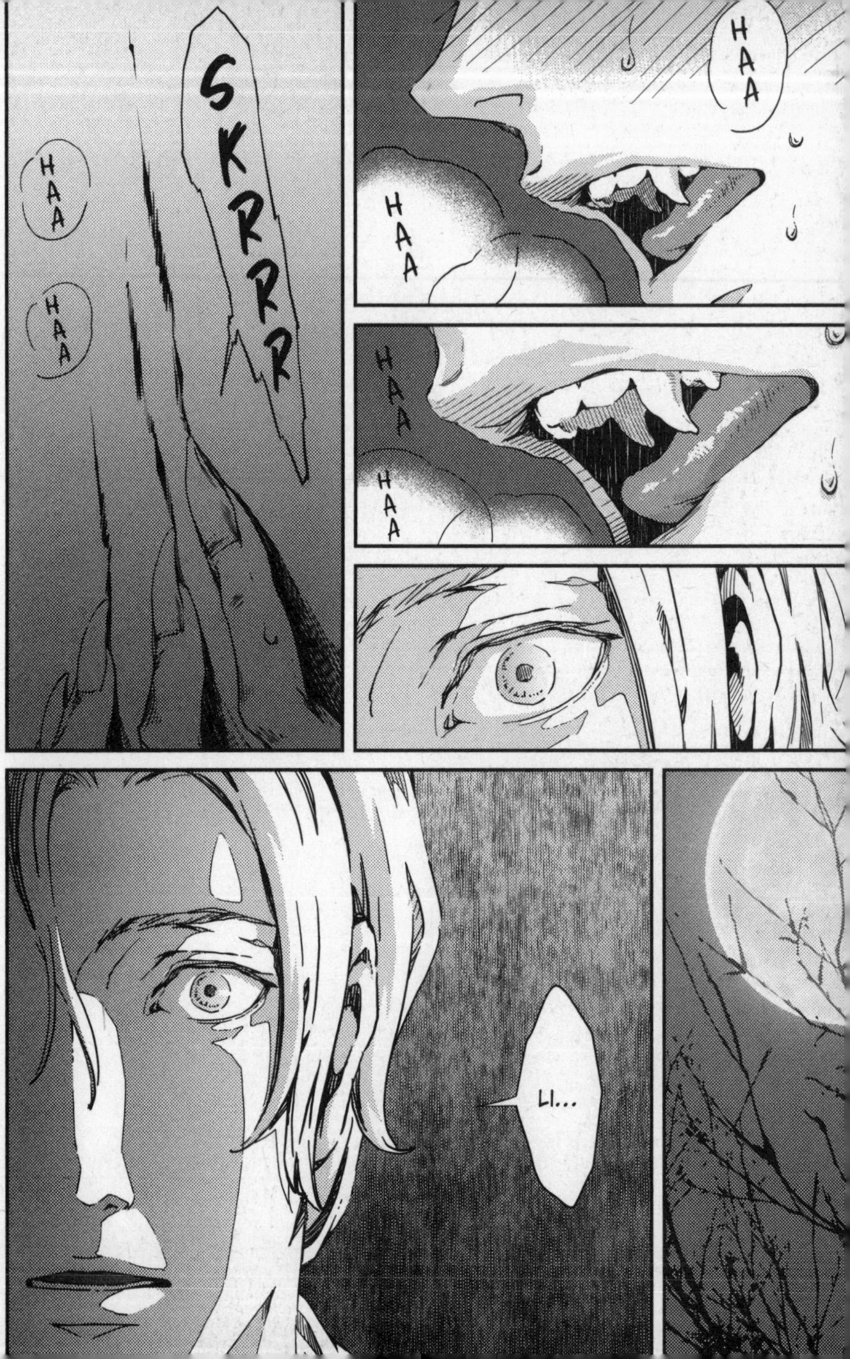
HAA
HAA
HAA
HAA
SKRRR
HAA
HAA
LI...

LILI?

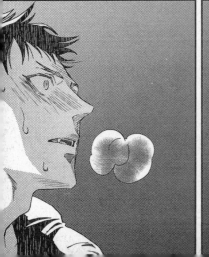

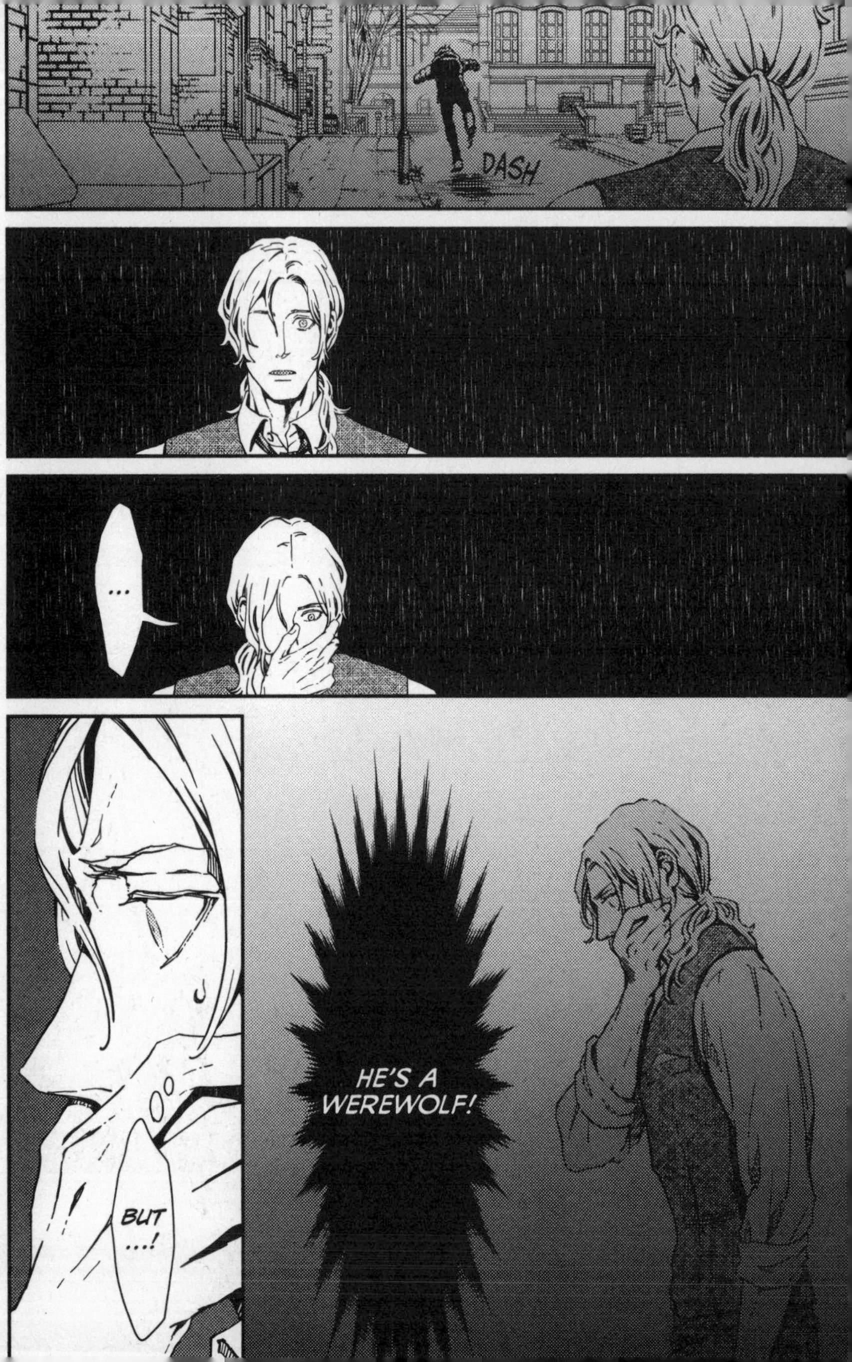
DASH
...
HE'S A WEREWOLF!
BUT ...!

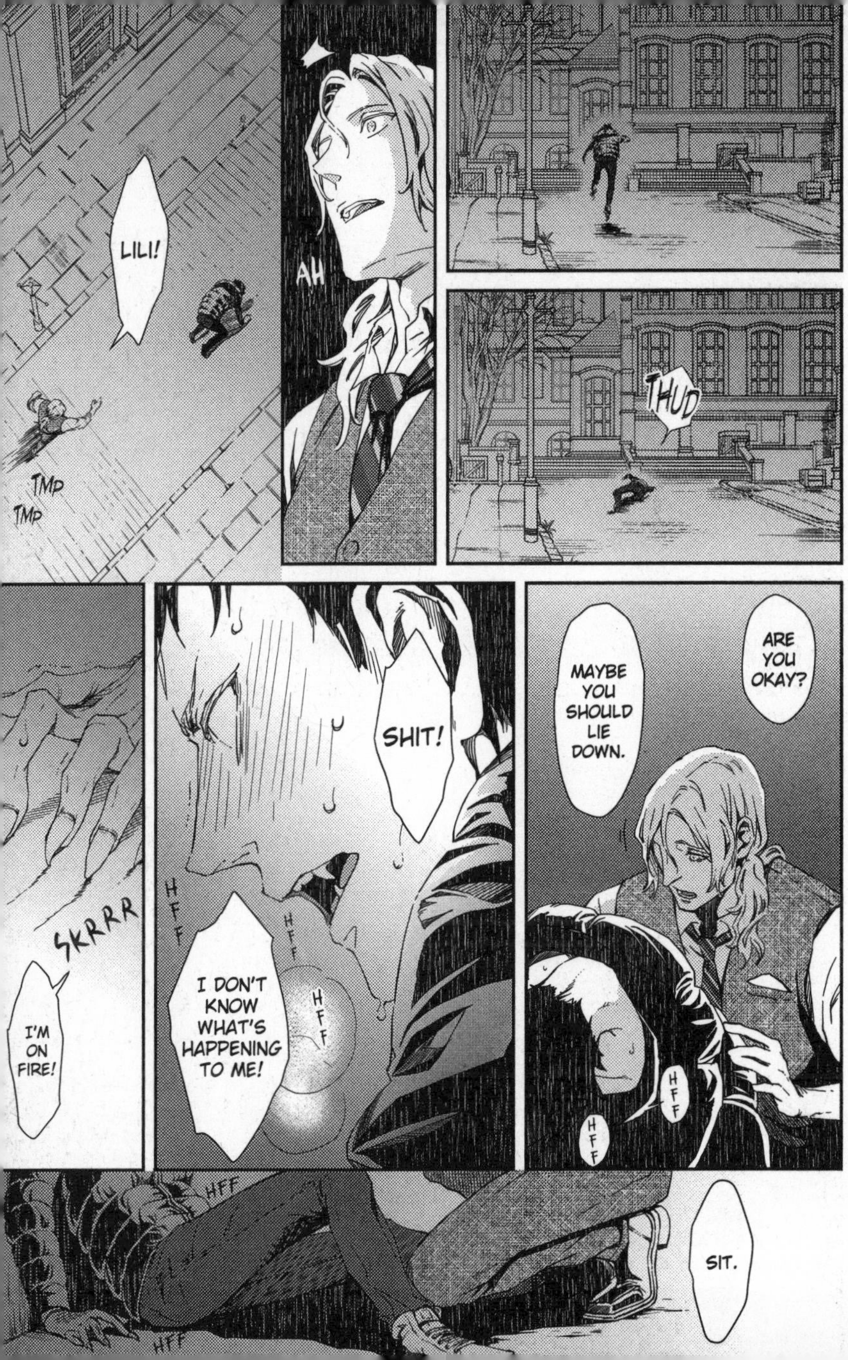
THUD
AH
LILI!
TMP
TMP
ARE YOU OKAY?
MAYBE YOU SHOULD LIE DOWN.
HFF
HFF
SHIT!
HFF
HFF
HFF
I DON'T KNOW WHAT'S HAPPENING TO ME!
SKRRR
I'M ON FIRE!
SIT.
HFF
HFF

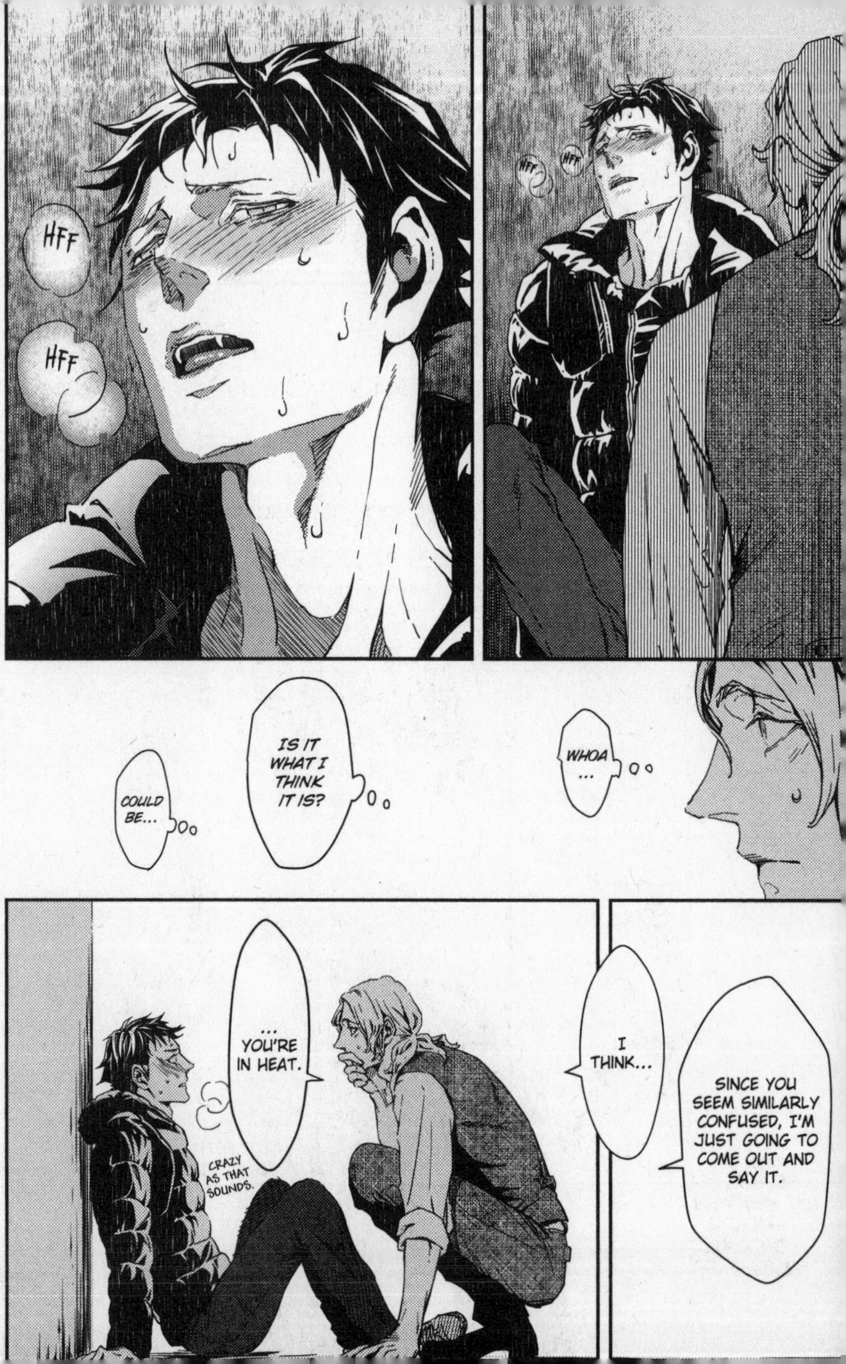
HFF
HFF
HFF
HFF
WHOA...
IS IT WHAT I THINK IT IS?
COULD BE...
SINCE YOU SEEM SIMILARLY CONFUSED, I'M JUST GOING TO COME OUT AND SAY IT.
I THINK...
...YOU'RE IN HEAT.
CRAZY AS THAT SOUNDS.

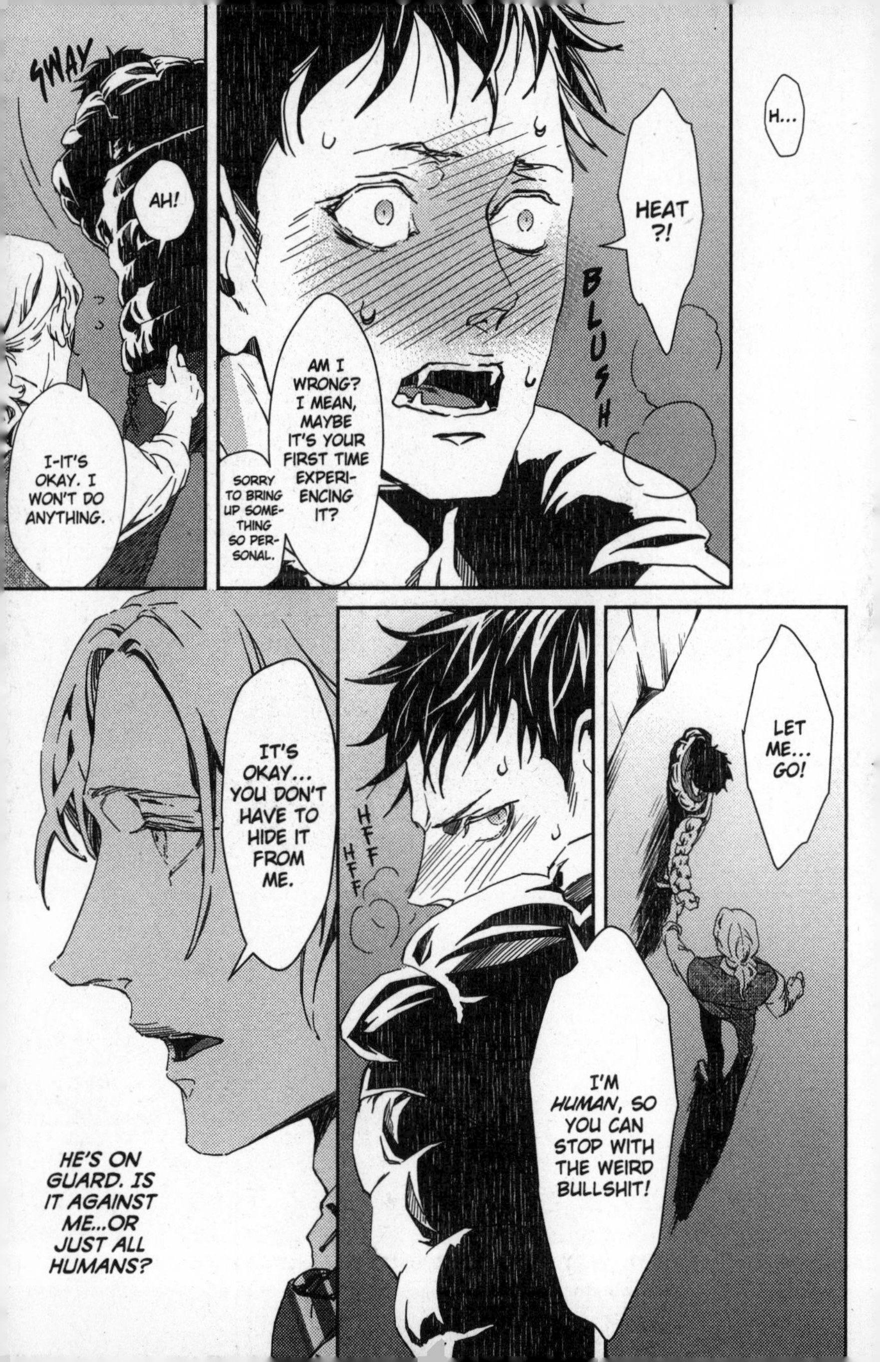
H...
HEAT ?!
BLUSH
AM I WRONG? I MEAN, MAYBE IT'S YOUR FIRST TIME EXPERIENCING IT?
SORRY TO BRING UP SOMETHING SO PERSONAL.
SWAY
AH!
I-IT'S OKAY. I WON'T DO ANYTHING.
LET ME... GO!
I'M *HUMAN*, SO YOU CAN STOP WITH THE WEIRD BULLSHIT!
HFF HFF
IT'S OKAY... YOU DON'T HAVE TO HIDE IT FROM ME.
HE'S ON GUARD. IS IT AGAINST ME...OR JUST ALL HUMANS?

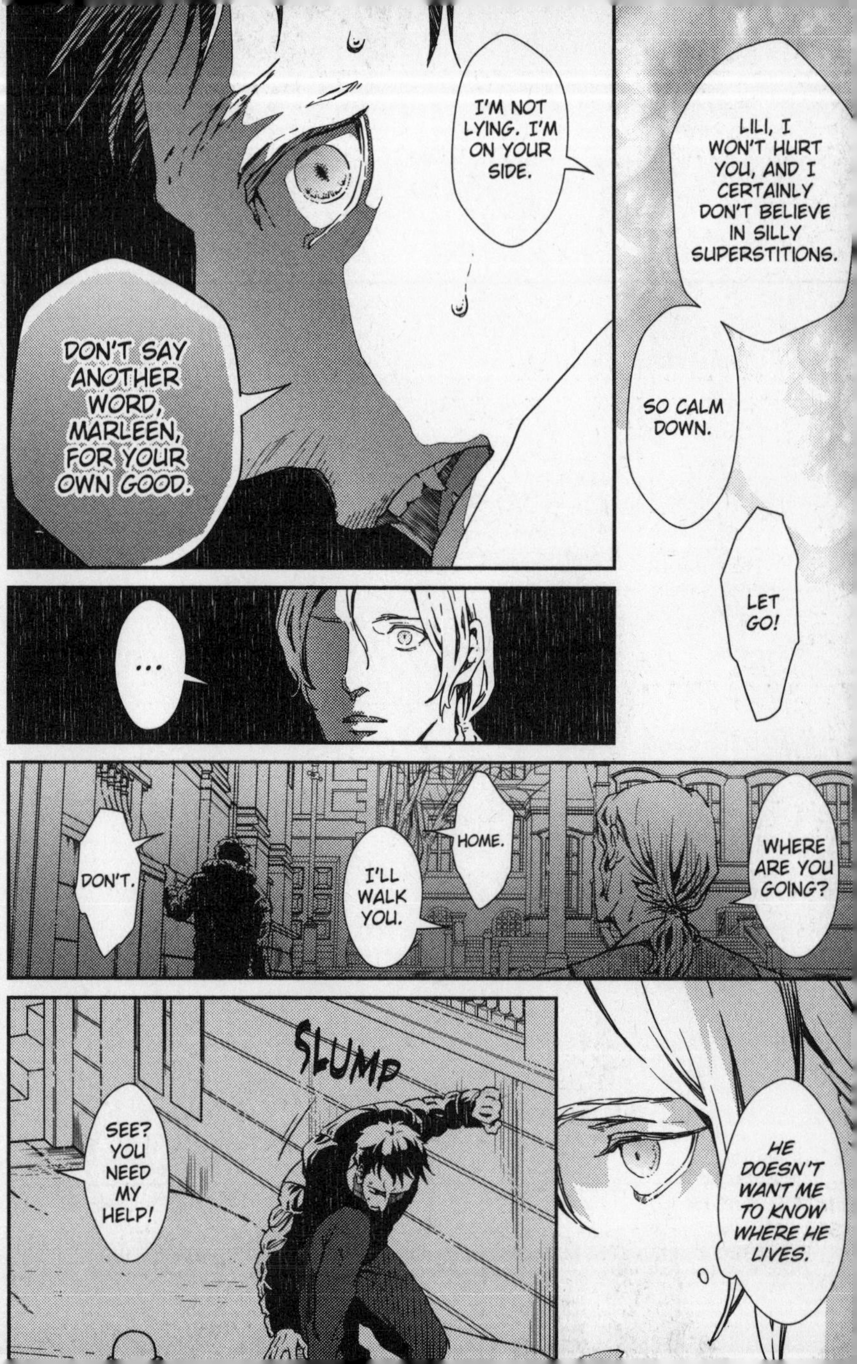
LILI, I WON'T HURT YOU, AND I CERTAINLY DON'T BELIEVE IN SILLY SUPERSTITIONS.
SO CALM DOWN.
LET GO!
I'M NOT LYING. I'M ON YOUR SIDE.
DON'T SAY ANOTHER WORD, MARLEEN, FOR YOUR OWN GOOD.
...
WHERE ARE YOU GOING?
HOME.
I'LL WALK YOU.
DON'T.
HE DOESN'T WANT ME TO KNOW WHERE HE LIVES.
SLUMP
SEE? YOU NEED MY HELP!

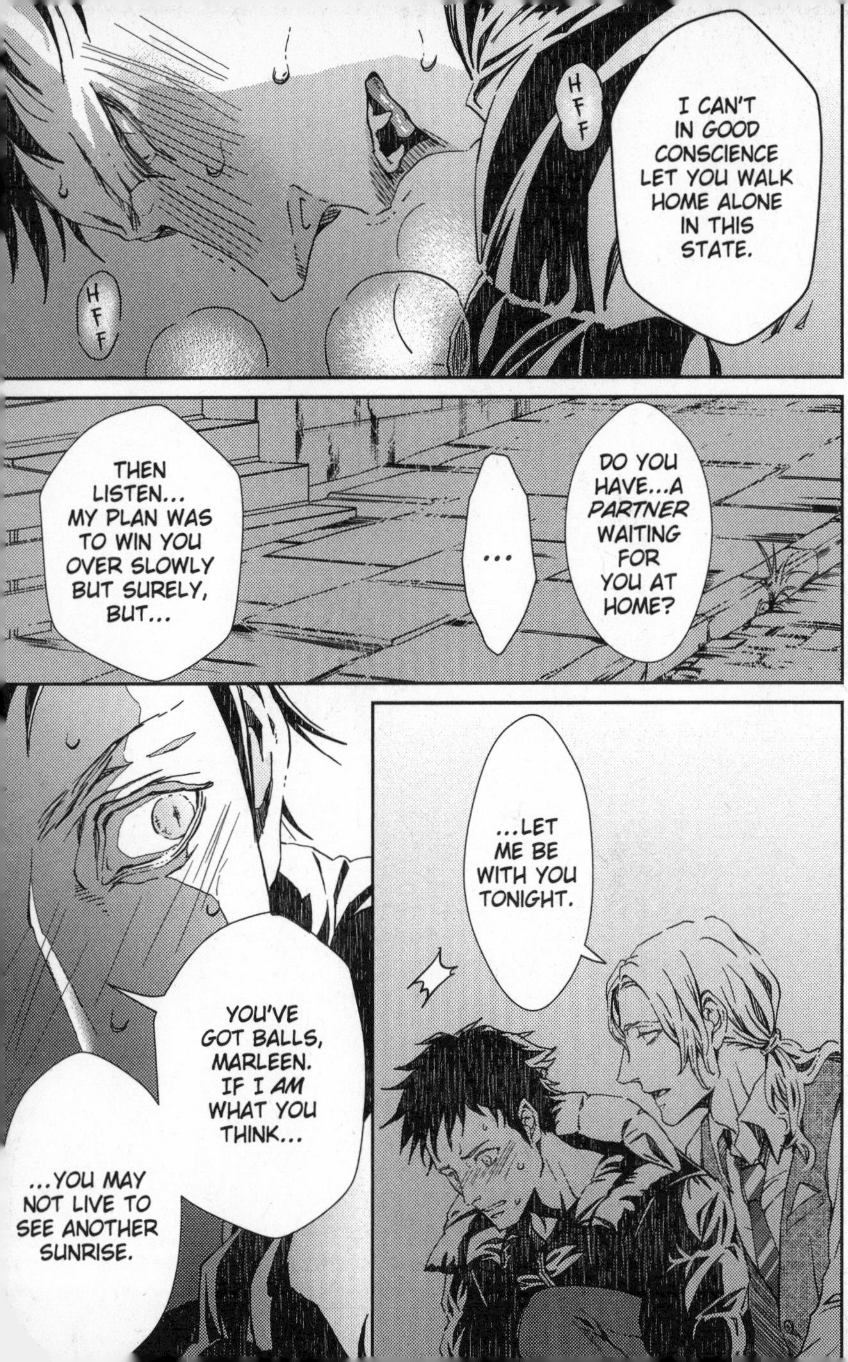
I CAN'T IN GOOD CONSCIENCE LET YOU WALK HOME ALONE IN THIS STATE.
HFF
HFF
DO YOU HAVE...A *PARTNER* WAITING FOR YOU AT HOME?
...
THEN LISTEN... MY PLAN WAS TO WIN YOU OVER SLOWLY BUT SURELY, BUT...
...LET ME BE WITH YOU TONIGHT.
YOU'VE GOT BALLS, MARLEEN. IF I *AM* WHAT YOU THINK...
...YOU MAY NOT LIVE TO SEE ANOTHER SUNRISE.

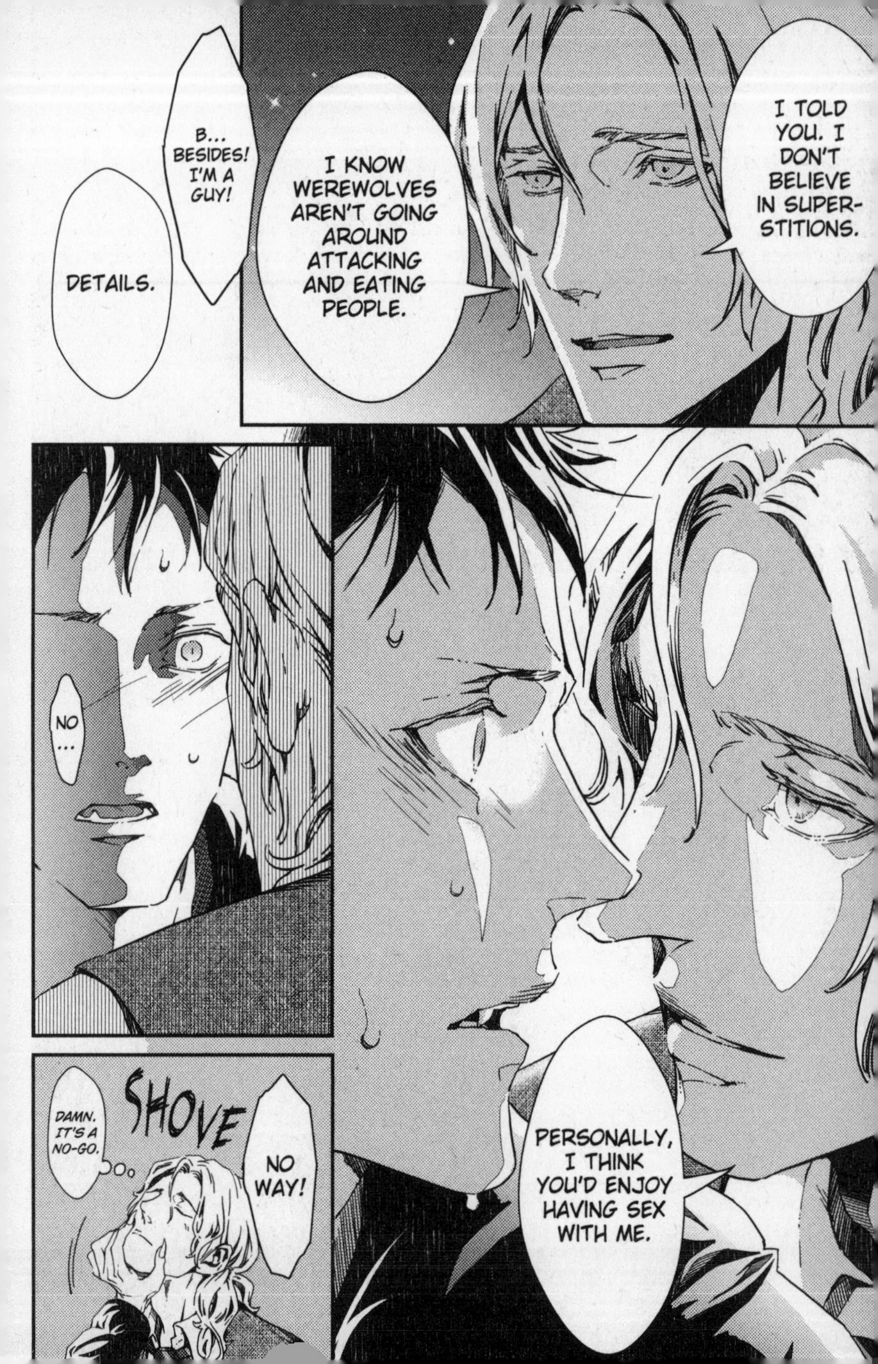
I TOLD YOU. I DON'T BELIEVE IN SUPER-STITIONS.
I KNOW WEREWOLVES AREN'T GOING AROUND ATTACKING AND EATING PEOPLE.
B... BESIDES! I'M A GUY!
DETAILS.
PERSONALLY, I THINK YOU'D ENJOY HAVING SEX WITH ME.
NO...
NO WAY!
SHOVE
DAMN. IT'S A NO-GO.

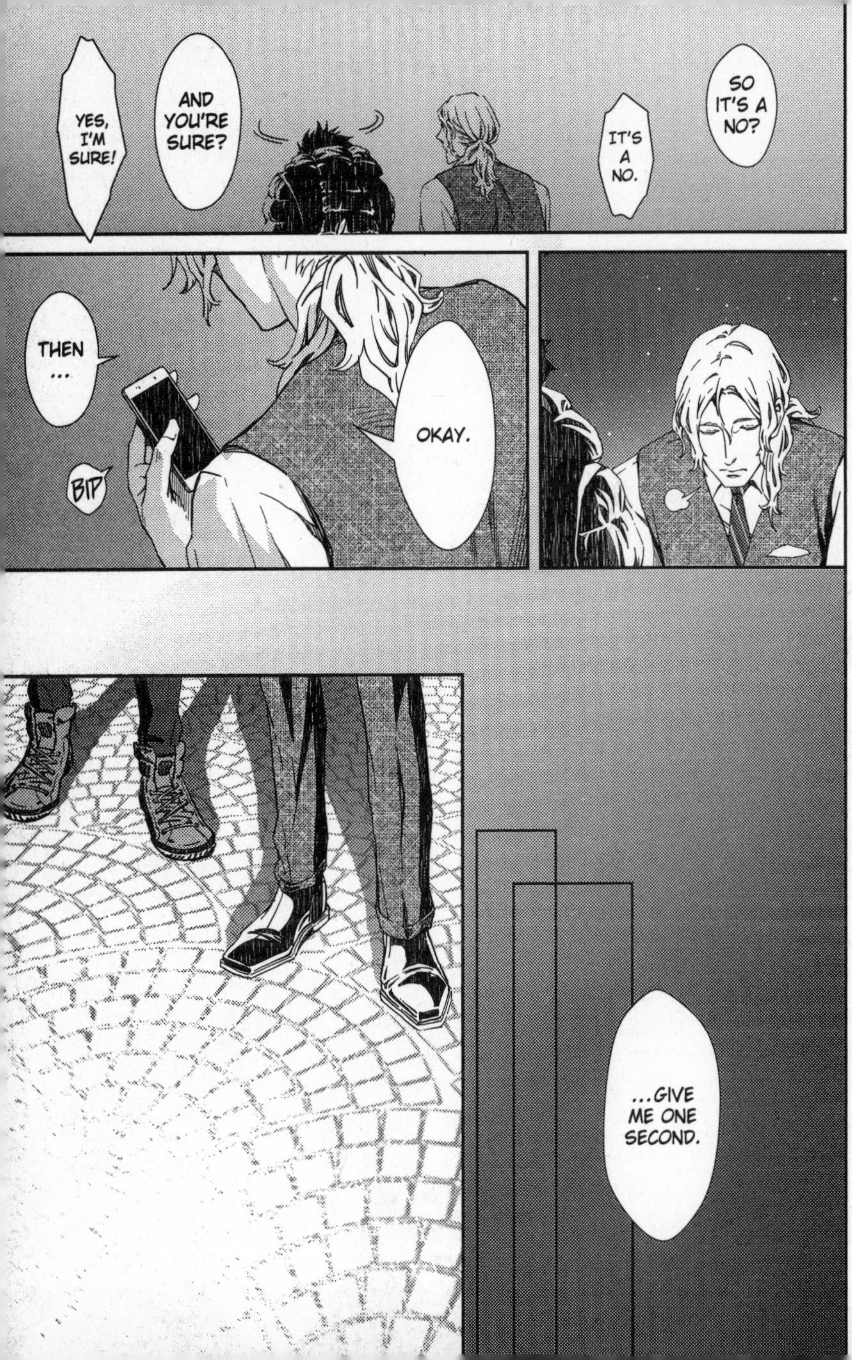
SO IT'S A NO?
IT'S A NO.
AND YOU'RE SURE?
YES, I'M SURE!
OKAY.
THEN ...
BIP
...GIVE ME ONE SECOND.

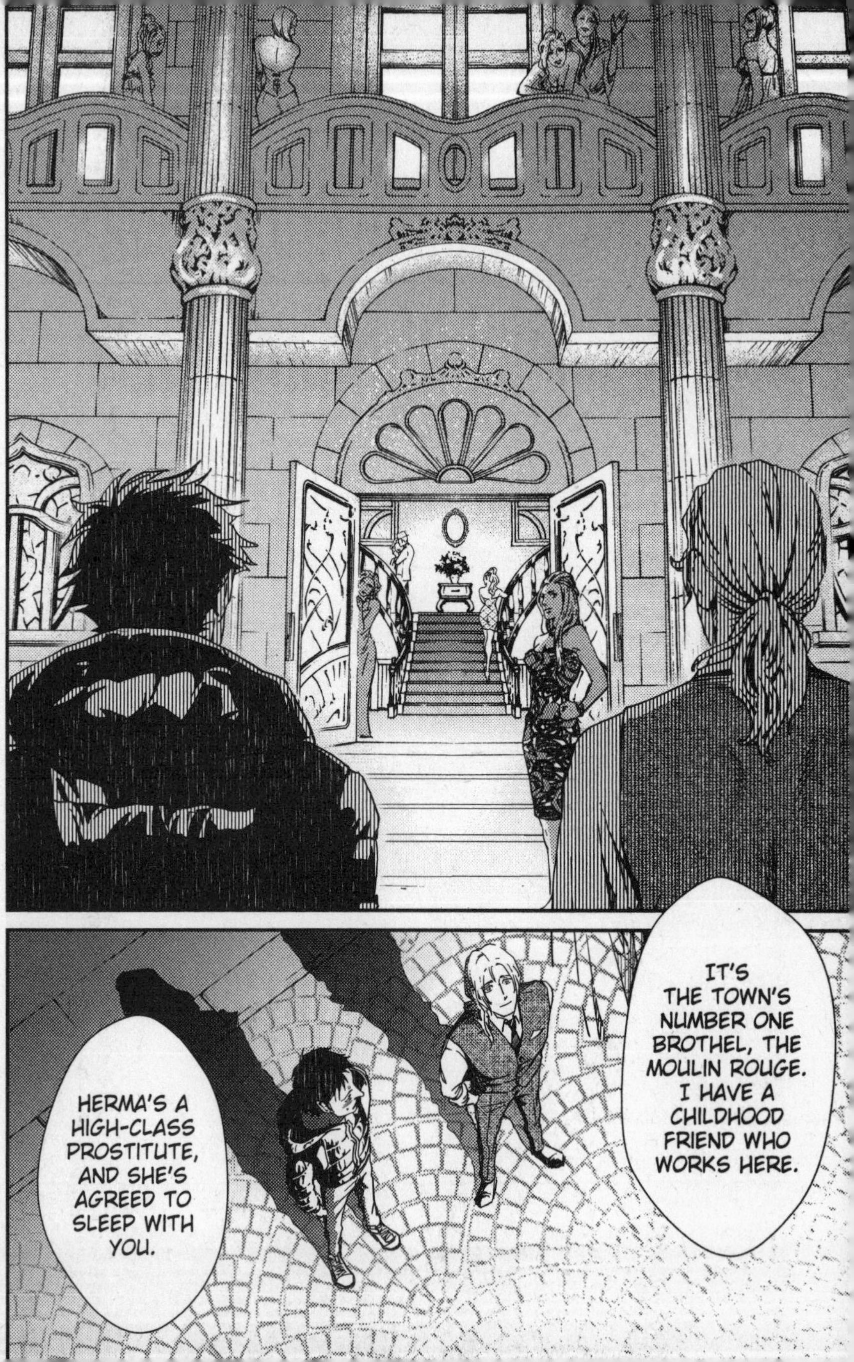
IT'S THE TOWN'S NUMBER ONE BROTHEL, THE MOULIN ROUGE. I HAVE A CHILDHOOD FRIEND WHO WORKS HERE.
HERMA'S A HIGH-CLASS PROSTITUTE, AND SHE'S AGREED TO SLEEP WITH YOU.

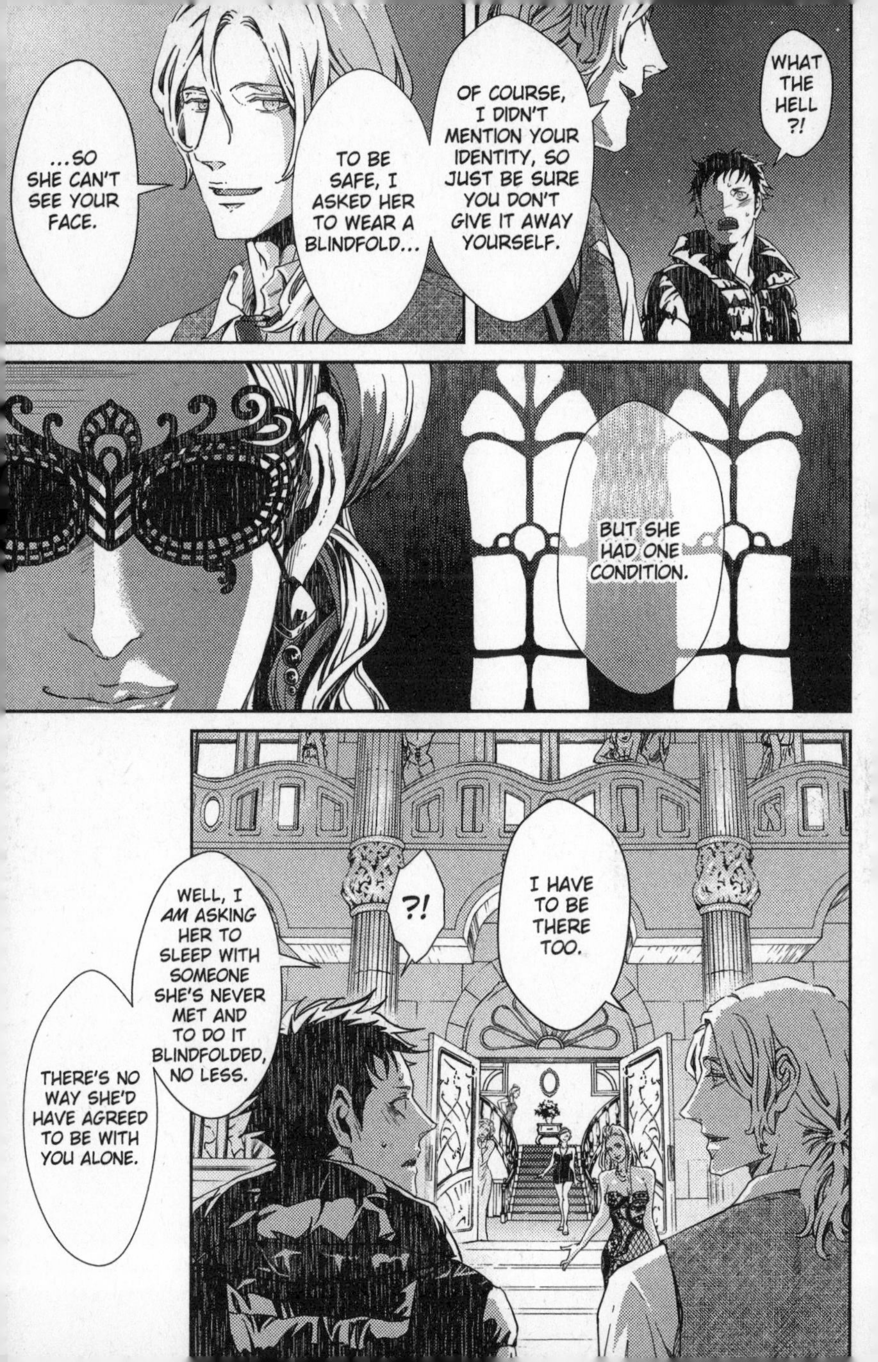
WHAT THE HELL ?!
OF COURSE, I DIDN'T MENTION YOUR IDENTITY, SO JUST BE SURE YOU DON'T GIVE IT AWAY YOURSELF.
TO BE SAFE, I ASKED HER TO WEAR A BLINDFOLD...
...SO SHE CAN'T SEE YOUR FACE.
BUT SHE HAD ONE CONDITION.
I HAVE TO BE THERE TOO.
?!
WELL, I *AM* ASKING HER TO SLEEP WITH SOMEONE SHE'S NEVER MET AND TO DO IT BLINDFOLDED, NO LESS.
THERE'S NO WAY SHE'D HAVE AGREED TO BE WITH YOU ALONE.

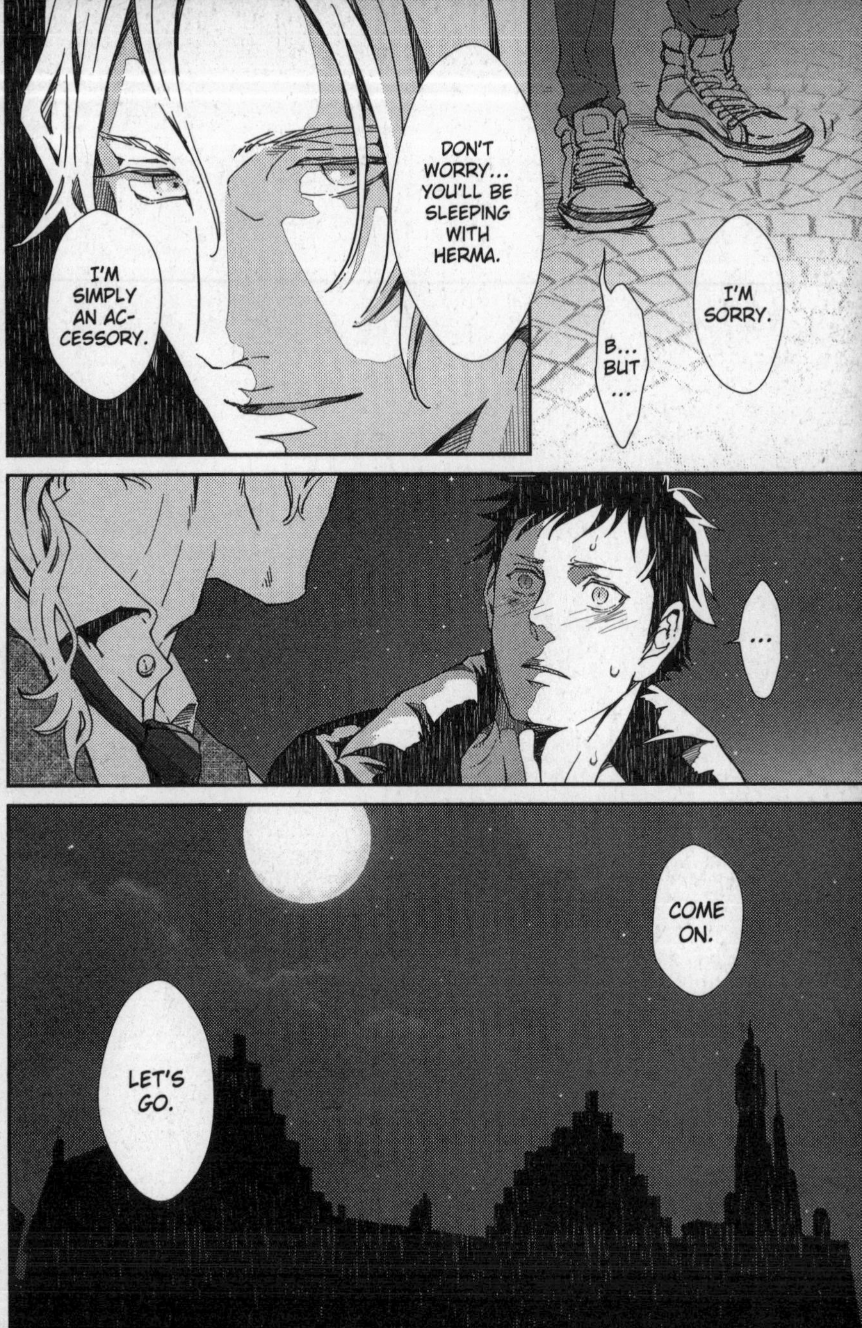
I'M SORRY.
B... BUT ...
DON'T WORRY... YOU'LL BE SLEEPING WITH HERMA.
I'M SIMPLY AN AC-CESSORY.
...
COME ON.
LET'S GO.

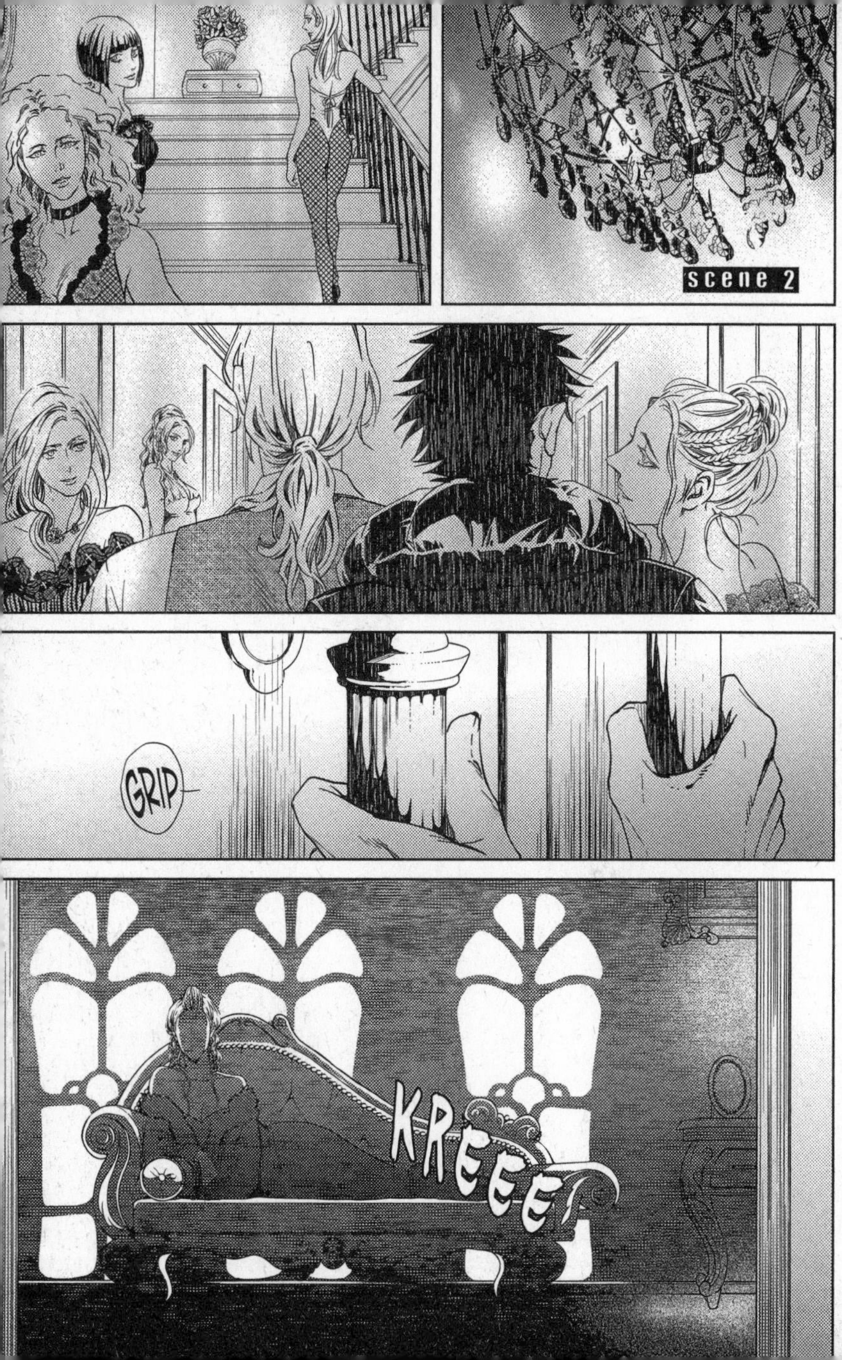
scene 2
GRIP
KREEE

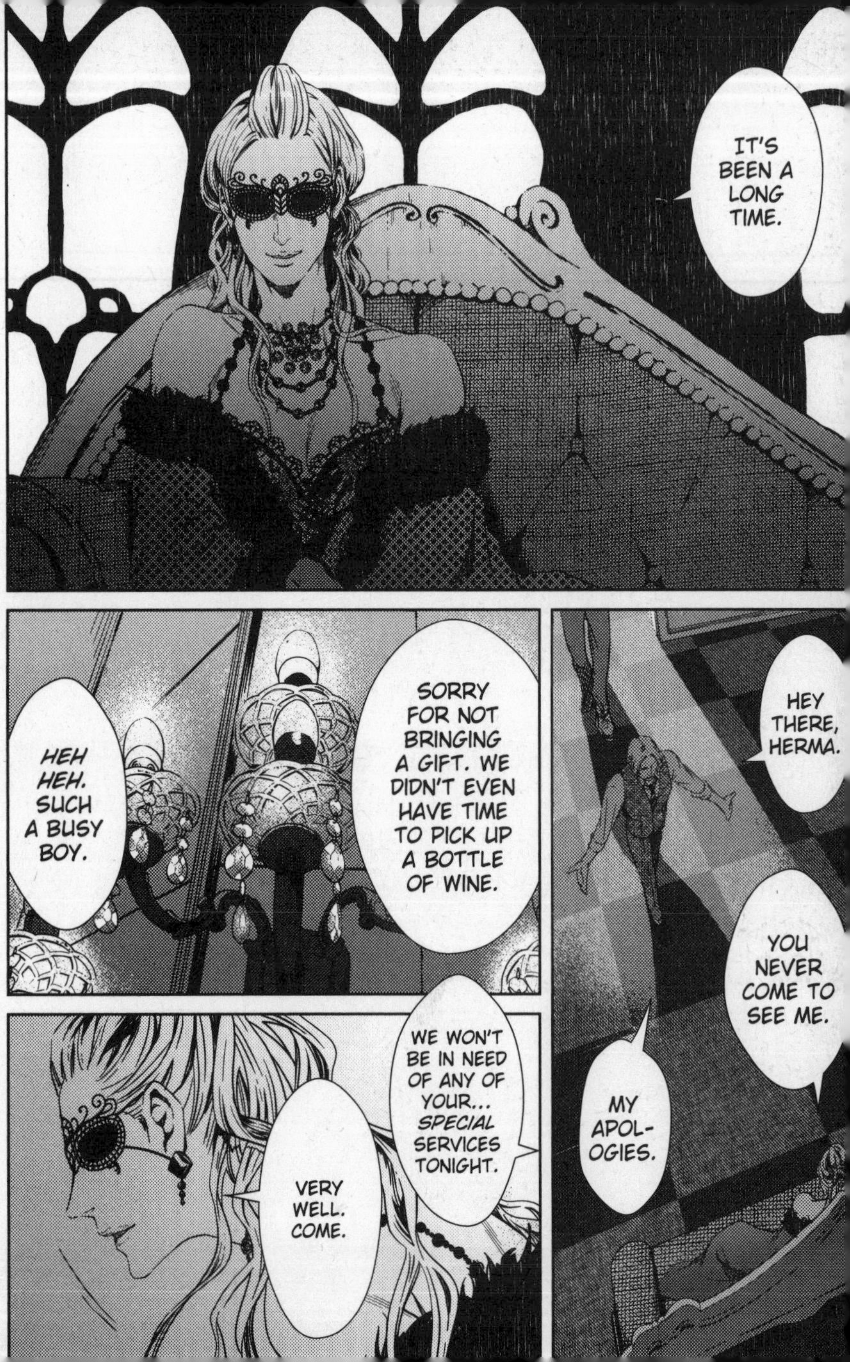
IT'S BEEN A LONG TIME.
HEY THERE, HERMA.
YOU NEVER COME TO SEE ME.
MY APOLOGIES.
SORRY FOR NOT BRINGING A GIFT. WE DIDN'T EVEN HAVE TIME TO PICK UP A BOTTLE OF WINE.
HEH HEH. SUCH A BUSY BOY.
WE WON'T BE IN NEED OF ANY OF YOUR... SPECIAL SERVICES TONIGHT.
VERY WELL. COME.

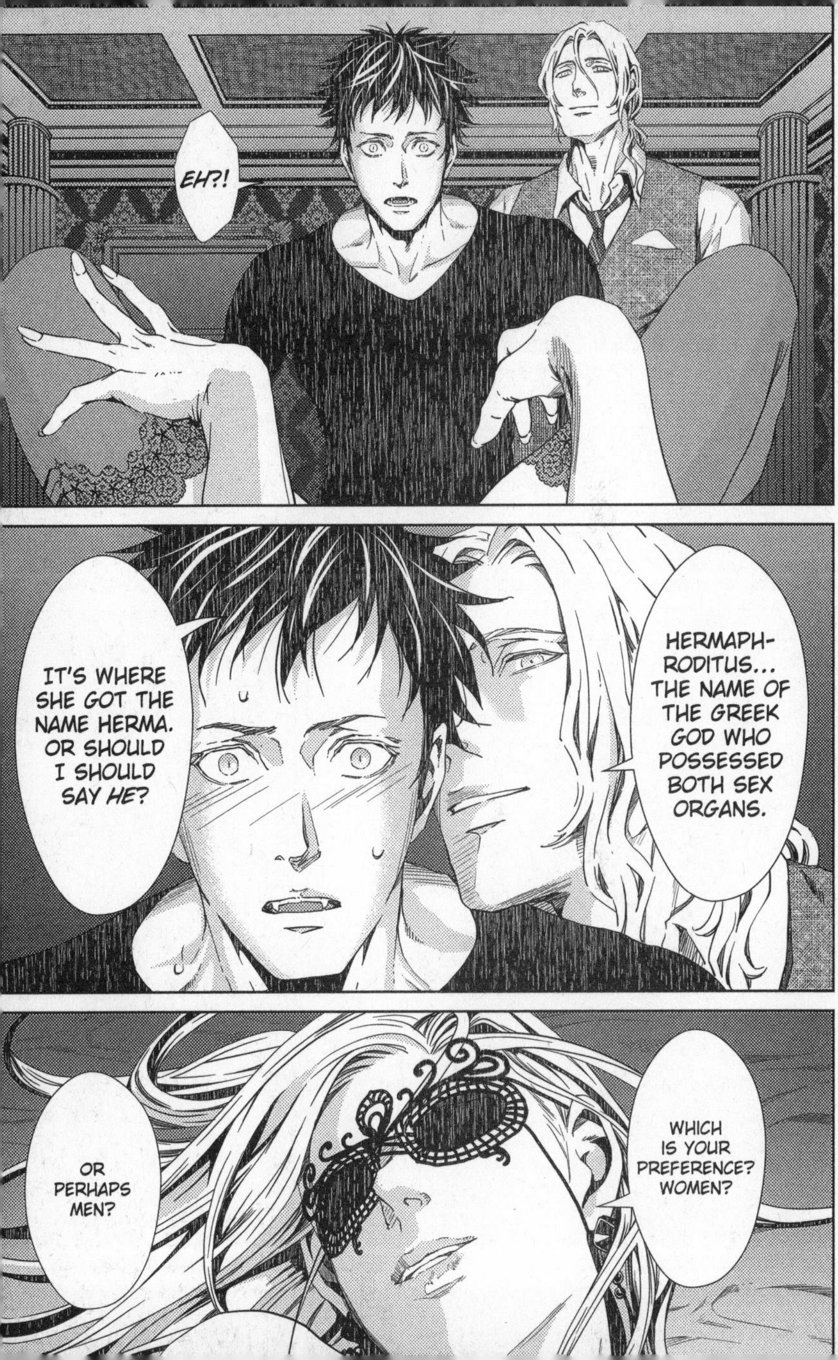
EH?!
HERMAPH-RODITUS... THE NAME OF THE GREEK GOD WHO POSSESSED BOTH SEX ORGANS.
IT'S WHERE SHE GOT THE NAME HERMA. OR SHOULD I SHOULD SAY *HE*?
WHICH IS YOUR PREFERENCE? WOMEN?
OR PERHAPS MEN?

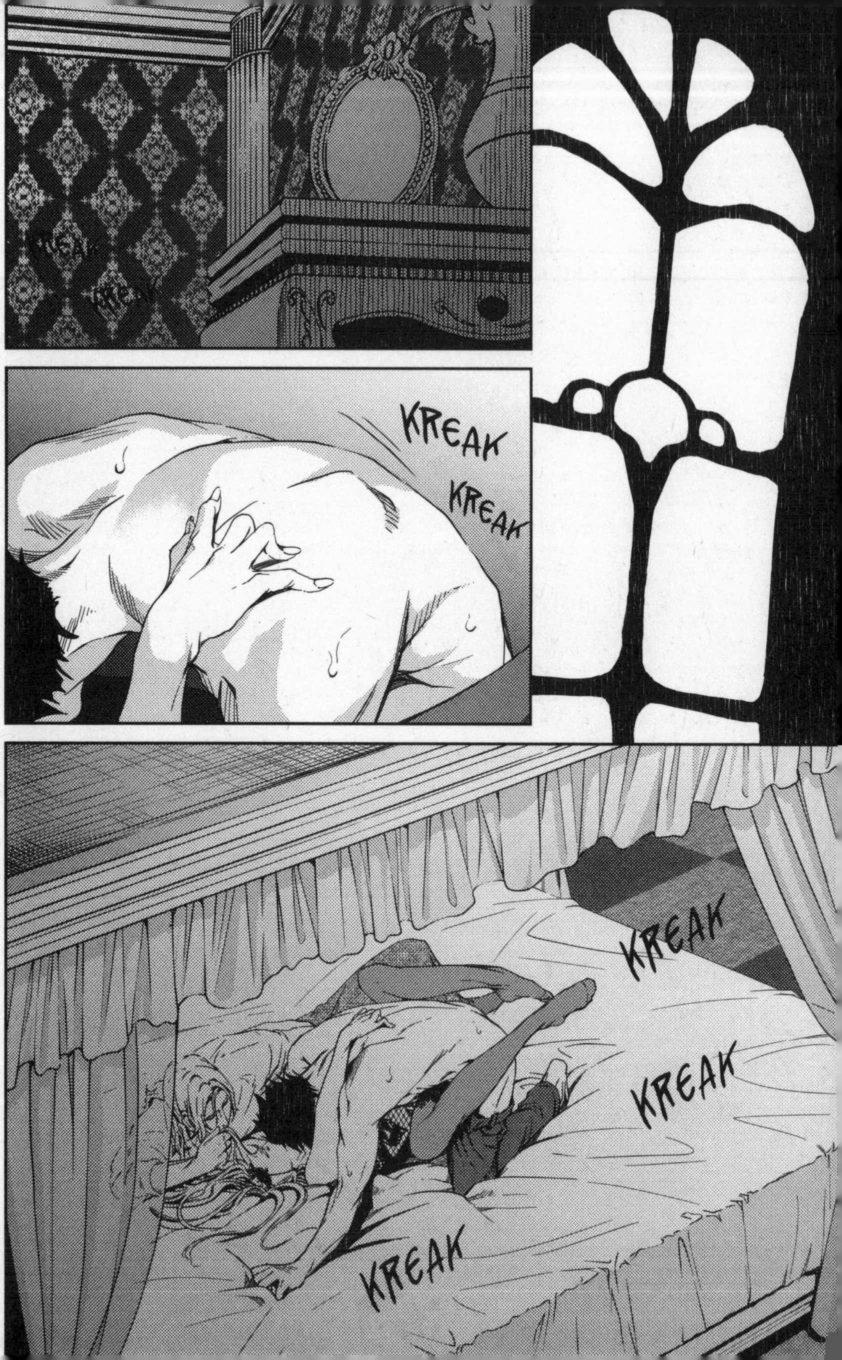
KREAK
KREAK
KREAK
KREAK
KREAK

KREAK KREAK

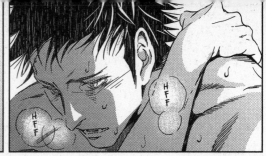

HFF

HFF

ARE YOU HOLDING BACK?

IT'S OKAY. YOU SHOULD ENJOY YOURSELF.

OH... MAYBE HE HAS A KNOT.

HE'D HAVE TO KEEP HIS MOVEMENTS SHALLOW SO HE DOESN'T PUSH IT INSIDE, AND GIVE AWAY HIS IDENTITY.

TRMBL

HFF

HFF

HFF

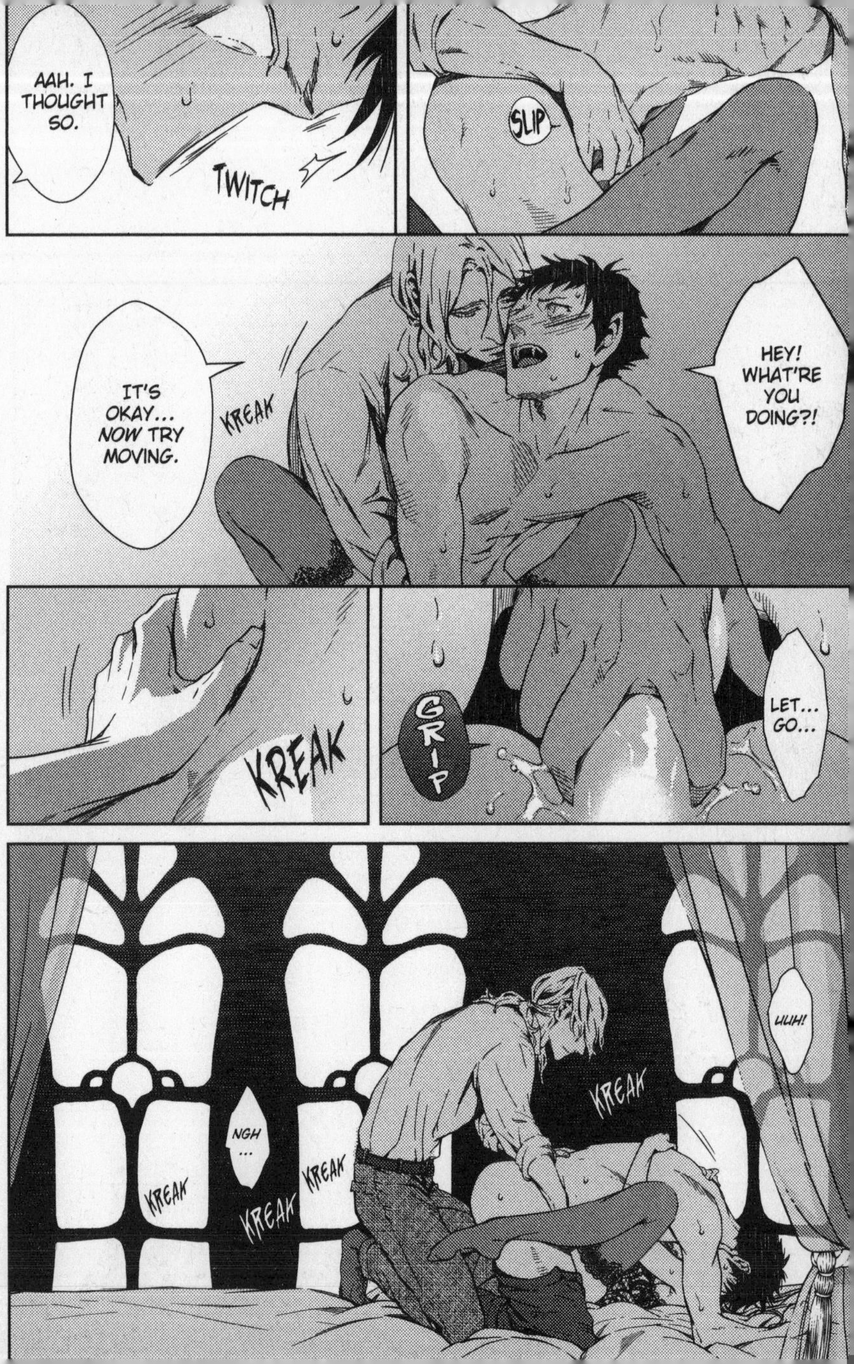
SLIP
AAH. I THOUGHT SO.
TWITCH
HEY! WHAT'RE YOU DOING?!
KREAK
IT'S OKAY... NOW TRY MOVING.
LET... GO...
GRIP
KREAK
UUH!
KREAK
NGH...
KREAK
KREAK
KREAK

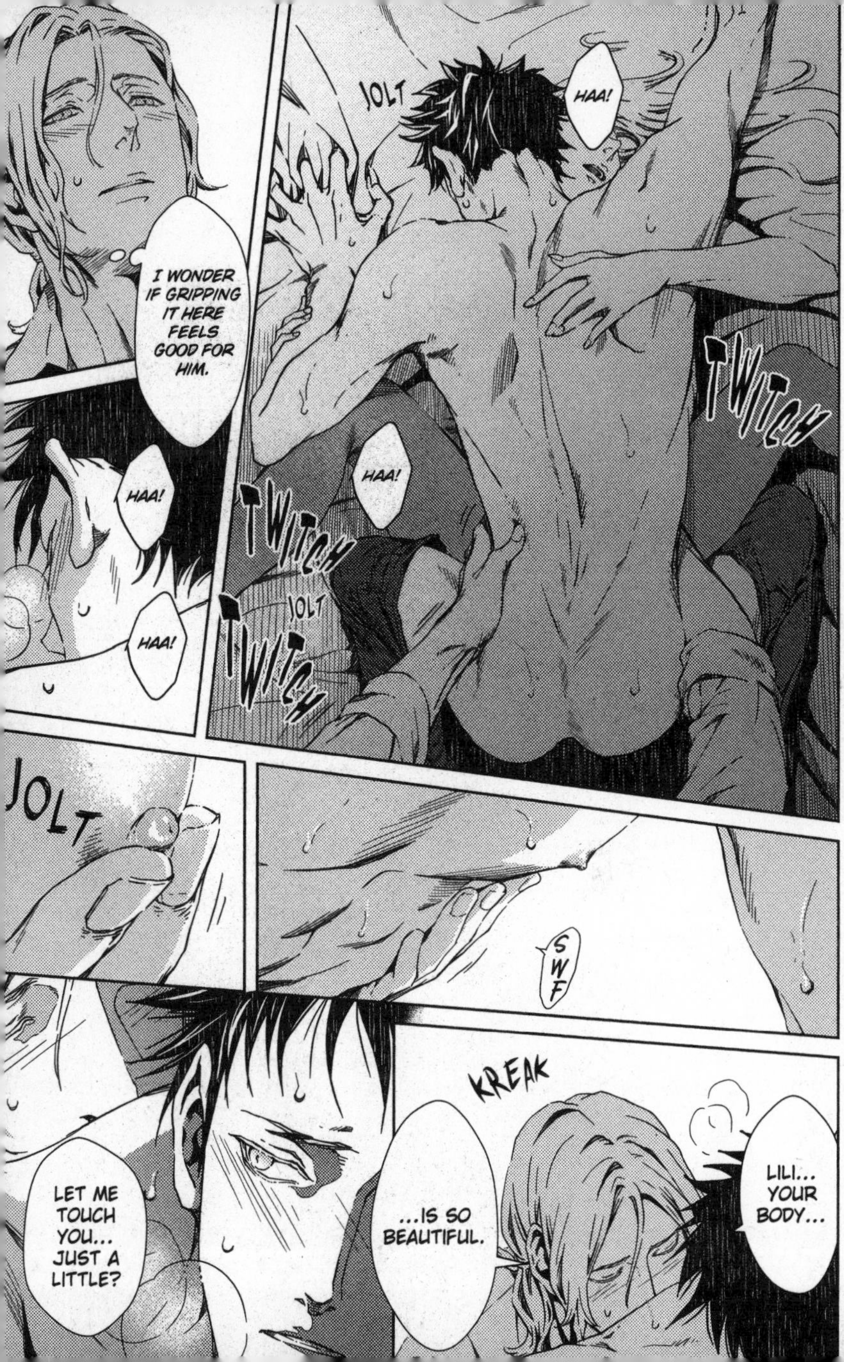
JOLT
HAA!
TWITCH
HAA!
TWITCH
JOLT
TWITCH
I WONDER IF GRIPPING IT HERE FEELS GOOD FOR HIM.
HAA!
HAA!
SWF
JOLT
KREAK
LILI... YOUR BODY...
...IS SO BEAUTIFUL.
LET ME TOUCH YOU... JUST A LITTLE?

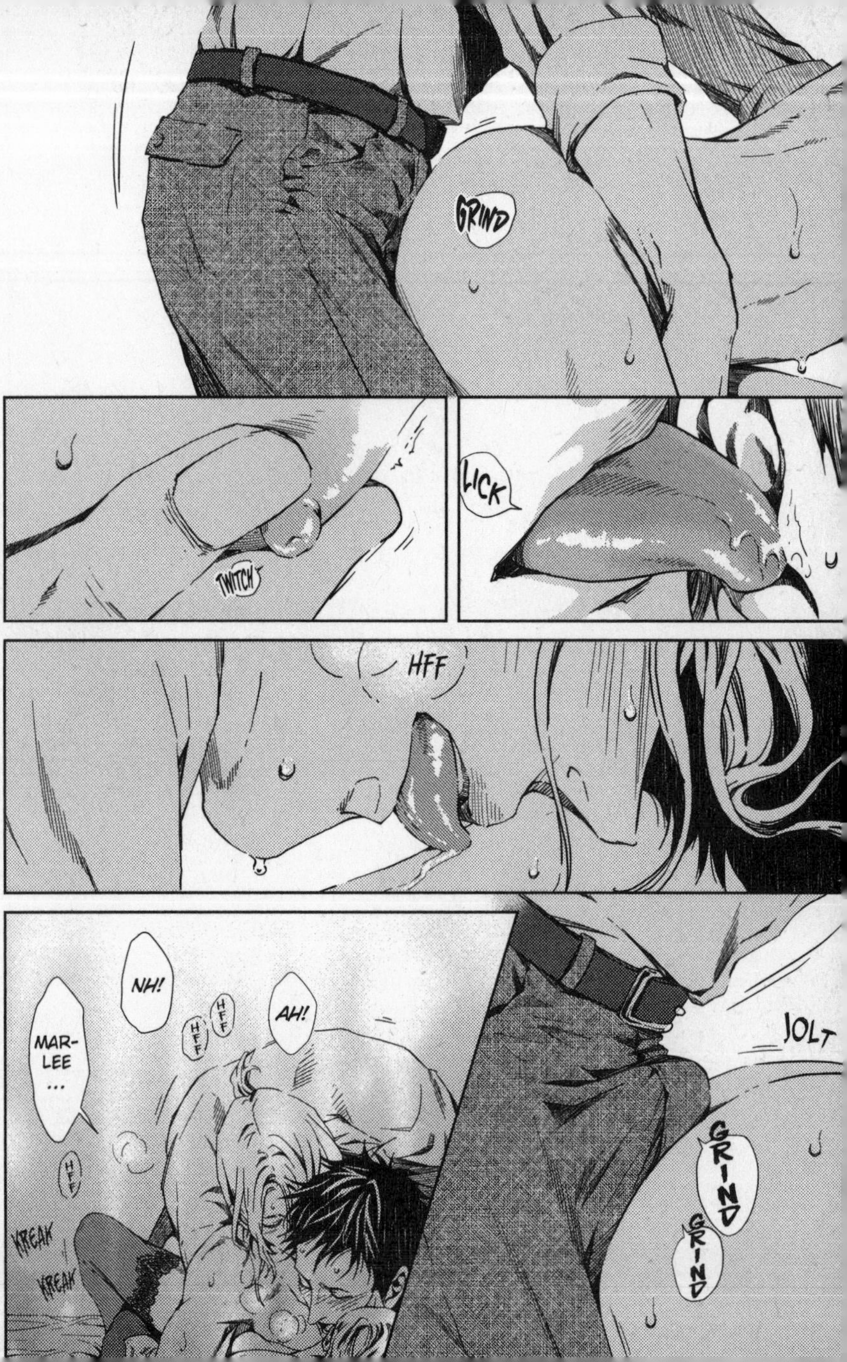
GRIND
LICK
TWITCH
HFF
JOLT
GRIND
GRIND
AH!
HFF
HFF
NH!
MAR-LEE ...
HFF
KREAK
KREAK

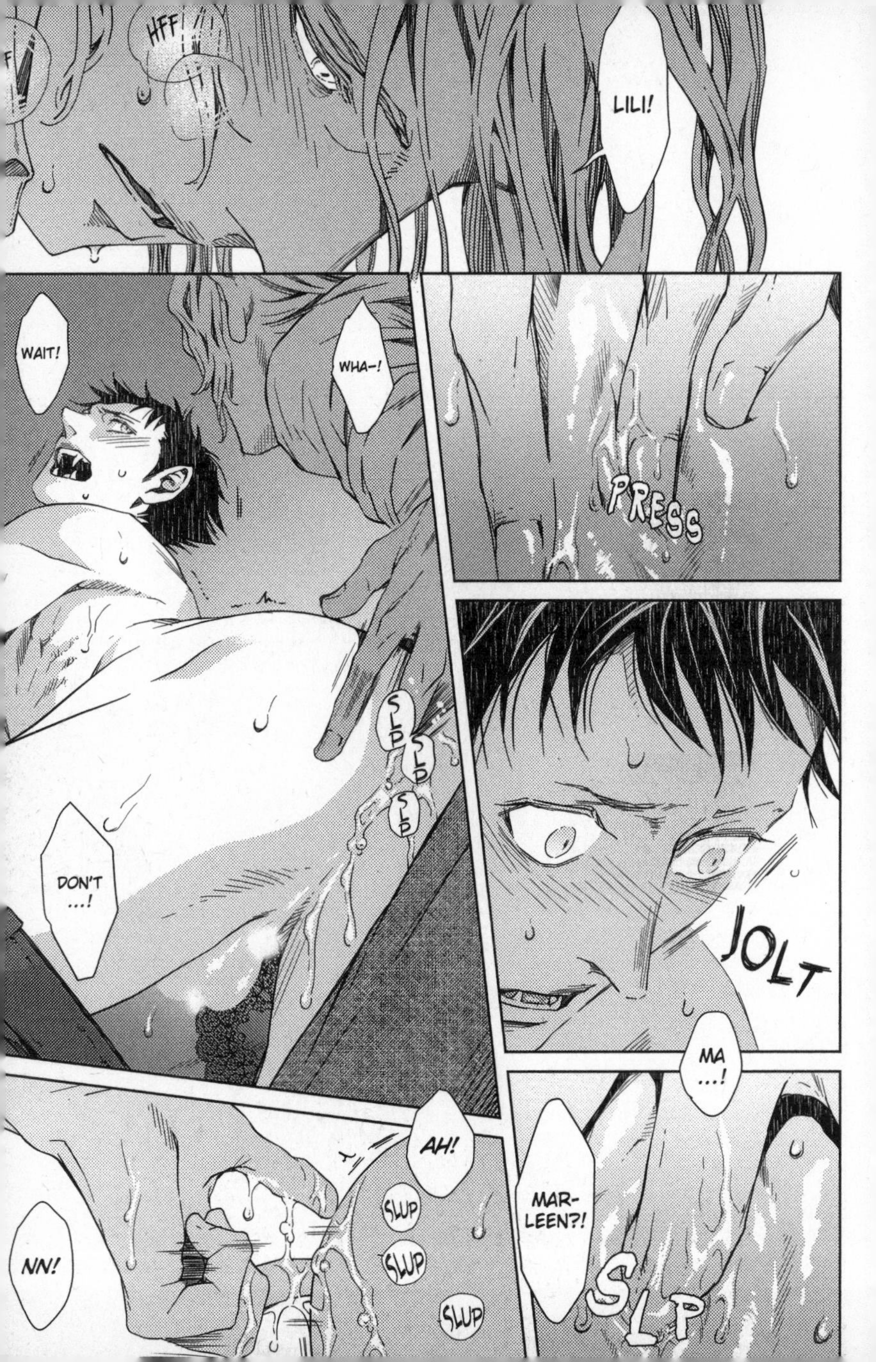
LILI!
HFF!
PRESS
JOLT
WHA-!
WAIT!
SLP SLP SLP
DON'T ...!
MA ...!
MAR-LEEN?!
SLP
AH!
SLUP
SLUP
SLUP
NN!

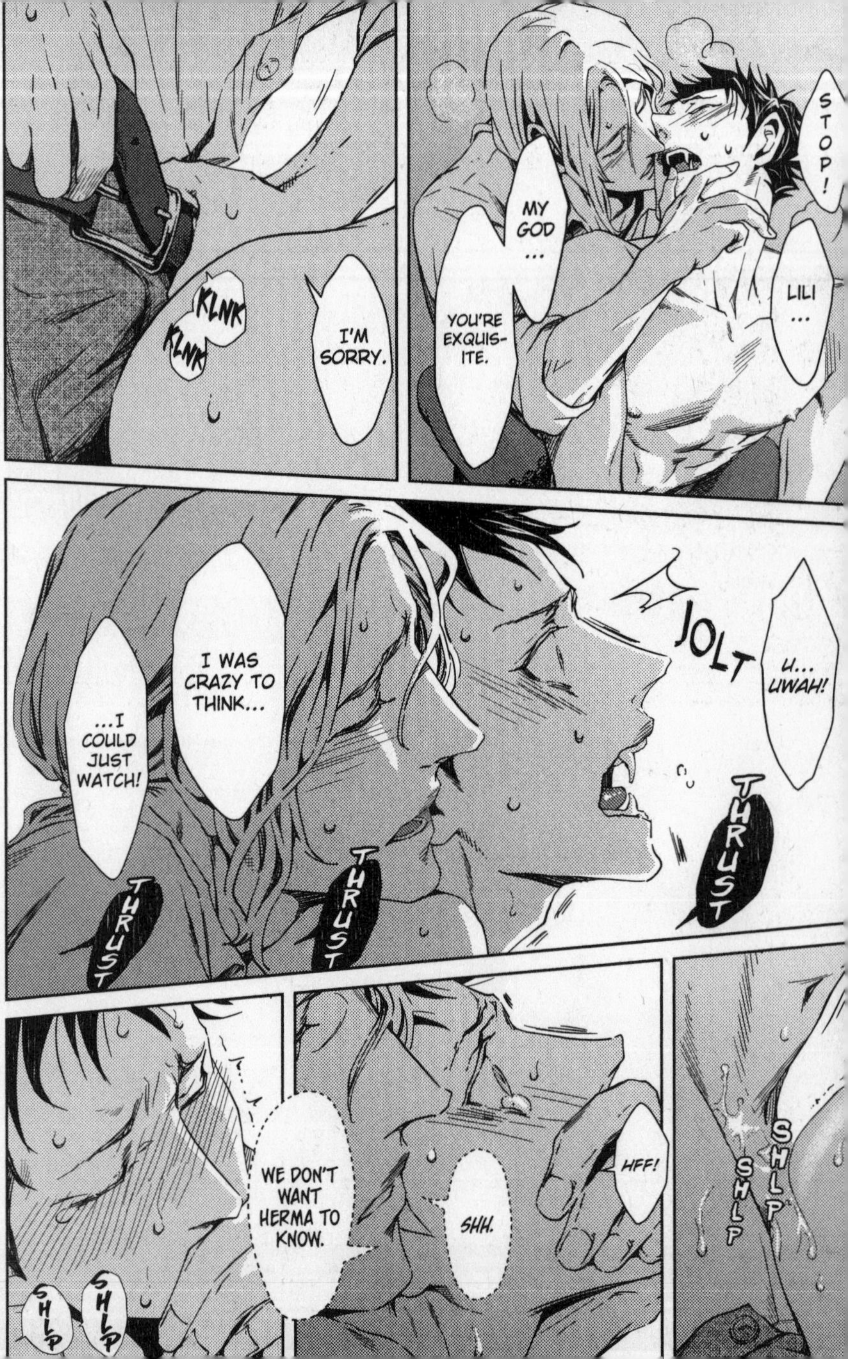
STOP!
LILI...
MY GOD...
YOU'RE EXQUIS-ITE.
I'M SORRY.
KLNK KLNK
U... UWAH!
JOLT
THRUST
I WAS CRAZY TO THINK...
...I COULD JUST WATCH!
THRUST
THRUST
SHLP SHLP
HFF!
SHH.
WE DON'T WANT HERMA TO KNOW.
SHLP SHLP

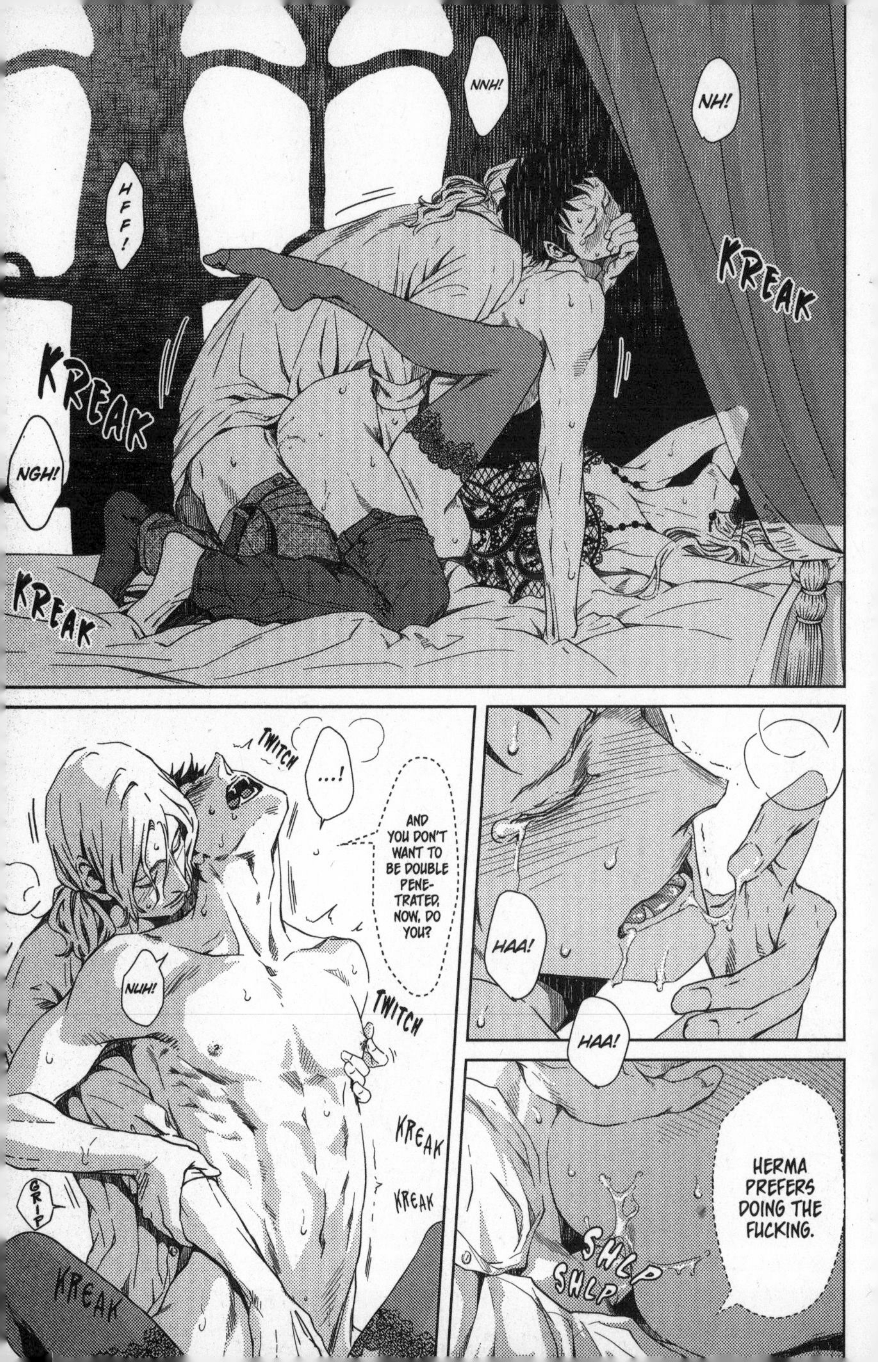
NH!
KREAK
NNH!
HFF!
KREAK
NGH!
KREAK
HAA!
HAA!
HERMA PREFERS DOING THE FUCKING.
SHLP
SHLP
...!
TWITCH
AND YOU DON'T WANT TO BE DOUBLE PENE-TRATED, NOW, DO YOU?
NUH!
TWITCH
KREAK
KREAK
GRIP
KREAK

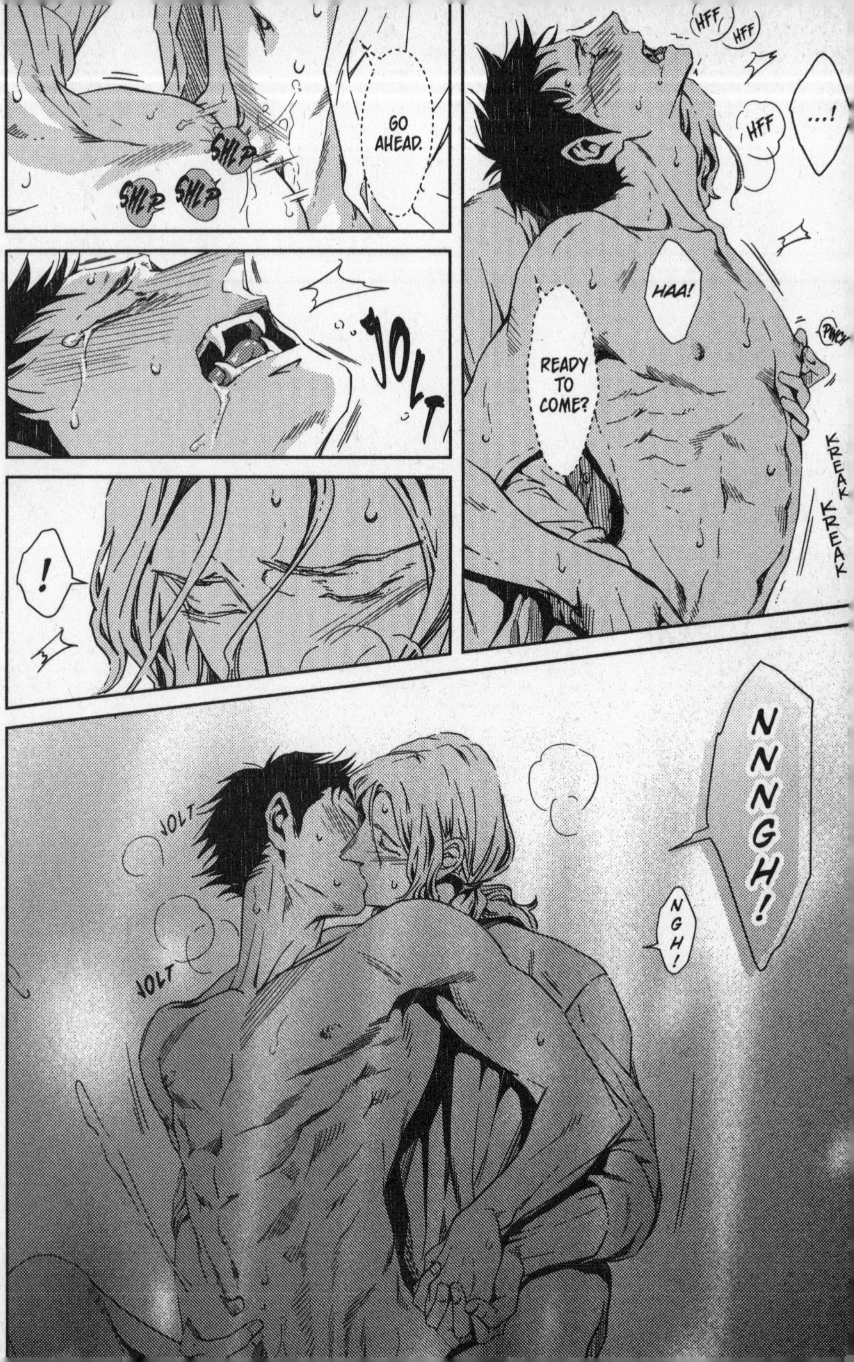
HFF
HFF
...!
HFF
HAA!
READY TO COME?
PINCH
KREAK
KREAK
GO AHEAD.
SHLP
SHLP
SHLP
JOLT
!
NNNGH!
NGH!
JOLT
JOLT

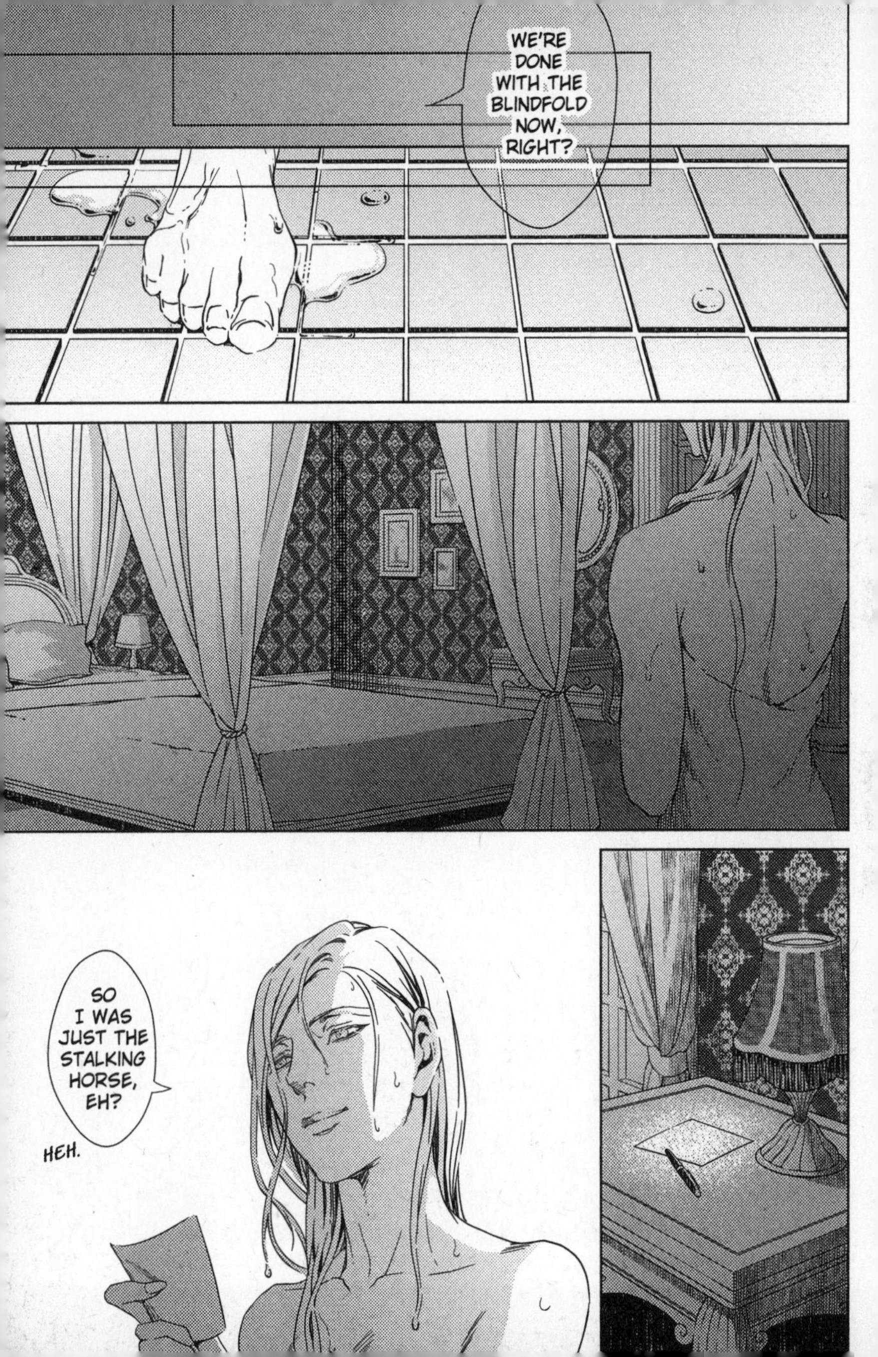
WE'RE DONE WITH THE BLINDFOLD NOW, RIGHT?
SO I WAS JUST THE STALKING HORSE, EH?
HEH.

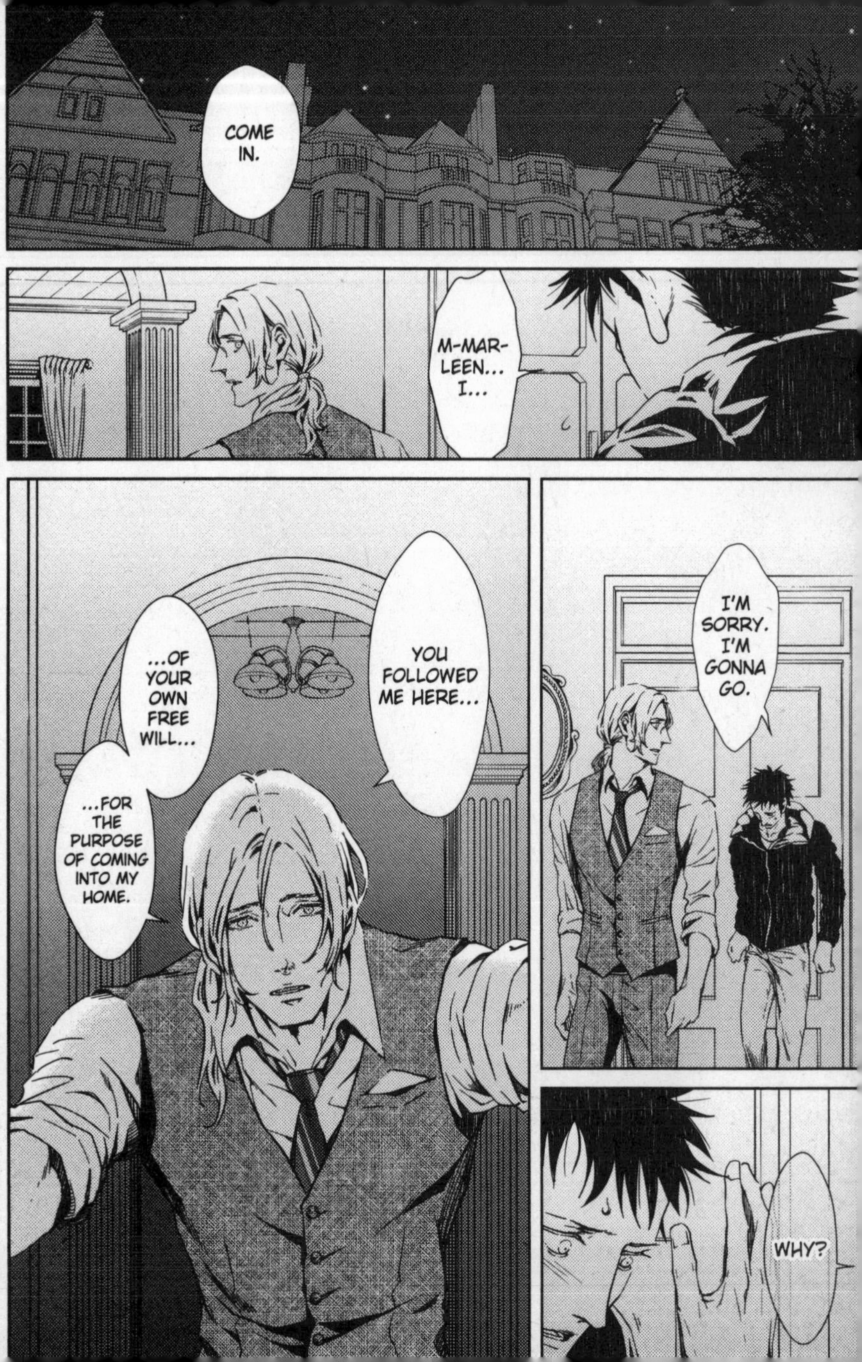
COME IN.
M-MAR-LEEN... I...
I'M SORRY. I'M GONNA GO.
WHY?
YOU FOLLOWED ME HERE...
...OF YOUR OWN FREE WILL...
...FOR THE PURPOSE OF COMING INTO MY HOME.

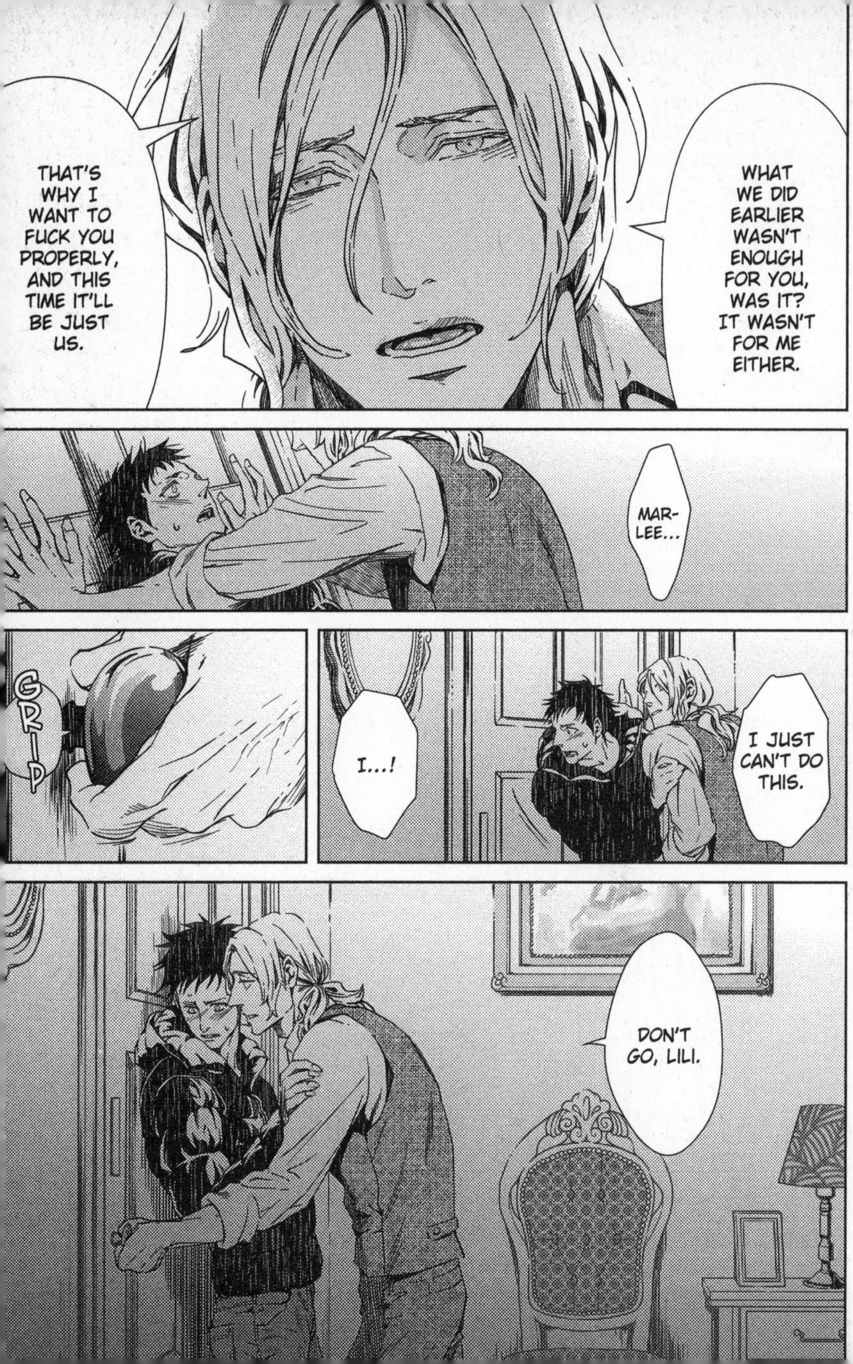
WHAT WE DID EARLIER WASN'T ENOUGH FOR YOU, WAS IT? IT WASN'T FOR ME EITHER.
THAT'S WHY I WANT TO FUCK YOU PROPERLY, AND THIS TIME IT'LL BE JUST US.
MAR-LEE...
I JUST CAN'T DO THIS.
I...!
GRIP
DON'T GO, LILI.

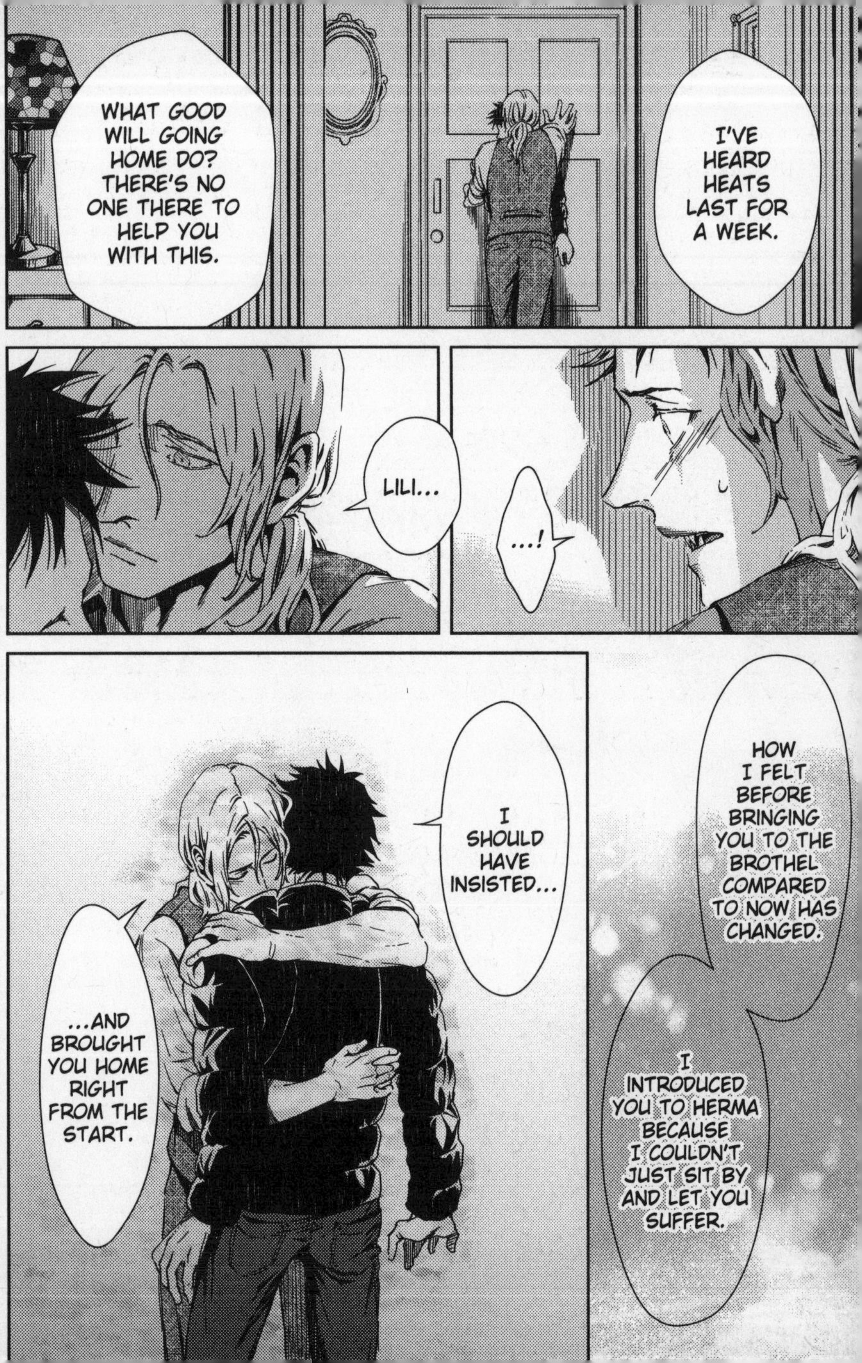
I'VE HEARD HEATS LAST FOR A WEEK.
WHAT GOOD WILL GOING HOME DO? THERE'S NO ONE THERE TO HELP YOU WITH THIS.
...!
LILI...
HOW I FELT BEFORE BRINGING YOU TO THE BROTHEL COMPARED TO NOW HAS CHANGED.
I INTRODUCED YOU TO HERMA BECAUSE I COULDN'T JUST SIT BY AND LET YOU SUFFER.
I SHOULD HAVE INSISTED...
...AND BROUGHT YOU HOME RIGHT FROM THE START.

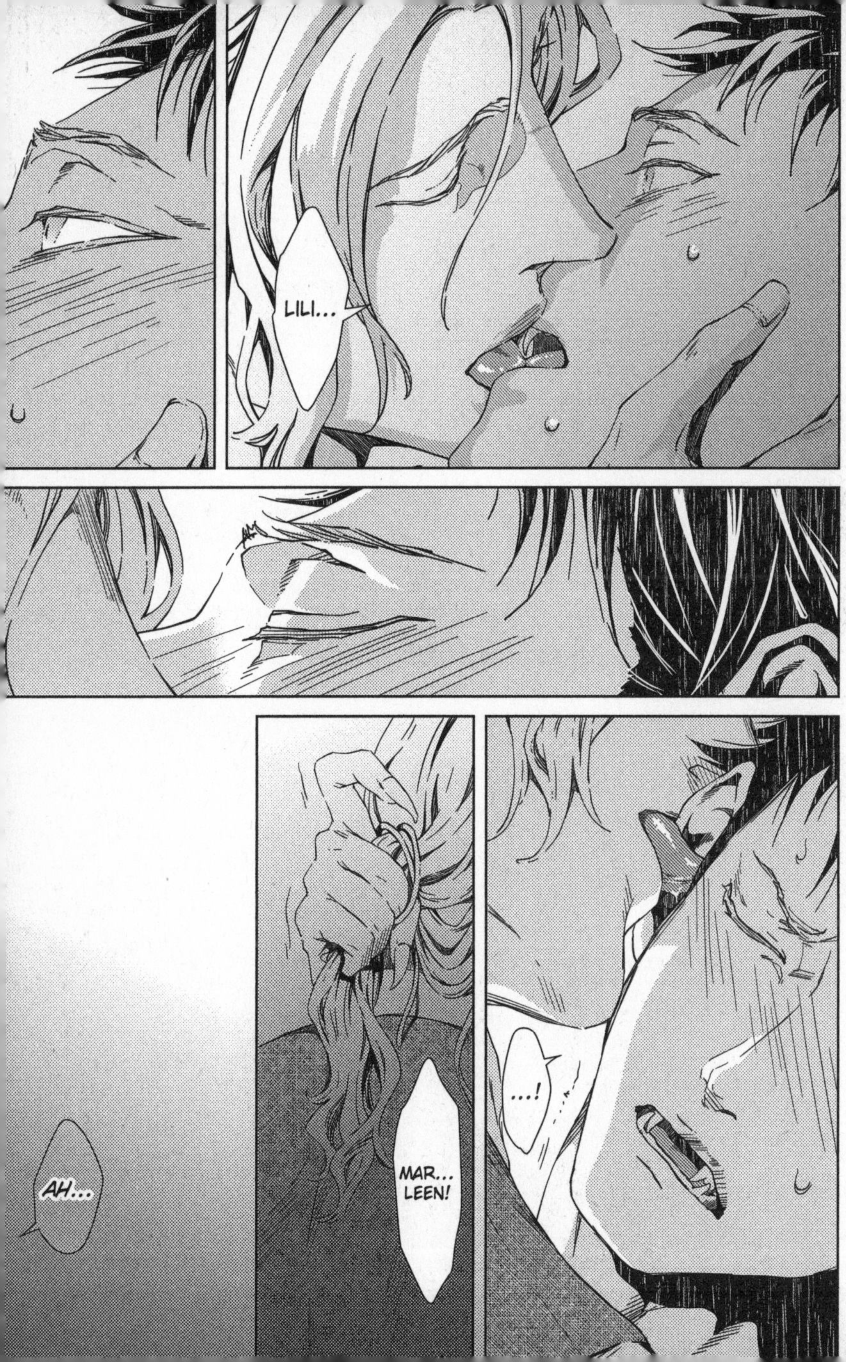
LILI...
...!
MAR... LEEN!
AH...

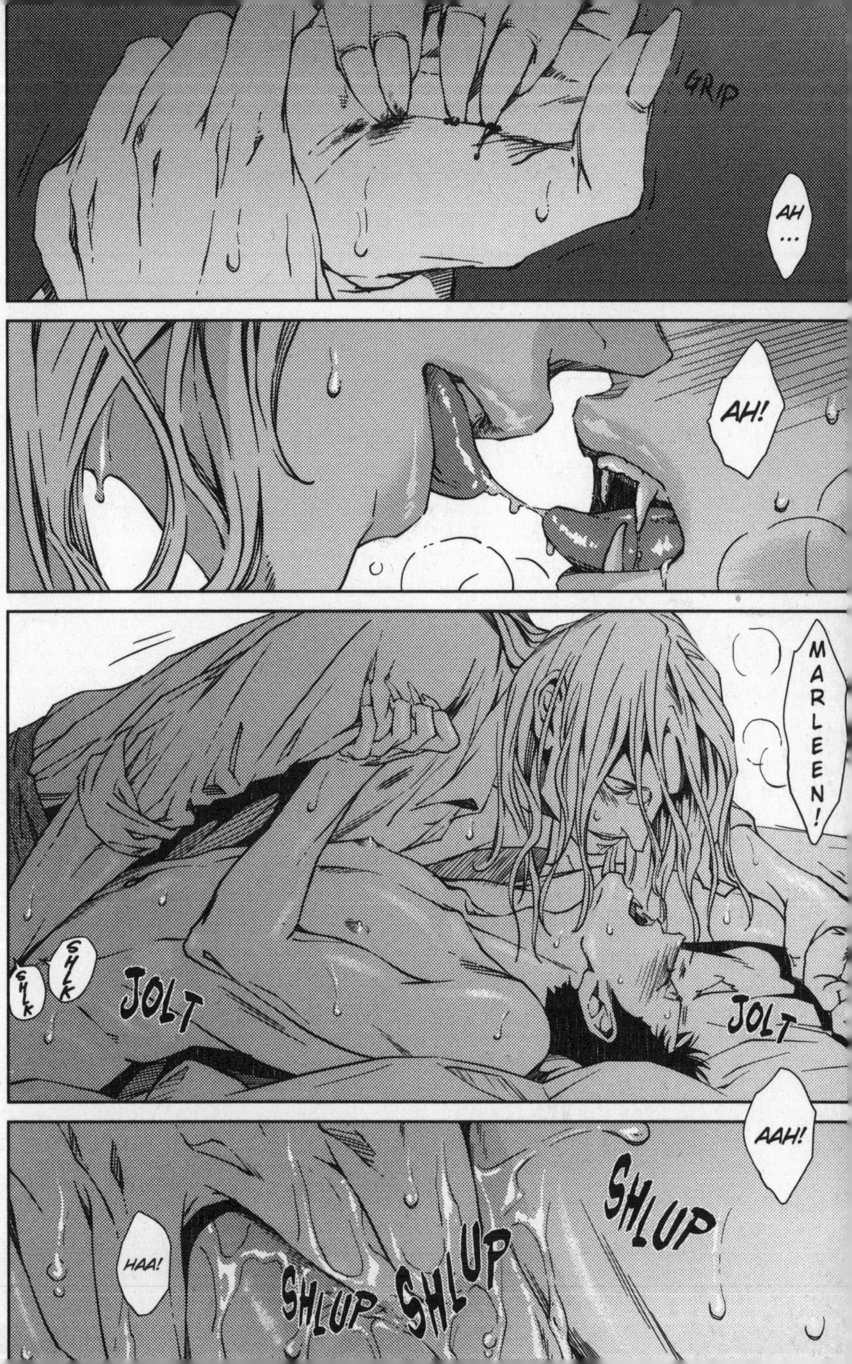
GRIP
AH...
AH!
MARLEEN!
JOLT
SHLK
SHLK
JOLT
AAH!
SHLUP
SHLUP
HAA!
SHLUP

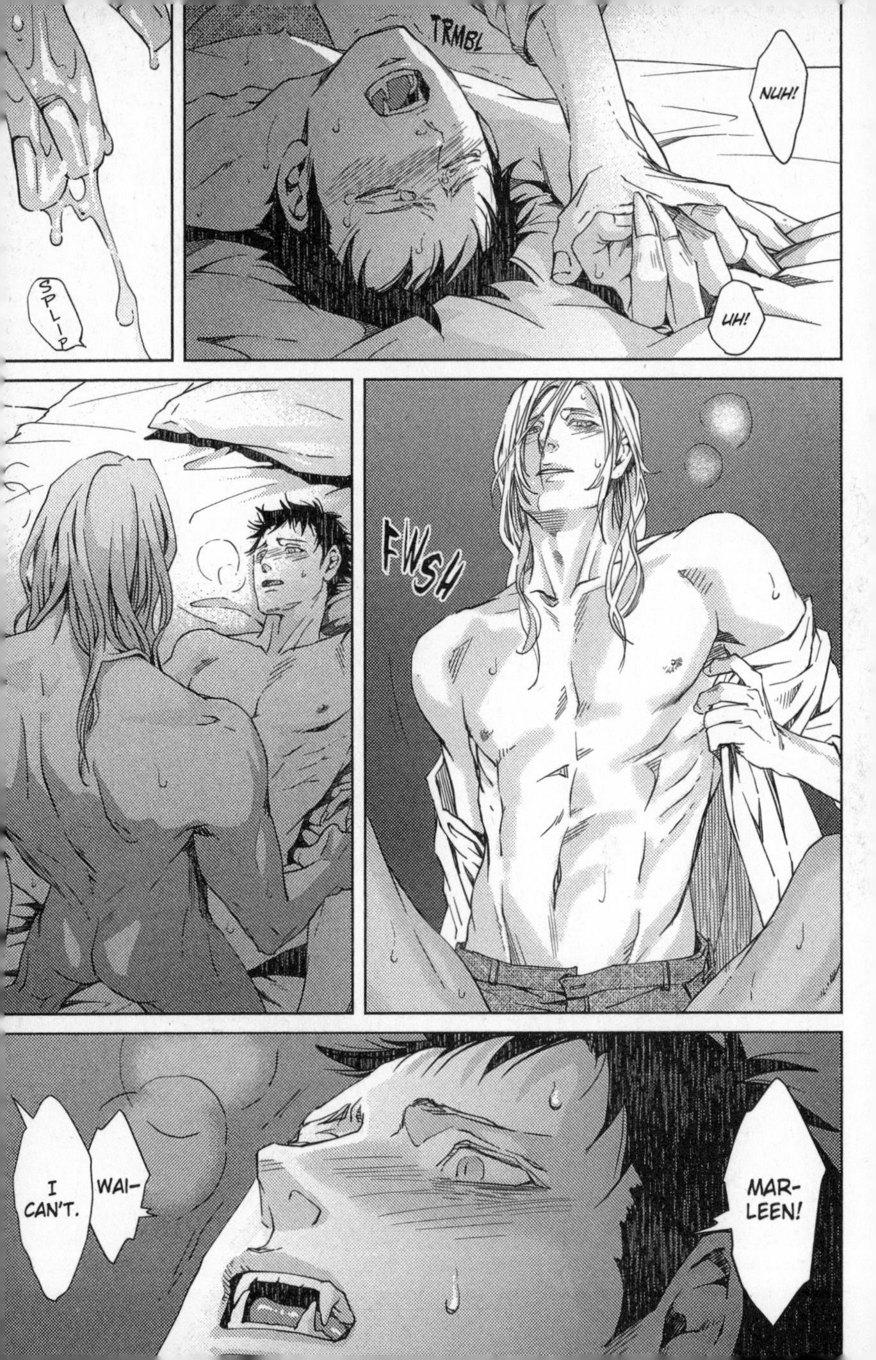
TRMBL
NUH!
UH!
SPLIP
FWSH
MAR-LEEN!
WAI-
I CAN'T.

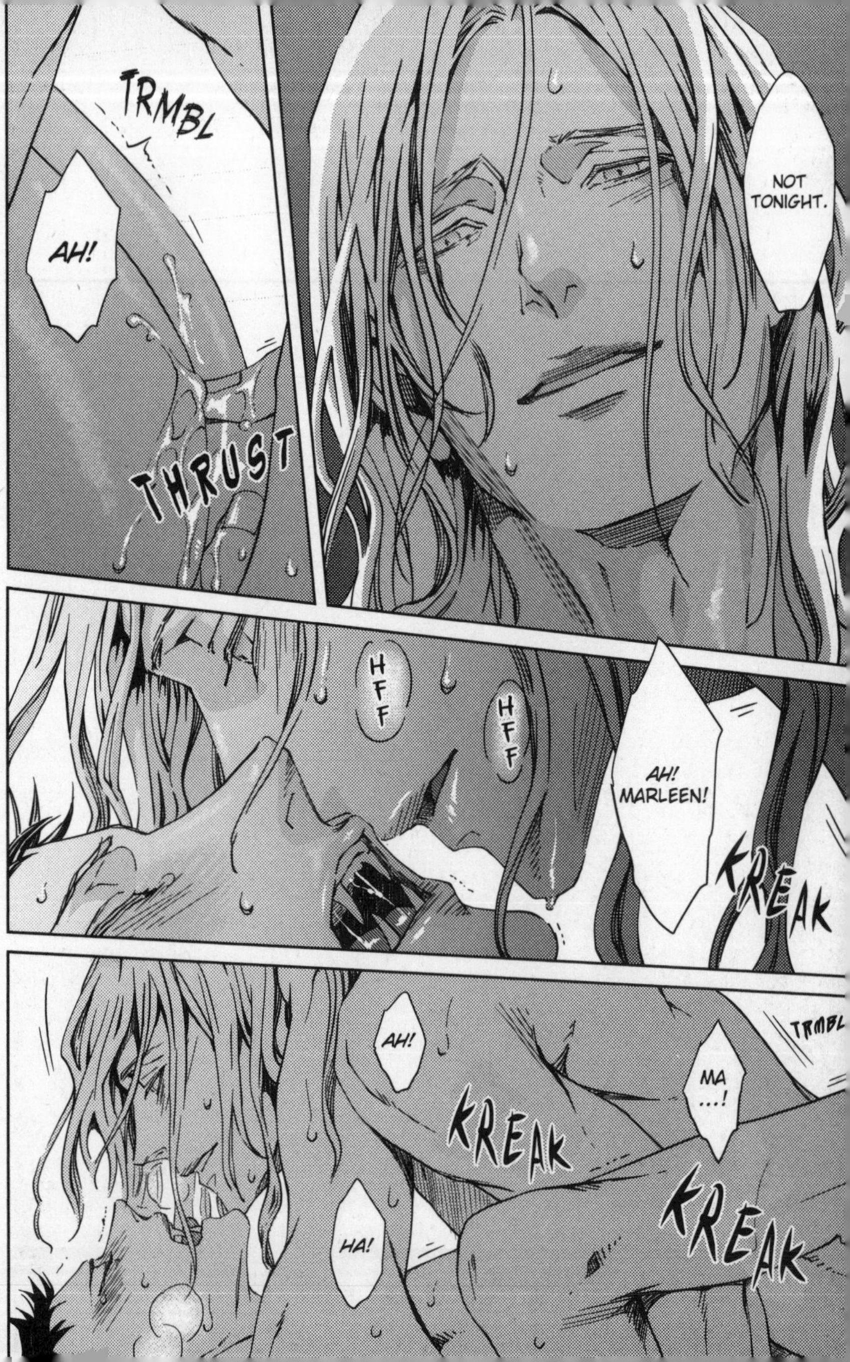
NOT TONIGHT.
TRMBL
AH!
THRUST
AH! MARLEEN!
KREAK
HFF
HFF
TRMBL
MA ...!
AH!
KREAK
KREAK
HA!

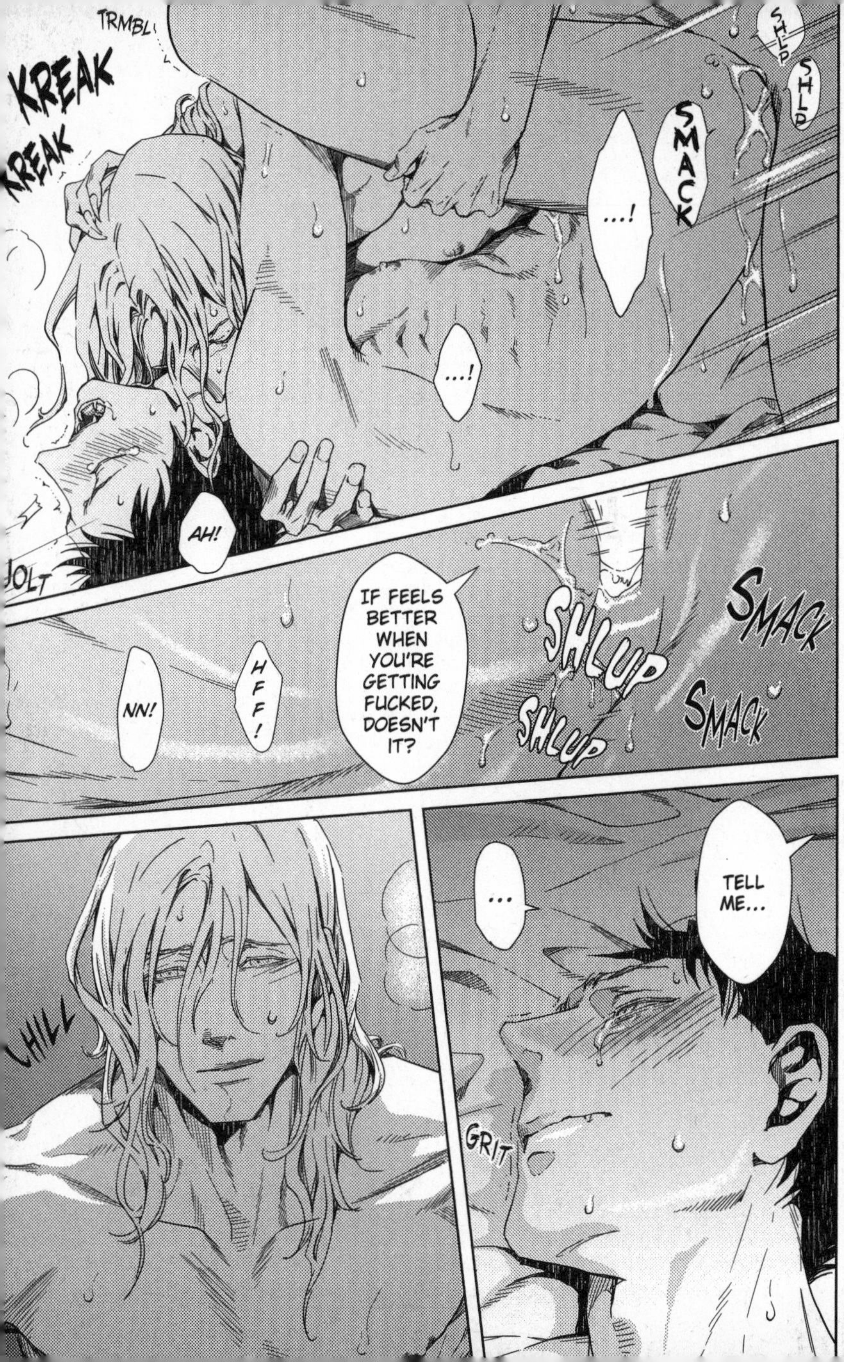
SHLP
SHLP
SMACK
...!
...!
TRMBL
KREAK
KREAK
AH!
JOLT
SMACK
SMACK
SHLUP
SHLUP
IF FEELS BETTER WHEN YOU'RE GETTING FUCKED, DOESN'T IT?
HFF!
NN!
TELL ME...
...
GRIT
CHILL

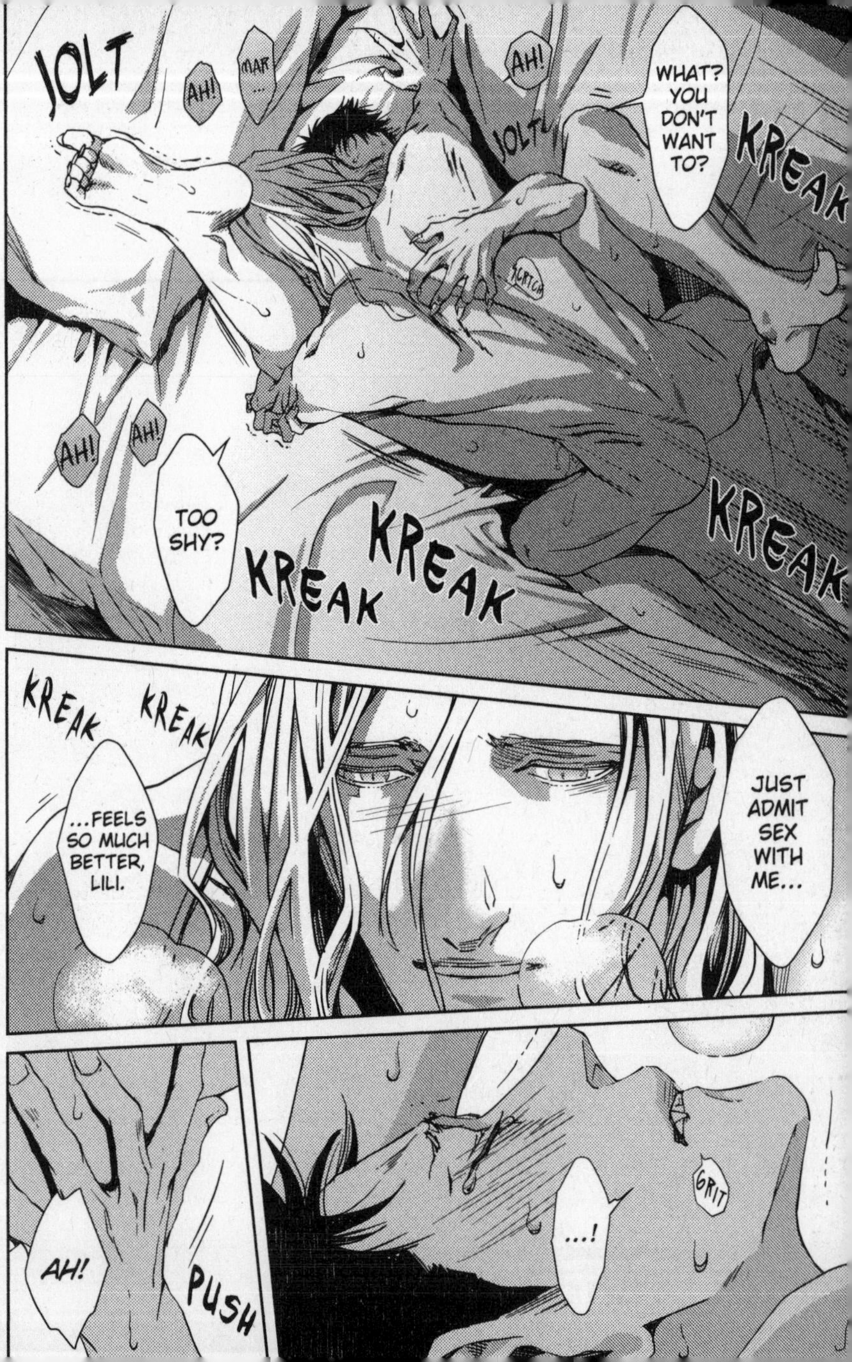
WHAT? YOU DON'T WANT TO?
KREAK
AH!
JOLT
MAR...
AH!
JOLT
SCRTCH
KREAK
AH!
AH!
TOO SHY?
KREAK
KREAK
JUST ADMIT SEX WITH ME...
...FEELS SO MUCH BETTER, LILI.
KREAK
KREAK
GRIT
...!
PUSH
AH!

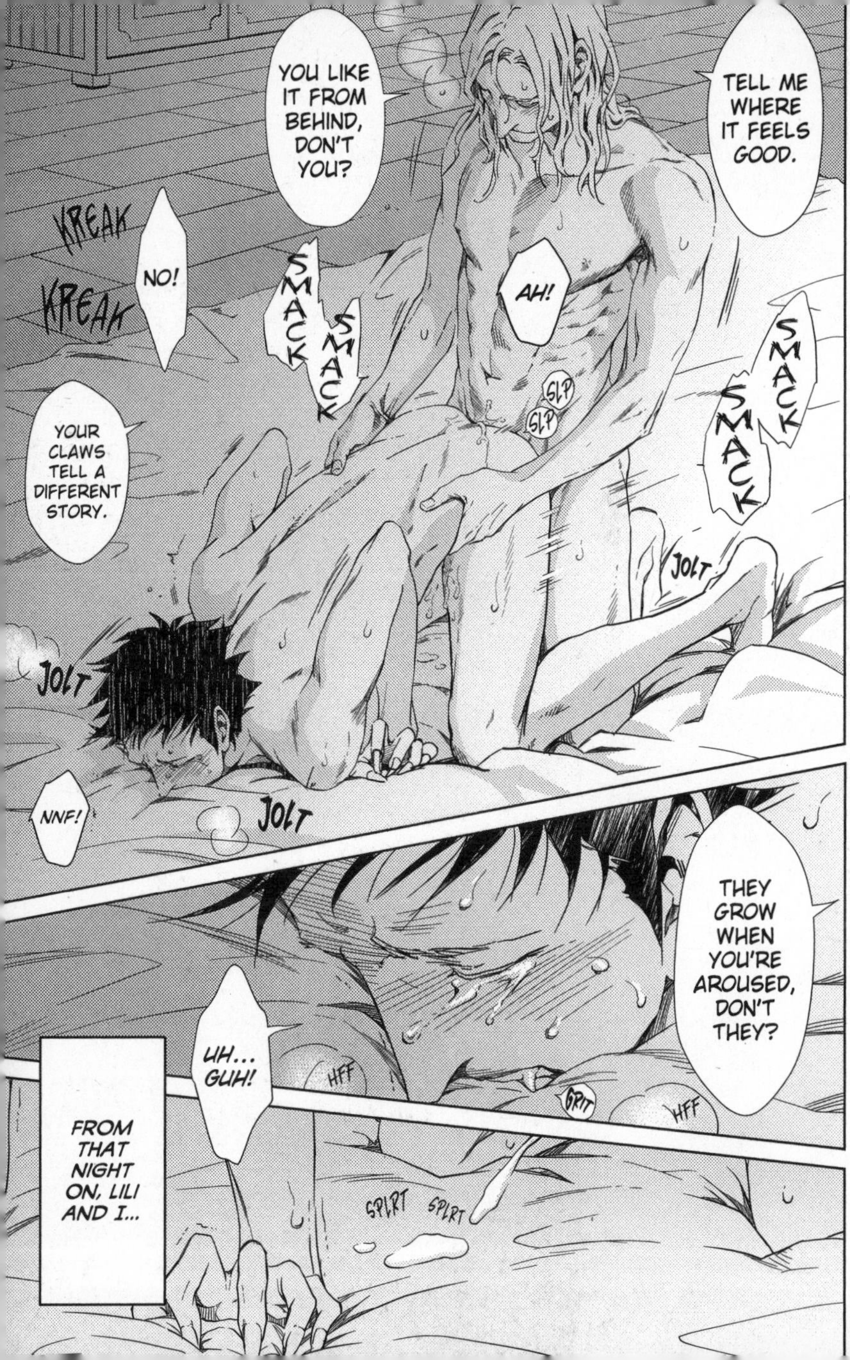
TELL ME WHERE IT FEELS GOOD.
YOU LIKE IT FROM BEHIND, DON'T YOU?
SMACK SMACK
AH!
SLP SLP
SMACK SMACK
NO!
KREAK KREAK
YOUR CLAWS TELL A DIFFERENT STORY.
JOLT
JOLT
JOLT
NNF!
THEY GROW WHEN YOU'RE AROUSED, DON'T THEY?
HFF
GRIT
HFF
UH... GUH!
SPLRT SPLRT
FROM THAT NIGHT ON, LILI AND I...

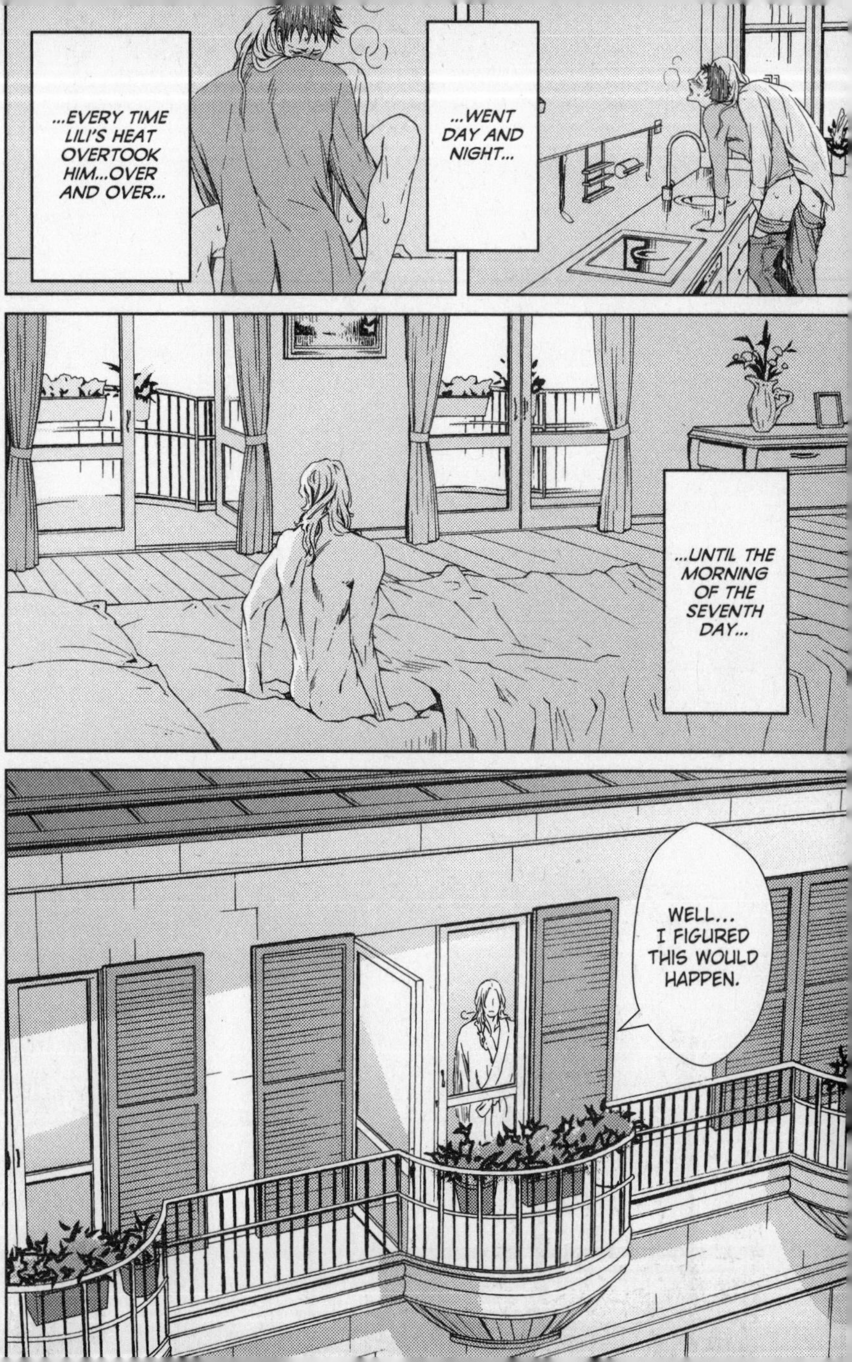
...WENT DAY AND NIGHT...
...EVERY TIME LILI'S HEAT OVERTOOK HIM...OVER AND OVER...
...UNTIL THE MORNING OF THE SEVENTH DAY...
WELL... I FIGURED THIS WOULD HAPPEN.

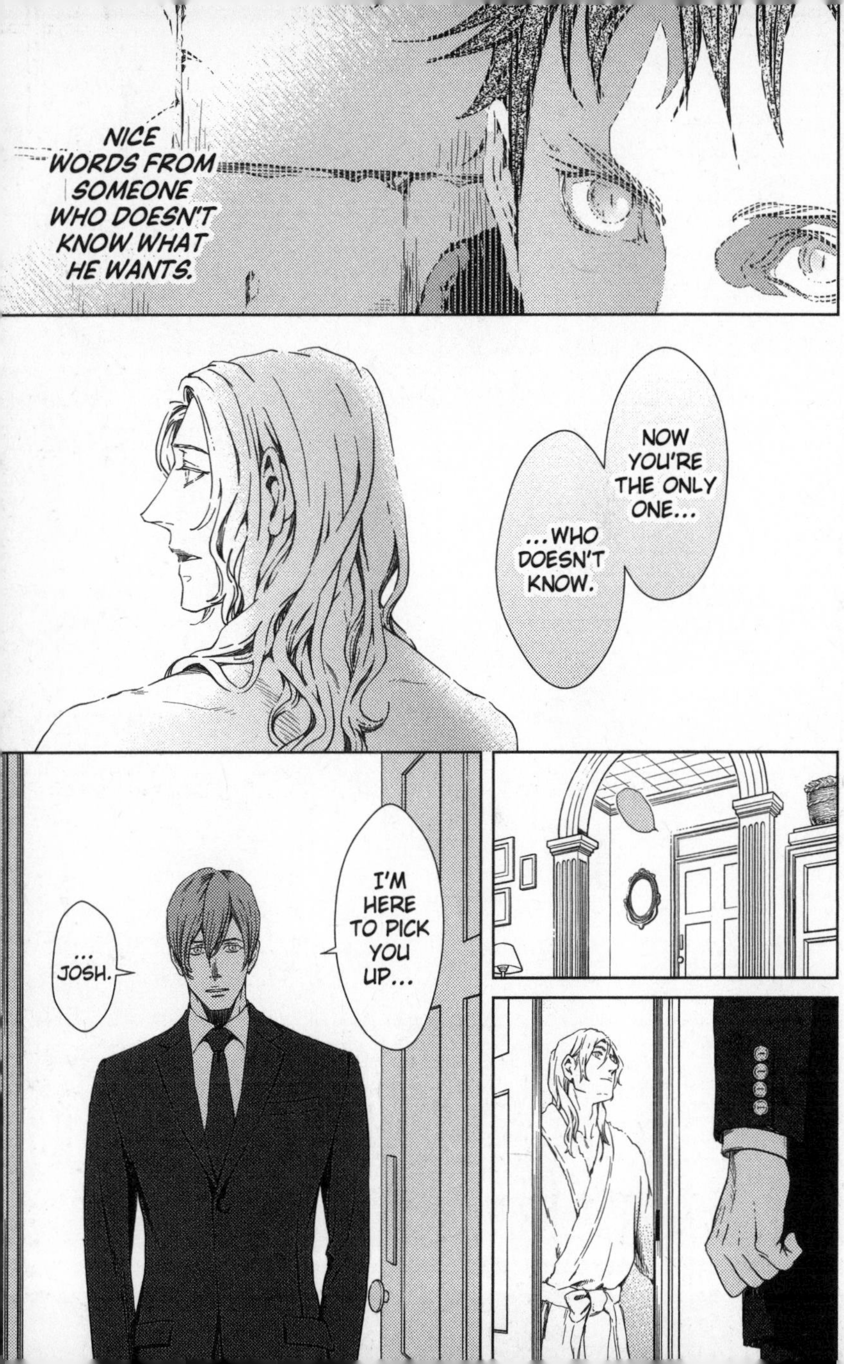
NICE WORDS FROM SOMEONE WHO DOESN'T KNOW WHAT HE WANTS.
NOW YOU'RE THE ONLY ONE...
...WHO DOESN'T KNOW.
I'M HERE TO PICK YOU UP...
...JOSH.

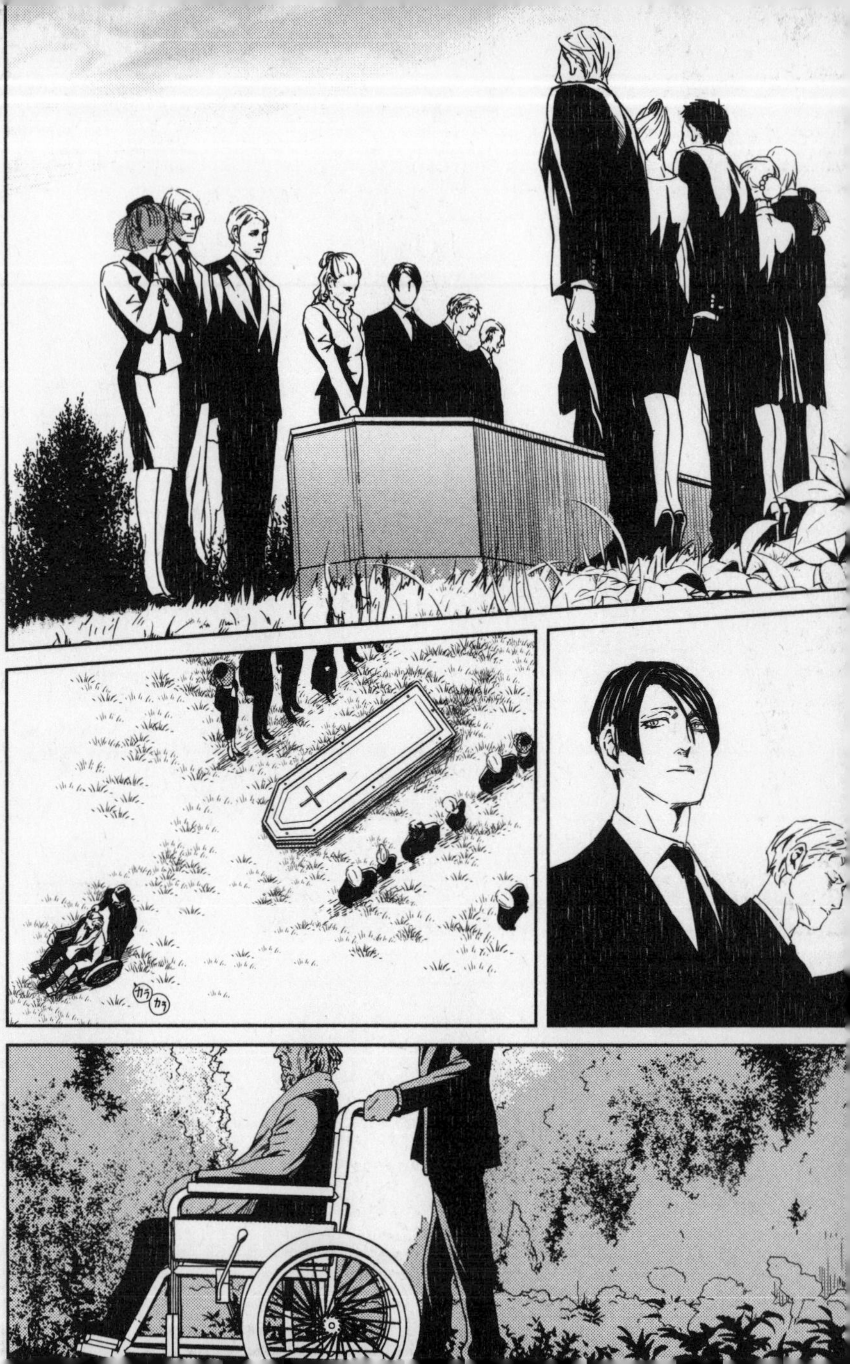
カラ
カラ

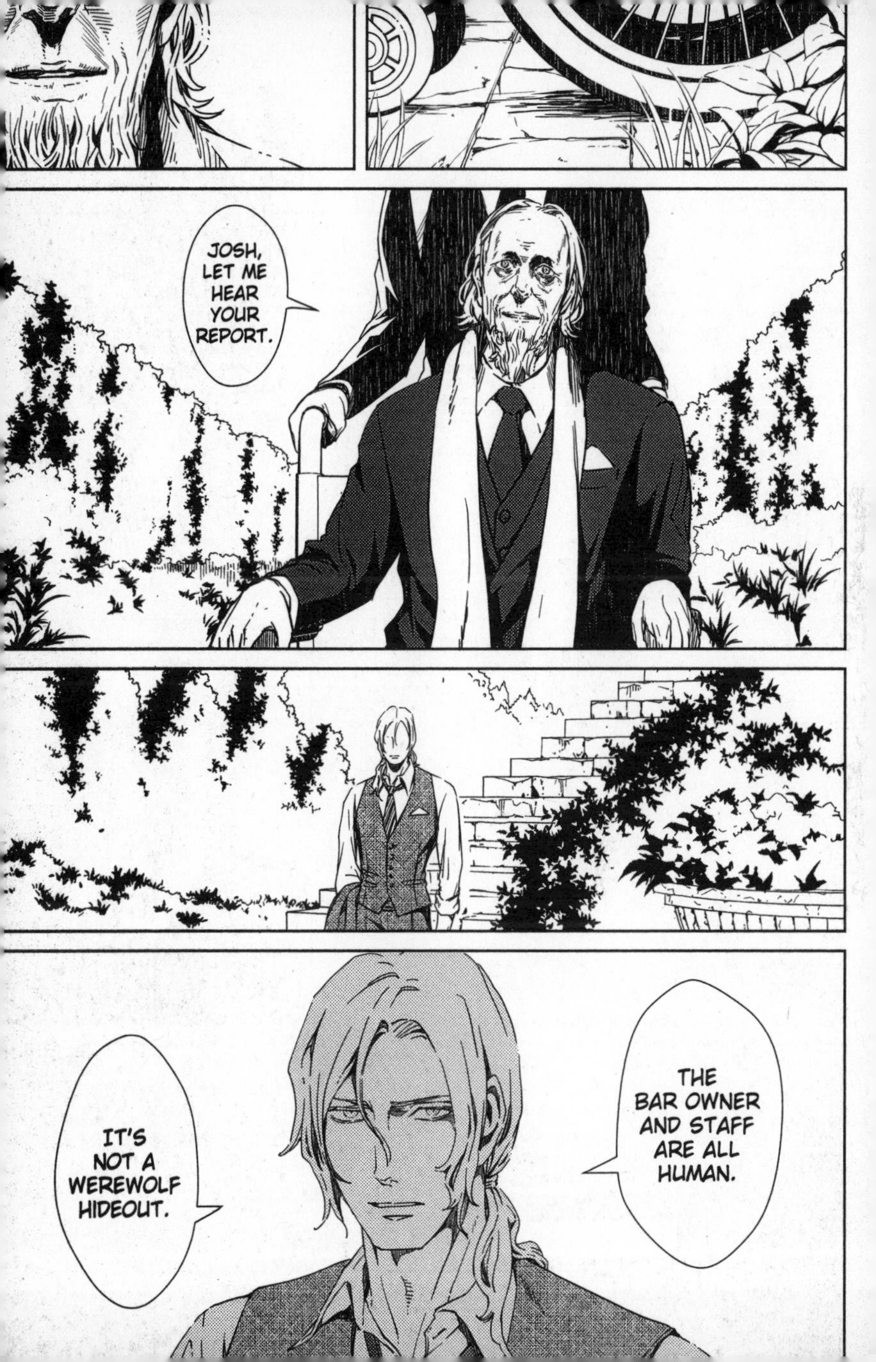
JOSH, LET ME HEAR YOUR REPORT.
THE BAR OWNER AND STAFF ARE ALL HUMAN.
IT'S NOT A WEREWOLF HIDEOUT.

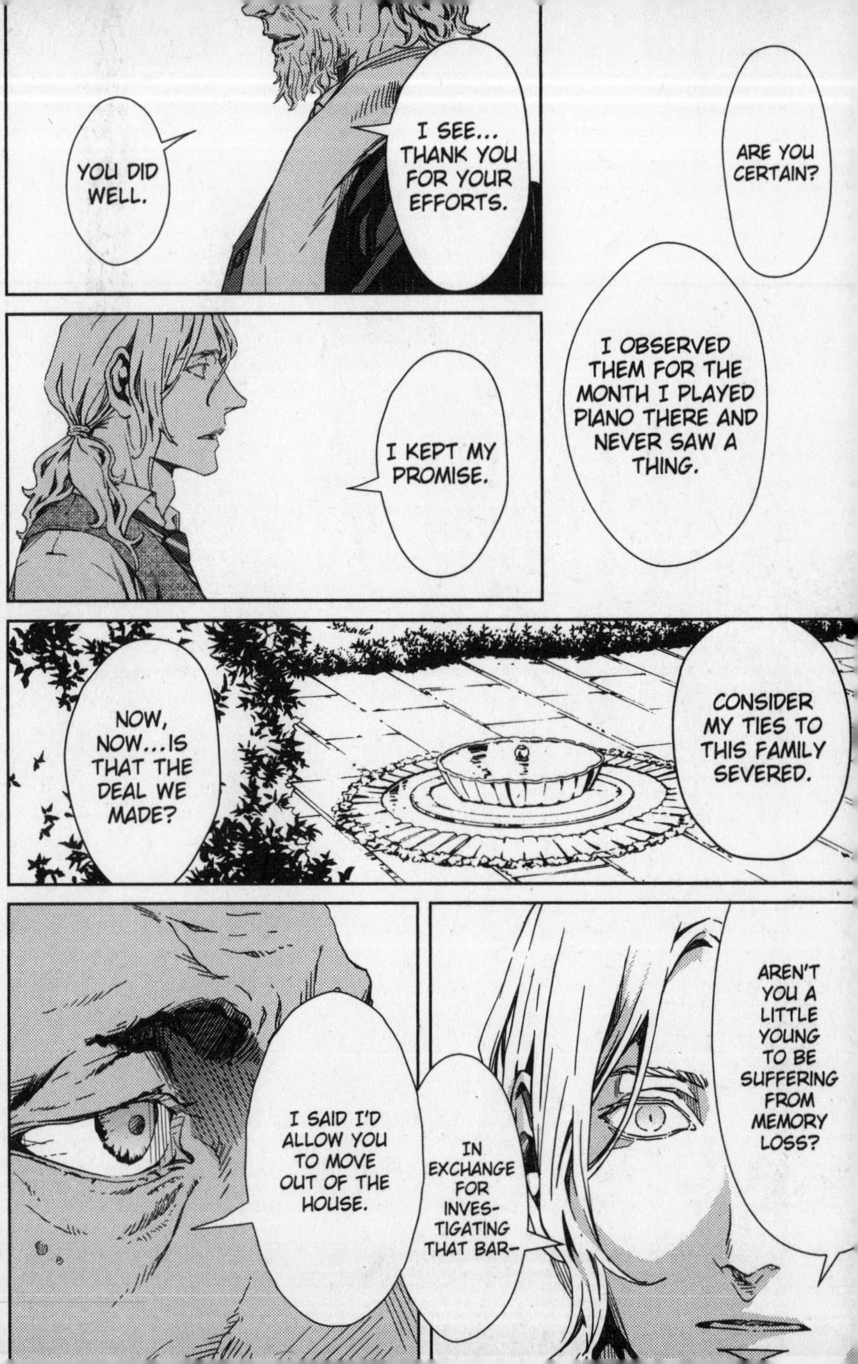
I SEE... THANK YOU FOR YOUR EFFORTS.
YOU DID WELL.
ARE YOU CERTAIN?
I OBSERVED THEM FOR THE MONTH I PLAYED PIANO THERE AND NEVER SAW A THING.
I KEPT MY PROMISE.
CONSIDER MY TIES TO THIS FAMILY SEVERED.
NOW, NOW...IS THAT THE DEAL WE MADE?
AREN'T YOU A LITTLE YOUNG TO BE SUFFERING FROM MEMORY LOSS?
IN EXCHANGE FOR INVES-TIGATING THAT BAR-
I SAID I'D ALLOW YOU TO MOVE OUT OF THE HOUSE.

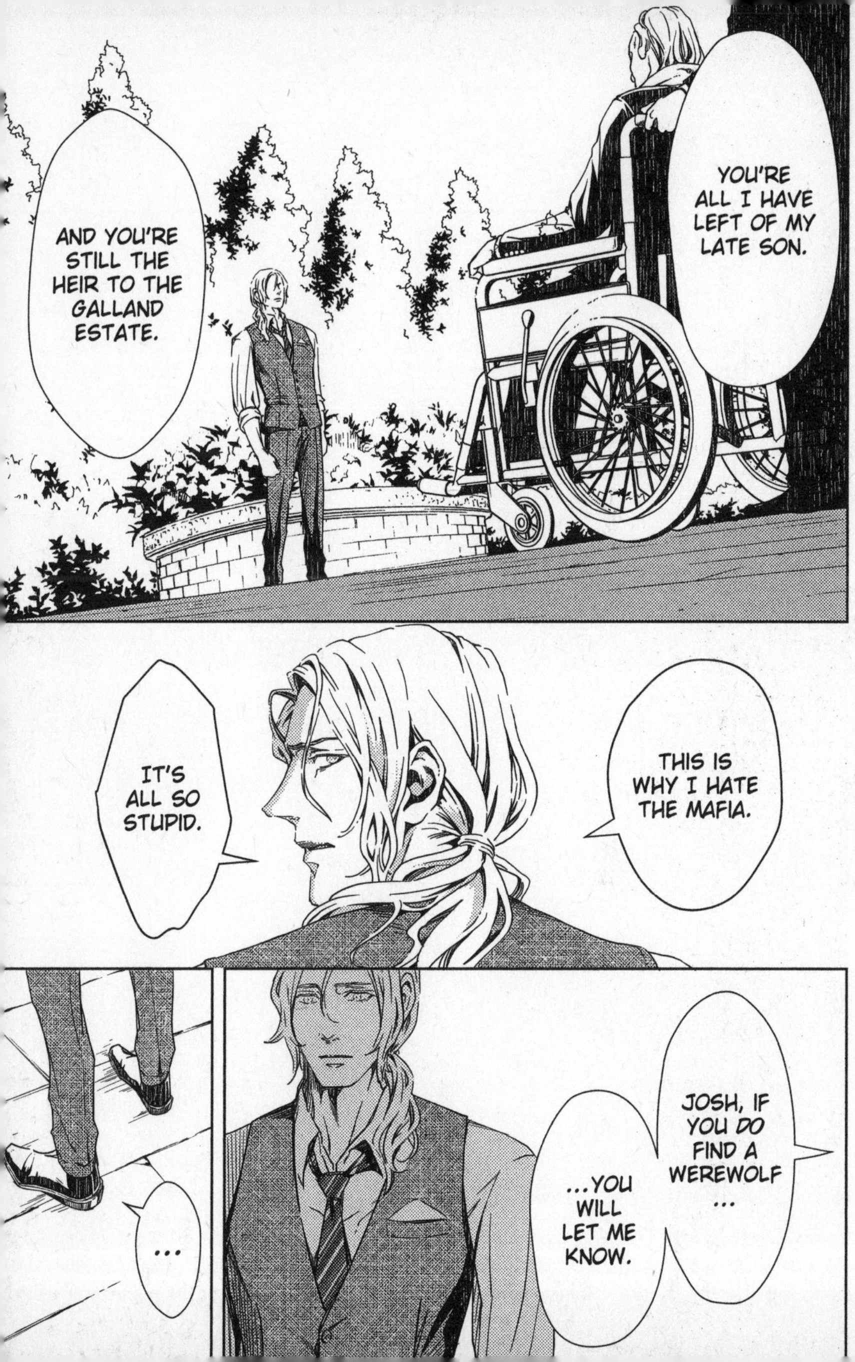
YOU'RE ALL I HAVE LEFT OF MY LATE SON.
AND YOU'RE STILL THE HEIR TO THE GALLAND ESTATE.
THIS IS WHY I HATE THE MAFIA.
IT'S ALL SO STUPID.
JOSH, IF YOU *DO* FIND A WEREWOLF ...
...YOU WILL LET ME KNOW.
...

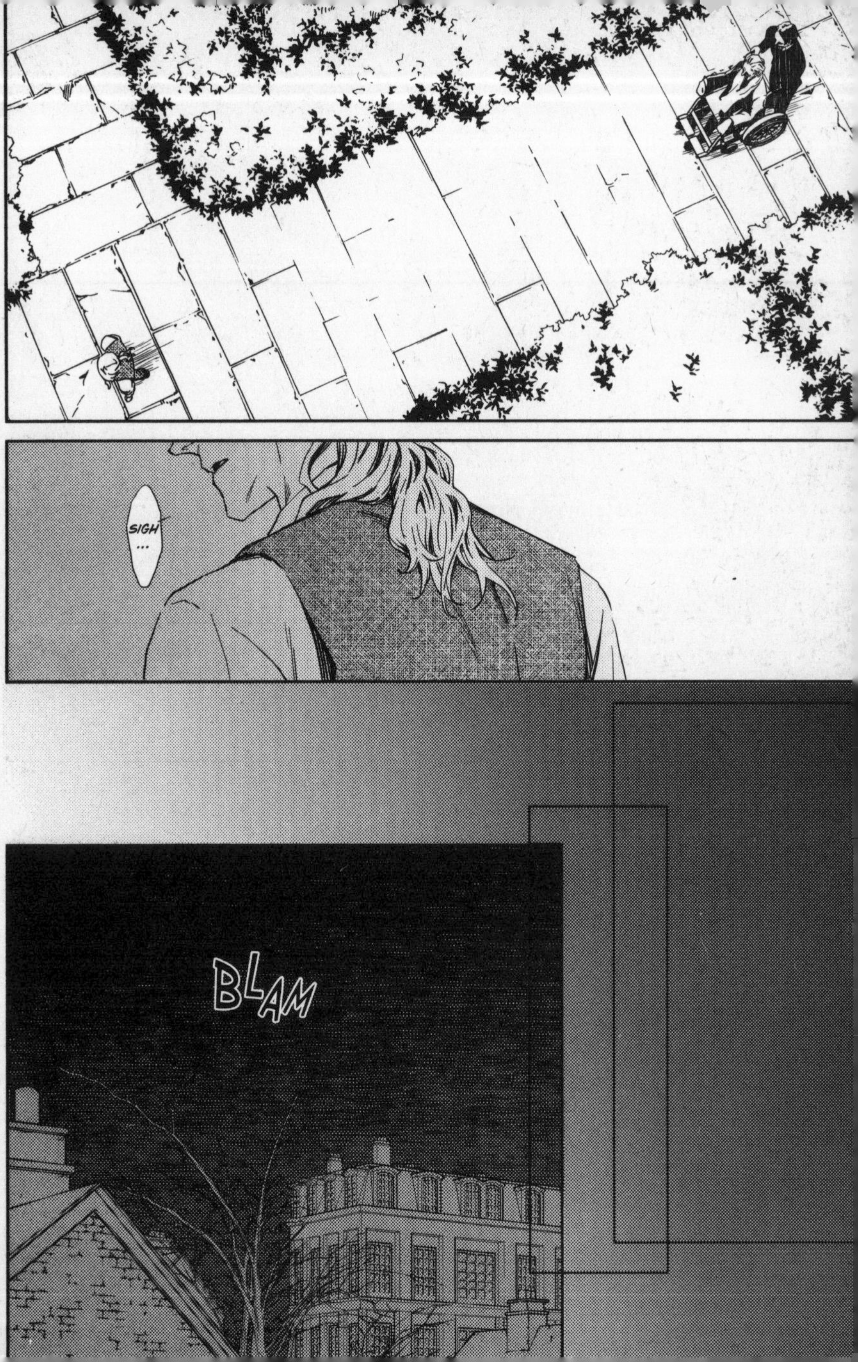
SIGH ...
BLAM

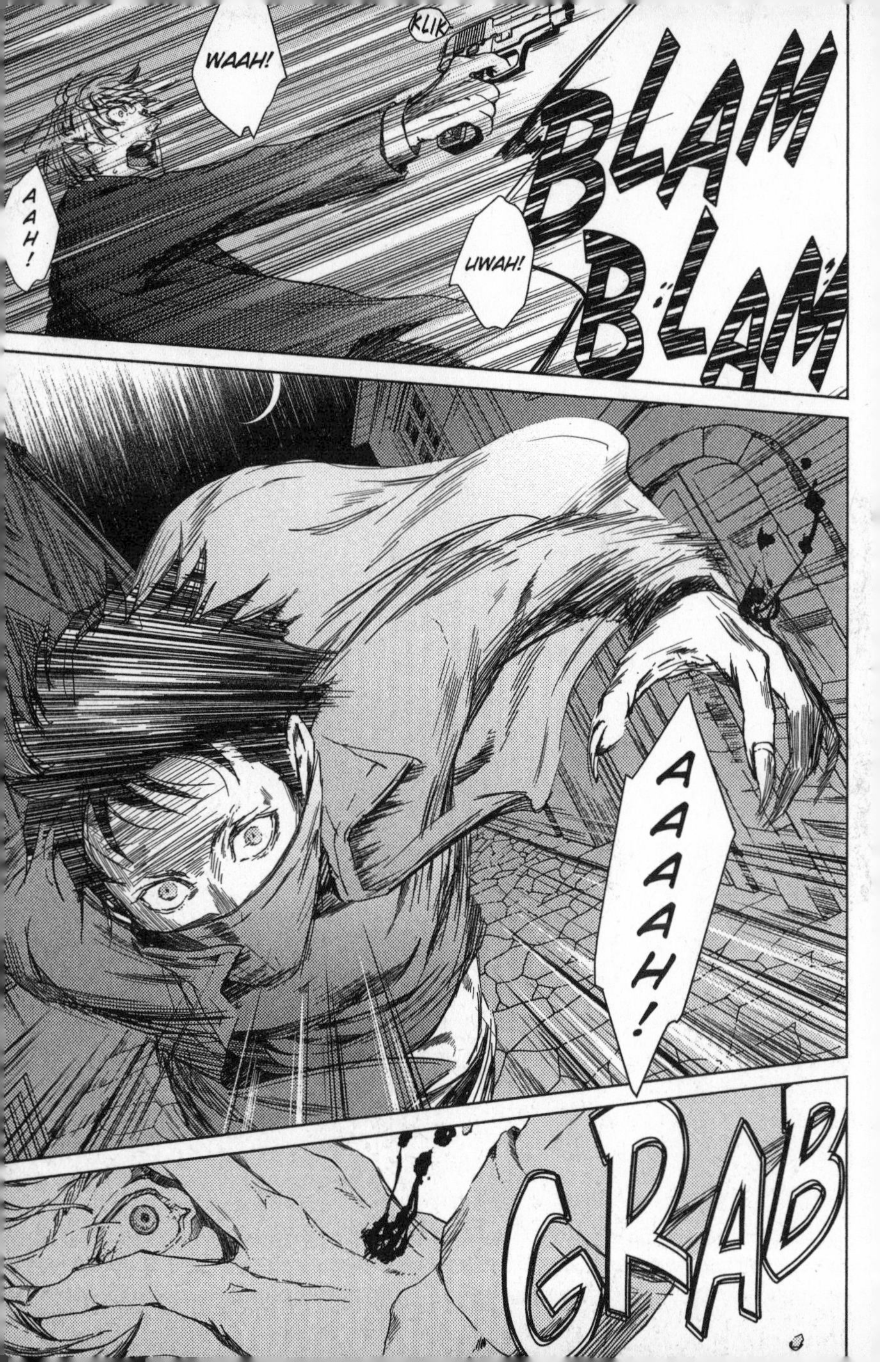
BLAM BLAM
KLIK
WAAH!
UWAH!
AAAH!
AAAAAH!
GRAB

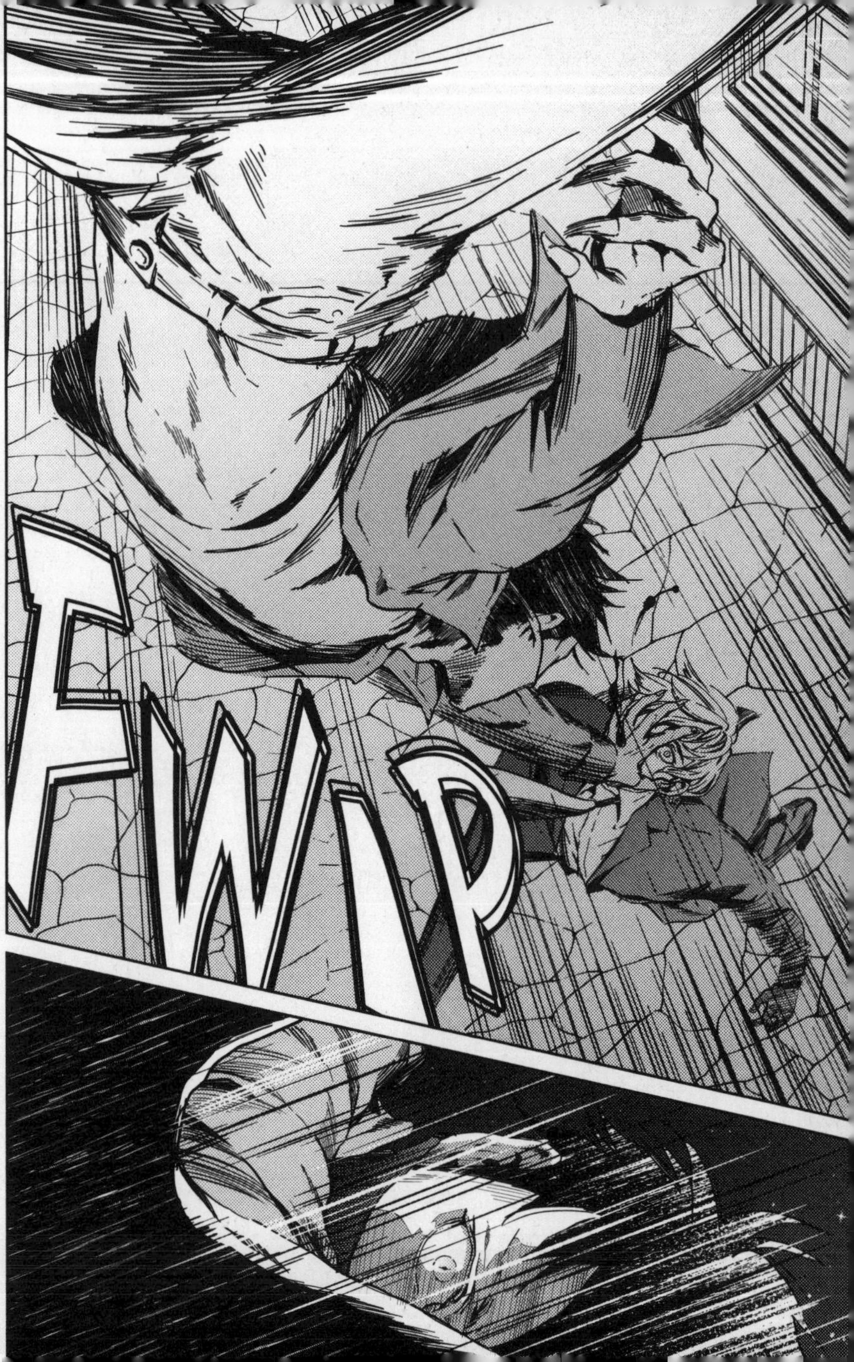
FWIP

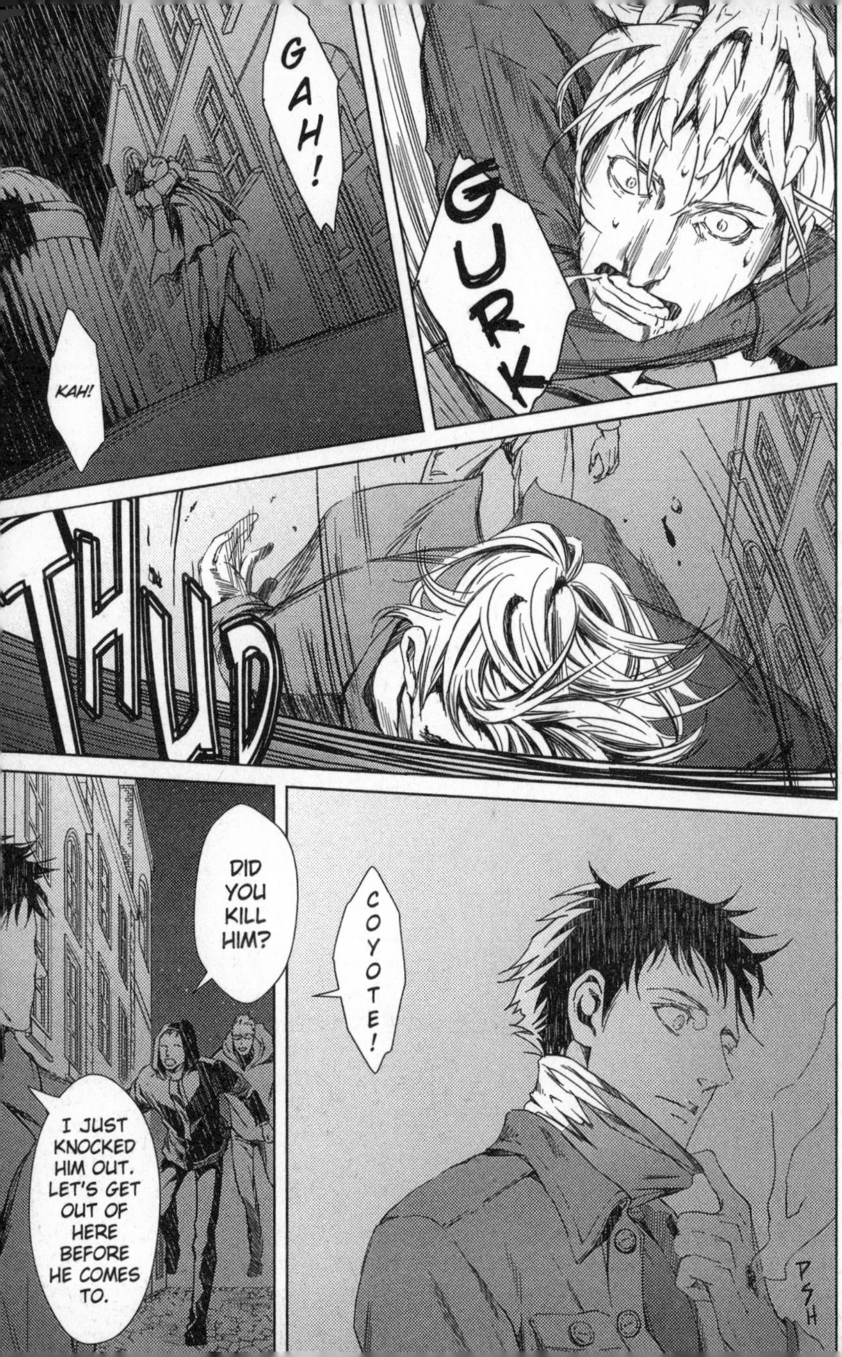
GURK
GAH!
KAH!
THUD
COYOTE!
PSH
DID YOU KILL HIM?
I JUST KNOCKED HIM OUT. LET'S GET OUT OF HERE BEFORE HE COMES TO.

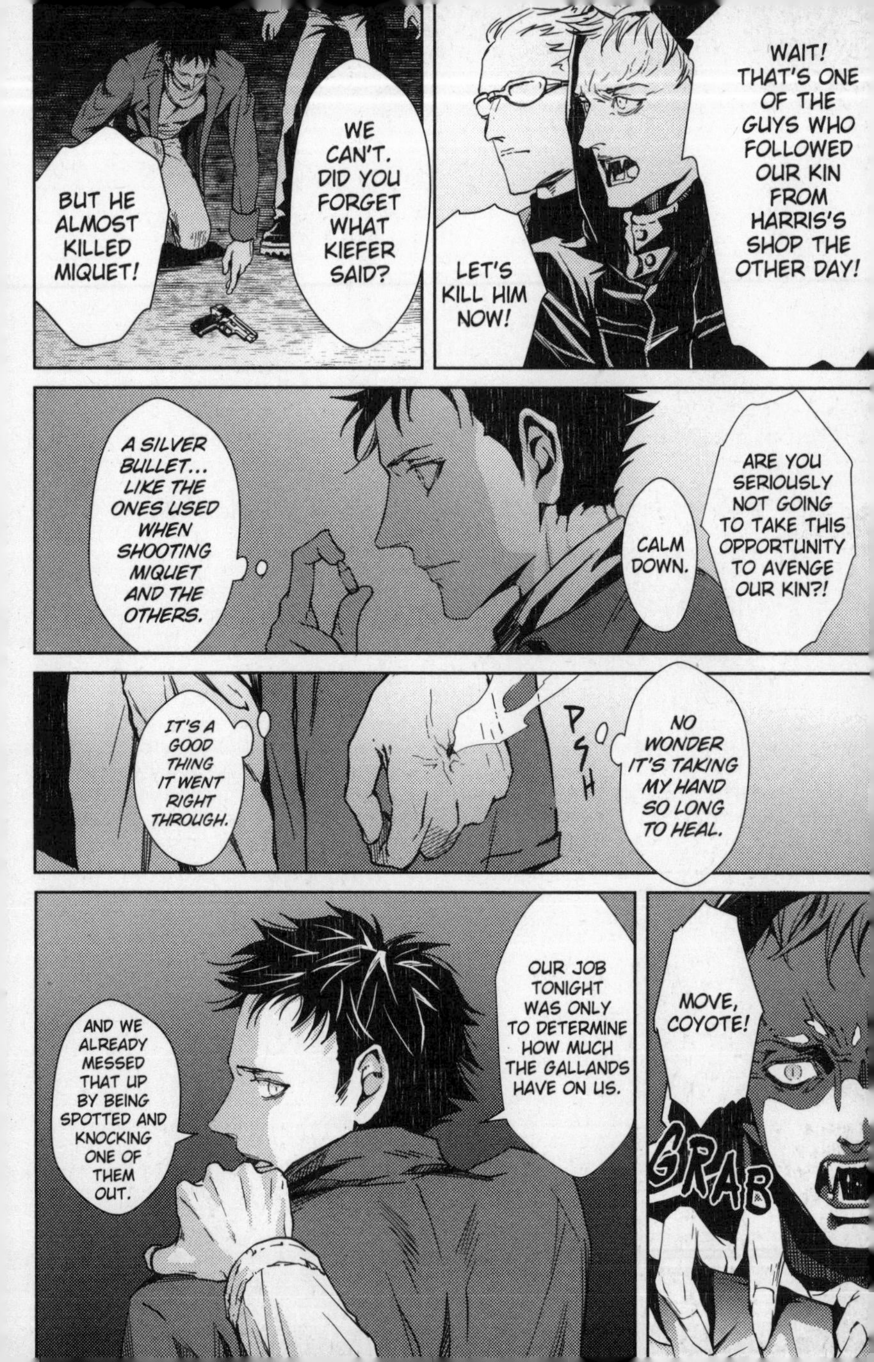
WAIT! THAT'S ONE OF THE GUYS WHO FOLLOWED OUR KIN FROM HARRIS'S SHOP THE OTHER DAY!
LET'S KILL HIM NOW!
WE CAN'T. DID YOU FORGET WHAT KIEFER SAID?
BUT HE ALMOST KILLED MIQUET!
ARE YOU SERIOUSLY NOT GOING TO TAKE THIS OPPORTUNITY TO AVENGE OUR KIN?!
CALM DOWN.
A SILVER BULLET... LIKE THE ONES USED WHEN SHOOTING MIQUET AND THE OTHERS.
NO WONDER IT'S TAKING MY HAND SO LONG TO HEAL.
PSH
IT'S A GOOD THING IT WENT RIGHT THROUGH.
MOVE, COYOTE!
GRAB
OUR JOB TONIGHT WAS ONLY TO DETERMINE HOW MUCH THE GALLANDS HAVE ON US.
AND WE ALREADY MESSED THAT UP BY BEING SPOTTED AND KNOCKING ONE OF THEM OUT.

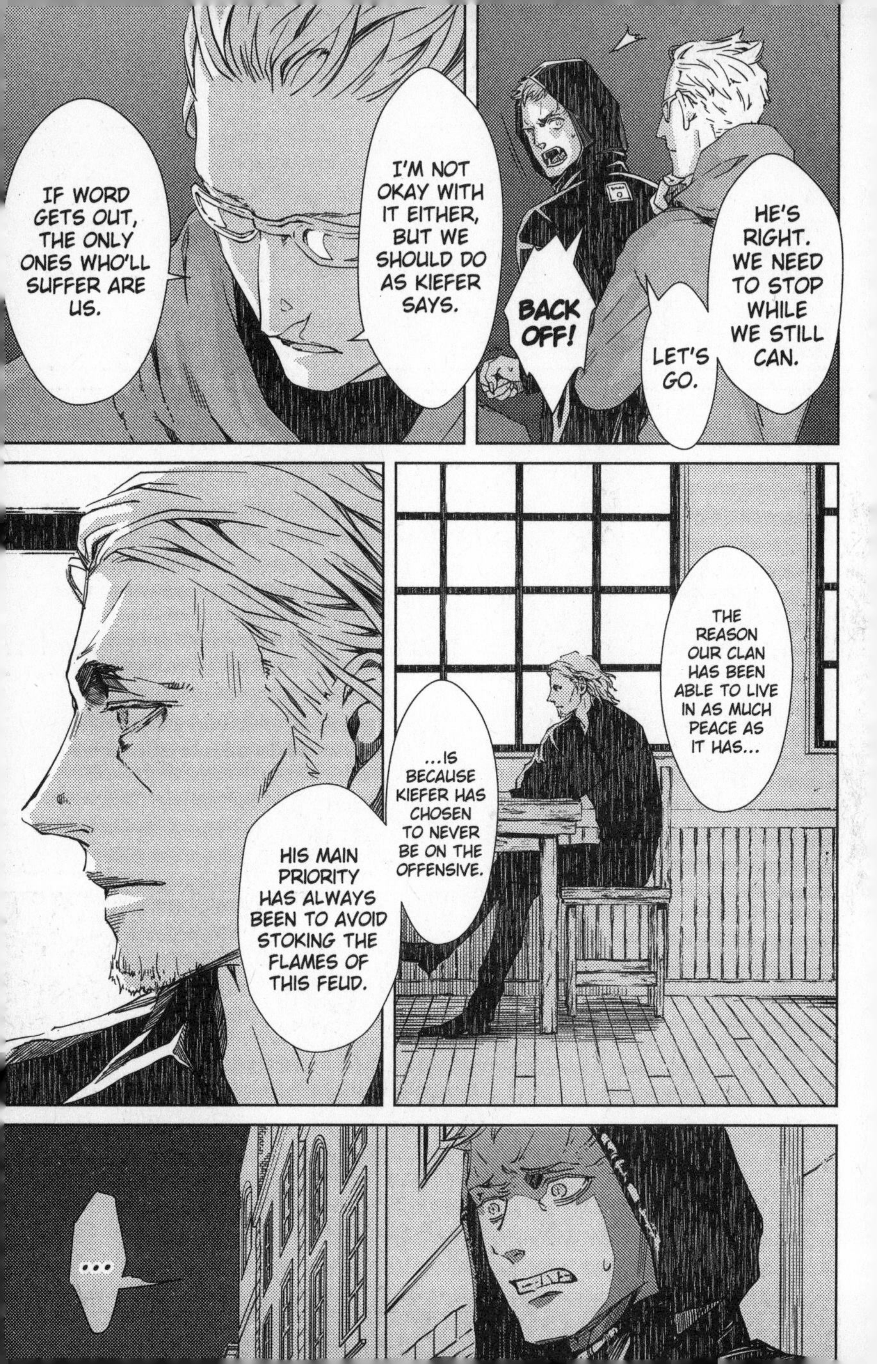
HE'S RIGHT. WE NEED TO STOP WHILE WE STILL CAN.
LET'S GO.
BACK OFF!
I'M NOT OKAY WITH IT EITHER, BUT WE SHOULD DO AS KIEFER SAYS.
IF WORD GETS OUT, THE ONLY ONES WHO'LL SUFFER ARE US.
THE REASON OUR CLAN HAS BEEN ABLE TO LIVE IN AS MUCH PEACE AS IT HAS...
...IS BECAUSE KIEFER HAS CHOSEN TO NEVER BE ON THE OFFENSIVE.
HIS MAIN PRIORITY HAS ALWAYS BEEN TO AVOID STOKING THE FLAMES OF THIS FEUD.
...

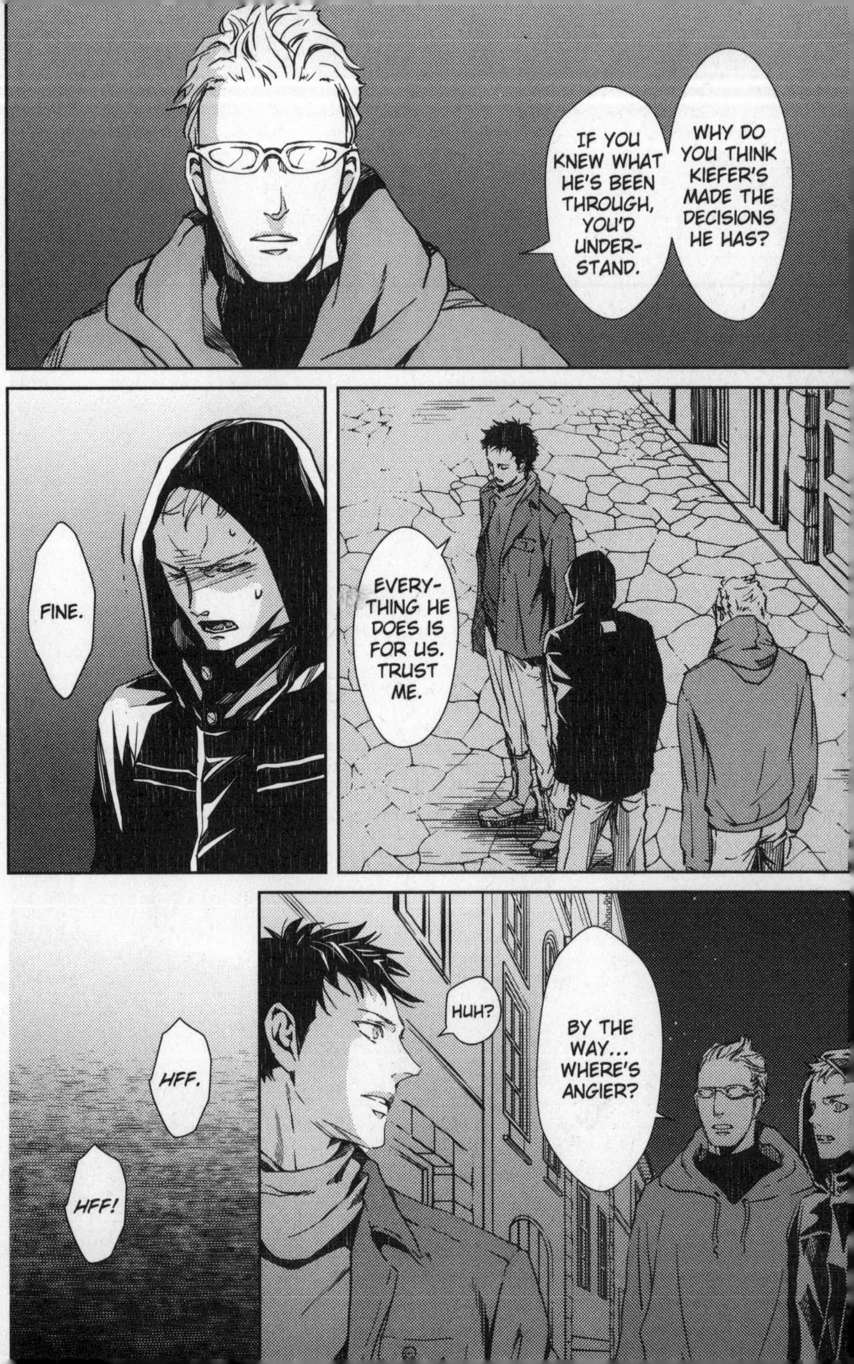
WHY DO YOU THINK KIEFER'S MADE THE DECISIONS HE HAS?
IF YOU KNEW WHAT HE'S BEEN THROUGH, YOU'D UNDER-STAND.
EVERY-THING HE DOES IS FOR US. TRUST ME.
FINE.
BY THE WAY... WHERE'S ANGIER?
HUH?
HFF.
HFF!

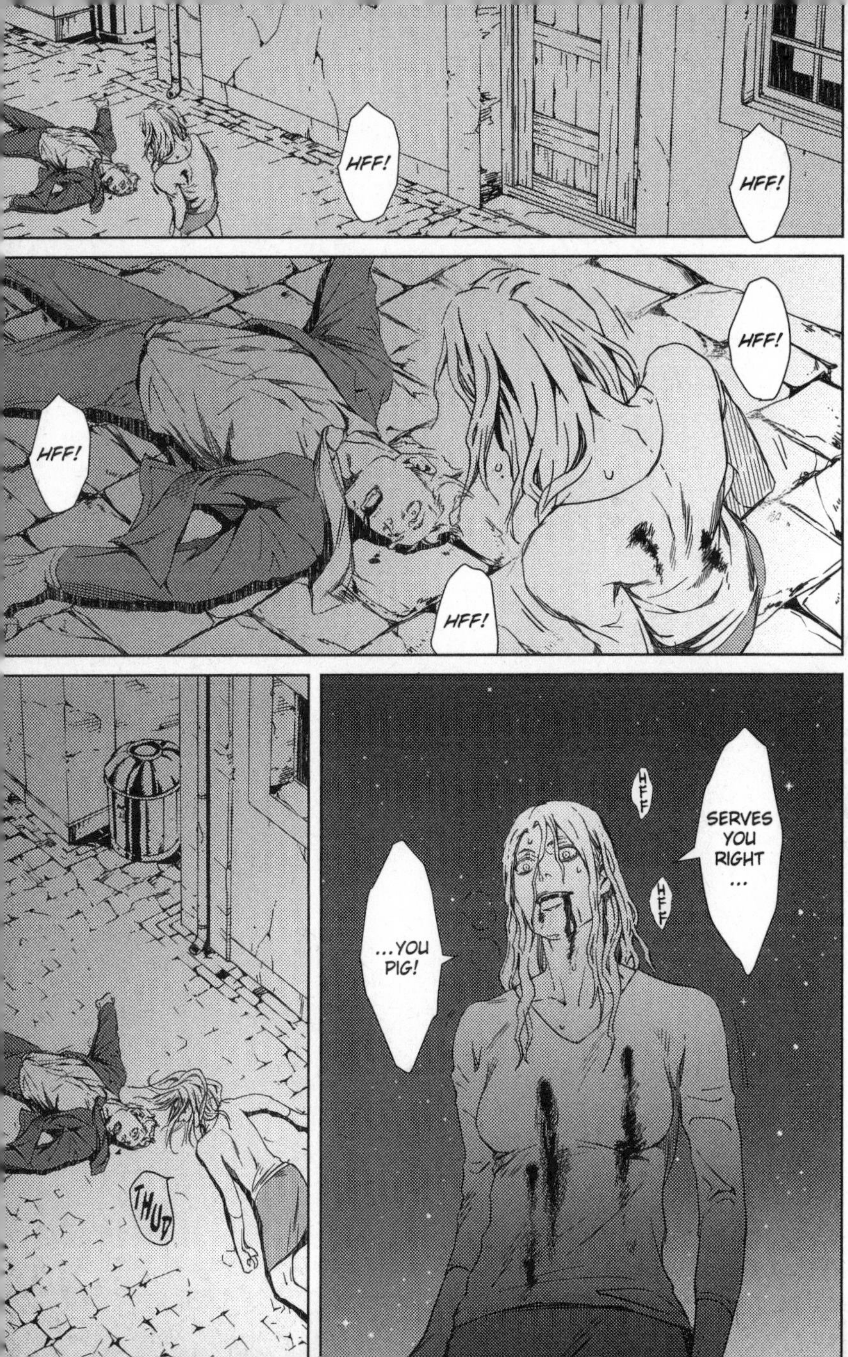
HFF!
HFF!
HFF!
HFF!
HFF!
HFF
SERVES YOU RIGHT ...
HFF
...YOU PIG!
THUD

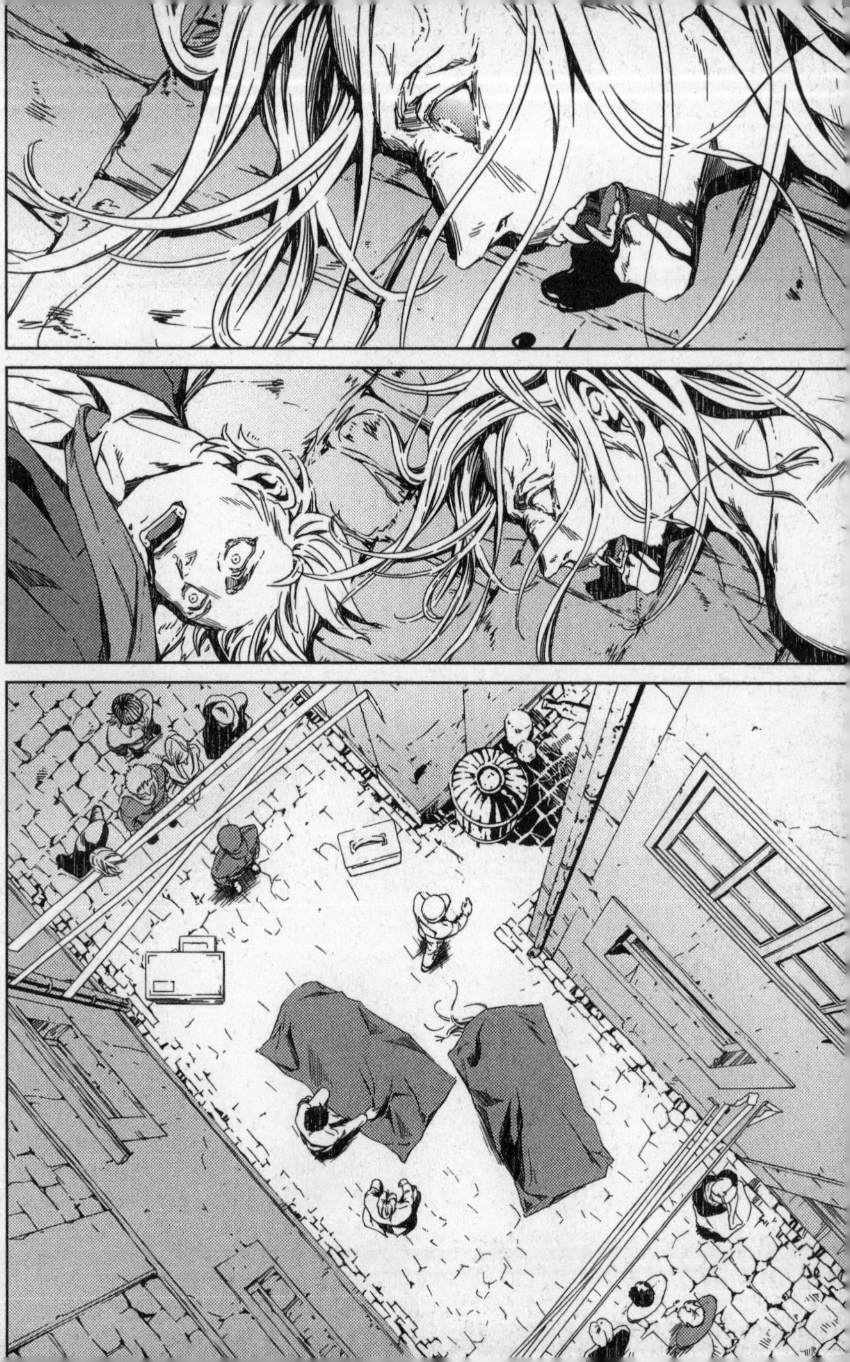

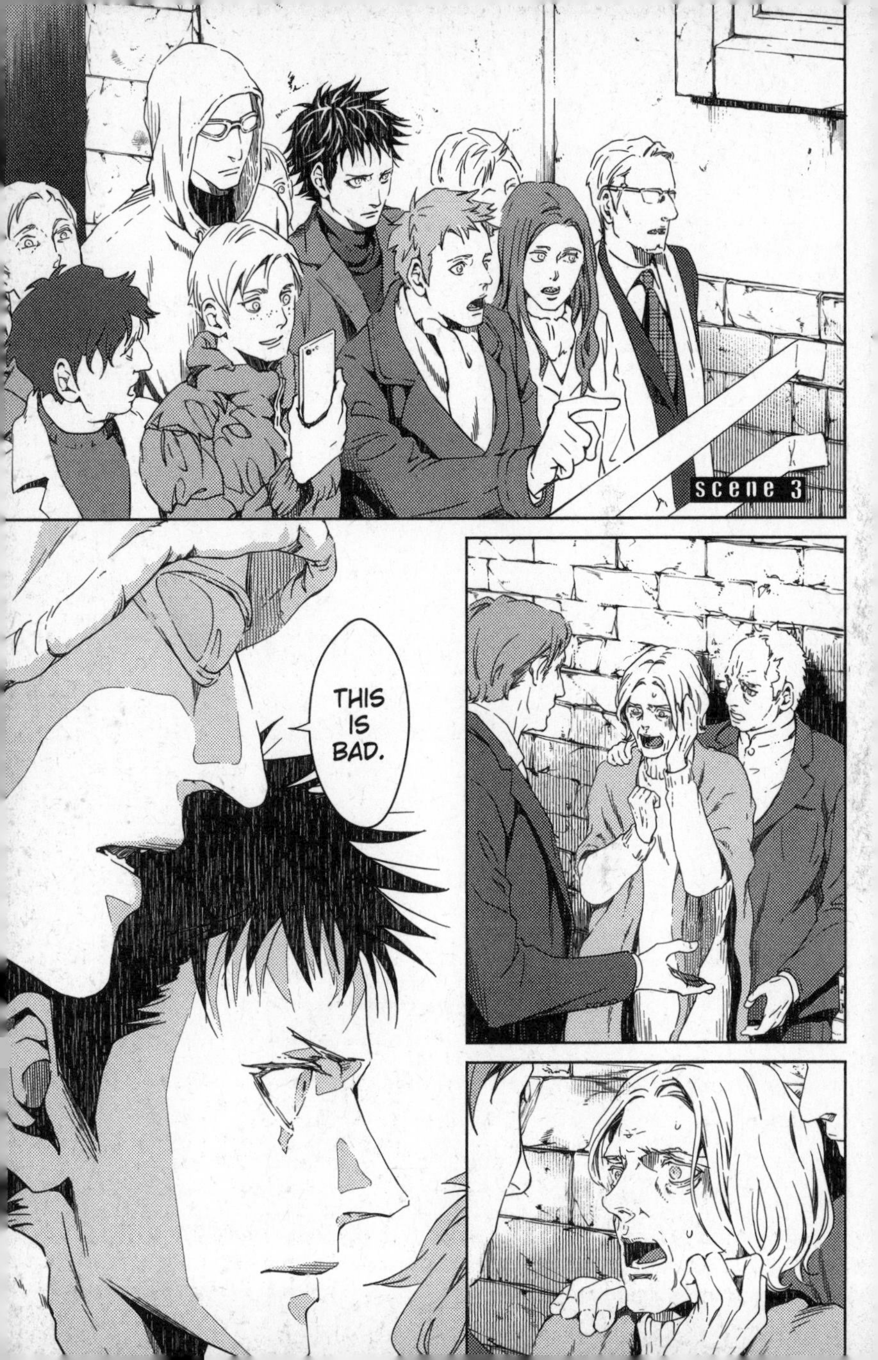
scene 3
THIS IS BAD.

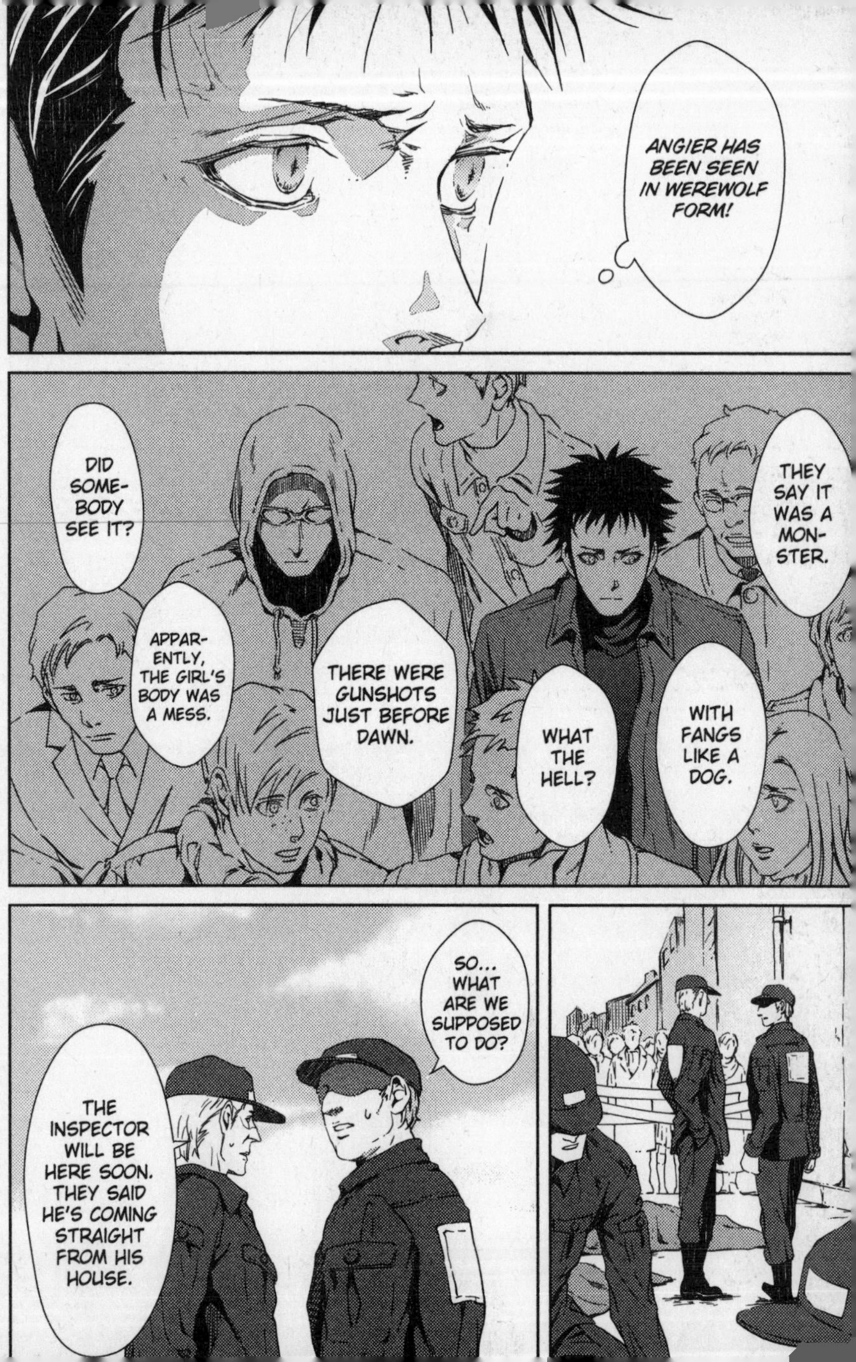
ANGIER HAS BEEN SEEN IN WEREWOLF FORM!
THEY SAY IT WAS A MONSTER.
DID SOMEBODY SEE IT?
WITH FANGS LIKE A DOG.
WHAT THE HELL?
THERE WERE GUNSHOTS JUST BEFORE DAWN.
APPARENTLY, THE GIRL'S BODY WAS A MESS.
SO... WHAT ARE WE SUPPOSED TO DO?
THE INSPECTOR WILL BE HERE SOON. THEY SAID HE'S COMING STRAIGHT FROM HIS HOUSE.

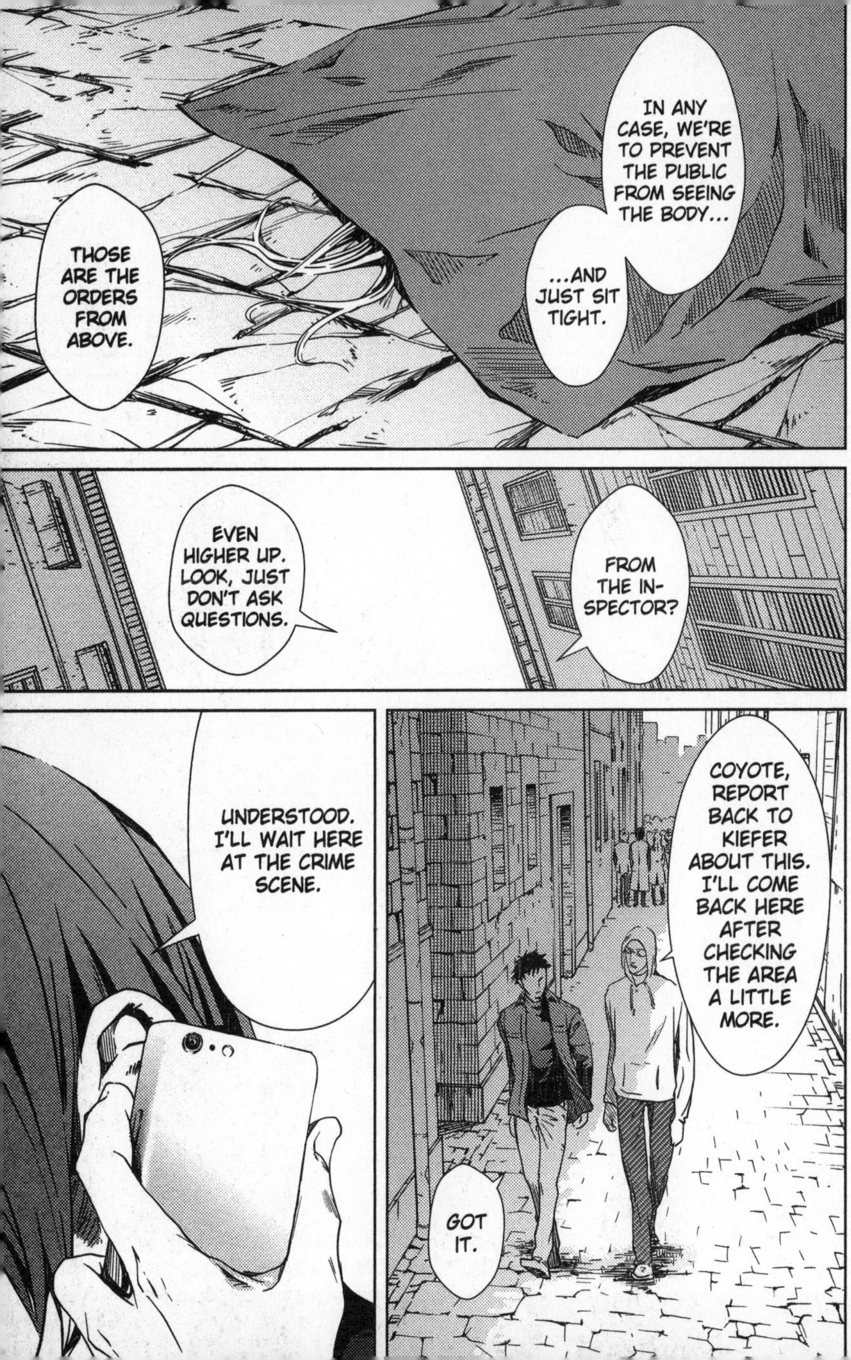
IN ANY CASE, WE'RE TO PREVENT THE PUBLIC FROM SEEING THE BODY...
...AND JUST SIT TIGHT.
THOSE ARE THE ORDERS FROM ABOVE.
FROM THE IN-SPECTOR?
EVEN HIGHER UP. LOOK, JUST DON'T ASK QUESTIONS.
COYOTE, REPORT BACK TO KIEFER ABOUT THIS. I'LL COME BACK HERE AFTER CHECKING THE AREA A LITTLE MORE.
GOT IT.
UNDERSTOOD. I'LL WAIT HERE AT THE CRIME SCENE.

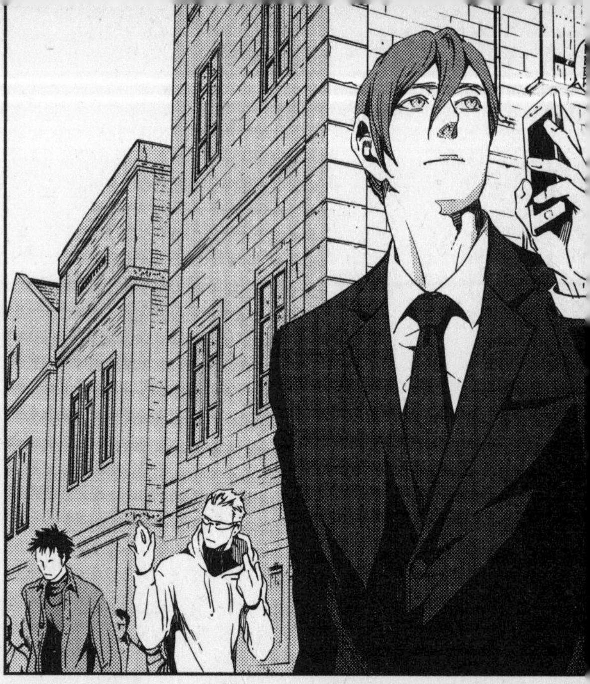

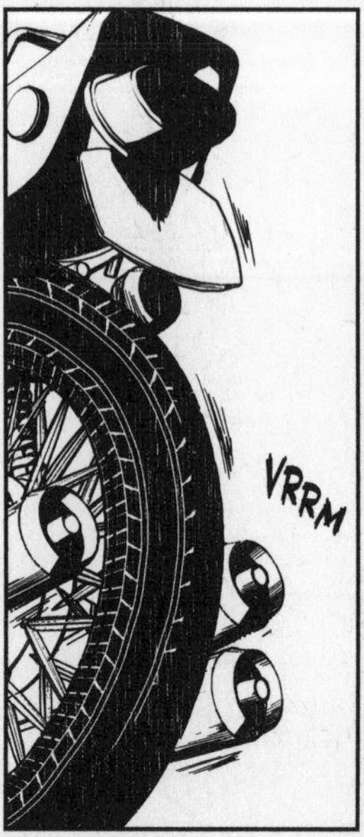
VRRM

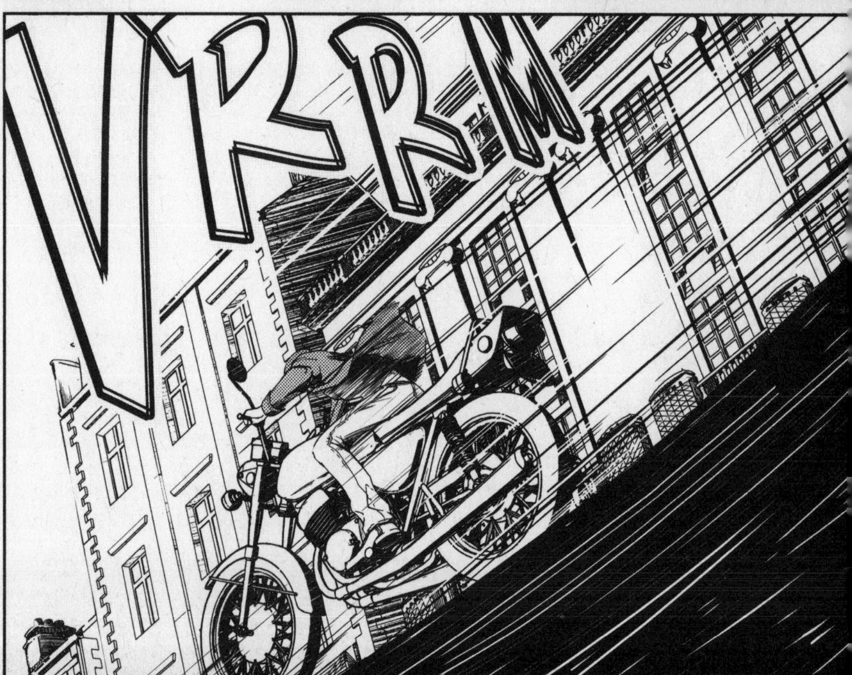
VRRM

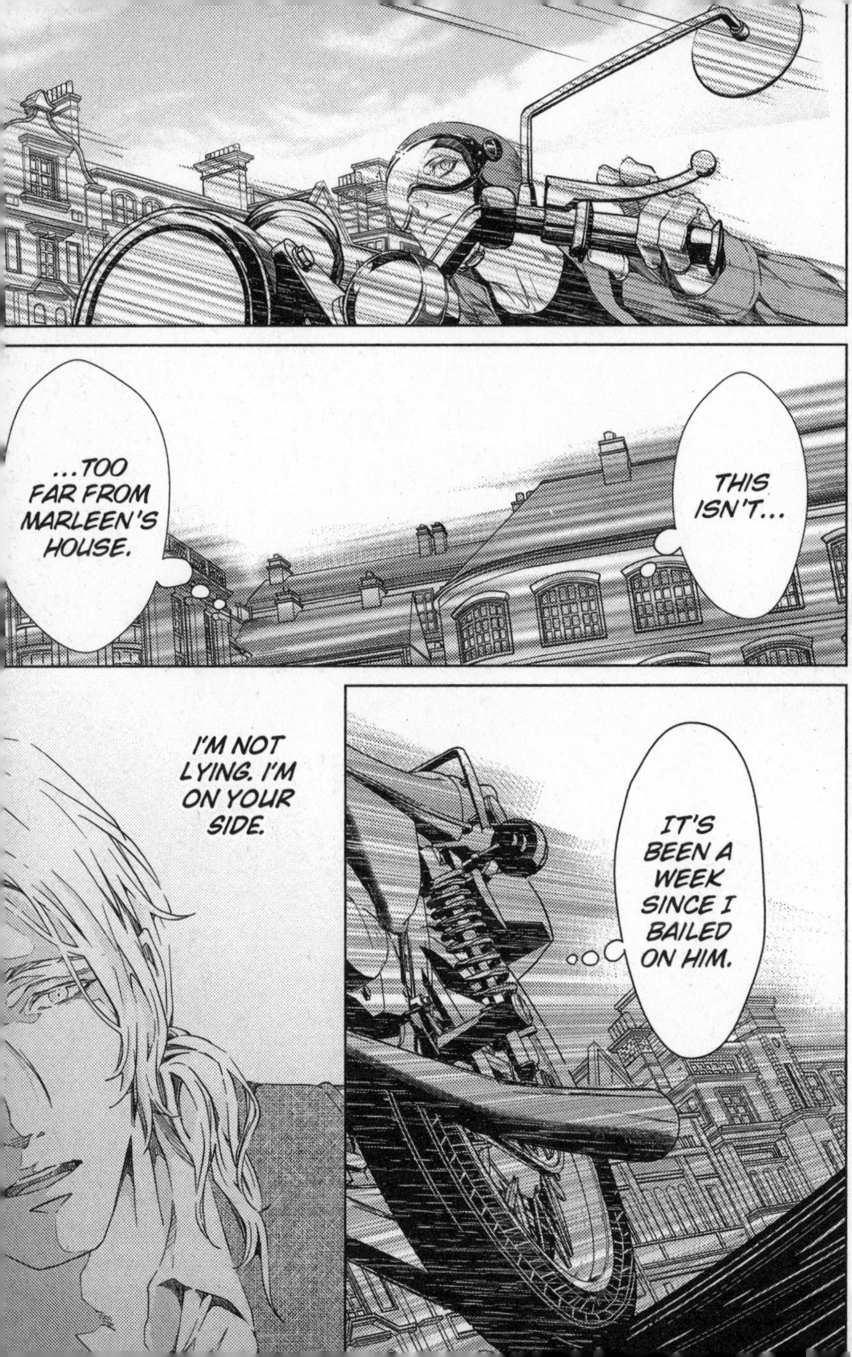
THIS ISN'T...
...TOO FAR FROM MARLEEN'S HOUSE.
IT'S BEEN A WEEK SINCE I BAILED ON HIM.
I'M NOT LYING. I'M ON YOUR SIDE.

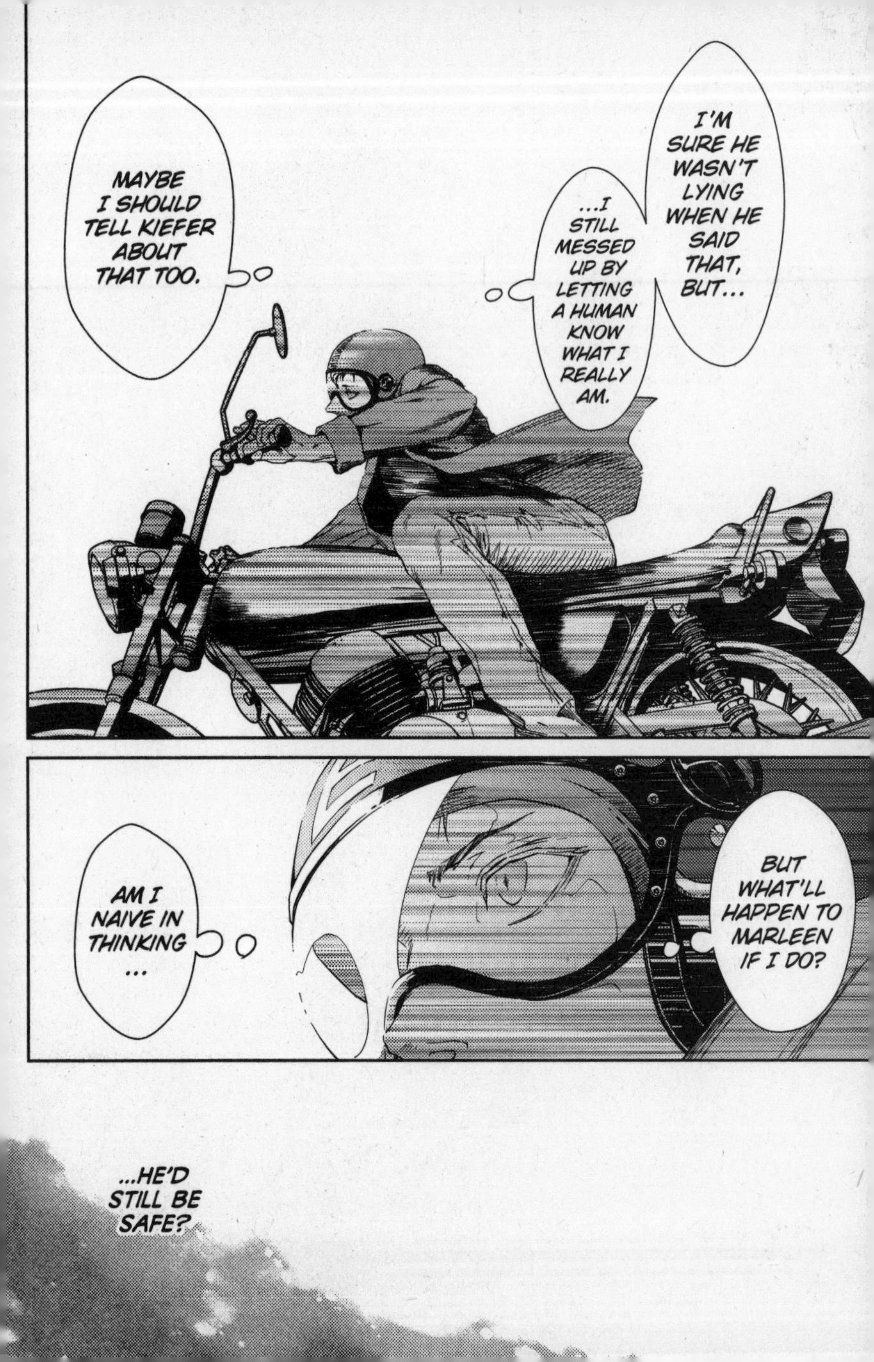
I'M SURE HE WASN'T LYING WHEN HE SAID THAT, BUT...
...I STILL MESSED UP BY LETTING A HUMAN KNOW WHAT I REALLY AM.
MAYBE I SHOULD TELL KIEFER ABOUT THAT TOO.
BUT WHAT'LL HAPPEN TO MARLEEN IF I DO?
AM I NAIVE IN THINKING ...
...HE'D STILL BE SAFE?

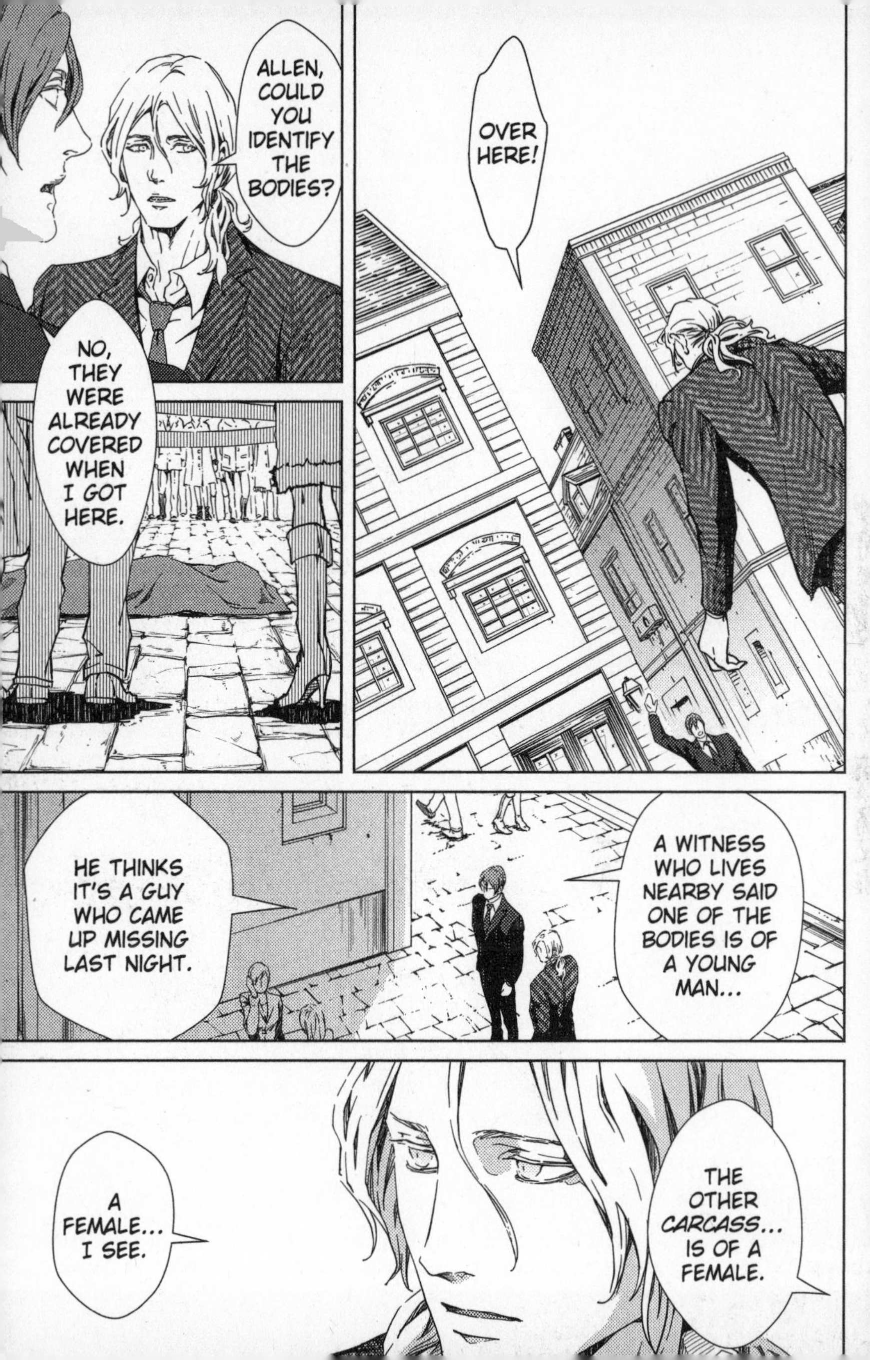
OVER HERE!
ALLEN, COULD YOU IDENTIFY THE BODIES?
NO, THEY WERE ALREADY COVERED WHEN I GOT HERE.
A WITNESS WHO LIVES NEARBY SAID ONE OF THE BODIES IS OF A YOUNG MAN...
HE THINKS IT'S A GUY WHO CAME UP MISSING LAST NIGHT.
THE OTHER *CARCASS*... IS OF A FEMALE.
A FEMALE... I SEE.

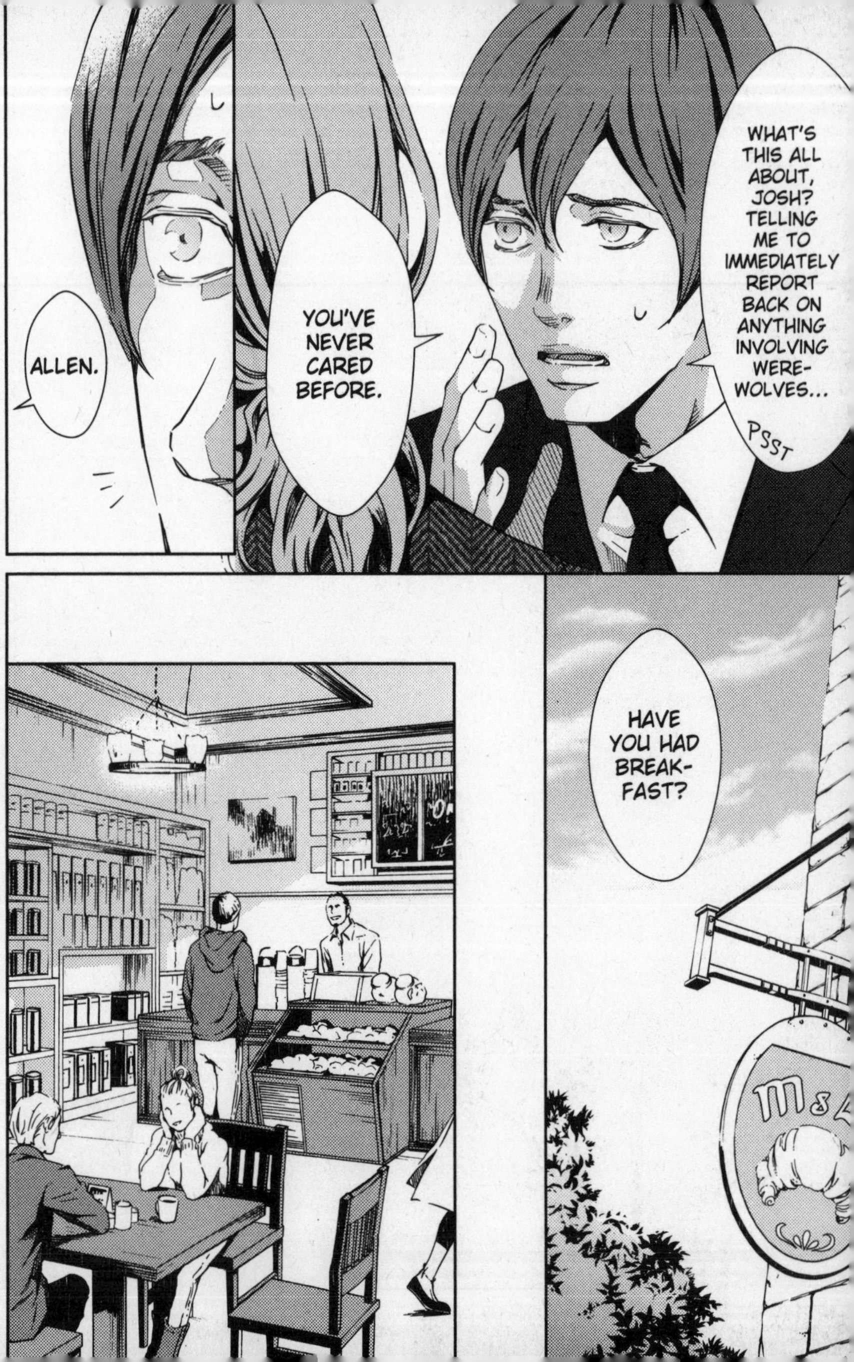
WHAT'S THIS ALL ABOUT, JOSH? TELLING ME TO IMMEDIATELY REPORT BACK ON ANYTHING INVOLVING WERE-WOLVES...
PSST
YOU'VE NEVER CARED BEFORE.
ALLEN.
HAVE YOU HAD BREAK-FAST?

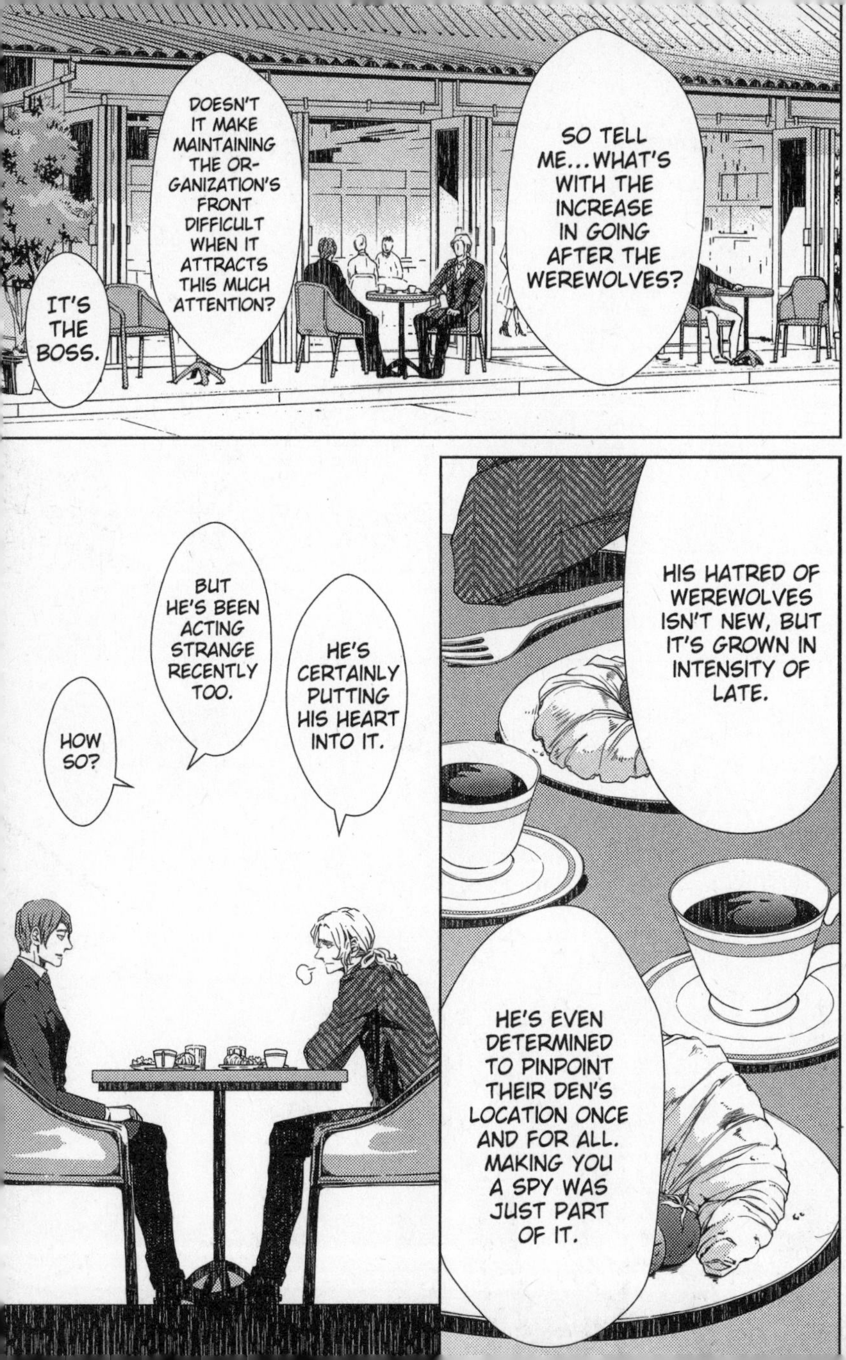
SO TELL ME...WHAT'S WITH THE INCREASE IN GOING AFTER THE WEREWOLVES?
DOESN'T IT MAKE MAINTAINING THE OR-GANIZATION'S FRONT DIFFICULT WHEN IT ATTRACTS THIS MUCH ATTENTION?
IT'S THE BOSS.
HIS HATRED OF WEREWOLVES ISN'T NEW, BUT IT'S GROWN IN INTENSITY OF LATE.
HE'S EVEN DETERMINED TO PINPOINT THEIR DEN'S LOCATION ONCE AND FOR ALL. MAKING YOU A SPY WAS JUST PART OF IT.
HE'S CERTAINLY PUTTING HIS HEART INTO IT.
BUT HE'S BEEN ACTING STRANGE RECENTLY TOO.
HOW SO?

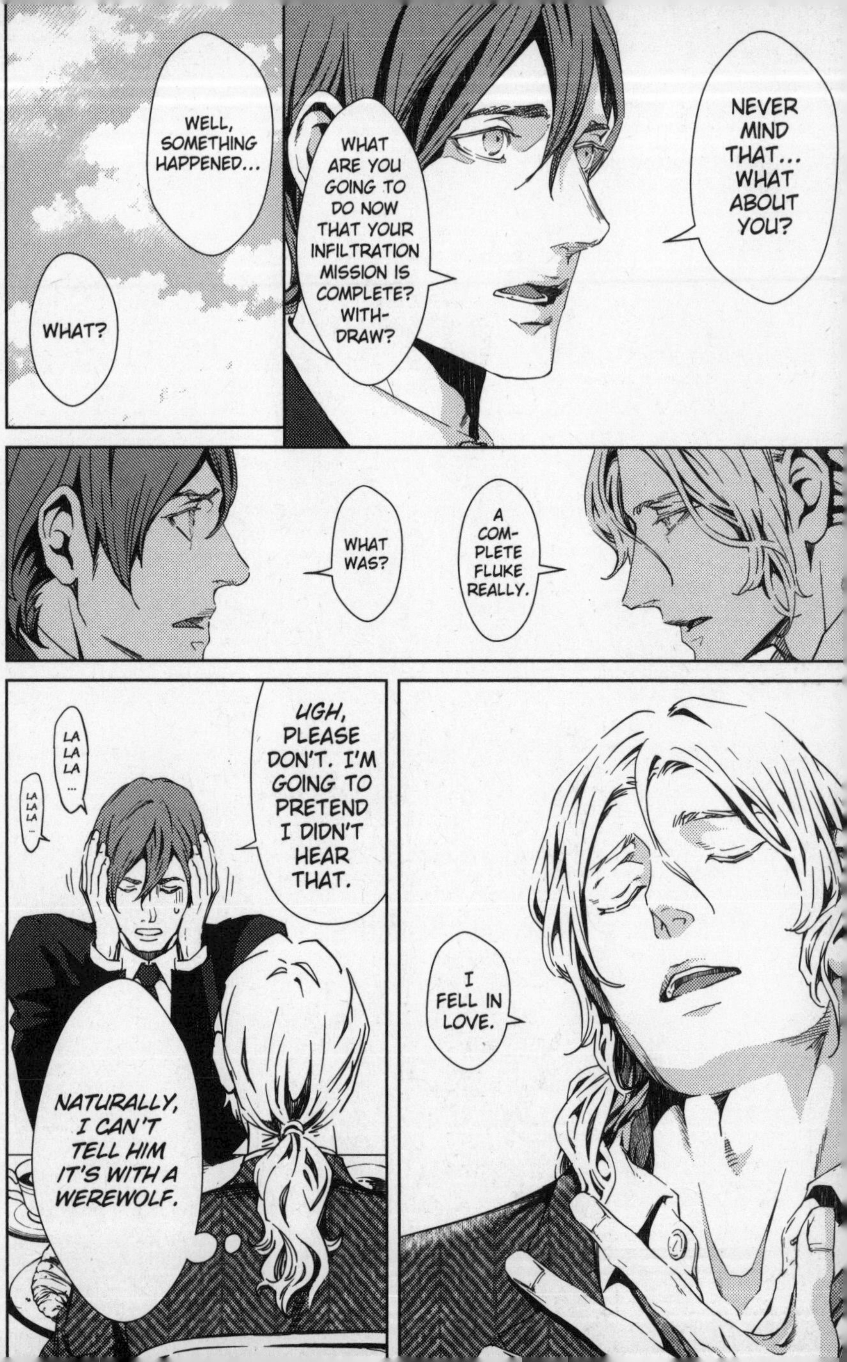
NEVER MIND THAT... WHAT ABOUT YOU?
WHAT ARE YOU GOING TO DO NOW THAT YOUR INFILTRATION MISSION IS COMPLETE? WITH-DRAW?
WELL, SOMETHING HAPPENED...
WHAT?
A COM-PLETE FLUKE REALLY.
WHAT WAS?
I FELL IN LOVE.
UGH, PLEASE DON'T. I'M GOING TO PRETEND I DIDN'T HEAR THAT.
LA LA LA ...
LA LA LA ...
NATURALLY, I CAN'T TELL HIM IT'S WITH A WEREWOLF.

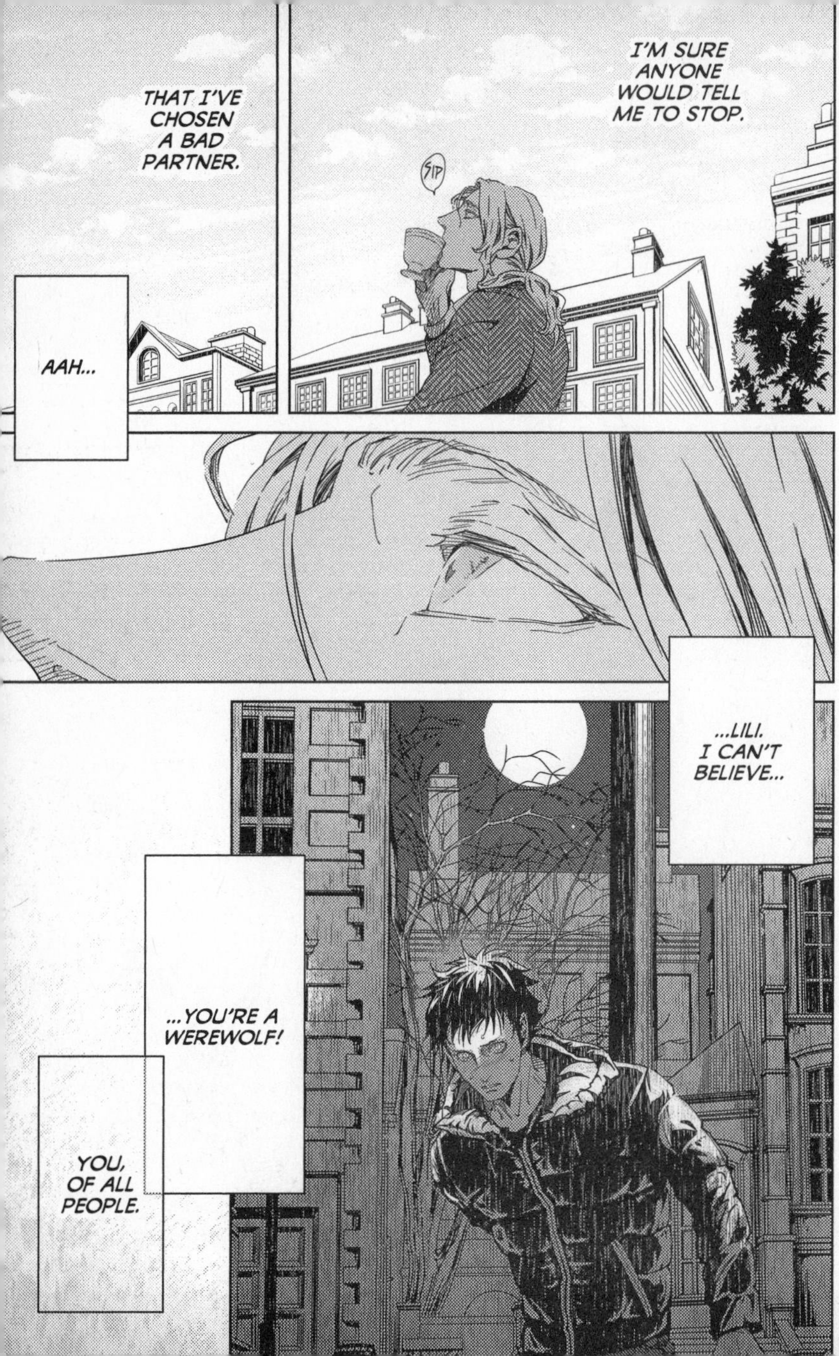
I'M SURE ANYONE WOULD TELL ME TO STOP.
SIP
THAT I'VE CHOSEN A BAD PARTNER.
AAH...
...LILI. I CAN'T BELIEVE...
...YOU'RE A WEREWOLF!
YOU, OF ALL PEOPLE.

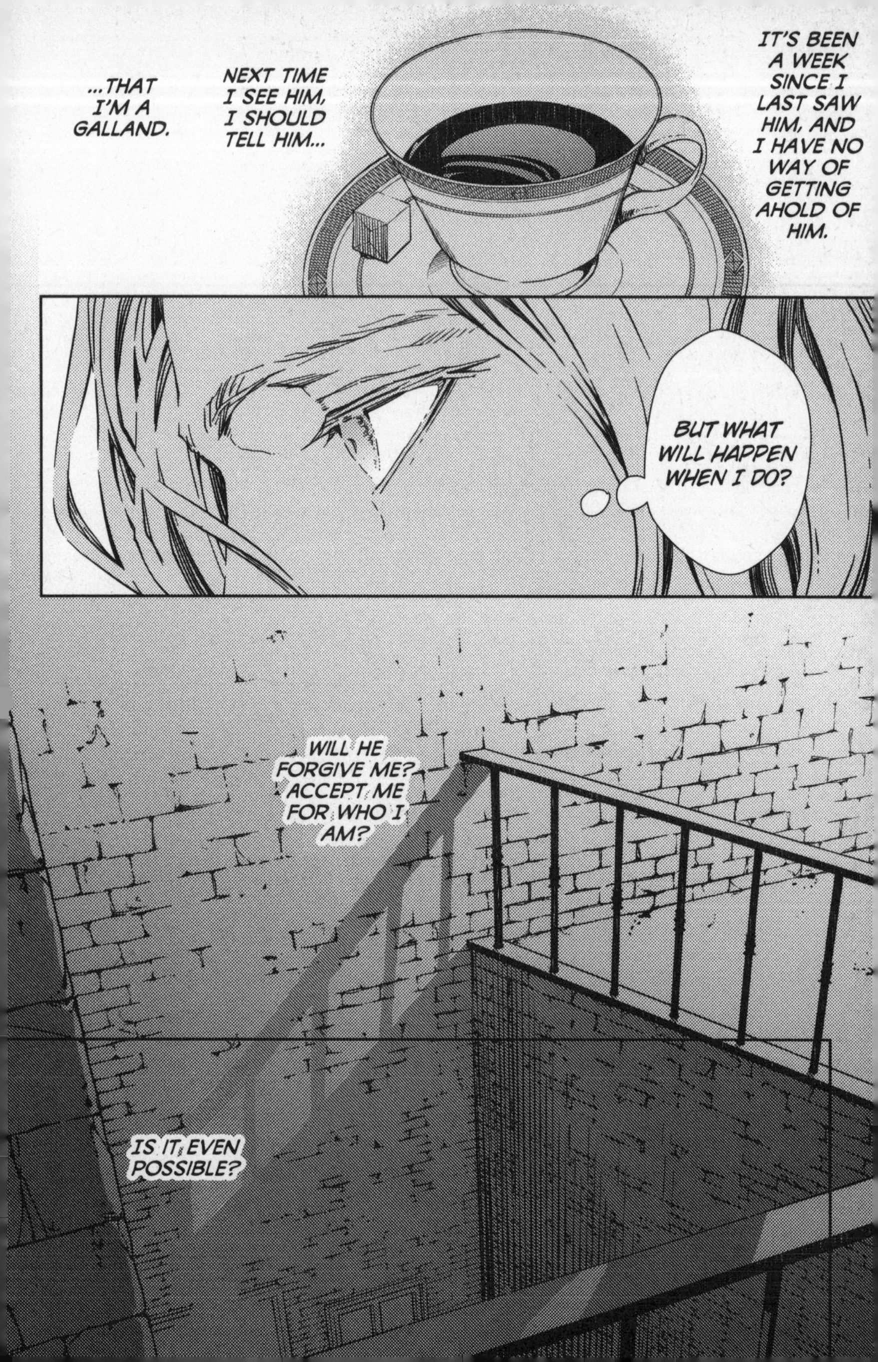
IT'S BEEN A WEEK SINCE I LAST SAW HIM, AND I HAVE NO WAY OF GETTING AHOLD OF HIM.
NEXT TIME I SEE HIM, I SHOULD TELL HIM...
...THAT I'M A GALLAND.
BUT WHAT WILL HAPPEN WHEN I DO?
WILL HE FORGIVE ME? ACCEPT ME FOR WHO I AM?
IS IT EVEN POSSIBLE?

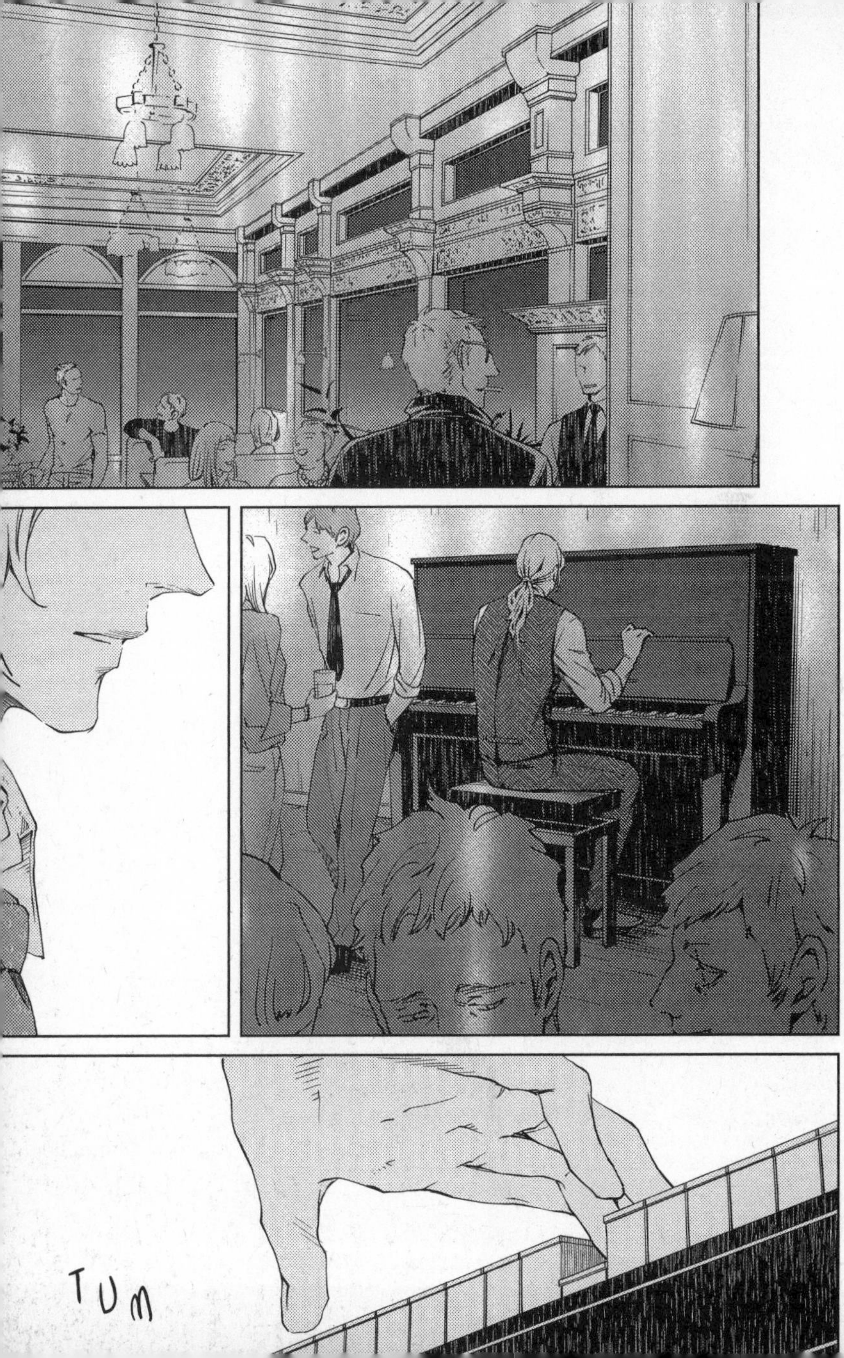
TUM

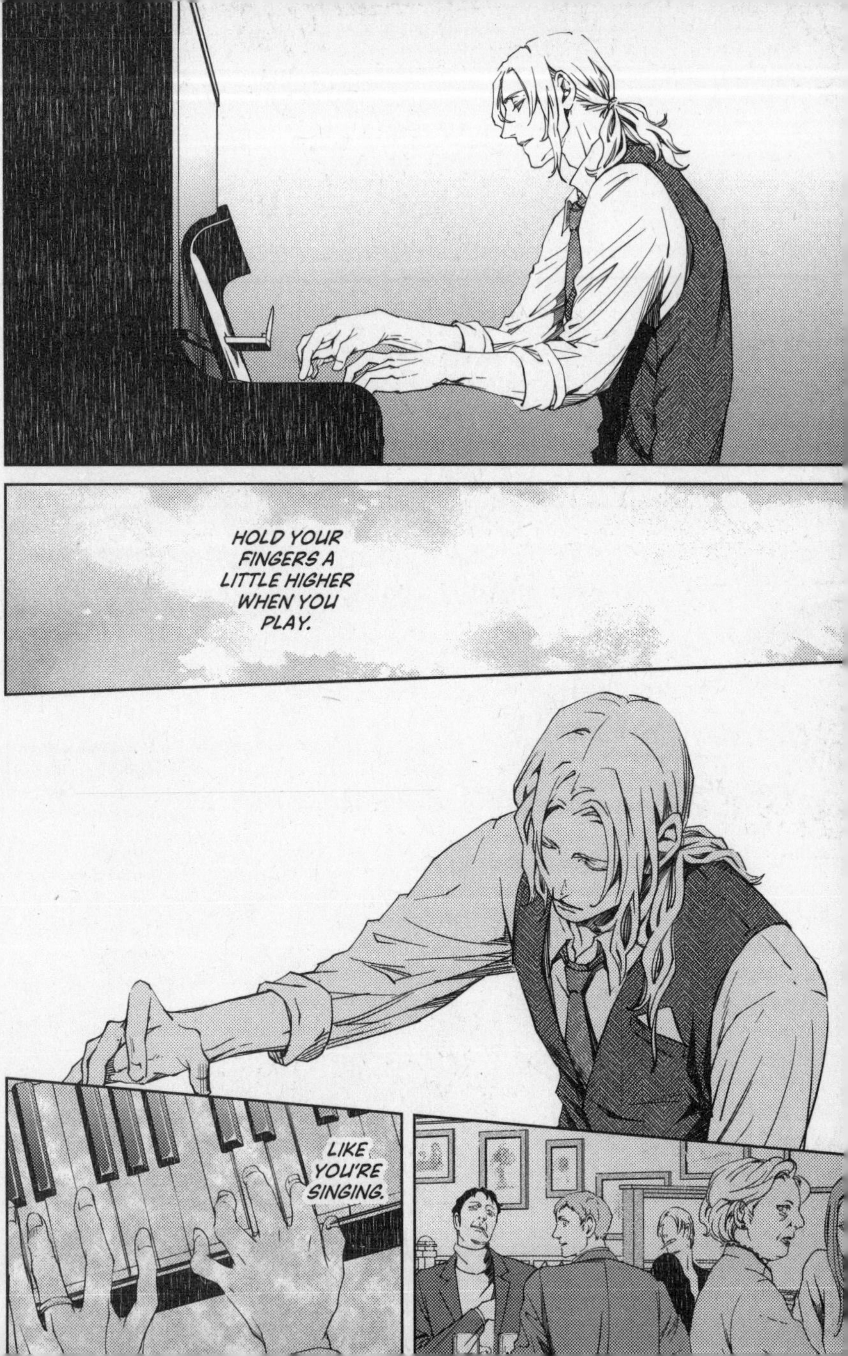
HOLD YOUR FINGERS A LITTLE HIGHER WHEN YOU PLAY.
LIKE YOU'RE SINGING.

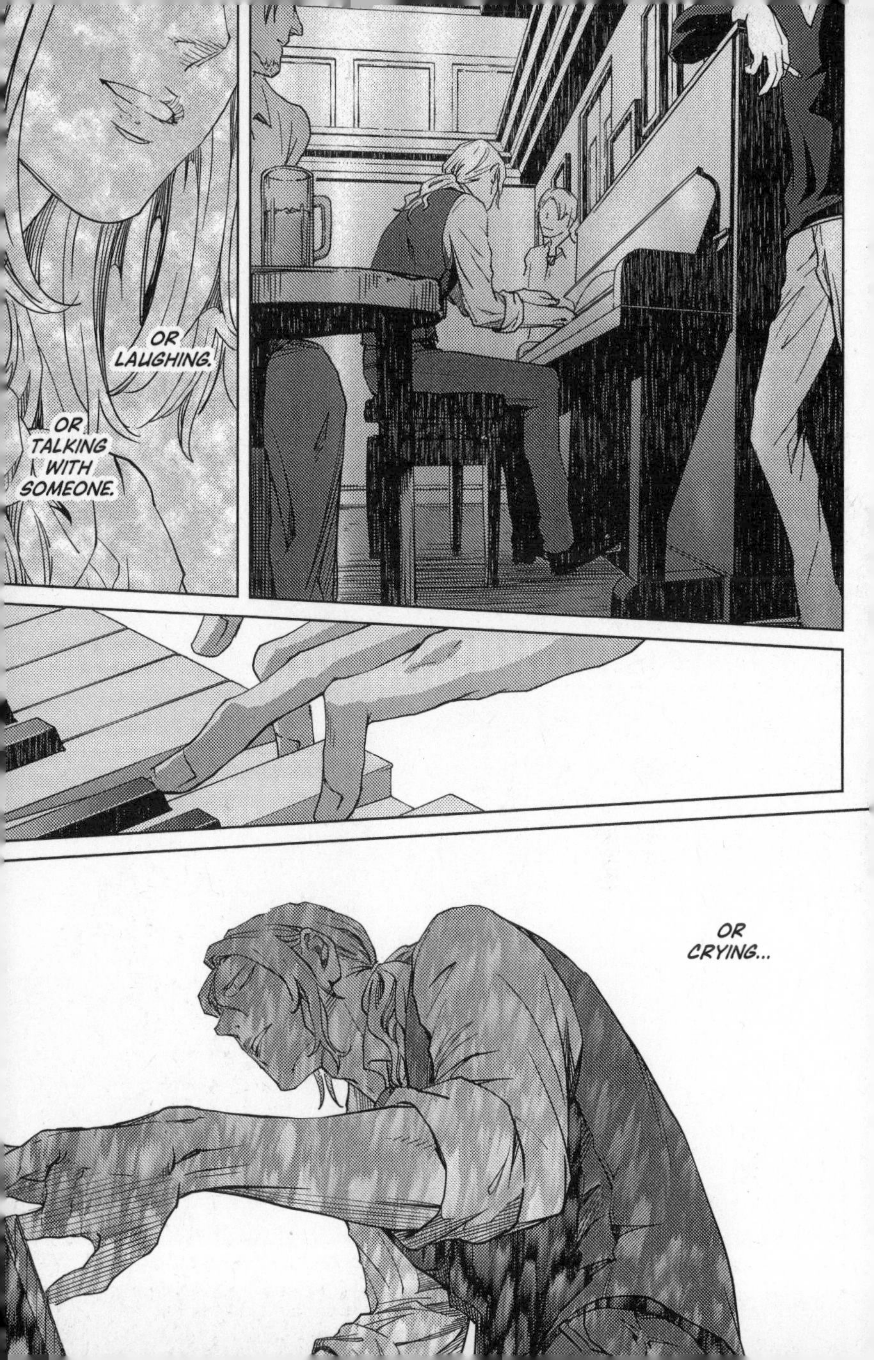
OR LAUGHING.
OR TALKING WITH SOMEONE.
OR CRYING...

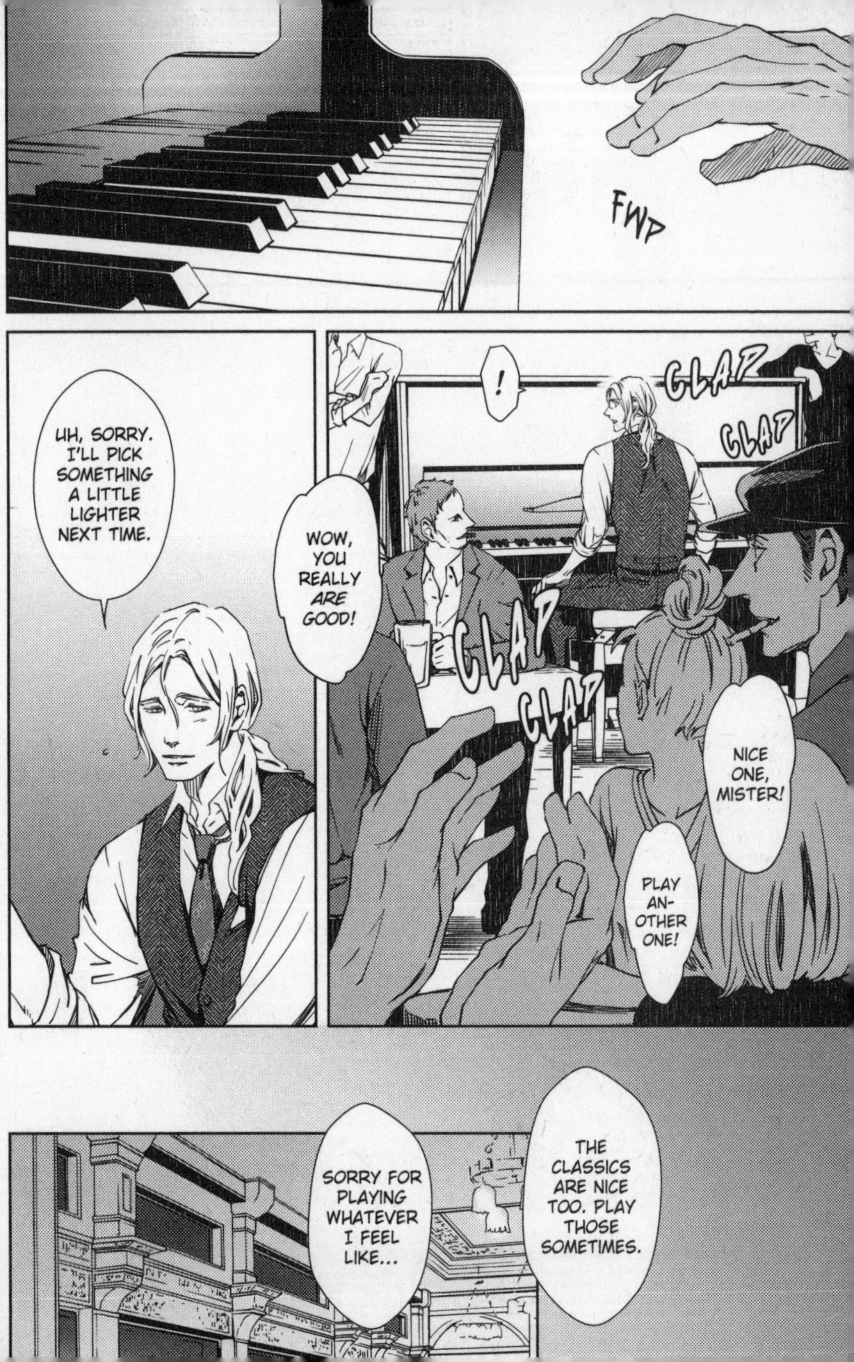
FWP
!
CLAP
CLAP
WOW, YOU REALLY ARE GOOD!
CLAP
CLAP
NICE ONE, MISTER!
PLAY AN-OTHER ONE!
UH, SORRY. I'LL PICK SOMETHING A LITTLE LIGHTER NEXT TIME.
THE CLASSICS ARE NICE TOO. PLAY THOSE SOMETIMES.
SORRY FOR PLAYING WHATEVER I FEEL LIKE...

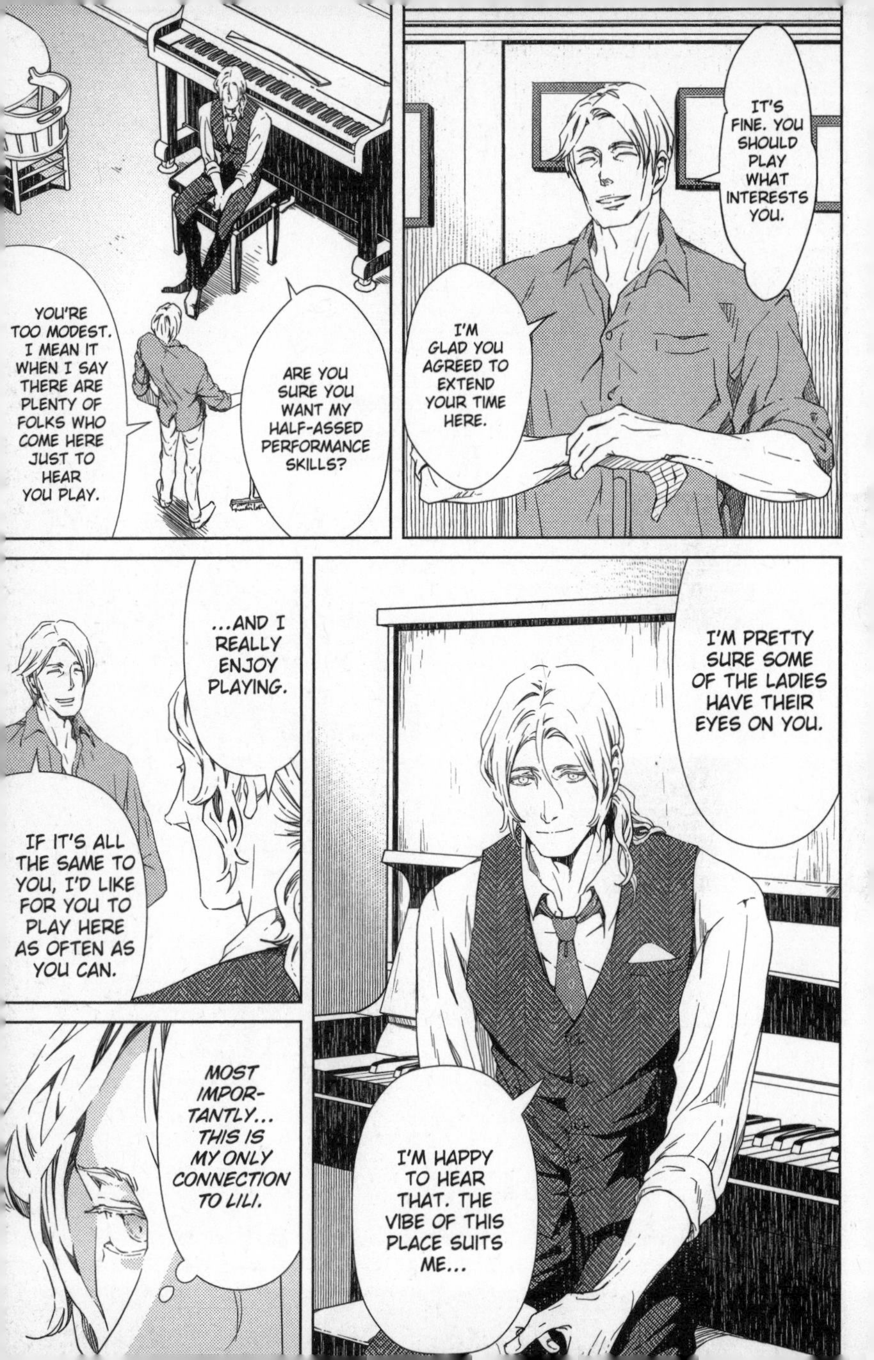
IT'S FINE. YOU SHOULD PLAY WHAT INTERESTS YOU.
I'M GLAD YOU AGREED TO EXTEND YOUR TIME HERE.
ARE YOU SURE YOU WANT MY HALF-ASSED PERFORMANCE SKILLS?
YOU'RE TOO MODEST. I MEAN IT WHEN I SAY THERE ARE PLENTY OF FOLKS WHO COME HERE JUST TO HEAR YOU PLAY.
I'M PRETTY SURE SOME OF THE LADIES HAVE THEIR EYES ON YOU.
I'M HAPPY TO HEAR THAT. THE VIBE OF THIS PLACE SUITS ME...
...AND I REALLY ENJOY PLAYING.
IF IT'S ALL THE SAME TO YOU, I'D LIKE FOR YOU TO PLAY HERE AS OFTEN AS YOU CAN.
MOST IMPOR-TANTLY... THIS IS MY ONLY CONNECTION TO LILI.

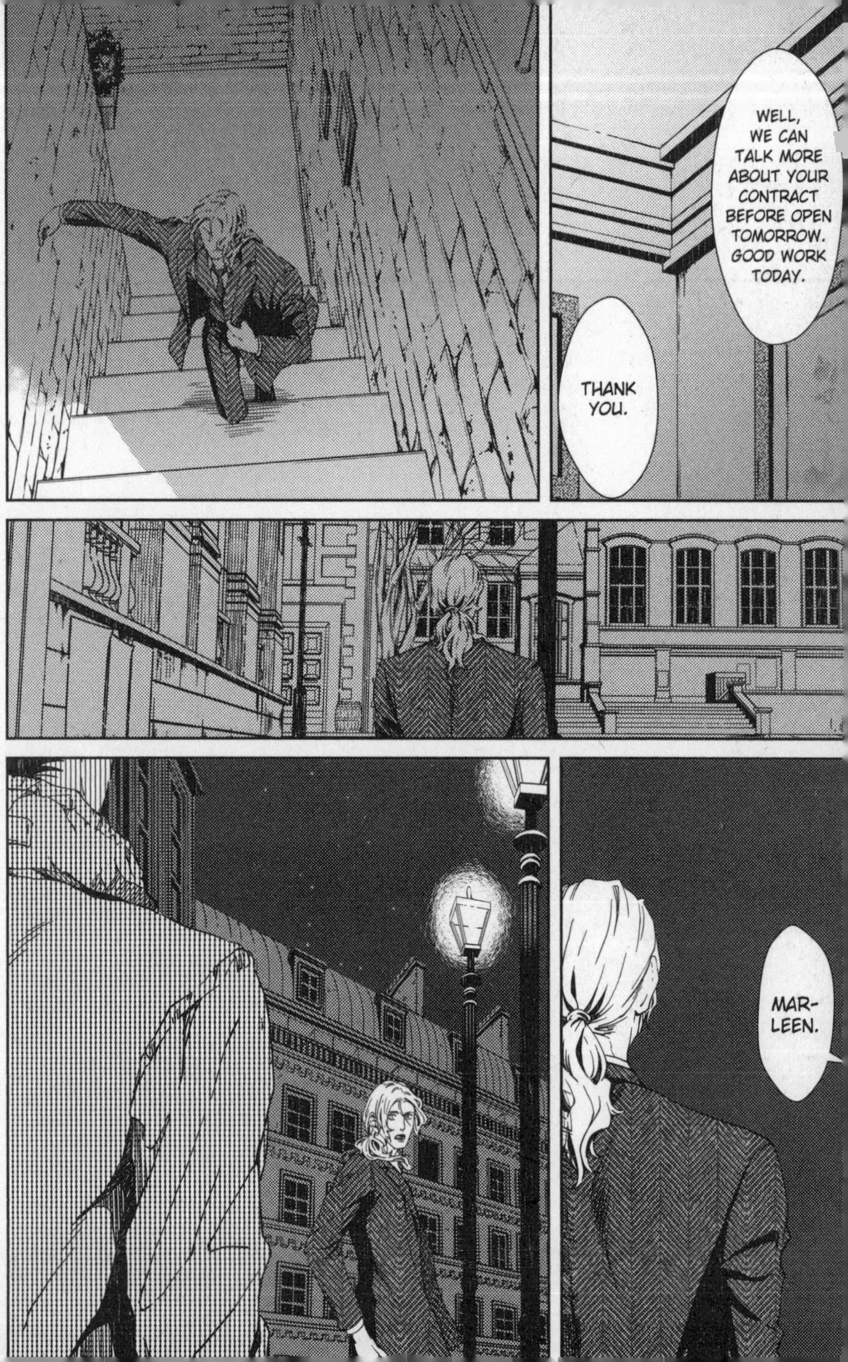
WELL, WE CAN TALK MORE ABOUT YOUR CONTRACT BEFORE OPEN TOMORROW. GOOD WORK TODAY.
THANK YOU.
MAR-LEEN.

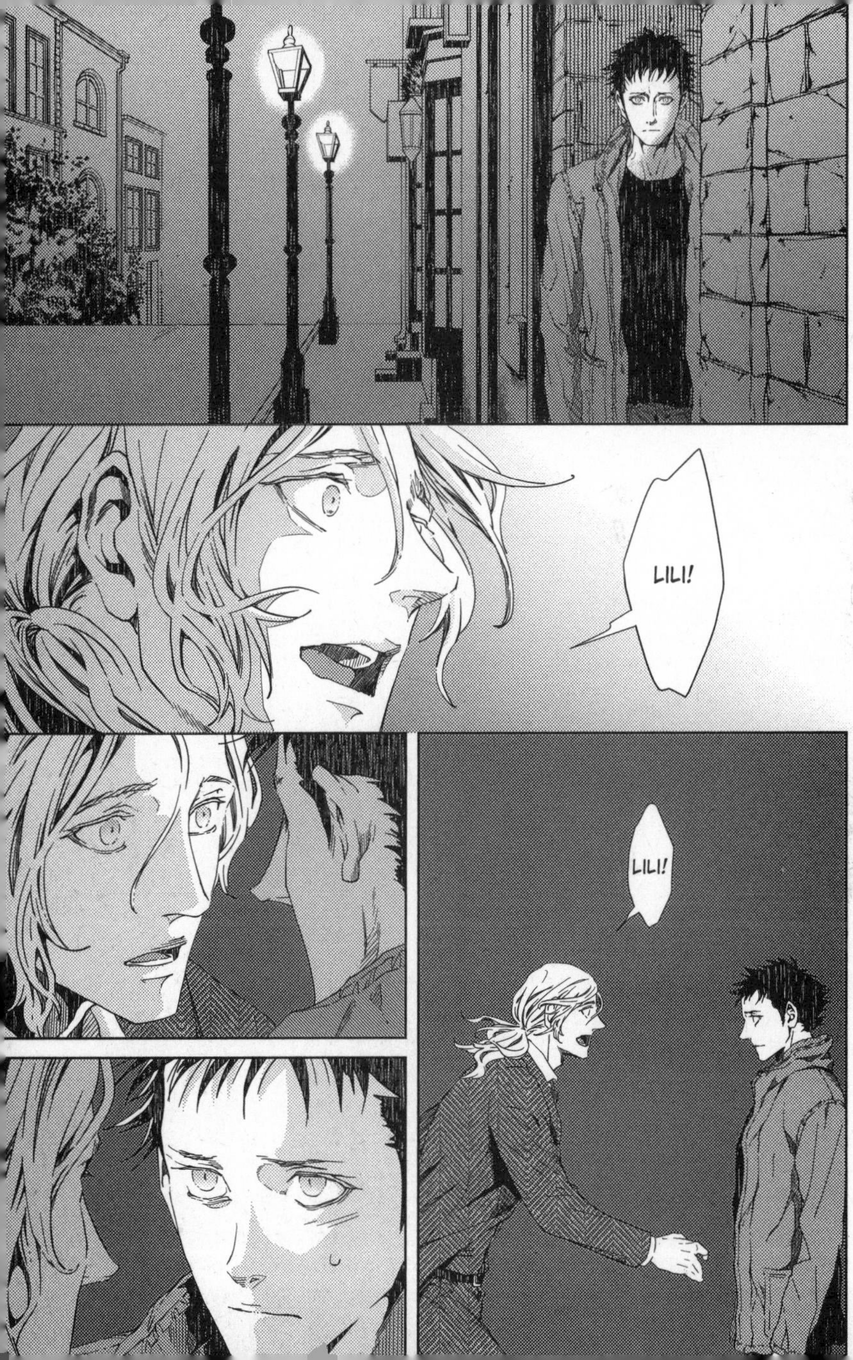
LILI!
LILI!

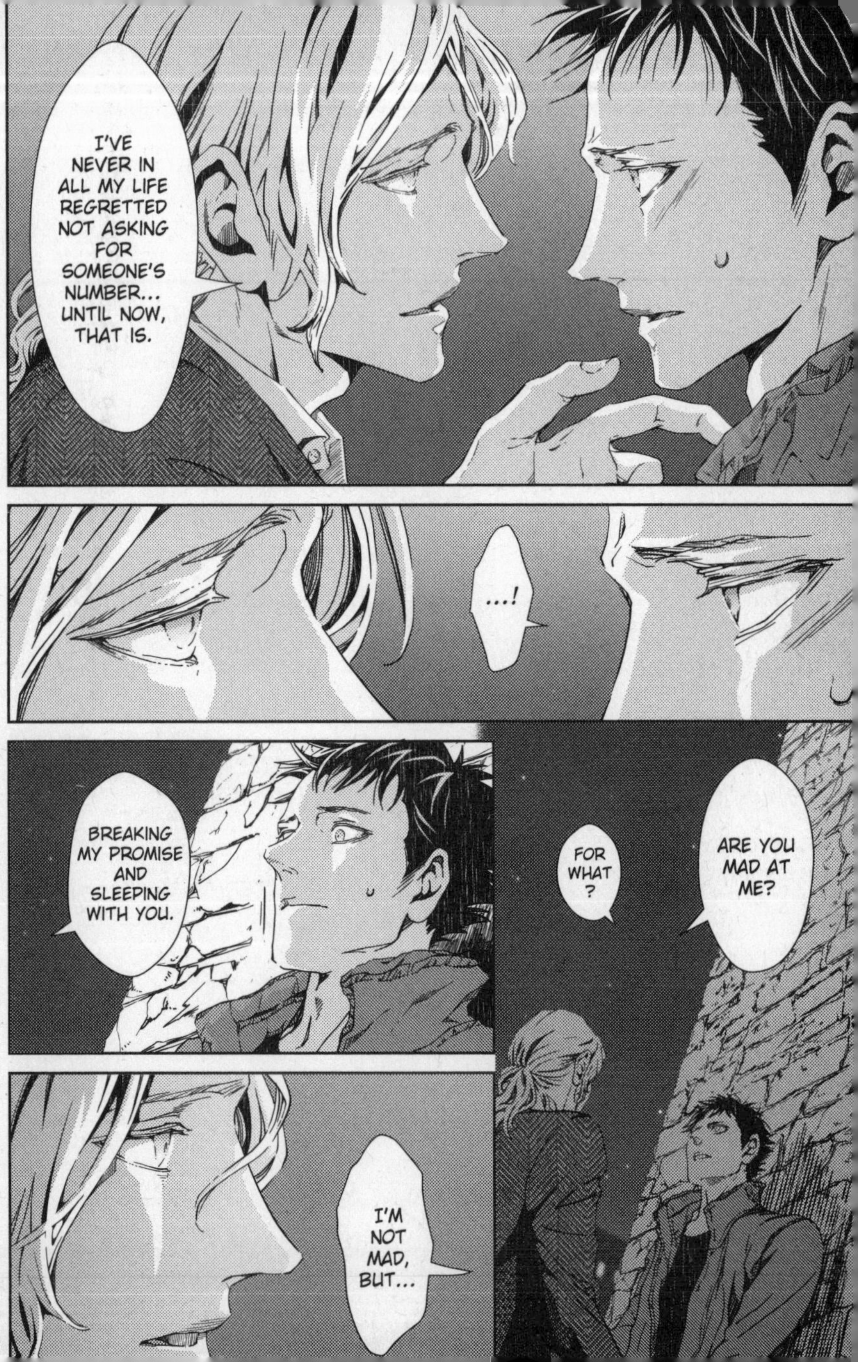
I'VE NEVER IN ALL MY LIFE REGRETTED NOT ASKING FOR SOMEONE'S NUMBER... UNTIL NOW, THAT IS.
...!
ARE YOU MAD AT ME?
FOR WHAT?
BREAKING MY PROMISE AND SLEEPING WITH YOU.
I'M NOT MAD, BUT...

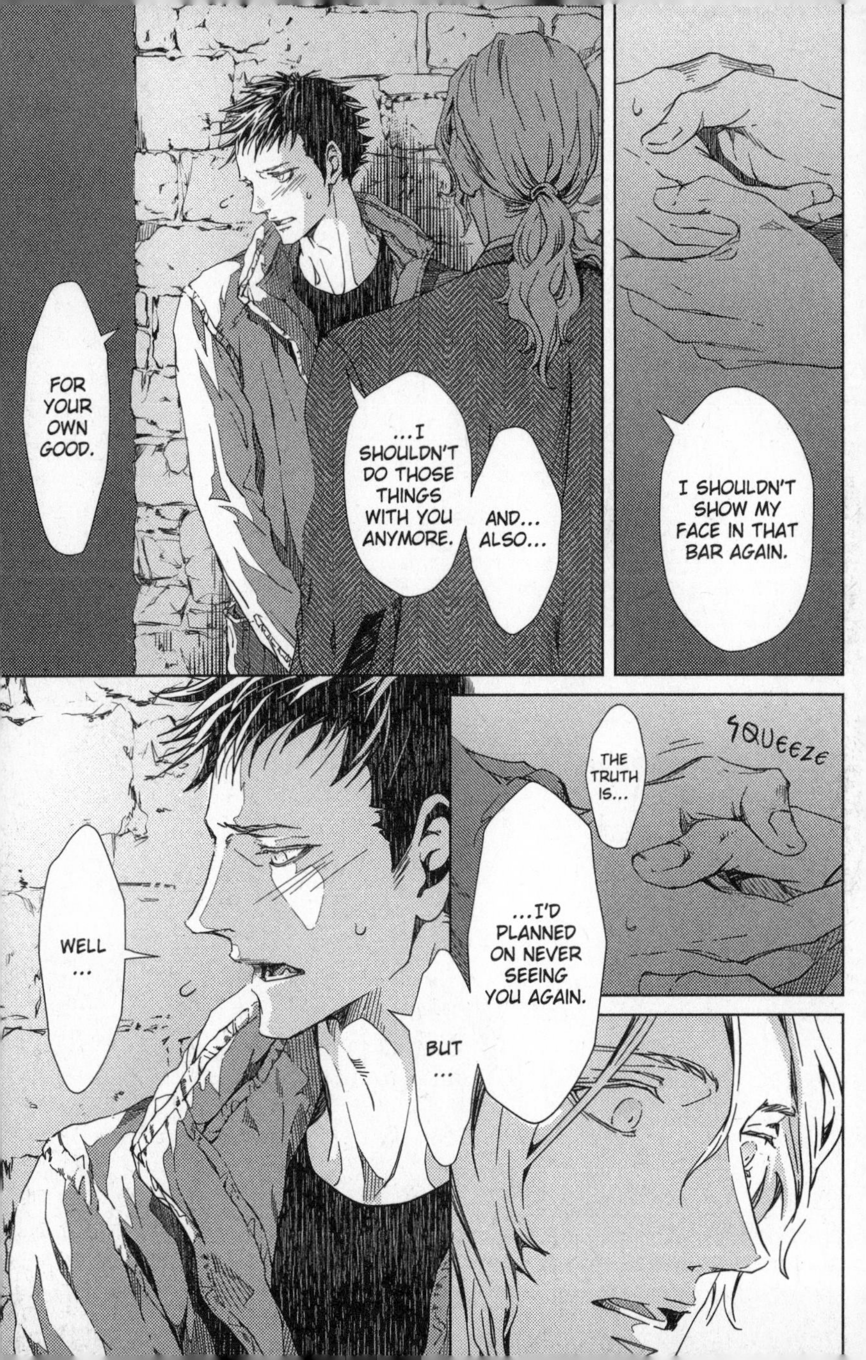
I SHOULDN'T SHOW MY FACE IN THAT BAR AGAIN.
AND... ALSO...
...I SHOULDN'T DO THOSE THINGS WITH YOU ANYMORE.
FOR YOUR OWN GOOD.
SQUEEZE
THE TRUTH IS...
...I'D PLANNED ON NEVER SEEING YOU AGAIN.
BUT ...
WELL ...

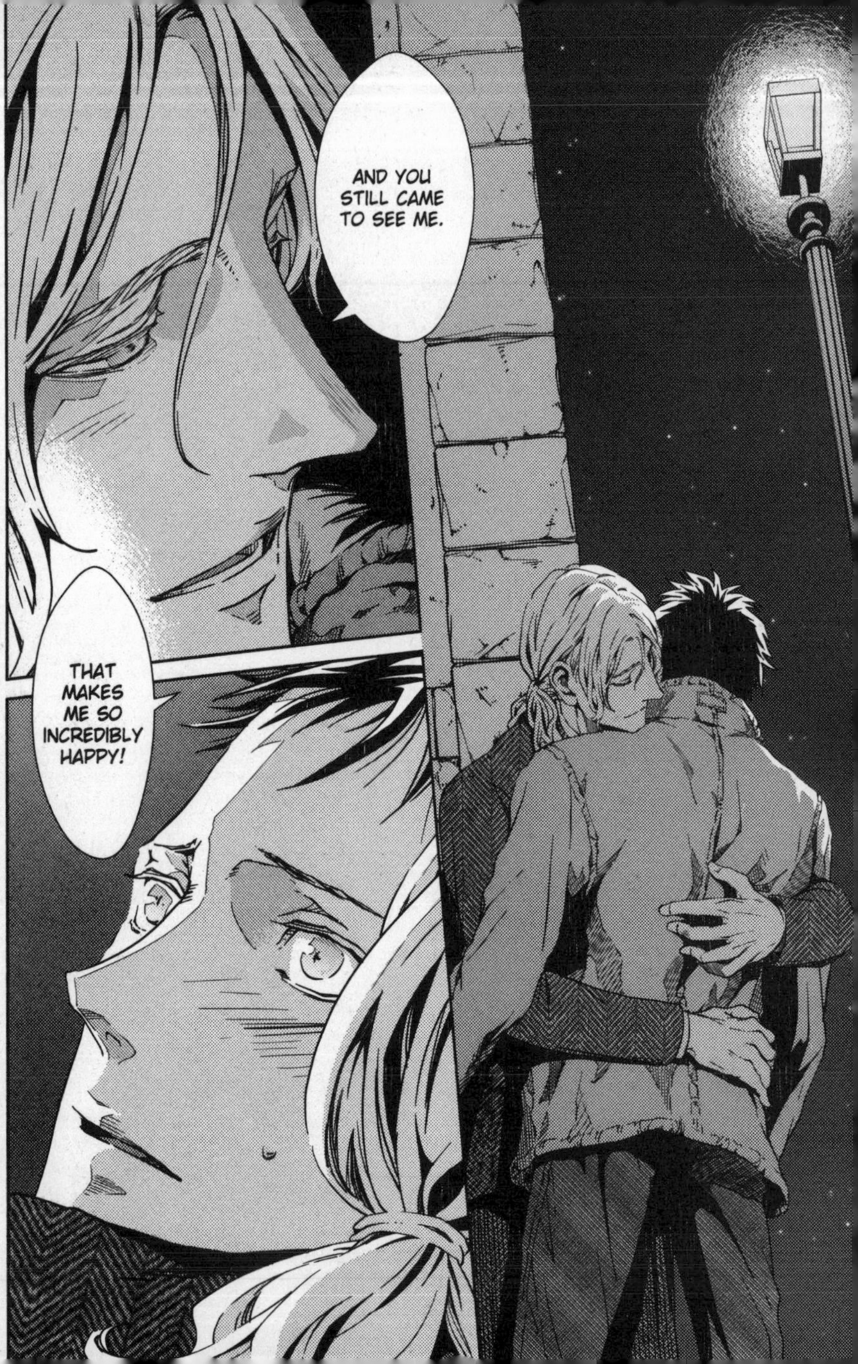
AND YOU STILL CAME TO SEE ME.
THAT MAKES ME SO INCREDIBLY HAPPY!

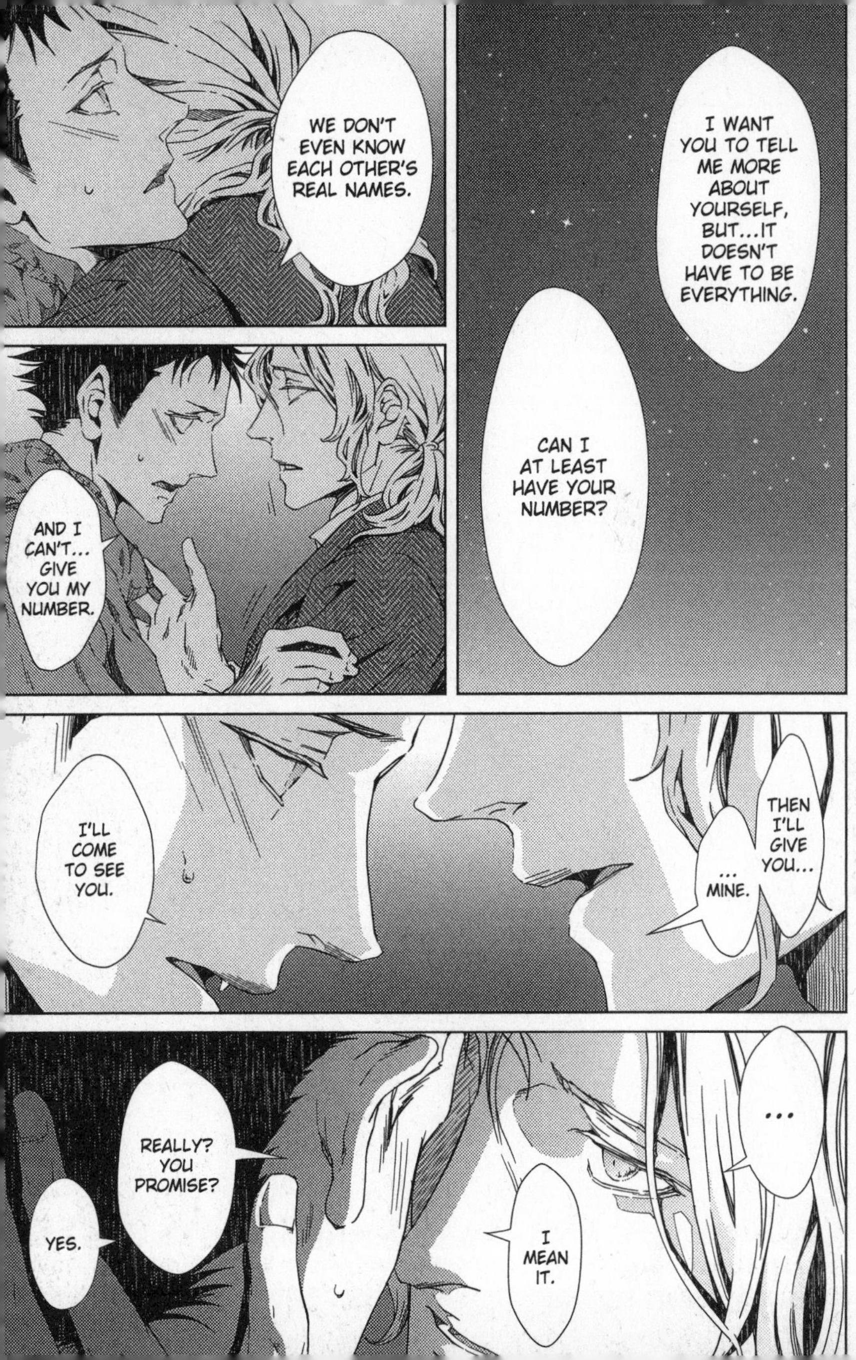
I WANT YOU TO TELL ME MORE ABOUT YOURSELF, BUT...IT DOESN'T HAVE TO BE EVERYTHING.
CAN I AT LEAST HAVE YOUR NUMBER?
WE DON'T EVEN KNOW EACH OTHER'S REAL NAMES.
AND I CAN'T... GIVE YOU MY NUMBER.
THEN I'LL GIVE YOU...
... MINE.
I'LL COME TO SEE YOU.
...
I MEAN IT.
REALLY? YOU PROMISE?
YES.

LILI, LISTEN ...

NEXT TIME ...

NEXT TIME I SEE YOU, I HAVE SOMETHING TO TELL YOU.

IT'S NOT SOMETHING I WANT OTHERS TO KNOW, JUST YOU.

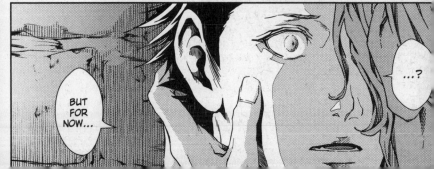

BUT FOR NOW...

...?

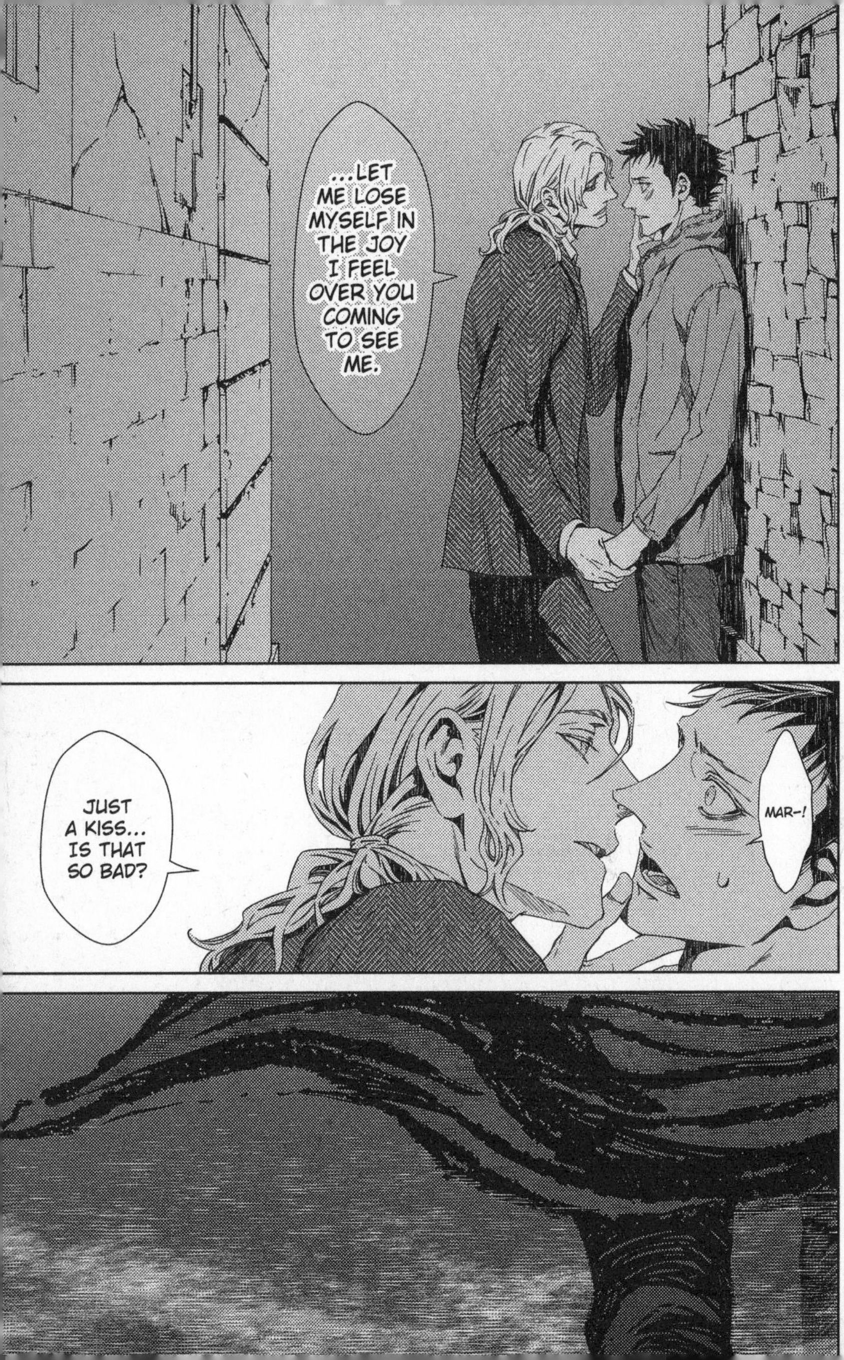
...LET ME LOSE MYSELF IN THE JOY I FEEL OVER YOU COMING TO SEE ME.
MAR-!
JUST A KISS... IS THAT SO BAD?

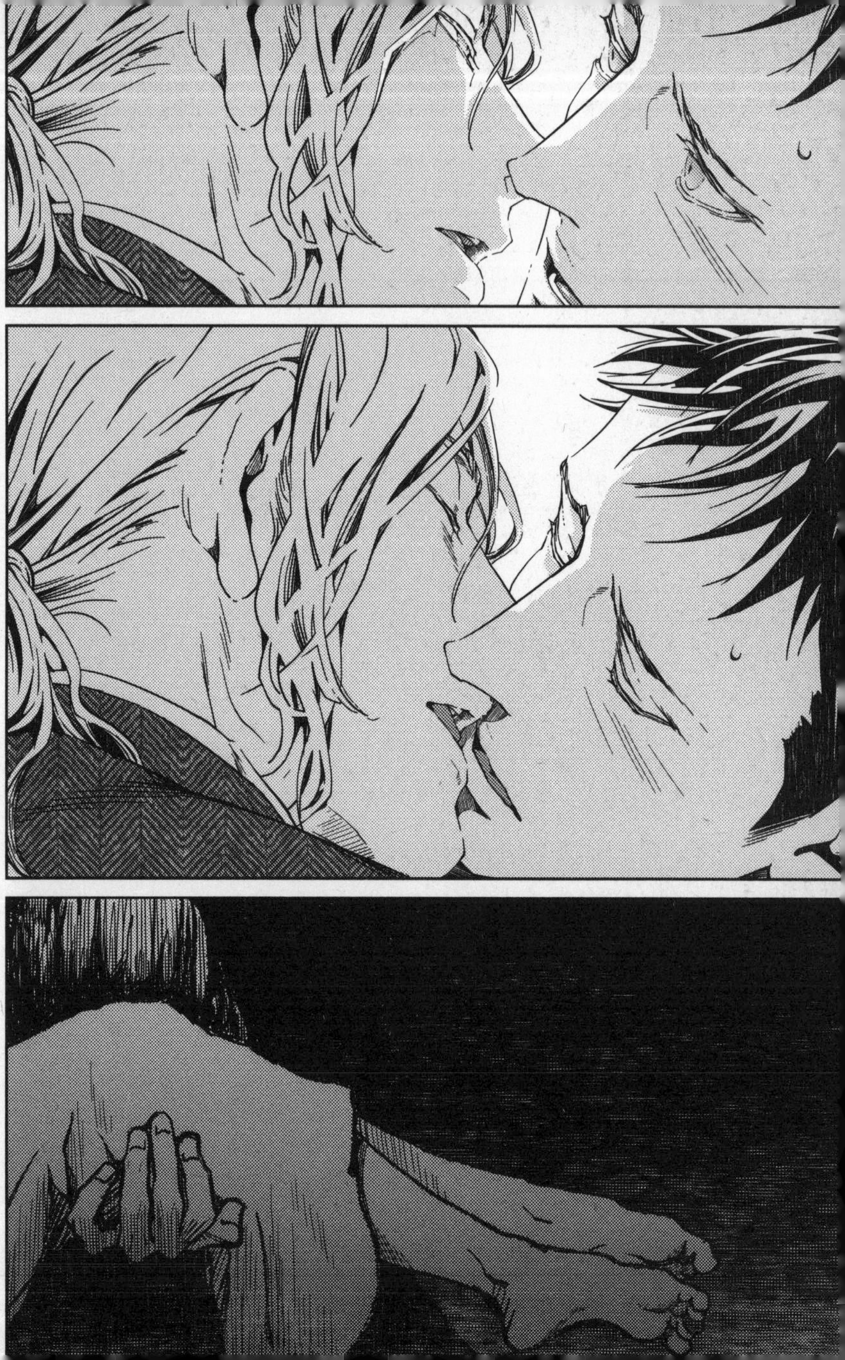

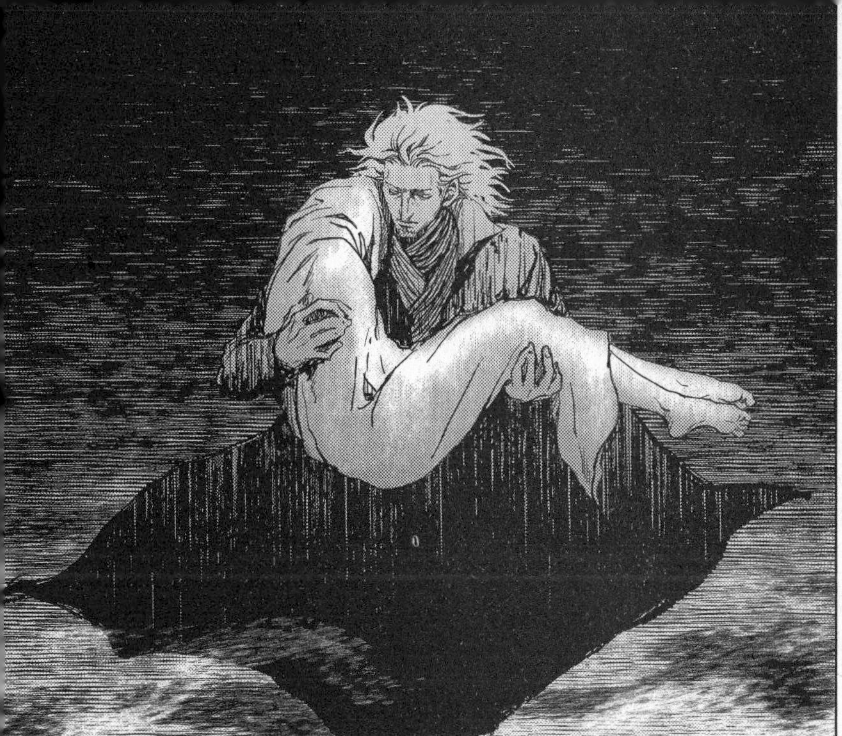
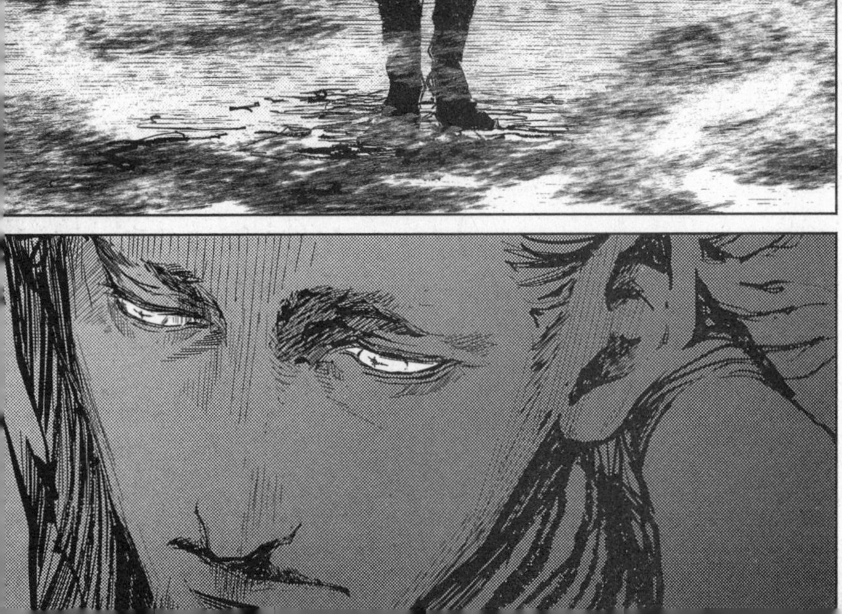

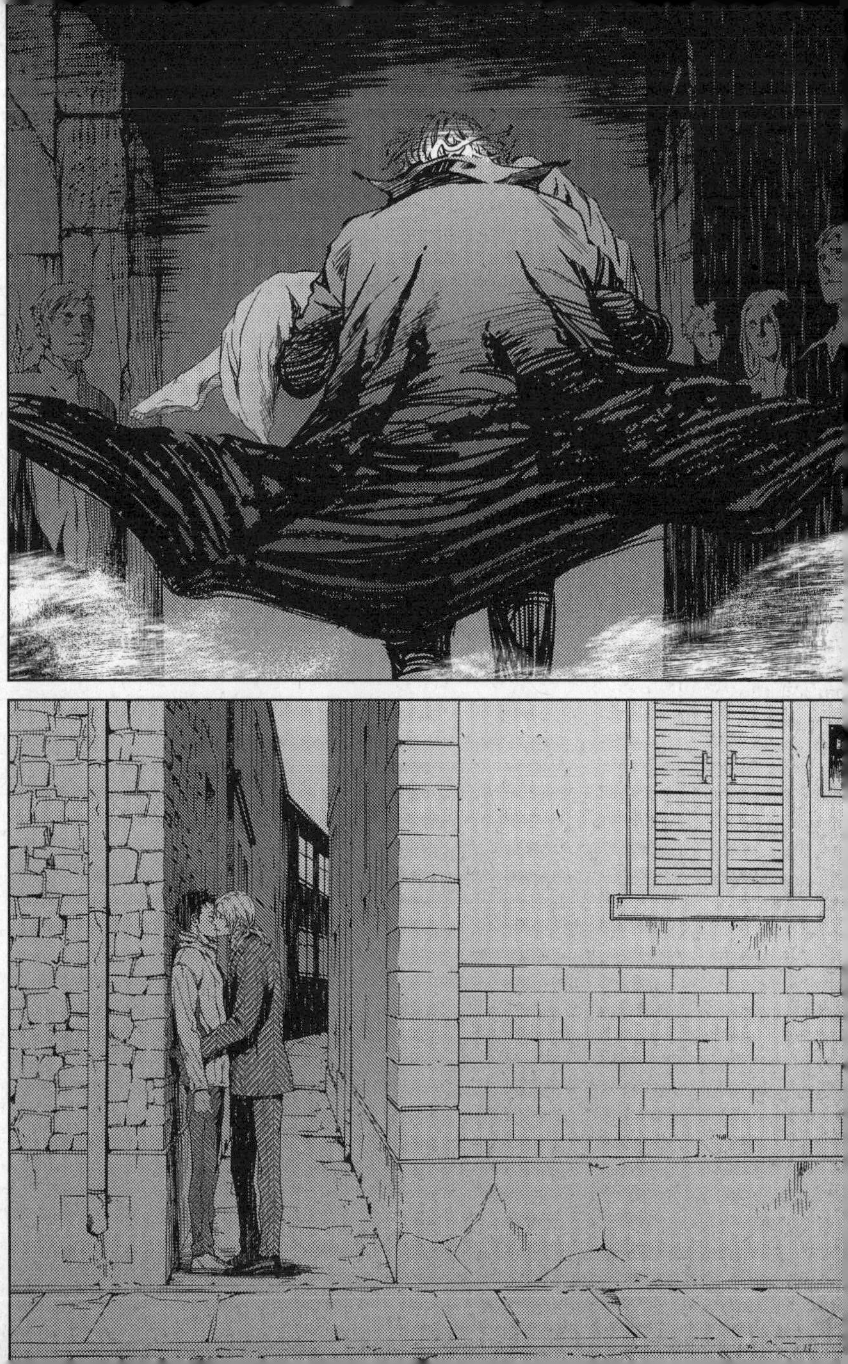

Coyote

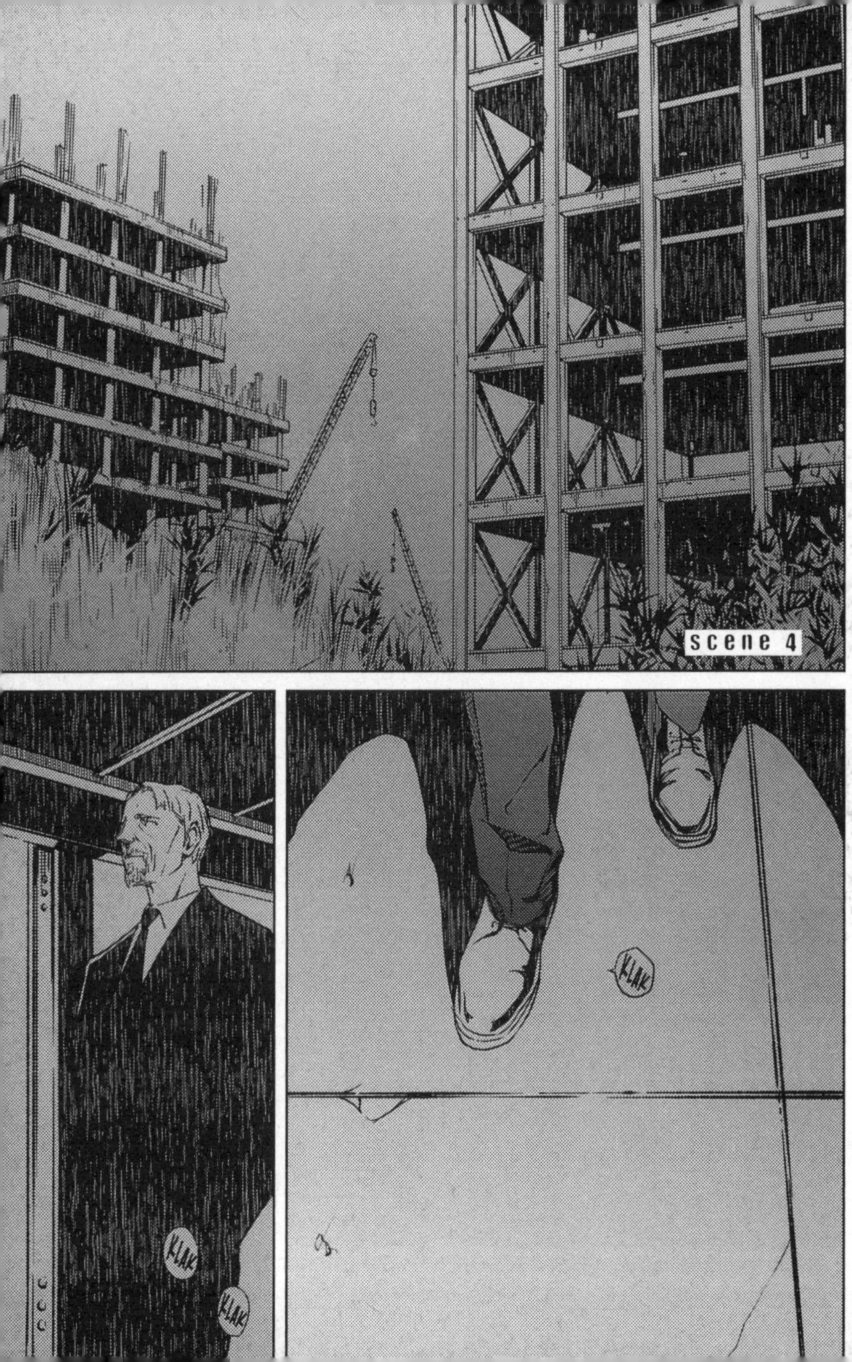
scene 4
KLAK
KLAK
KLAK

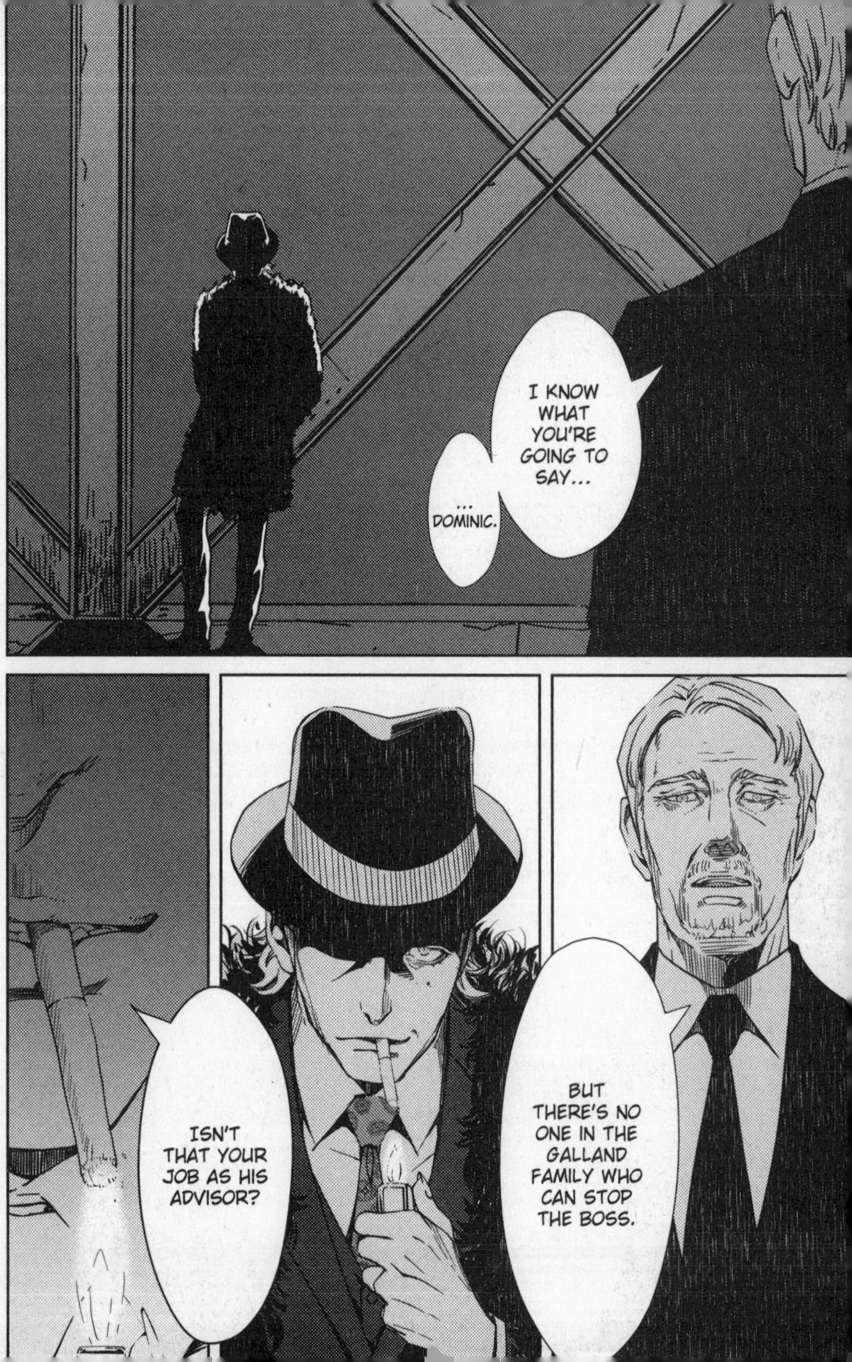
I KNOW WHAT YOU'RE GOING TO SAY...
...DOMINIC.
BUT THERE'S NO ONE IN THE GALLAND FAMILY WHO CAN STOP THE BOSS.
ISN'T THAT YOUR JOB AS HIS ADVISOR?

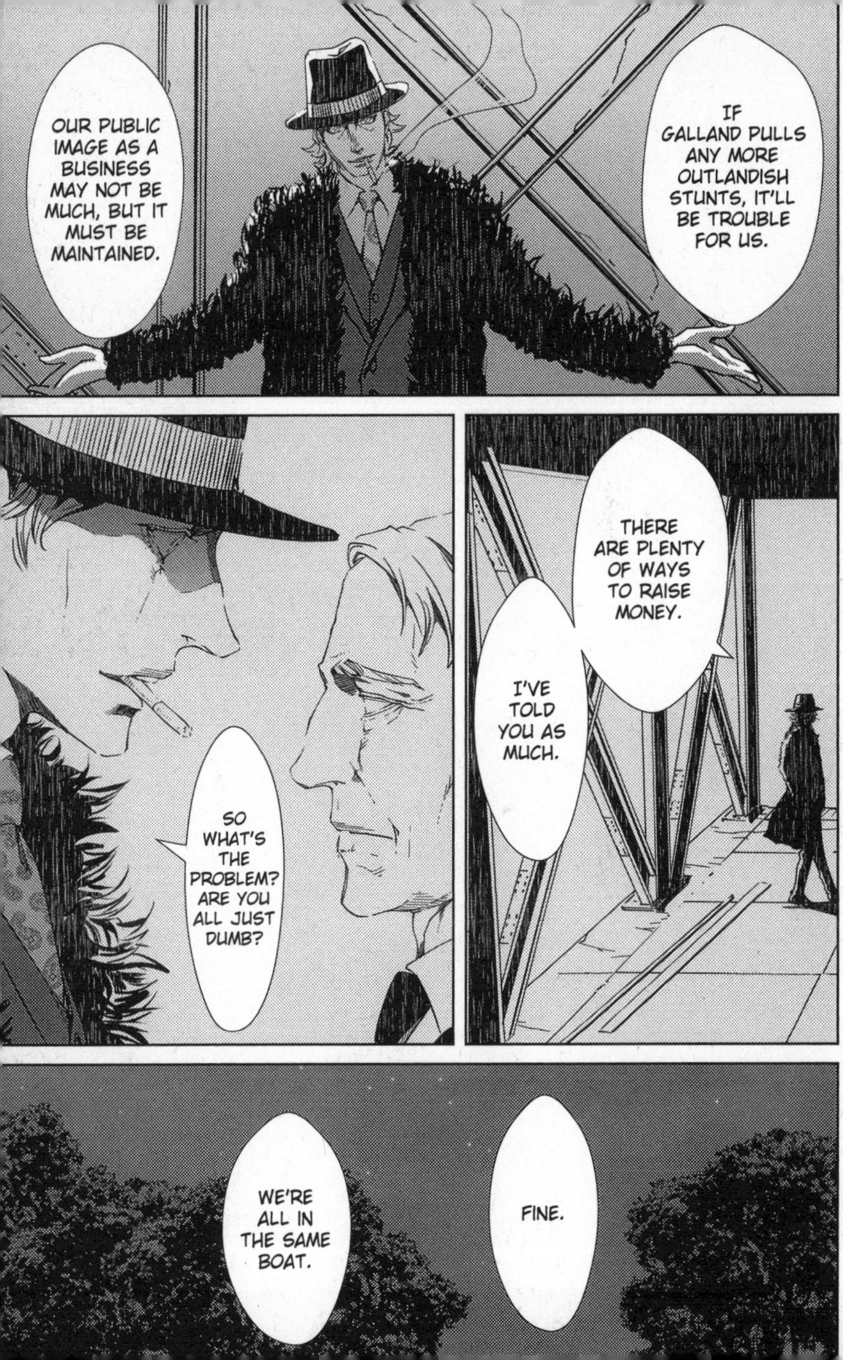
IF GALLAND PULLS ANY MORE OUTLANDISH STUNTS, IT'LL BE TROUBLE FOR US.
OUR PUBLIC IMAGE AS A BUSINESS MAY NOT BE MUCH, BUT IT MUST BE MAINTAINED.
THERE ARE PLENTY OF WAYS TO RAISE MONEY.
I'VE TOLD YOU AS MUCH.
SO WHAT'S THE PROBLEM? ARE YOU ALL JUST DUMB?
FINE.
WE'RE ALL IN THE SAME BOAT.

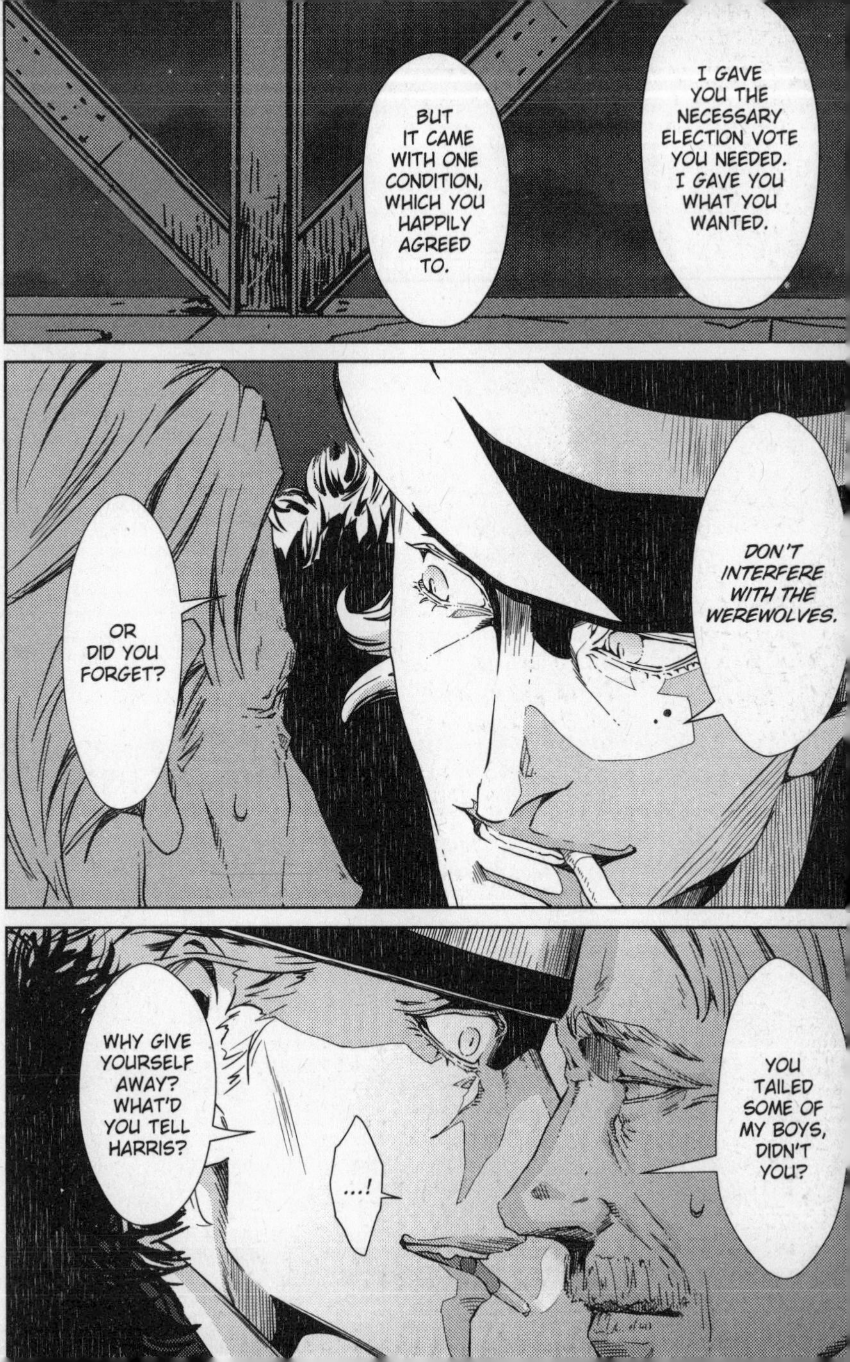
I GAVE YOU THE NECESSARY ELECTION VOTE YOU NEEDED. I GAVE YOU WHAT YOU WANTED.
BUT IT CAME WITH ONE CONDITION, WHICH YOU HAPPILY AGREED TO.
DON'T INTERFERE WITH THE WEREWOLVES.
OR DID YOU FORGET?
YOU TAILED SOME OF MY BOYS, DIDN'T YOU?
...!
WHY GIVE YOURSELF AWAY? WHAT'D YOU TELL HARRIS?

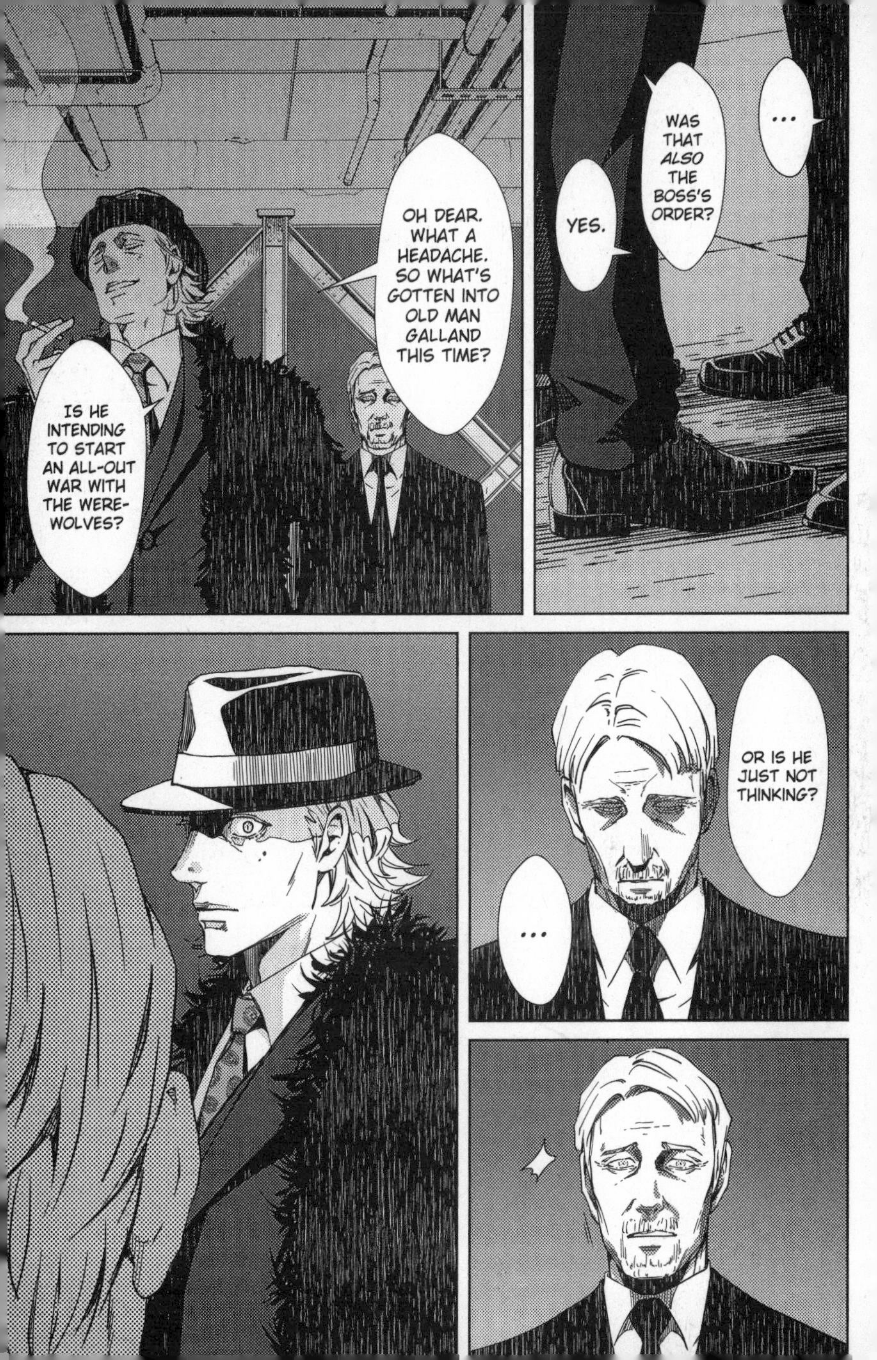
...
WAS THAT ALSO THE BOSS'S ORDER?
YES.
OH DEAR. WHAT A HEADACHE. SO WHAT'S GOTTEN INTO OLD MAN GALLAND THIS TIME?
IS HE INTENDING TO START AN ALL-OUT WAR WITH THE WERE-WOLVES?
OR IS HE JUST NOT THINKING?
...

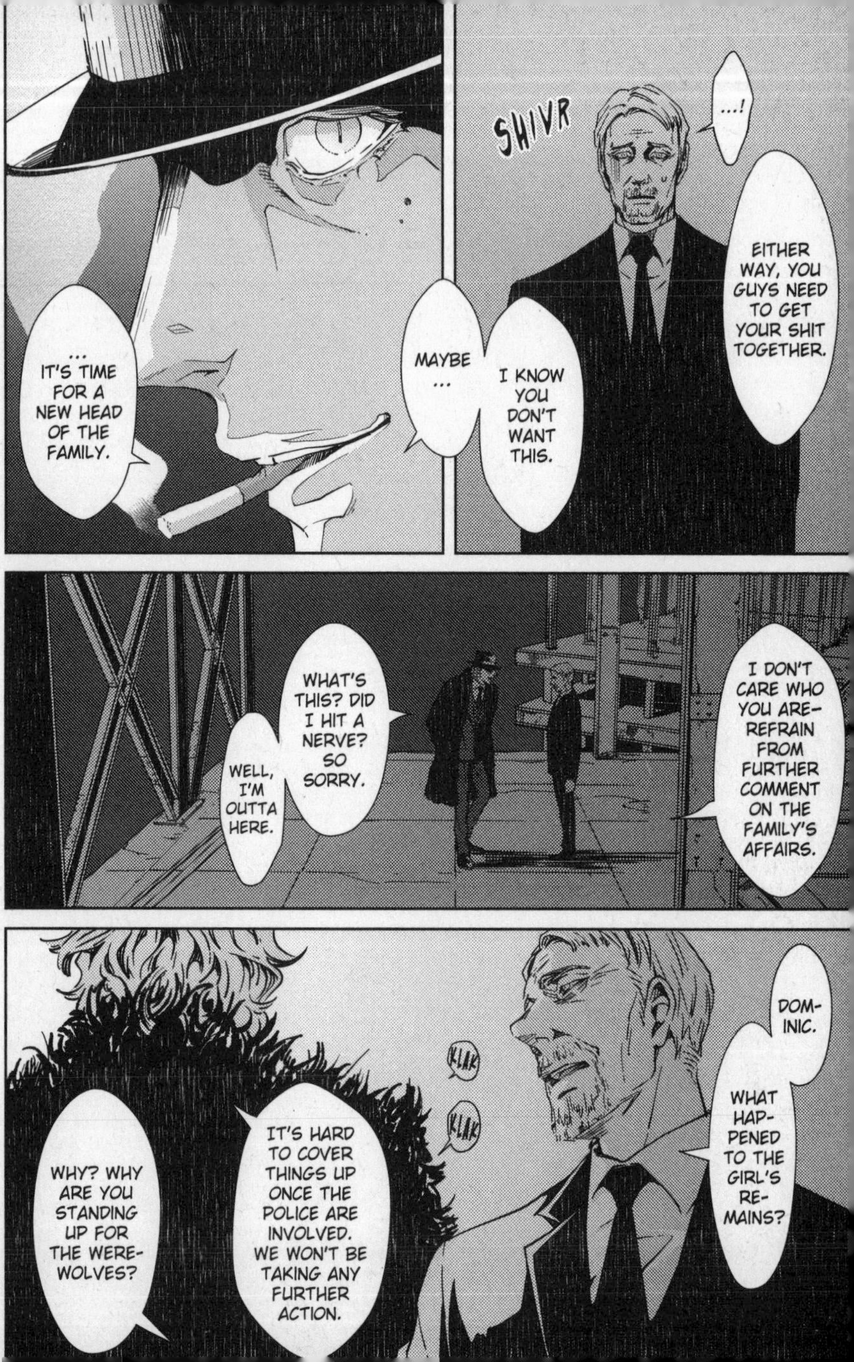
...!
SHIVR
EITHER WAY, YOU GUYS NEED TO GET YOUR SHIT TOGETHER.
I KNOW YOU DON'T WANT THIS.
MAYBE ...
... IT'S TIME FOR A NEW HEAD OF THE FAMILY.
I DON'T CARE WHO YOU ARE—REFRAIN FROM FURTHER COMMENT ON THE FAMILY'S AFFAIRS.
WHAT'S THIS? DID I HIT A NERVE? SO SORRY.
WELL, I'M OUTTA HERE.
DOM-INIC.
WHAT HAP-PENED TO THE GIRL'S RE-MAINS?
KLAK
KLAK
IT'S HARD TO COVER THINGS UP ONCE THE POLICE ARE INVOLVED. WE WON'T BE TAKING ANY FURTHER ACTION.
WHY? WHY ARE YOU STANDING UP FOR THE WERE-WOLVES?

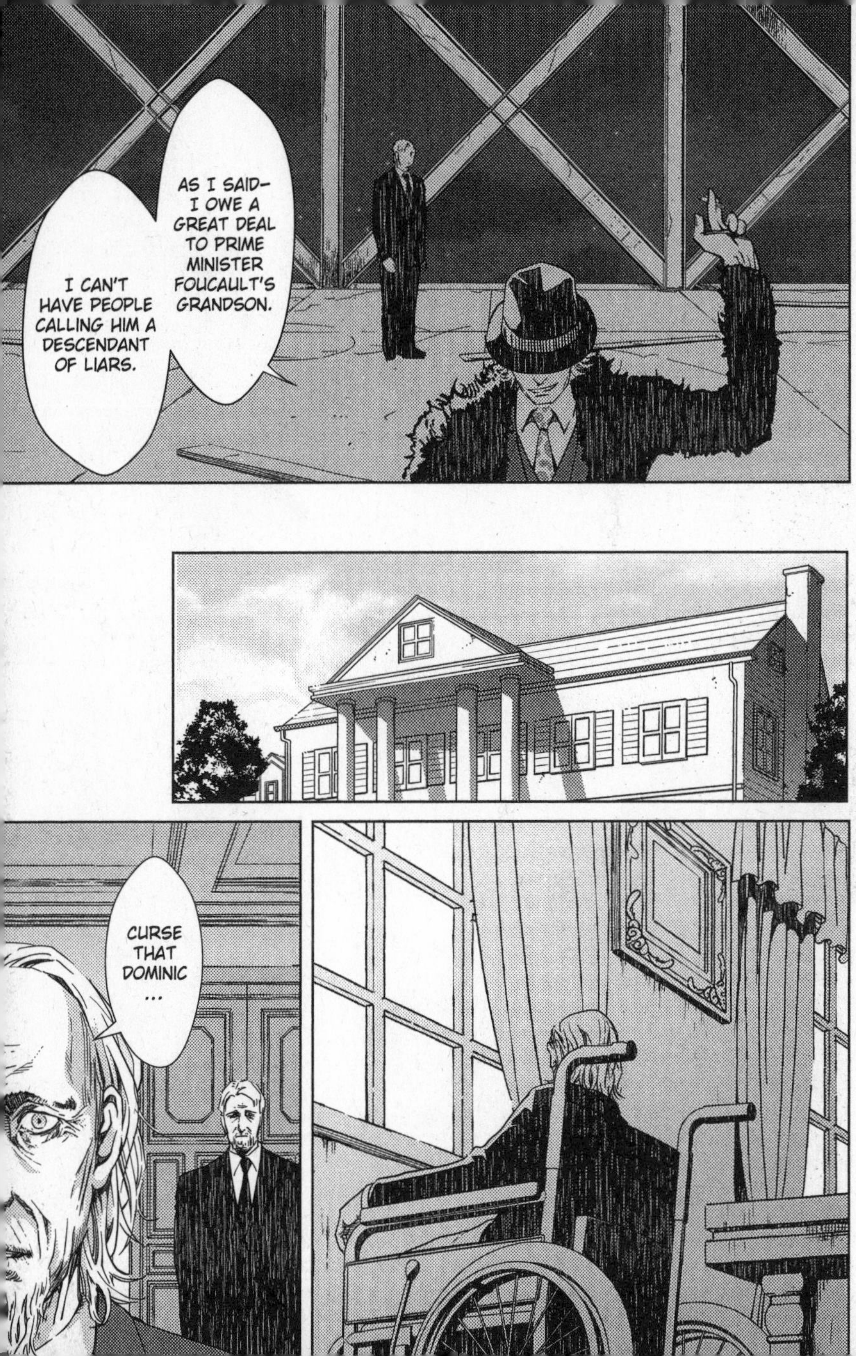
AS I SAID- I OWE A GREAT DEAL TO PRIME MINISTER FOUCAULT'S GRANDSON.
I CAN'T HAVE PEOPLE CALLING HIM A DESCENDANT OF LIARS.
CURSE THAT DOMINIC ...

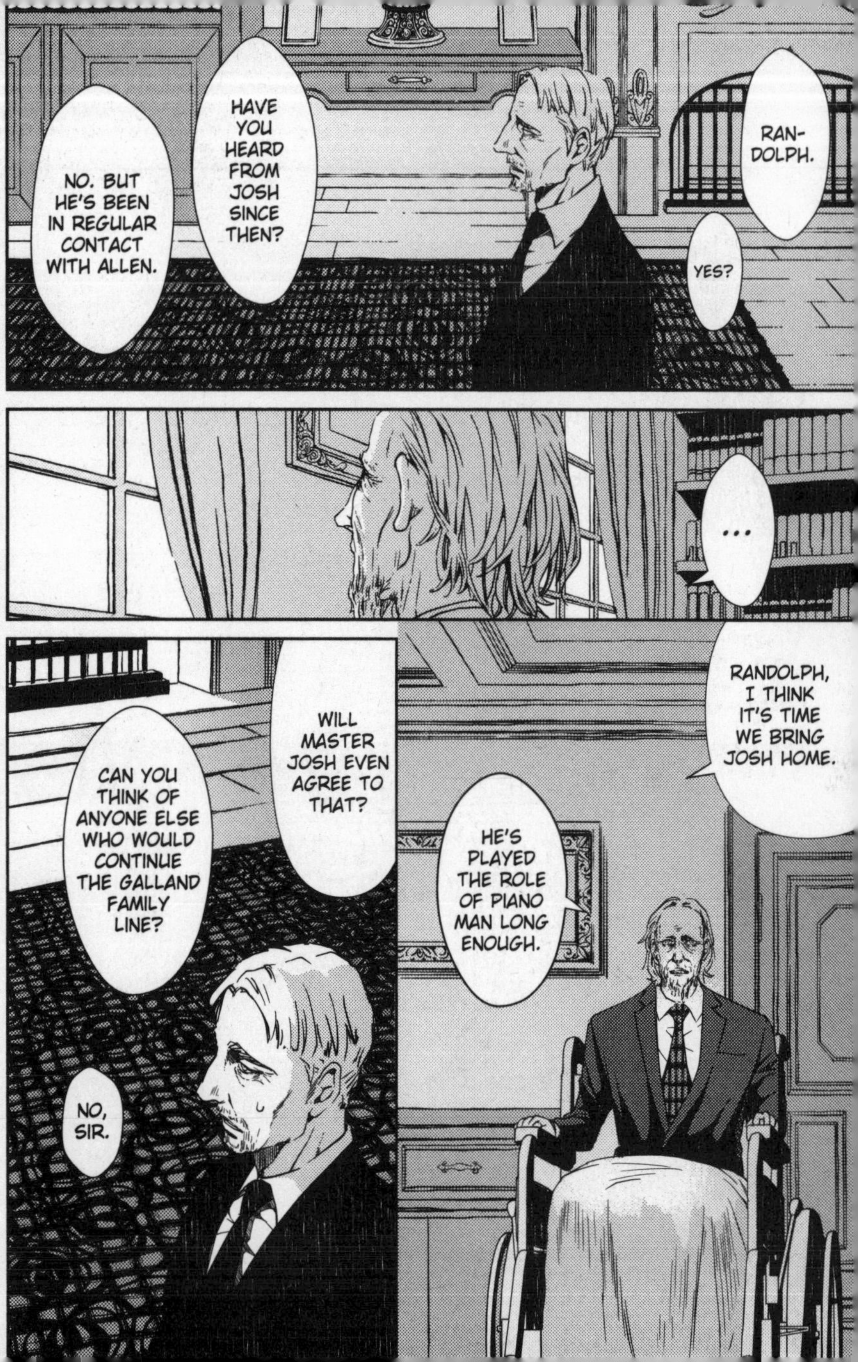
RAN-DOLPH.
YES?
HAVE YOU HEARD FROM JOSH SINCE THEN?
NO. BUT HE'S BEEN IN REGULAR CONTACT WITH ALLEN.
...
RANDOLPH, I THINK IT'S TIME WE BRING JOSH HOME.
HE'S PLAYED THE ROLE OF PIANO MAN LONG ENOUGH.
WILL MASTER JOSH EVEN AGREE TO THAT?
CAN YOU THINK OF ANYONE ELSE WHO WOULD CONTINUE THE GALLAND FAMILY LINE?
NO, SIR.

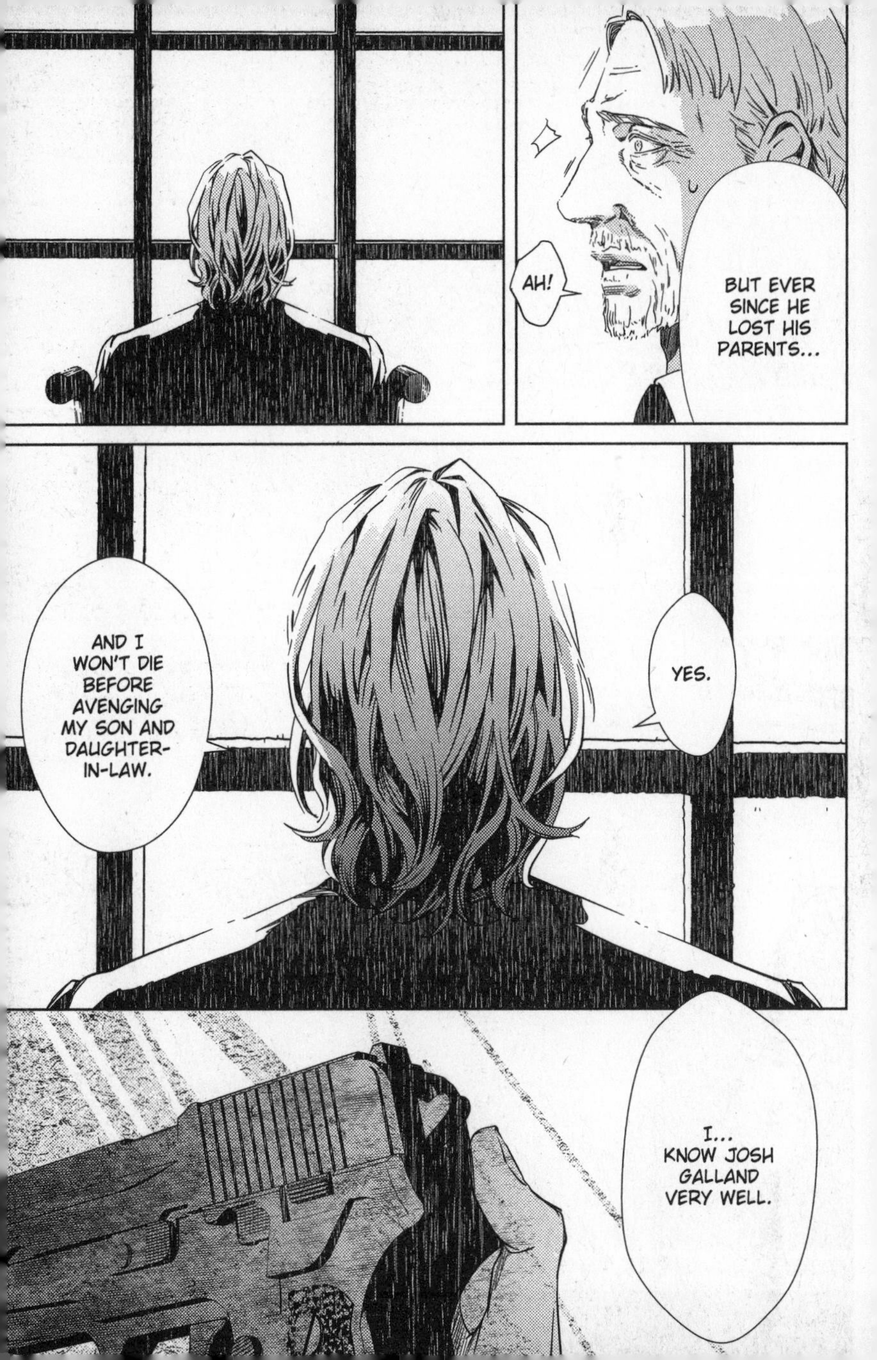
BUT EVER SINCE HE LOST HIS PARENTS...
AH!
YES.
AND I WON'T DIE BEFORE AVENGING MY SON AND DAUGHTER-IN-LAW.
I... KNOW JOSH GALLAND VERY WELL.

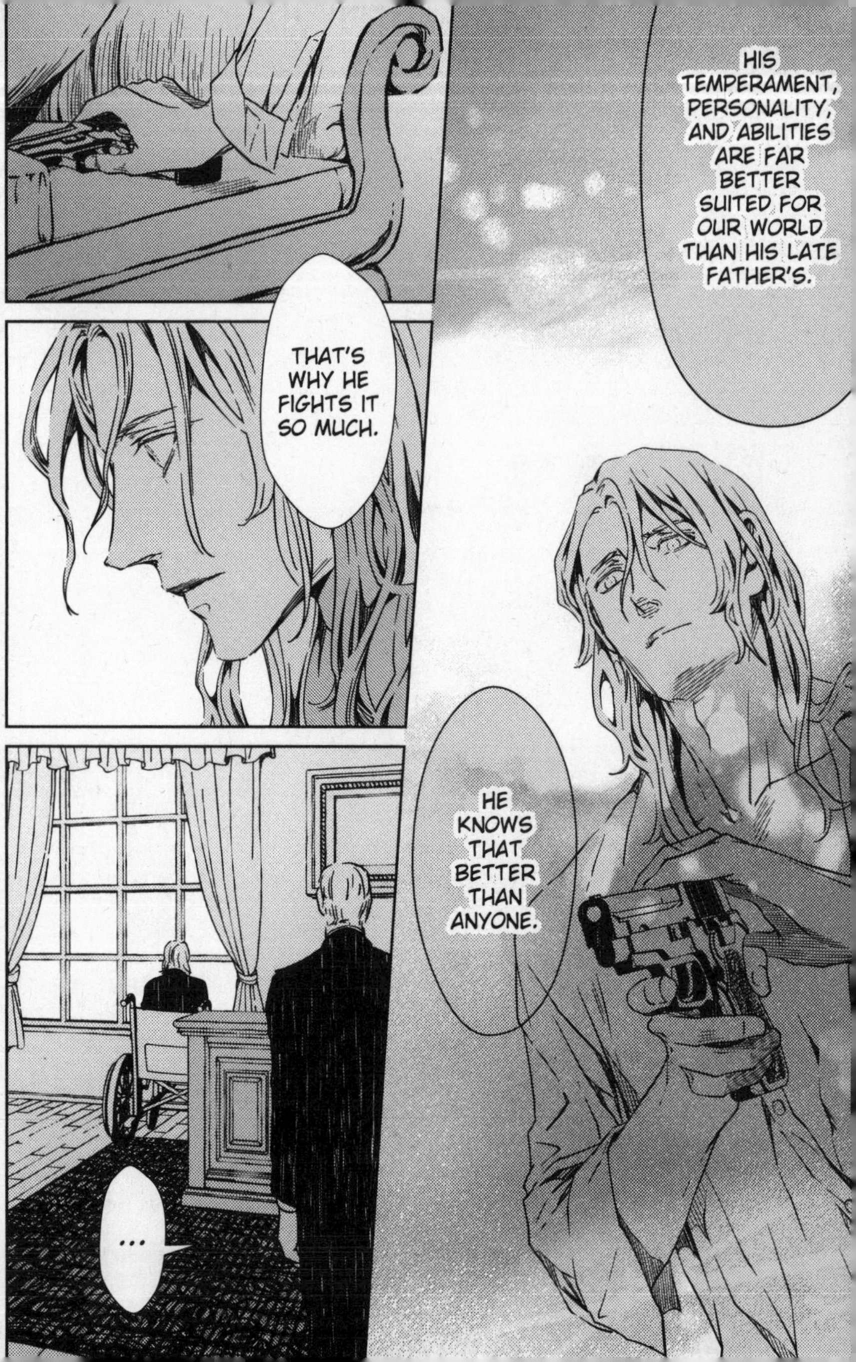
HIS TEMPERAMENT, PERSONALITY, AND ABILITIES ARE FAR BETTER SUITED FOR OUR WORLD THAN HIS LATE FATHER'S.
HE KNOWS THAT BETTER THAN ANYONE.
THAT'S WHY HE FIGHTS IT SO MUCH.
...

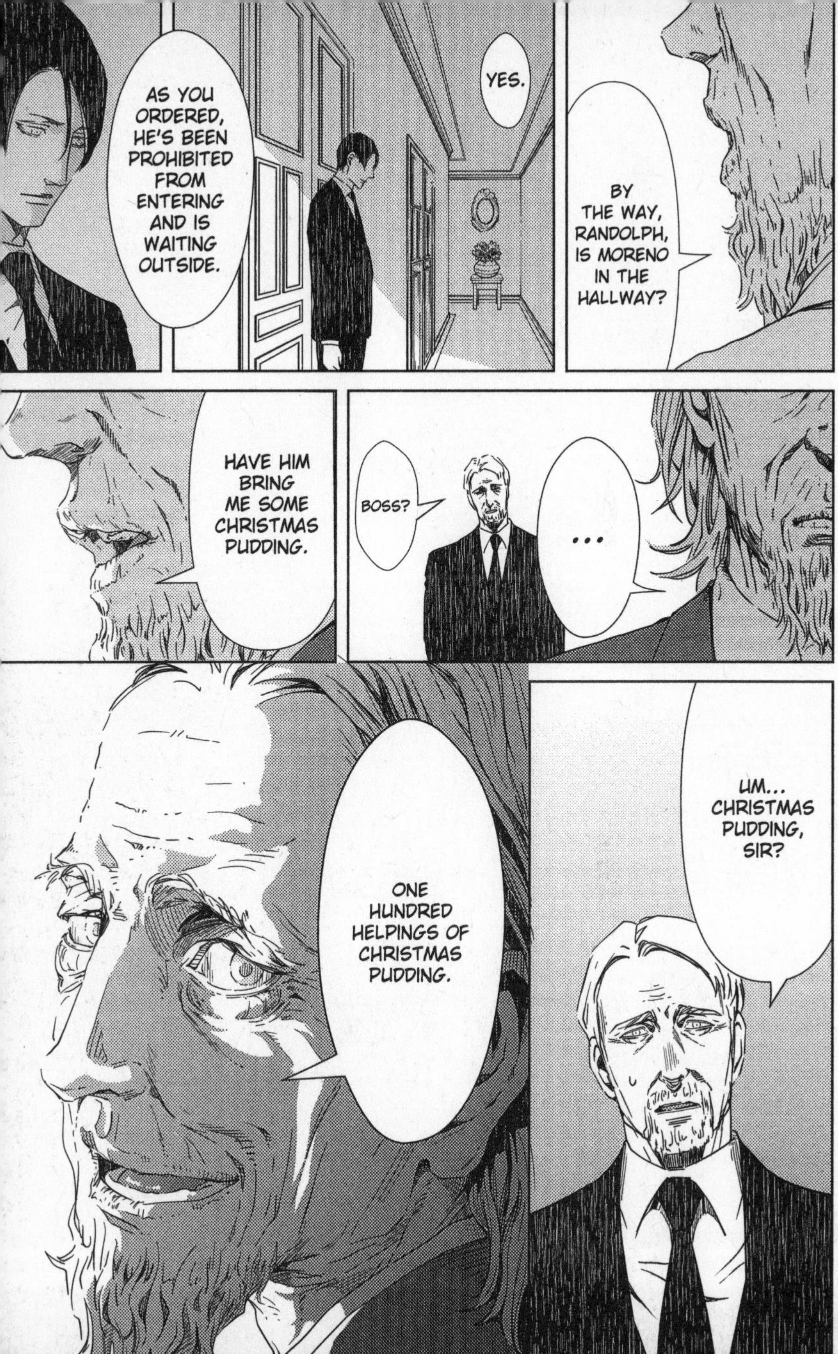
BY THE WAY, RANDOLPH, IS MORENO IN THE HALLWAY?
YES.
AS YOU ORDERED, HE'S BEEN PROHIBITED FROM ENTERING AND IS WAITING OUTSIDE.
...
BOSS?
HAVE HIM BRING ME SOME CHRISTMAS PUDDING.
UM... CHRISTMAS PUDDING, SIR?
ONE HUNDRED HELPINGS OF CHRISTMAS PUDDING.

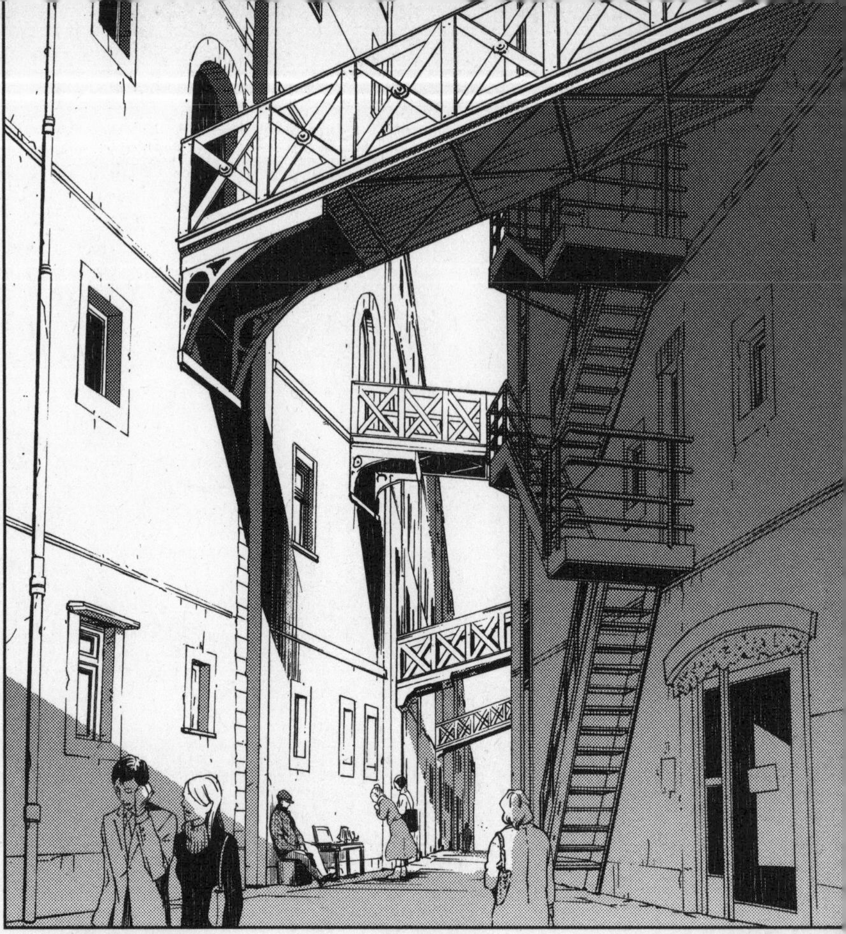
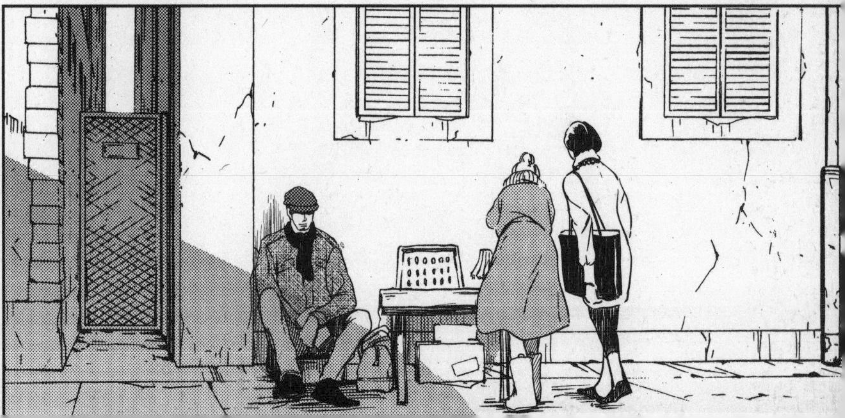

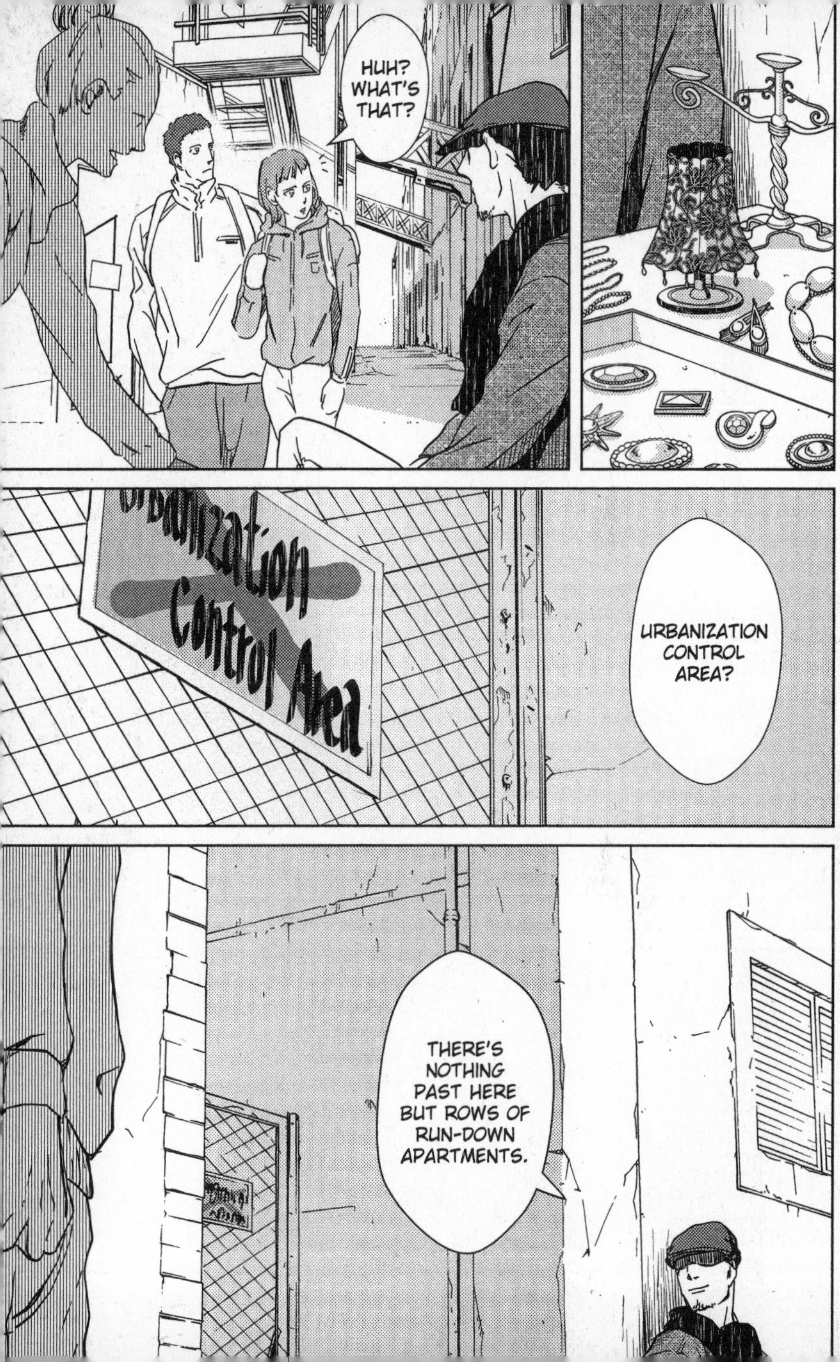
HUH? WHAT'S THAT?
URBANIZATION CONTROL AREA?
Control Area
THERE'S NOTHING PAST HERE BUT ROWS OF RUN-DOWN APARTMENTS.

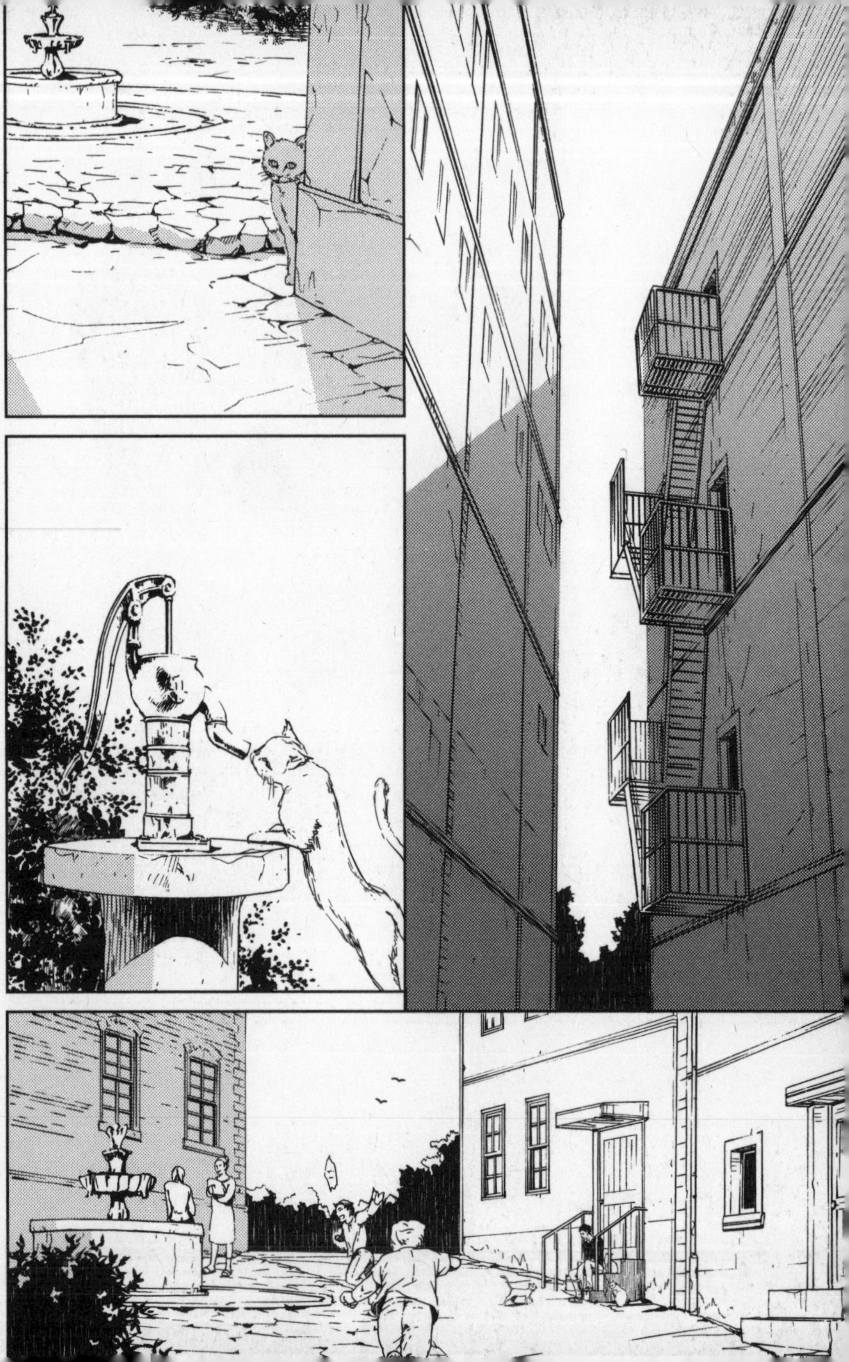

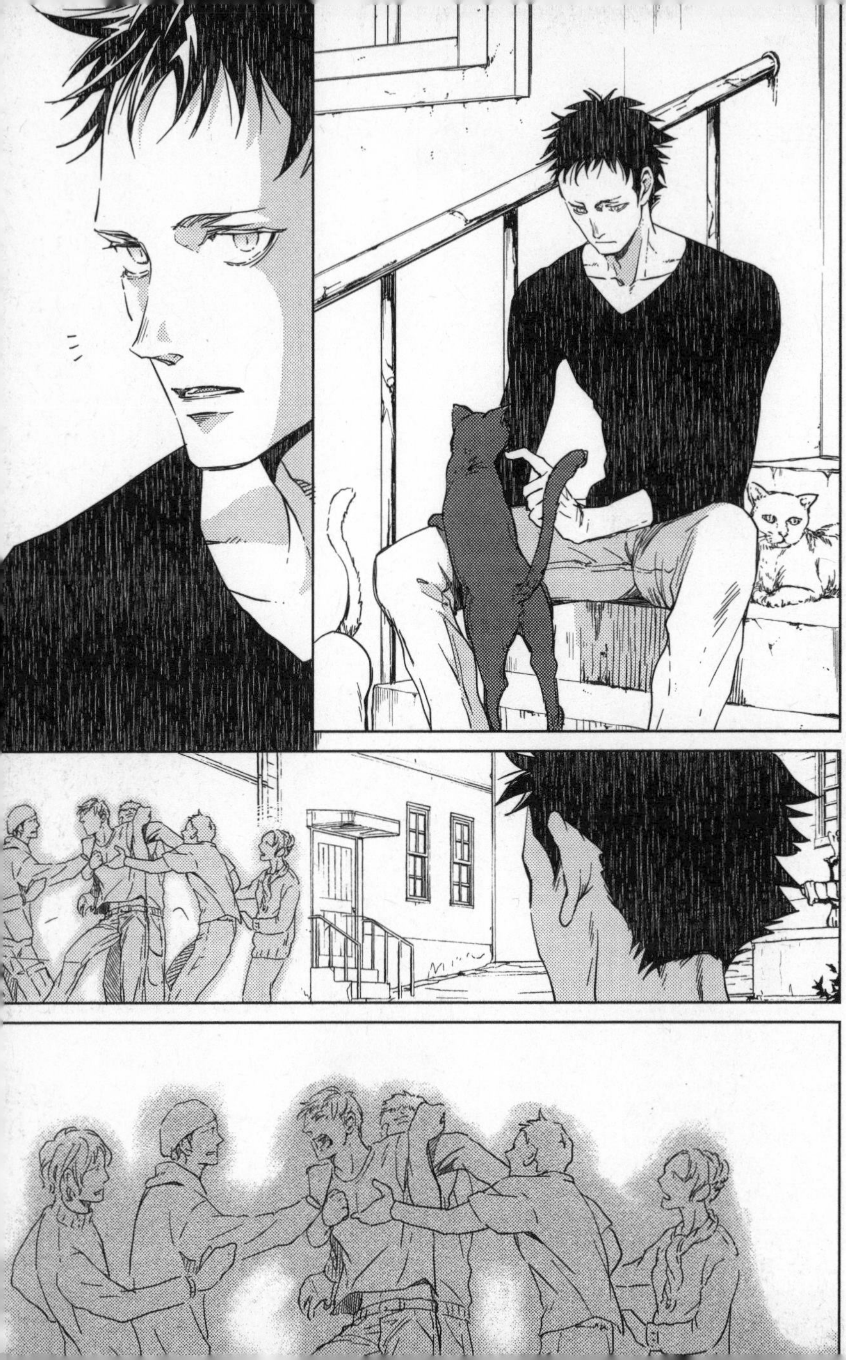

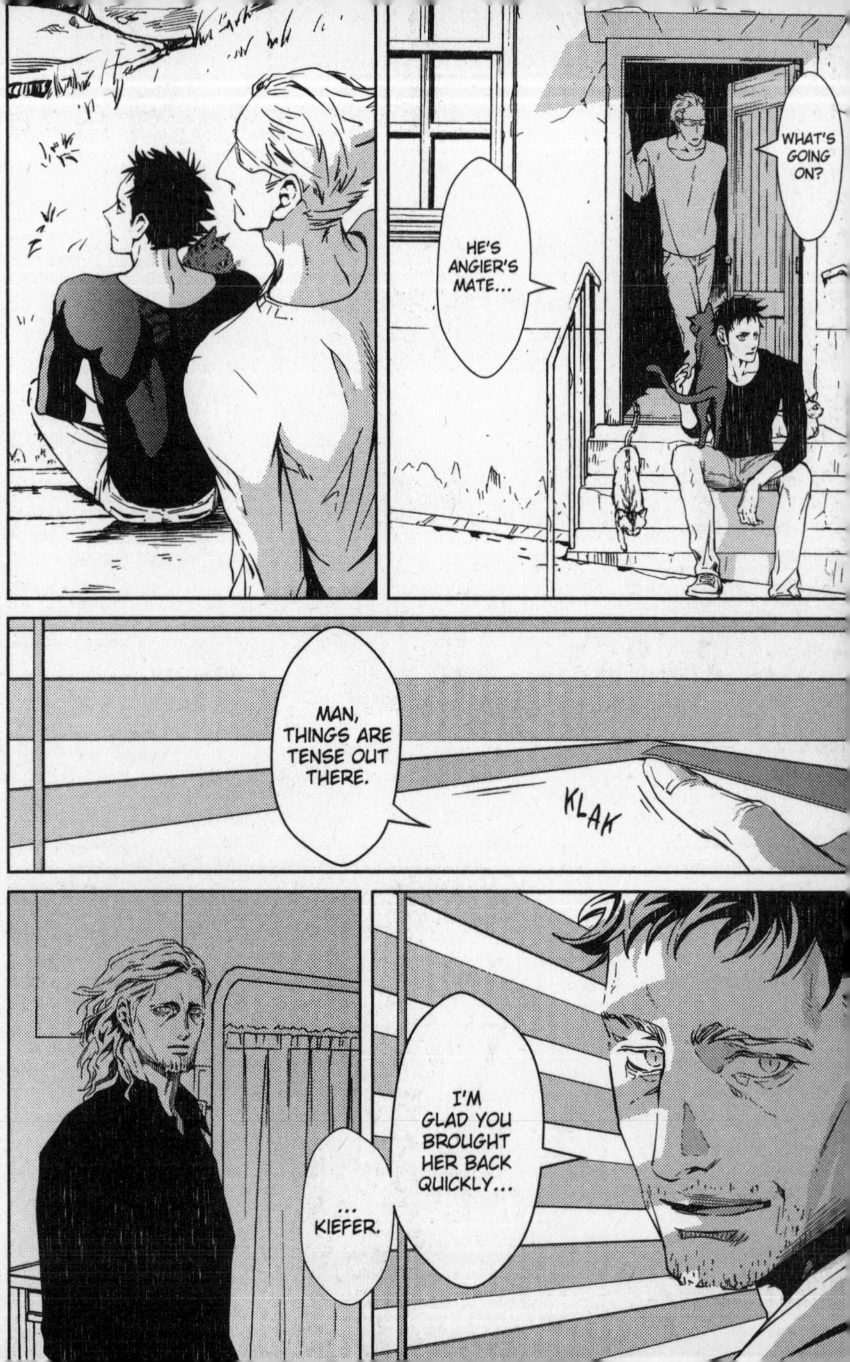
WHAT'S GOING ON?
HE'S ANGIER'S MATE...
MAN, THINGS ARE TENSE OUT THERE.
KLAK
I'M GLAD YOU BROUGHT HER BACK QUICKLY...
... KIEFER.

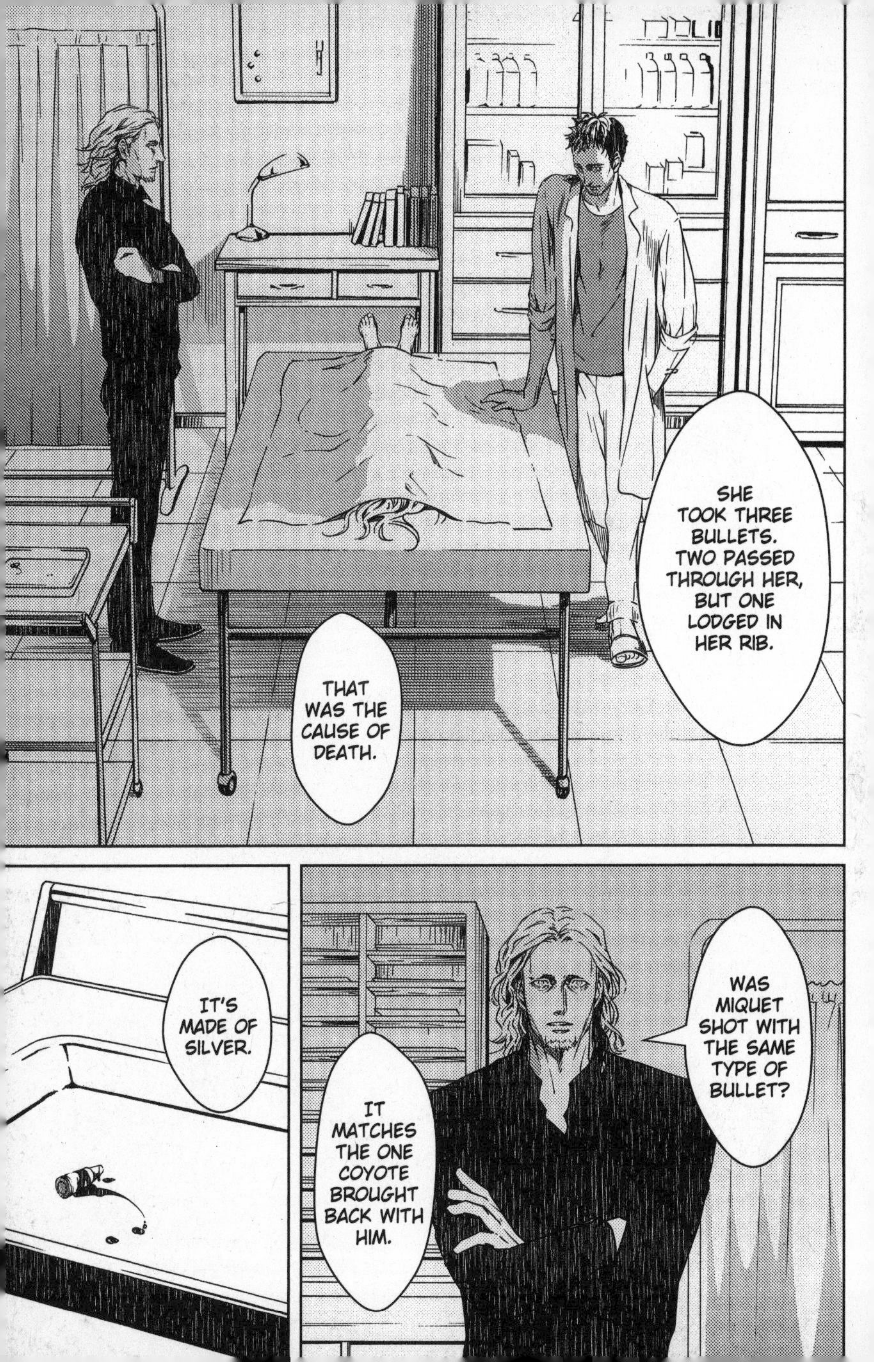
SHE TOOK THREE BULLETS. TWO PASSED THROUGH HER, BUT ONE LODGED IN HER RIB.
THAT WAS THE CAUSE OF DEATH.
WAS MIQUET SHOT WITH THE SAME TYPE OF BULLET?
IT MATCHES THE ONE COYOTE BROUGHT BACK WITH HIM.
IT'S MADE OF SILVER.

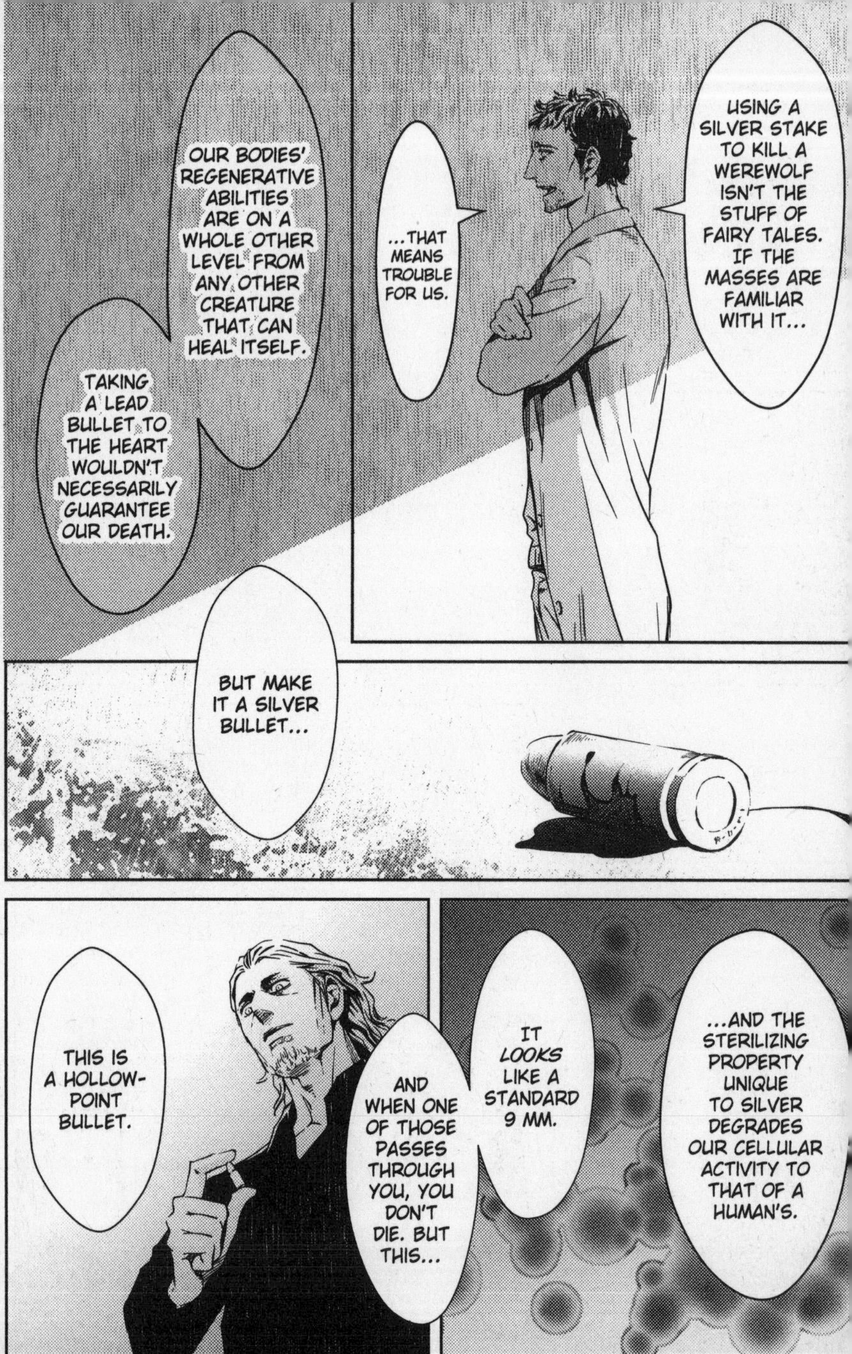
USING A SILVER STAKE TO KILL A WEREWOLF ISN'T THE STUFF OF FAIRY TALES. IF THE MASSES ARE FAMILIAR WITH IT...
...THAT MEANS TROUBLE FOR US.
OUR BODIES' REGENERATIVE ABILITIES ARE ON A WHOLE OTHER LEVEL FROM ANY OTHER CREATURE THAT CAN HEAL ITSELF.
TAKING A LEAD BULLET TO THE HEART WOULDN'T NECESSARILY GUARANTEE OUR DEATH.
BUT MAKE IT A SILVER BULLET...
...AND THE STERILIZING PROPERTY UNIQUE TO SILVER DEGRADES OUR CELLULAR ACTIVITY TO THAT OF A HUMAN'S.
IT LOOKS LIKE A STANDARD 9 MM.
AND WHEN ONE OF THOSE PASSES THROUGH YOU, YOU DON'T DIE. BUT THIS...
THIS IS A HOLLOW-POINT BULLET.

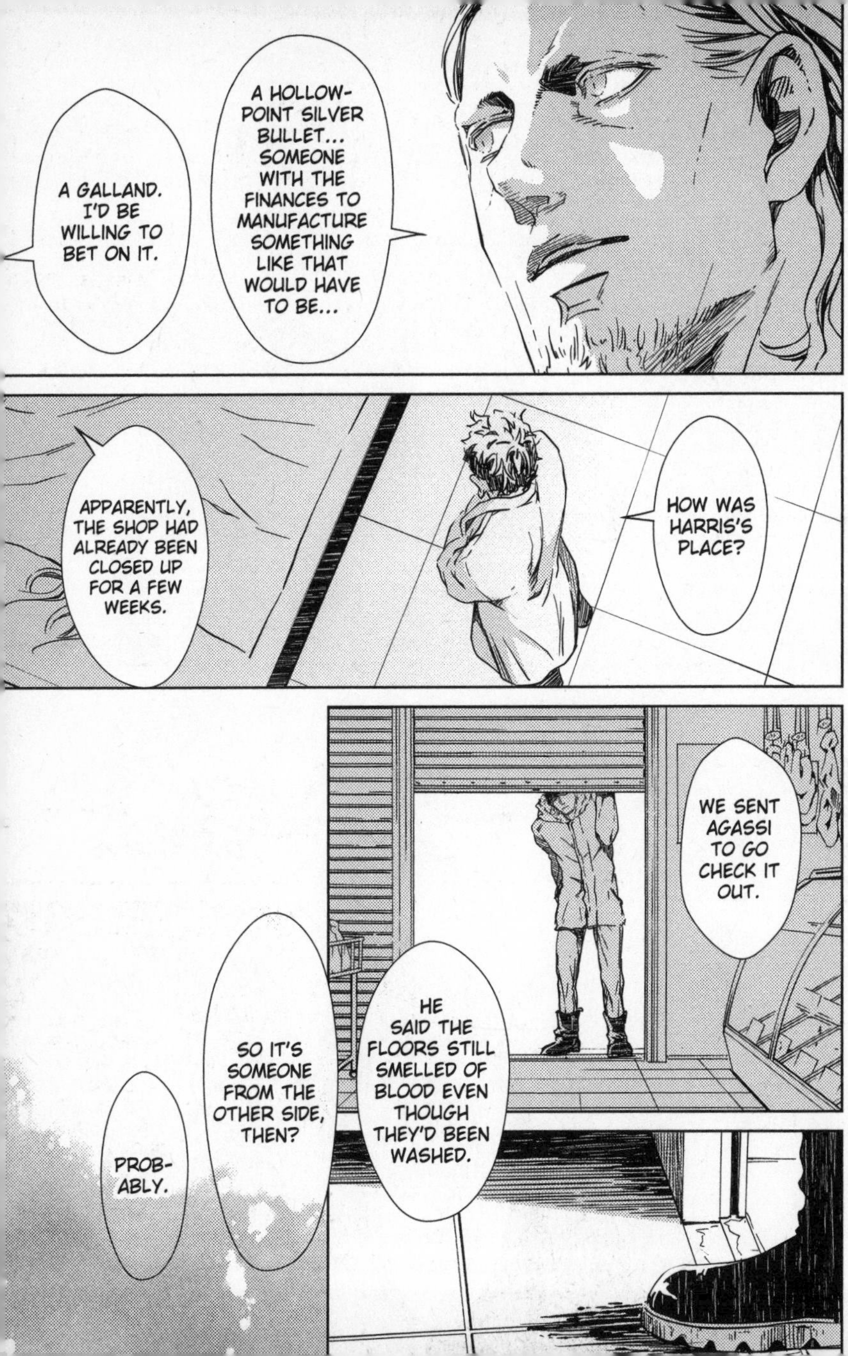
A HOLLOW-POINT SILVER BULLET... SOMEONE WITH THE FINANCES TO MANUFACTURE SOMETHING LIKE THAT WOULD HAVE TO BE...
A GALLAND. I'D BE WILLING TO BET ON IT.
HOW WAS HARRIS'S PLACE?
APPARENTLY, THE SHOP HAD ALREADY BEEN CLOSED UP FOR A FEW WEEKS.
WE SENT AGASSI TO GO CHECK IT OUT.
HE SAID THE FLOORS STILL SMELLED OF BLOOD EVEN THOUGH THEY'D BEEN WASHED.
SO IT'S SOMEONE FROM THE OTHER SIDE, THEN?
PROB-ABLY.

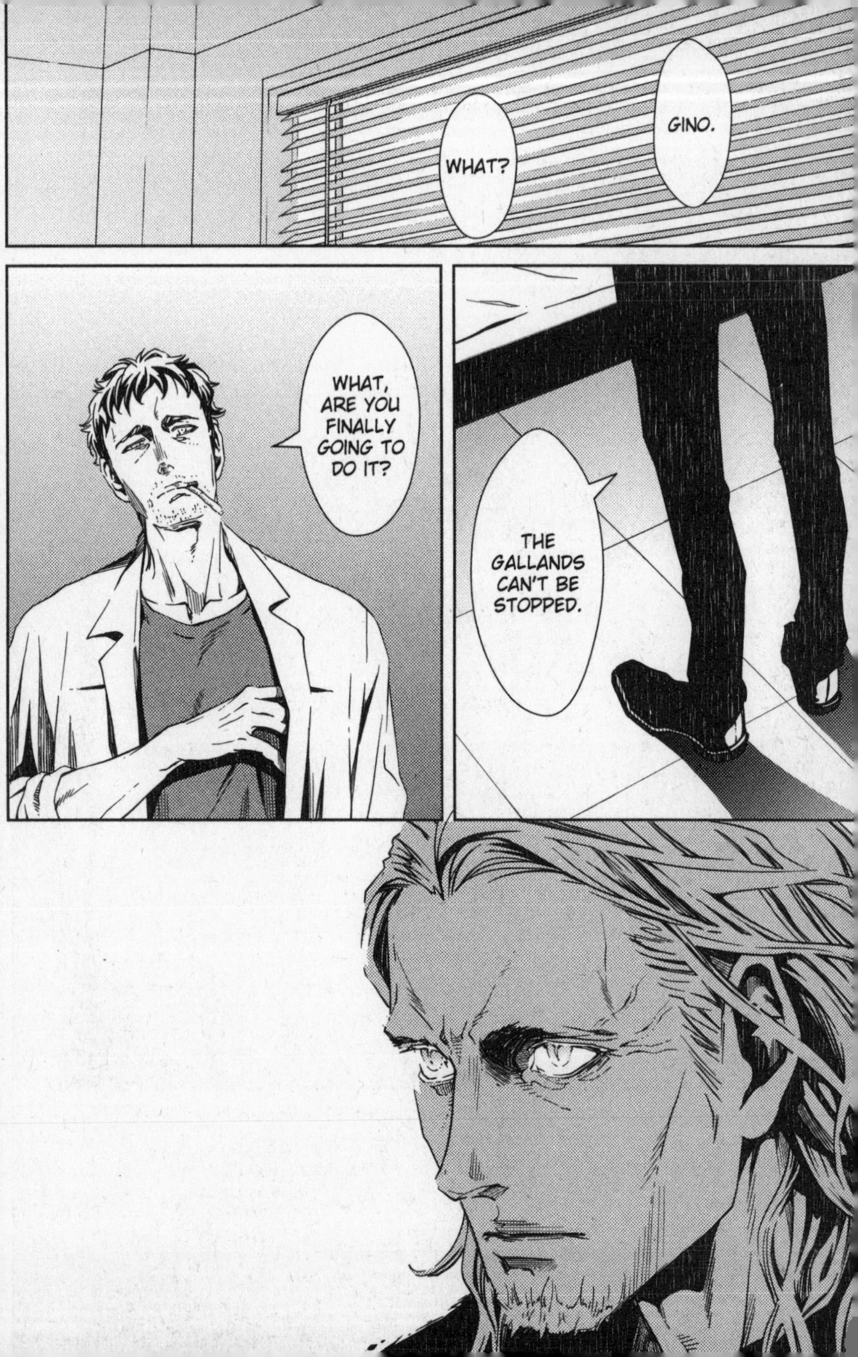
GINO.
WHAT?
THE GALLANDS CAN'T BE STOPPED.
WHAT, ARE YOU FINALLY GOING TO DO IT?

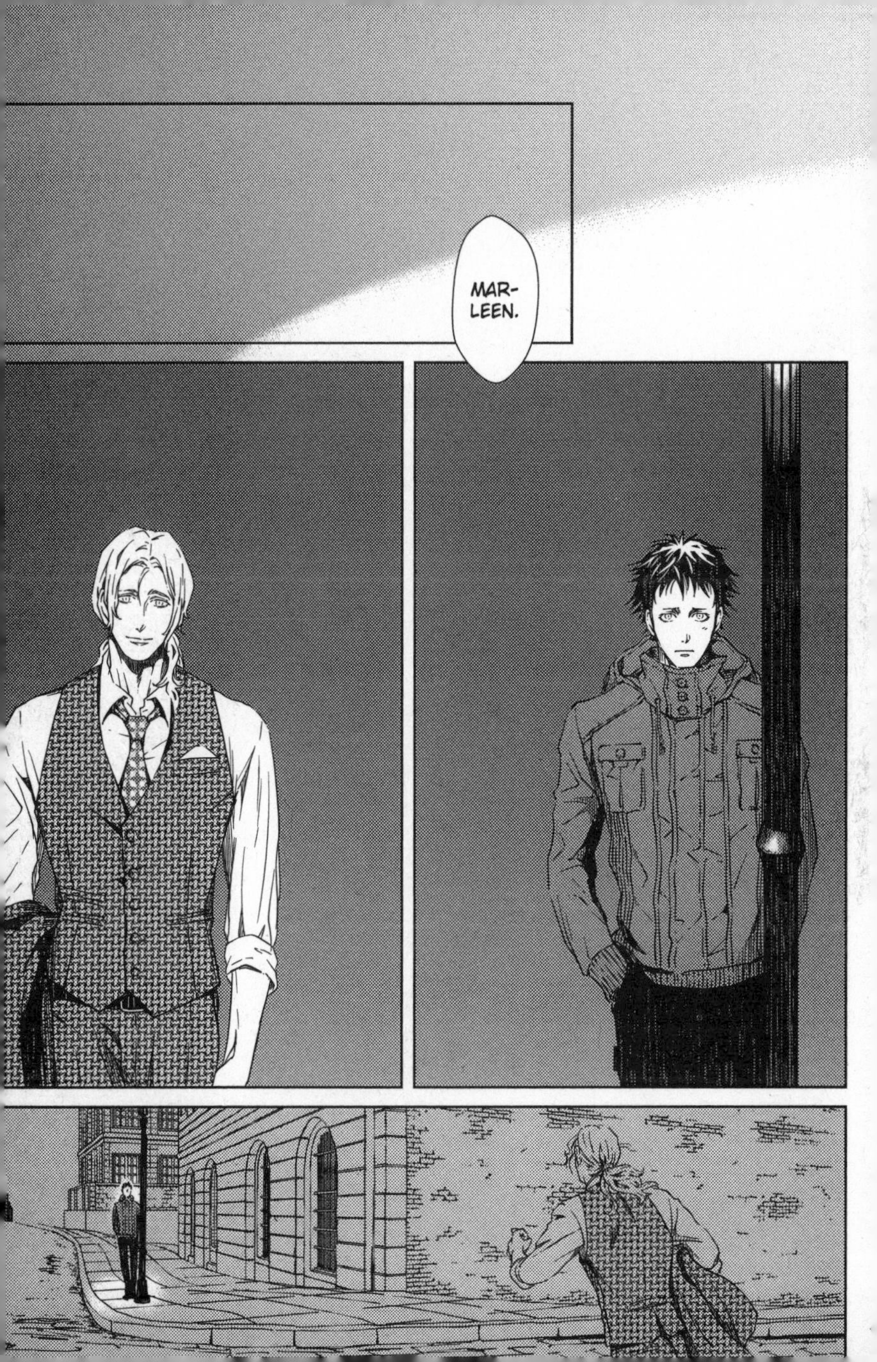
MAR-
LEEN.

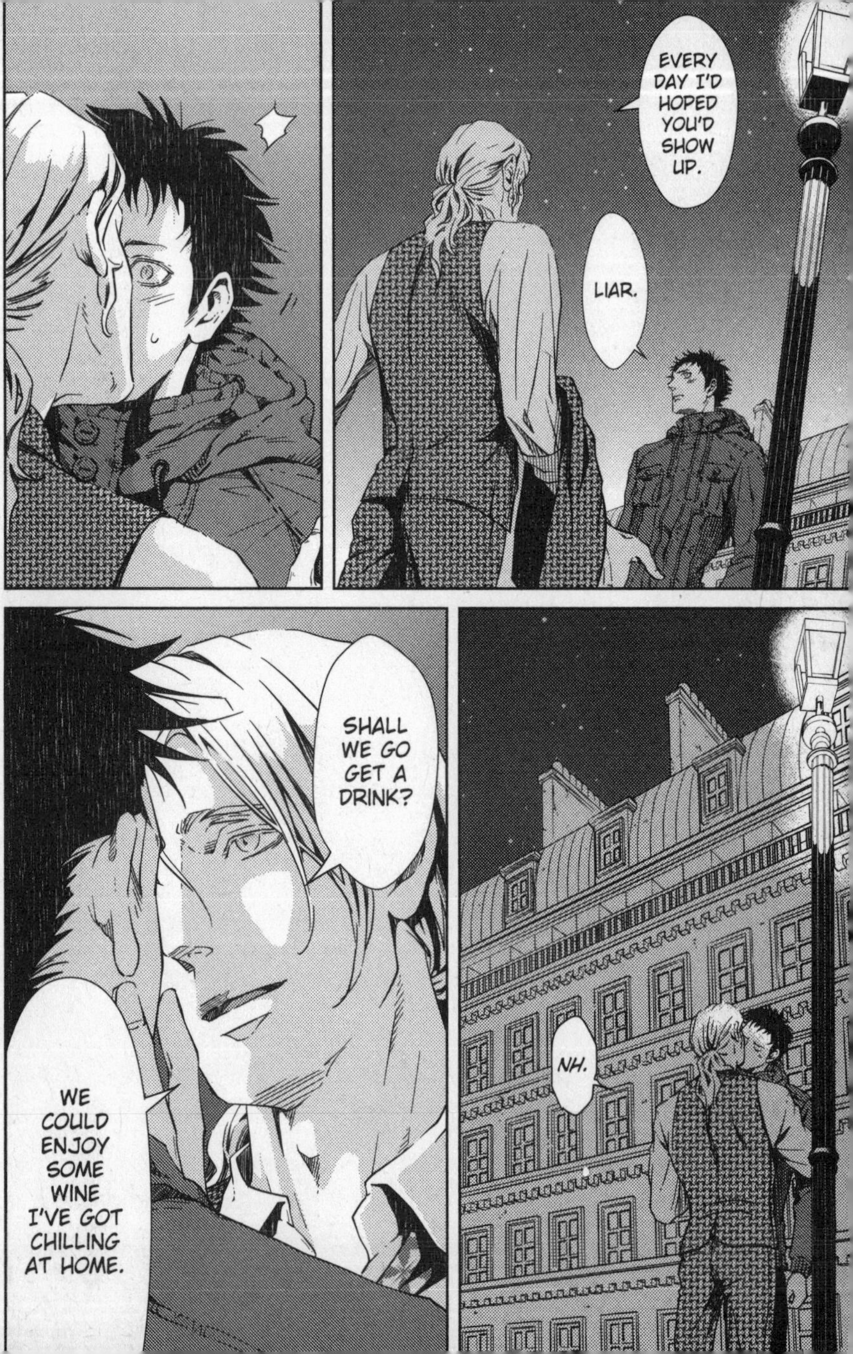
EVERY DAY I'D HOPED YOU'D SHOW UP.
LIAR.
NH.
SHALL WE GO GET A DRINK?
WE COULD ENJOY SOME WINE I'VE GOT CHILLING AT HOME.

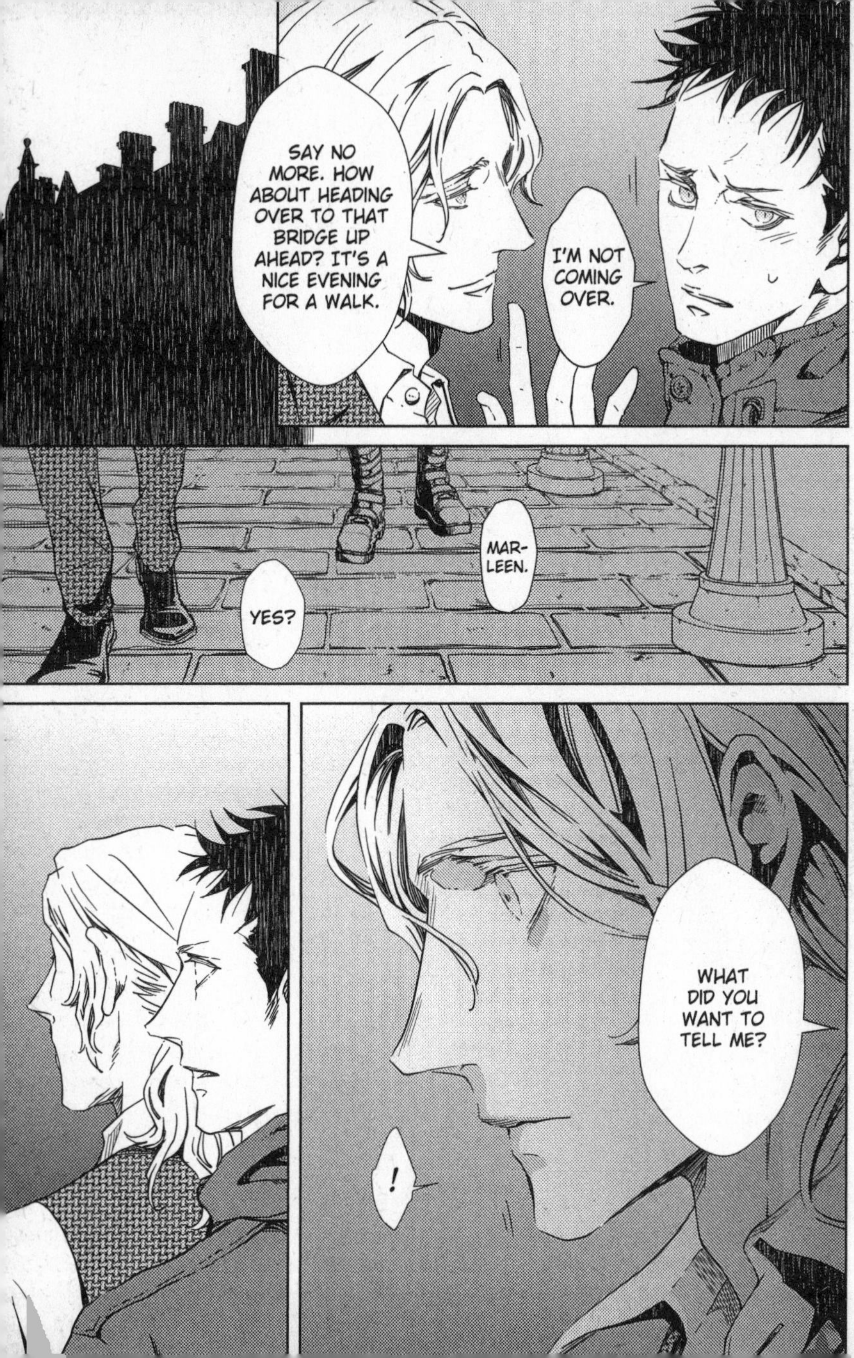
I'M NOT COMING OVER.
SAY NO MORE. HOW ABOUT HEADING OVER TO THAT BRIDGE UP AHEAD? IT'S A NICE EVENING FOR A WALK.
MAR-LEEN.
YES?
WHAT DID YOU WANT TO TELL ME?
!

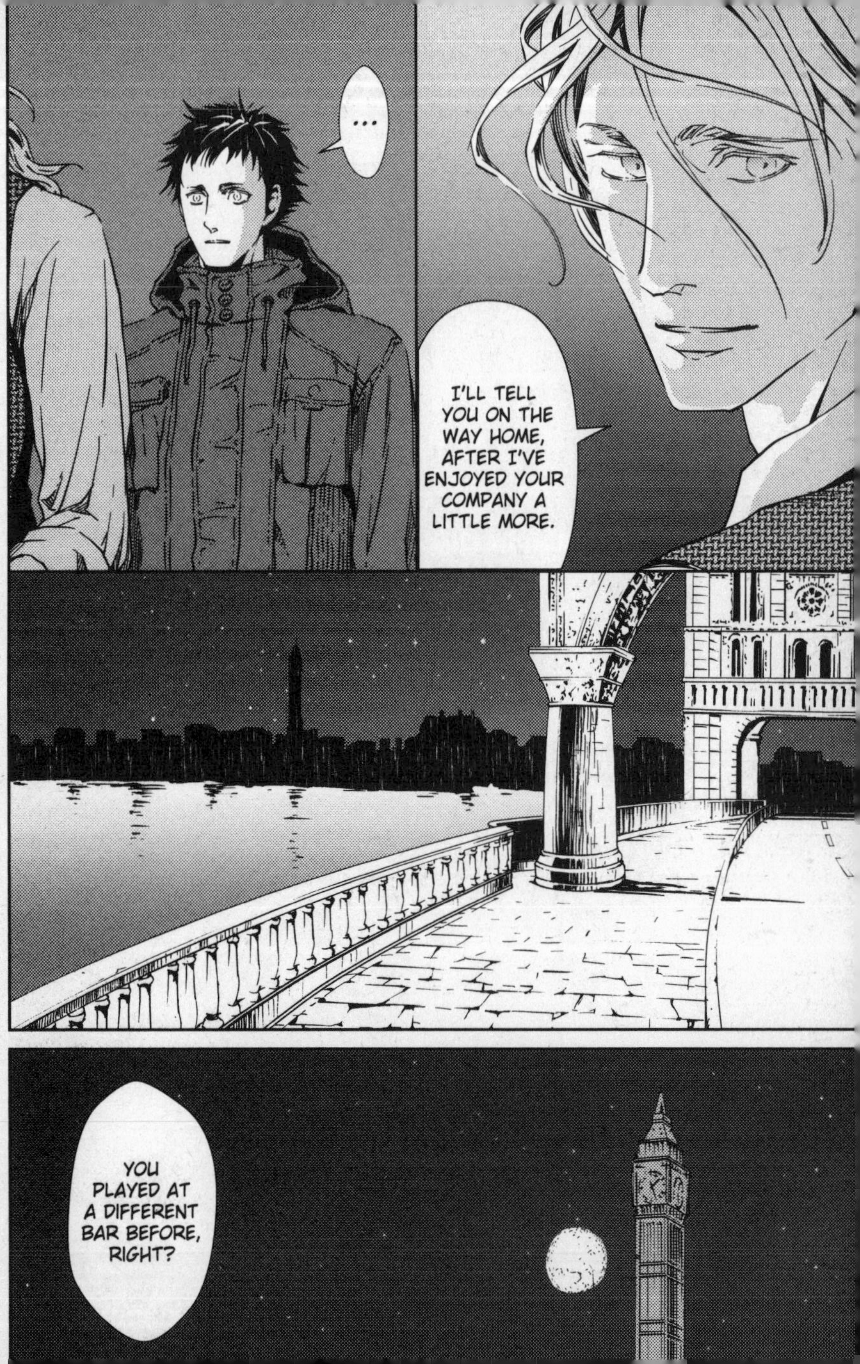
I'LL TELL YOU ON THE WAY HOME, AFTER I'VE ENJOYED YOUR COMPANY A LITTLE MORE.
...
YOU PLAYED AT A DIFFERENT BAR BEFORE, RIGHT?

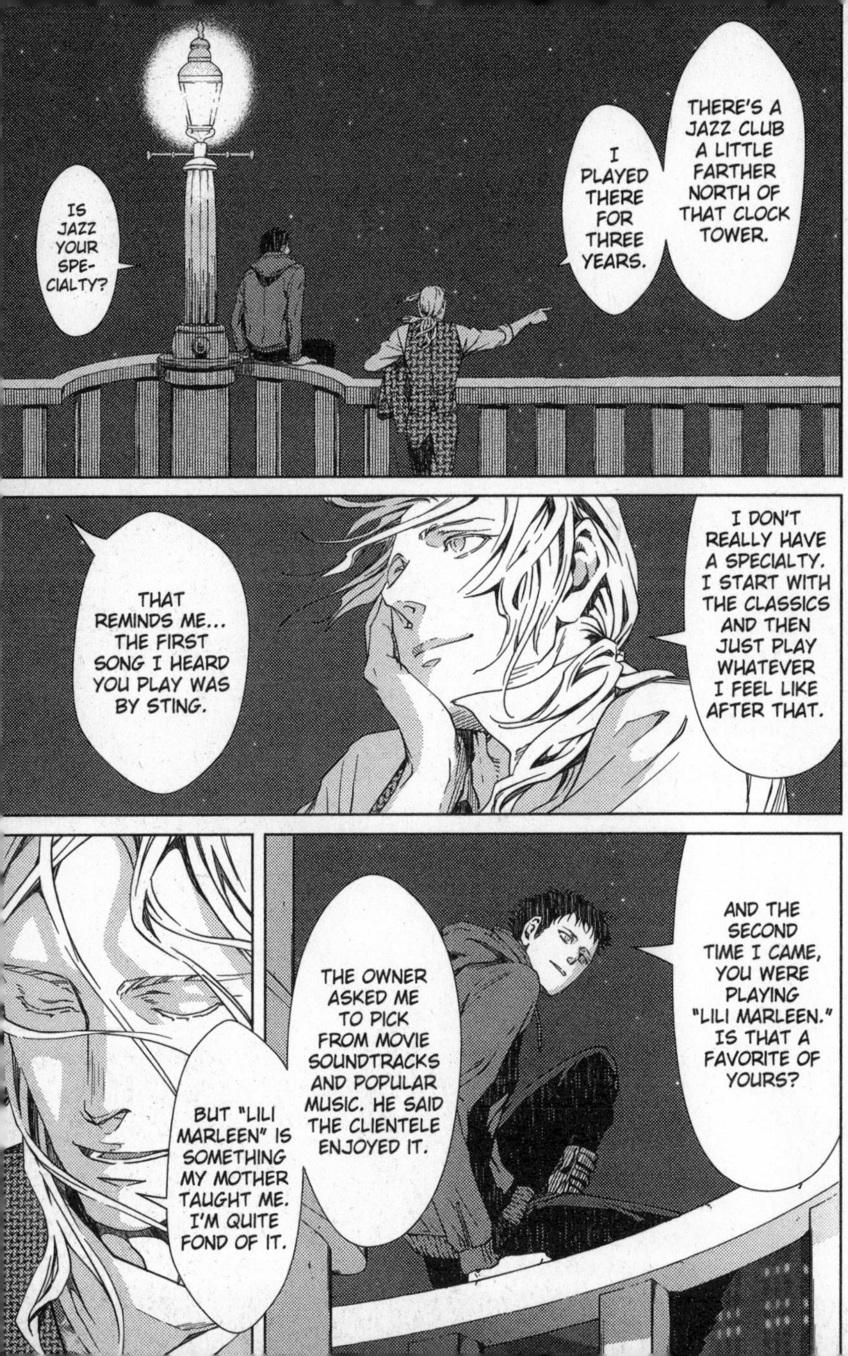
THERE'S A JAZZ CLUB A LITTLE FARTHER NORTH OF THAT CLOCK TOWER.
I PLAYED THERE FOR THREE YEARS.
IS JAZZ YOUR SPE-CIALTY?
I DON'T REALLY HAVE A SPECIALTY. I START WITH THE CLASSICS AND THEN JUST PLAY WHATEVER I FEEL LIKE AFTER THAT.
THAT REMINDS ME... THE FIRST SONG I HEARD YOU PLAY WAS BY STING.
AND THE SECOND TIME I CAME, YOU WERE PLAYING "LILI MARLEEN." IS THAT A FAVORITE OF YOURS?
THE OWNER ASKED ME TO PICK FROM MOVIE SOUNDTRACKS AND POPULAR MUSIC. HE SAID THE CLIENTELE ENJOYED IT.
BUT "LILI MARLEEN" IS SOMETHING MY MOTHER TAUGHT ME. I'M QUITE FOND OF IT.

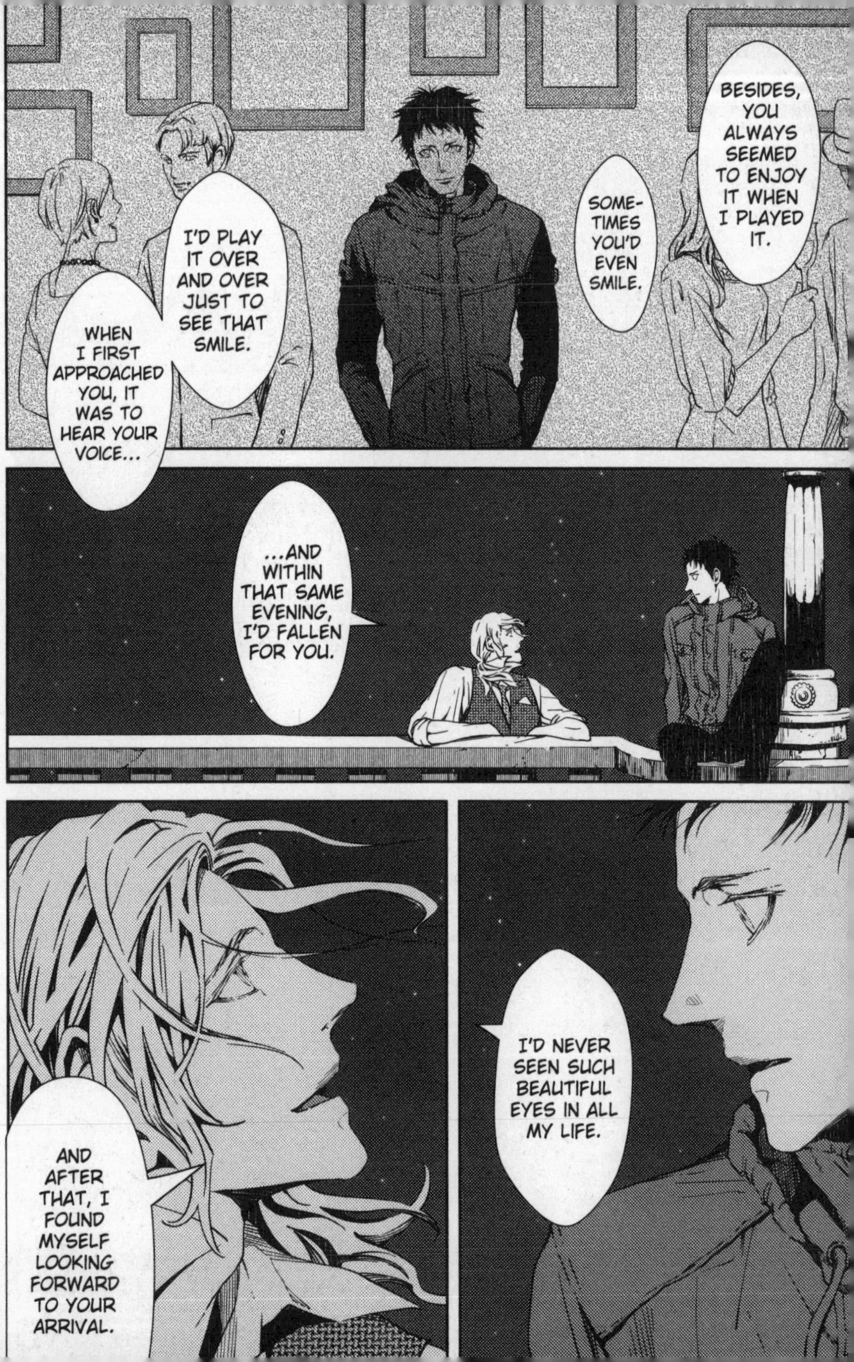
BESIDES, YOU ALWAYS SEEMED TO ENJOY IT WHEN I PLAYED IT.
SOMETIMES YOU'D EVEN SMILE.
I'D PLAY IT OVER AND OVER JUST TO SEE THAT SMILE.
WHEN I FIRST APPROACHED YOU, IT WAS TO HEAR YOUR VOICE...
...AND WITHIN THAT SAME EVENING, I'D FALLEN FOR YOU.
I'D NEVER SEEN SUCH BEAUTIFUL EYES IN ALL MY LIFE.
AND AFTER THAT, I FOUND MYSELF LOOKING FORWARD TO YOUR ARRIVAL.

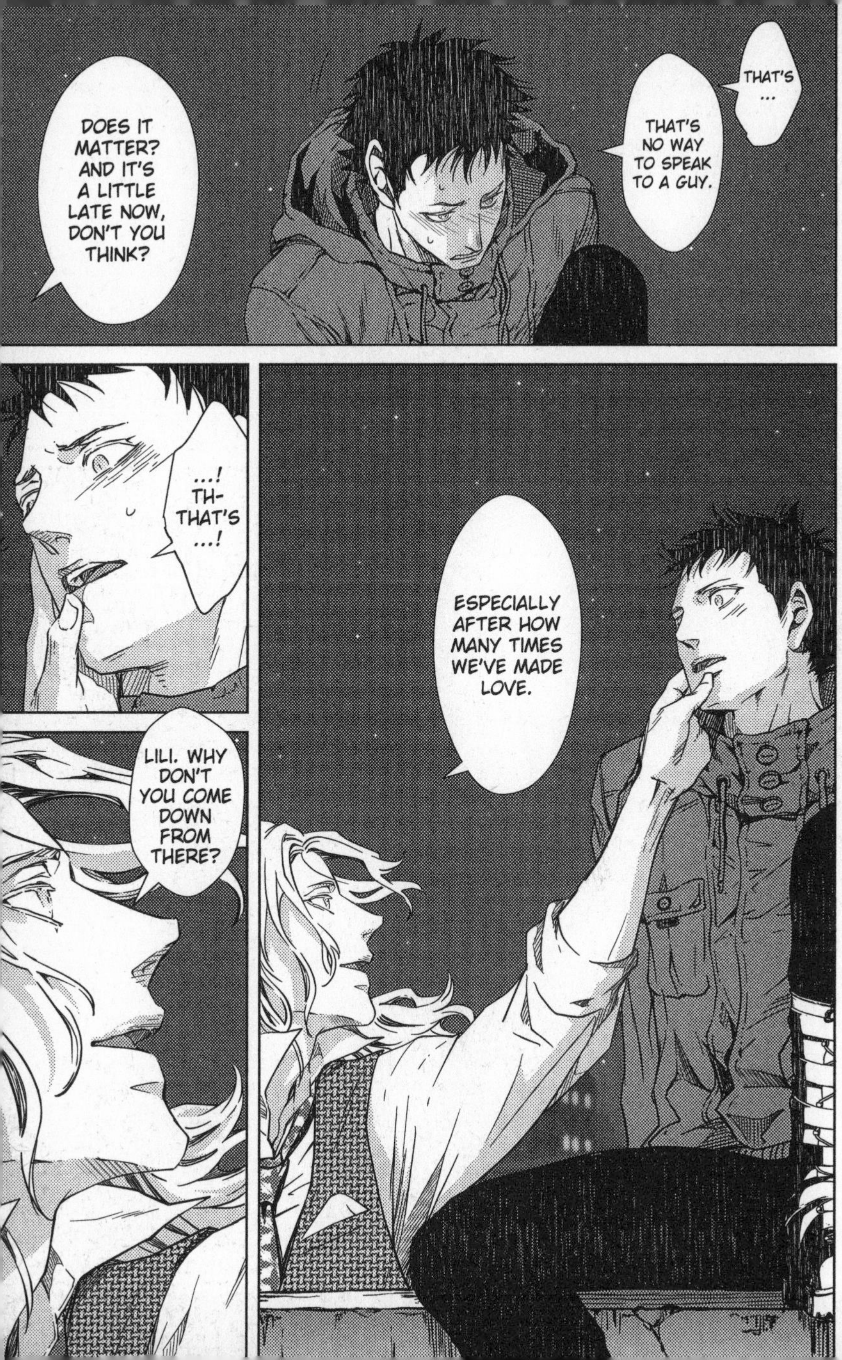
THAT'S ...
THAT'S NO WAY TO SPEAK TO A GUY.
DOES IT MATTER? AND IT'S A LITTLE LATE NOW, DON'T YOU THINK?
ESPECIALLY AFTER HOW MANY TIMES WE'VE MADE LOVE.
...! TH-THAT'S ...!
LILI. WHY DON'T YOU COME DOWN FROM THERE?

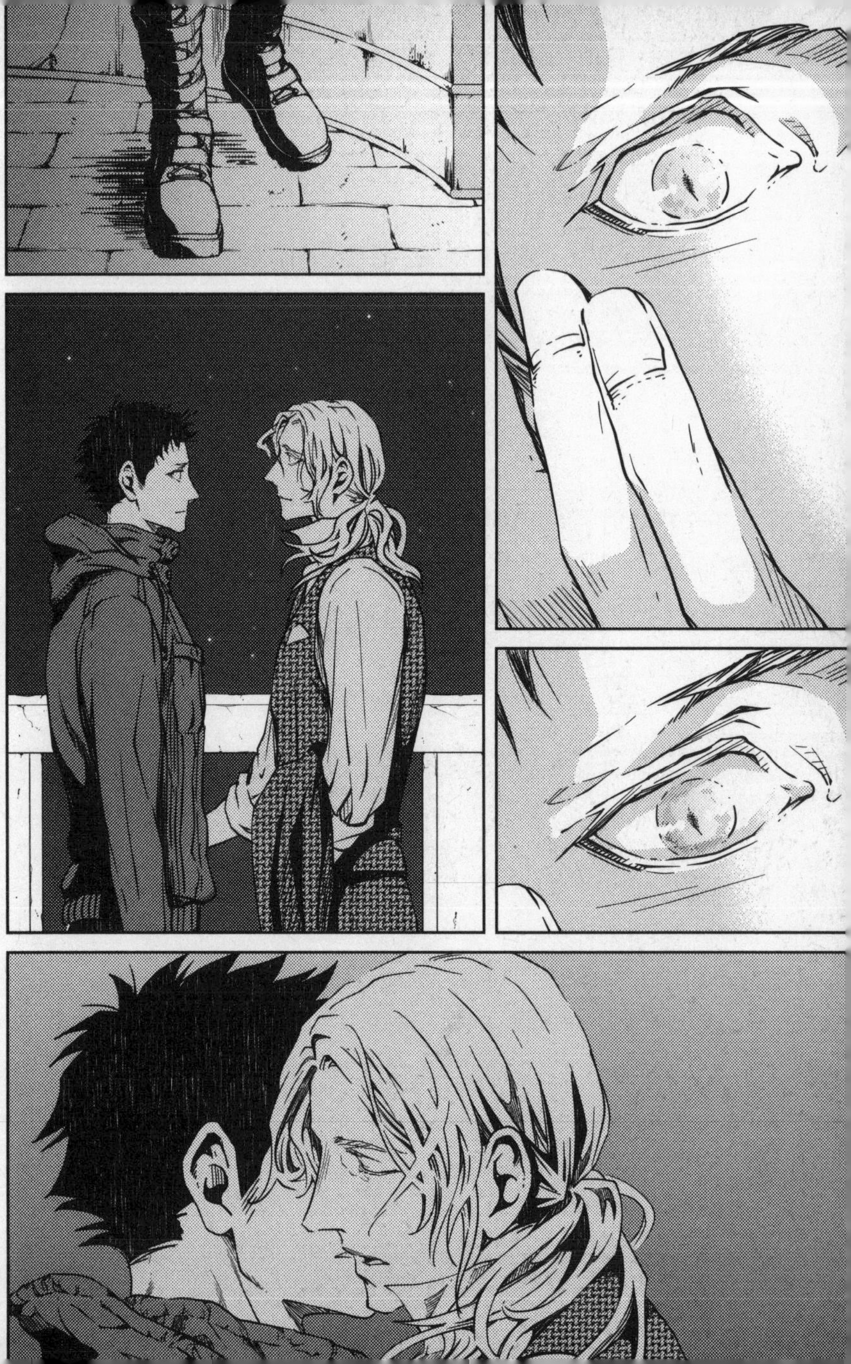

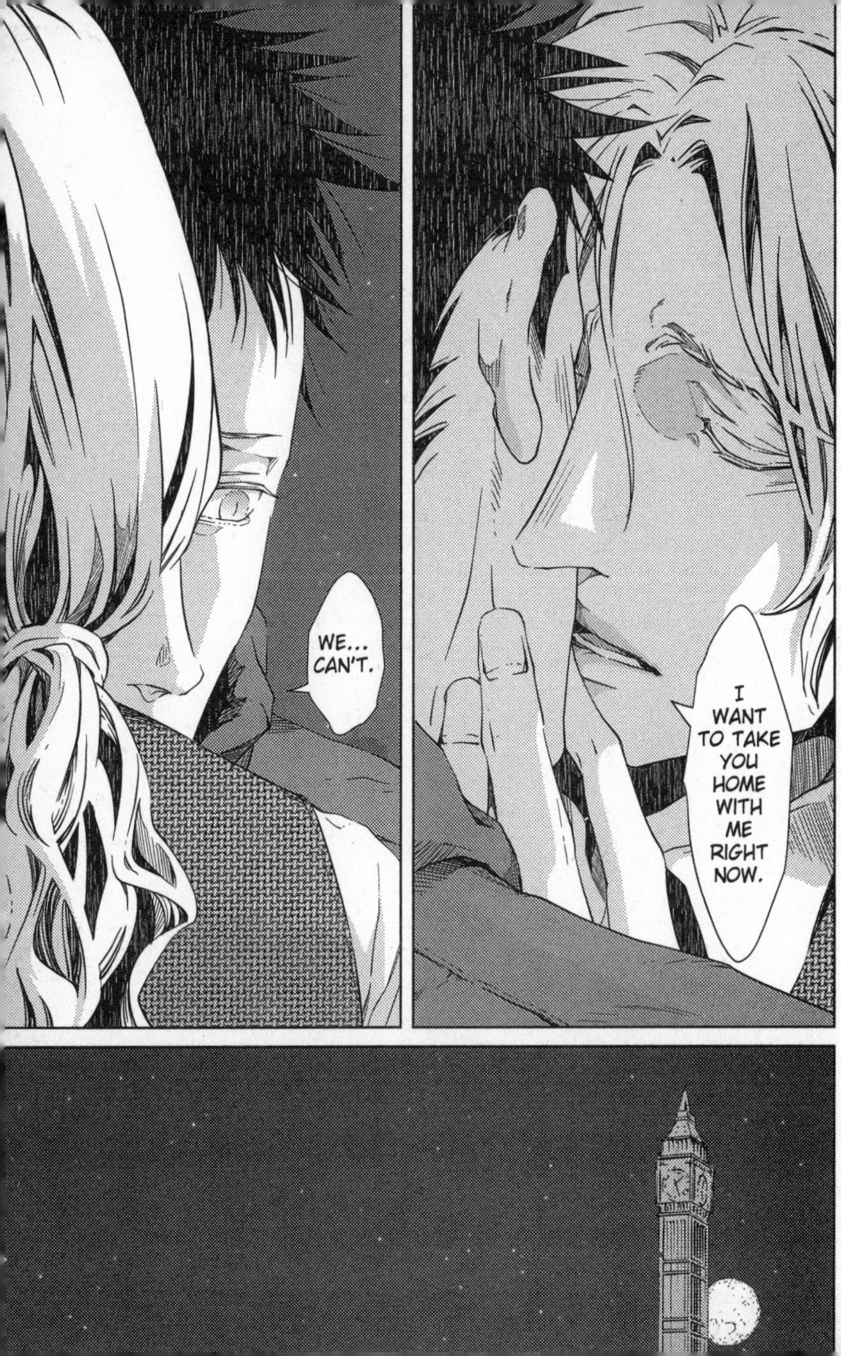
I WANT TO TAKE YOU HOME WITH ME RIGHT NOW.
WE... CAN'T.

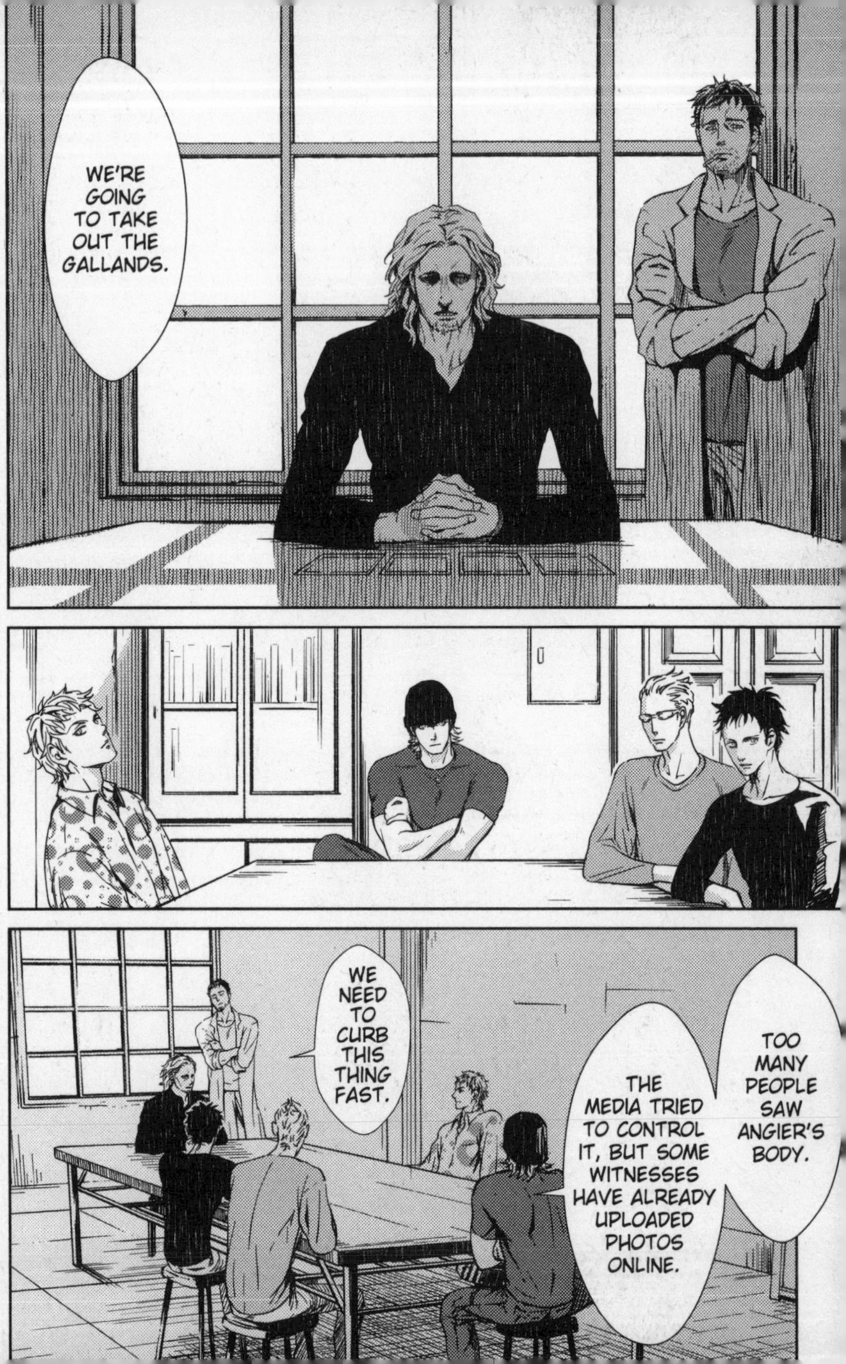
WE'RE GOING TO TAKE OUT THE GALLANDS.
TOO MANY PEOPLE SAW ANGIER'S BODY.
THE MEDIA TRIED TO CONTROL IT, BUT SOME WITNESSES HAVE ALREADY UPLOADED PHOTOS ONLINE.
WE NEED TO CURB THIS THING FAST.

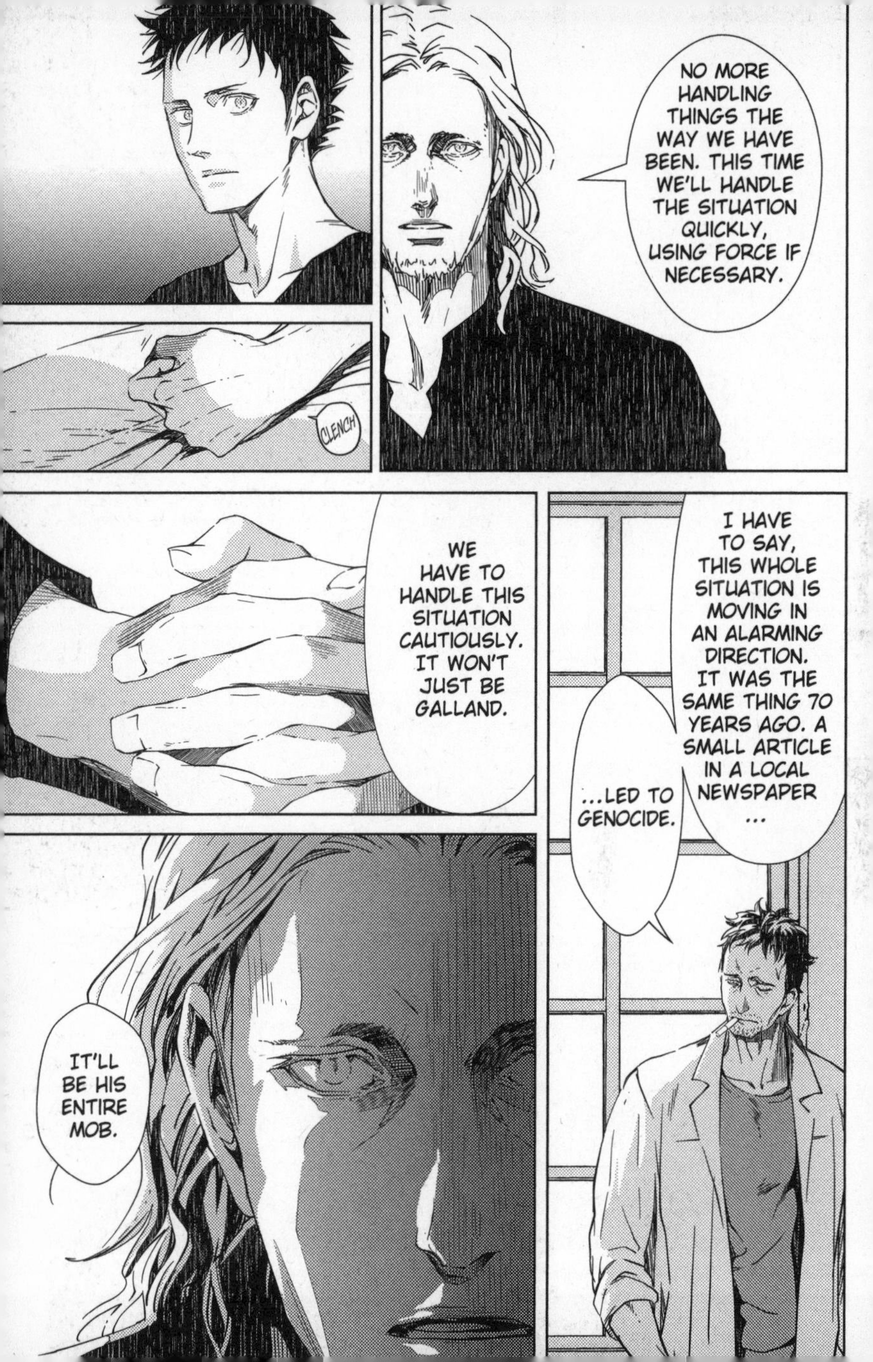
NO MORE HANDLING THINGS THE WAY WE HAVE BEEN. THIS TIME WE'LL HANDLE THE SITUATION QUICKLY, USING FORCE IF NECESSARY.
CLENCH
I HAVE TO SAY, THIS WHOLE SITUATION IS MOVING IN AN ALARMING DIRECTION. IT WAS THE SAME THING 70 YEARS AGO. A SMALL ARTICLE IN A LOCAL NEWSPAPER ...
...LED TO GENOCIDE.
WE HAVE TO HANDLE THIS SITUATION CAUTIOUSLY. IT WON'T JUST BE GALLAND.
IT'LL BE HIS ENTIRE MOB.

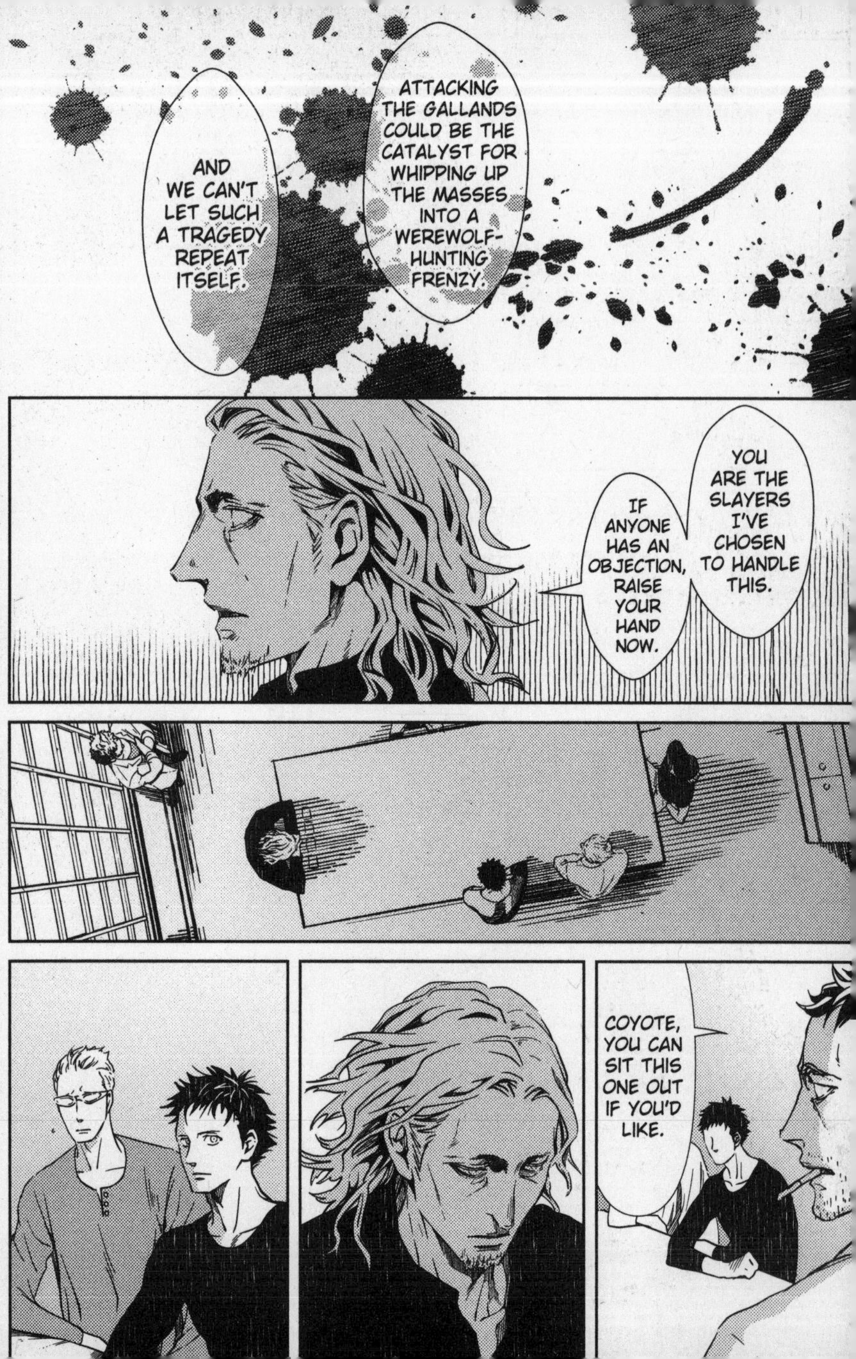
ATTACKING THE GALLANDS COULD BE THE CATALYST FOR WHIPPING UP THE MASSES INTO A WEREWOLF-HUNTING FRENZY.
AND WE CAN'T LET SUCH A TRAGEDY REPEAT ITSELF.
YOU ARE THE SLAYERS I'VE CHOSEN TO HANDLE THIS.
IF ANYONE HAS AN OBJECTION, RAISE YOUR HAND NOW.
COYOTE, YOU CAN SIT THIS ONE OUT IF YOU'D LIKE.

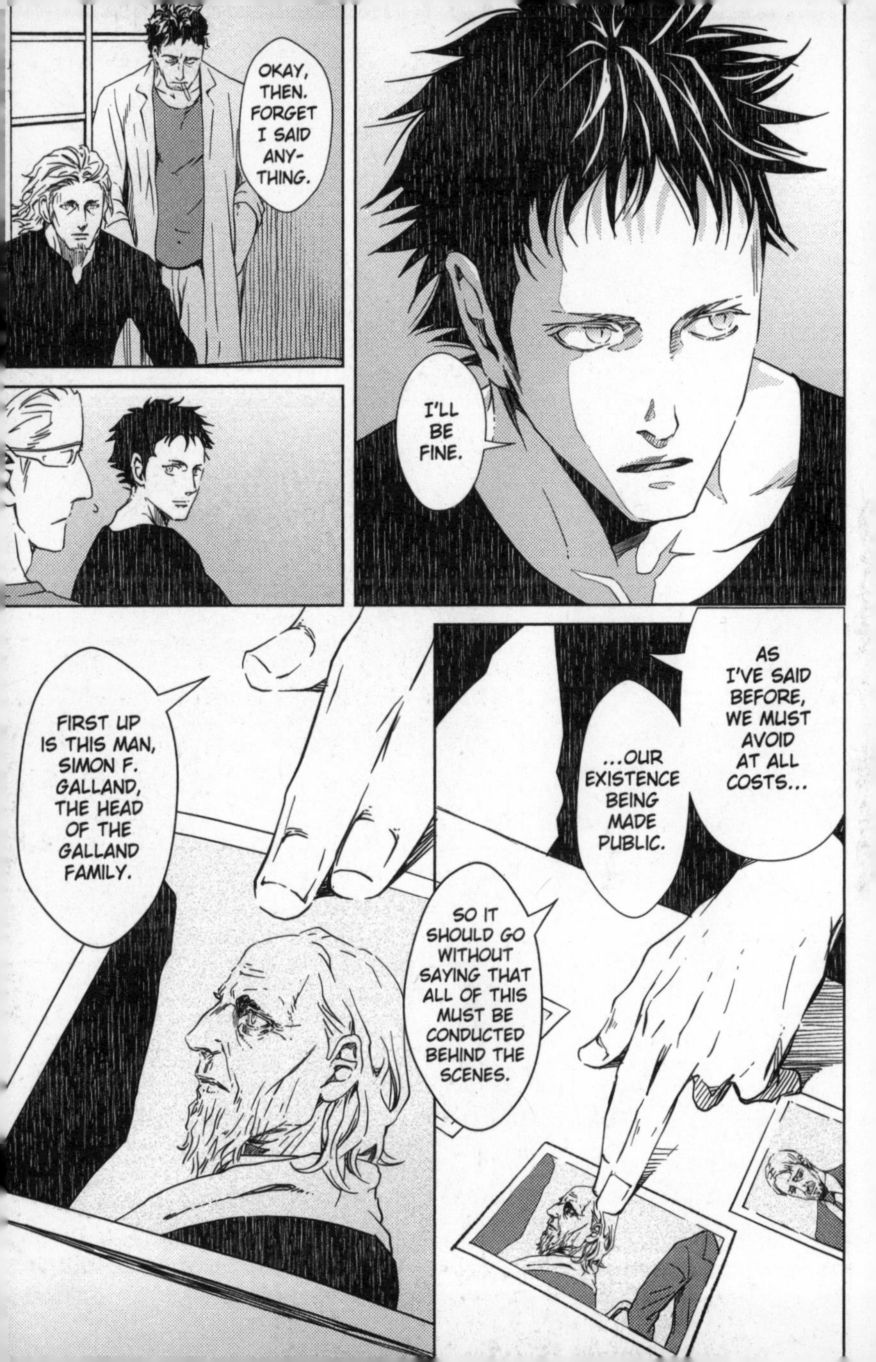
I'LL BE FINE.
OKAY, THEN. FORGET I SAID ANYTHING.
AS I'VE SAID BEFORE, WE MUST AVOID AT ALL COSTS...
...OUR EXISTENCE BEING MADE PUBLIC.
SO IT SHOULD GO WITHOUT SAYING THAT ALL OF THIS MUST BE CONDUCTED BEHIND THE SCENES.
FIRST UP IS THIS MAN, SIMON F. GALLAND, THE HEAD OF THE GALLAND FAMILY.

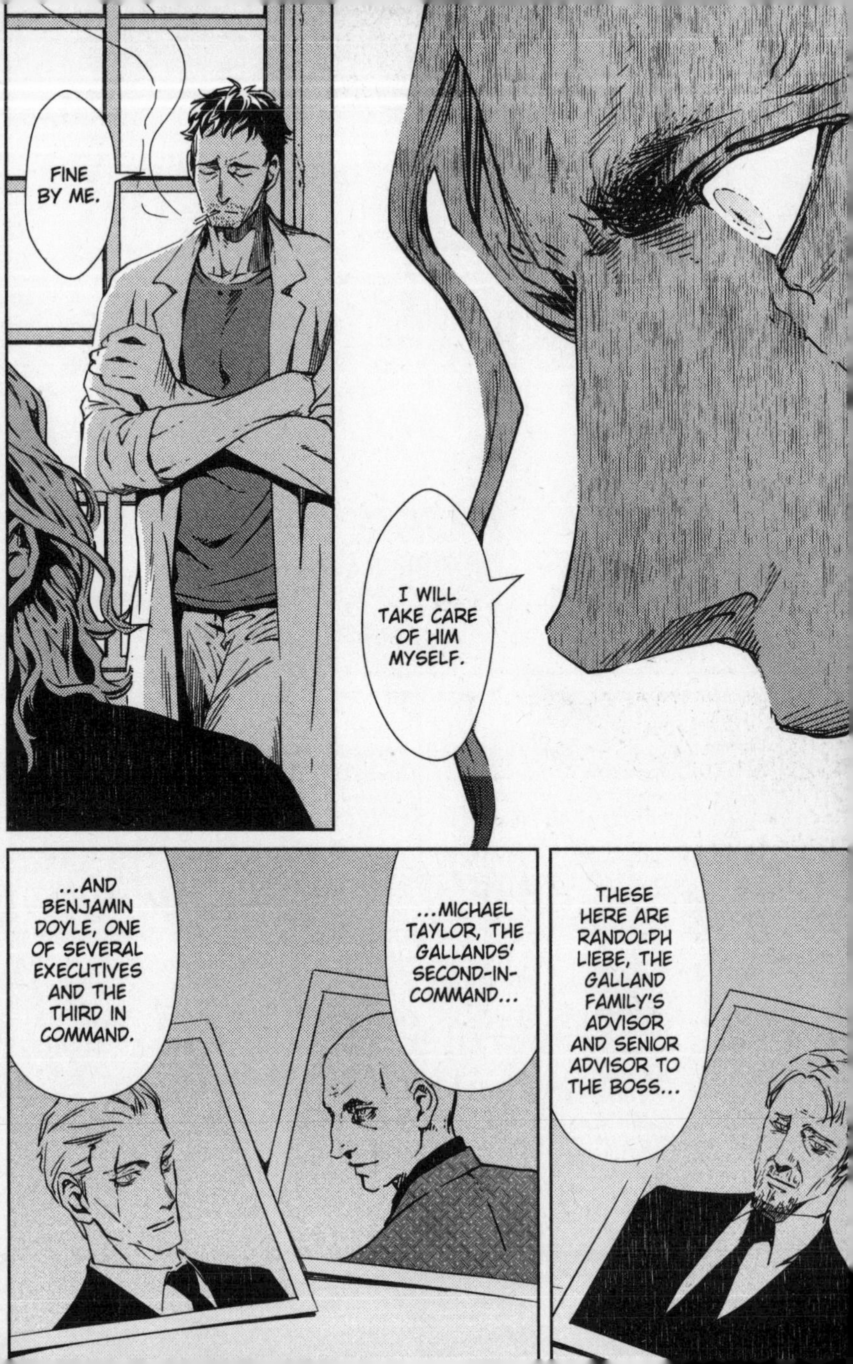
I WILL TAKE CARE OF HIM MYSELF.
FINE BY ME.
THESE HERE ARE RANDOLPH LIEBE, THE GALLAND FAMILY'S ADVISOR AND SENIOR ADVISOR TO THE BOSS...
...MICHAEL TAYLOR, THE GALLANDS' SECOND-IN-COMMAND...
...AND BENJAMIN DOYLE, ONE OF SEVERAL EXECUTIVES AND THE THIRD IN COMMAND.

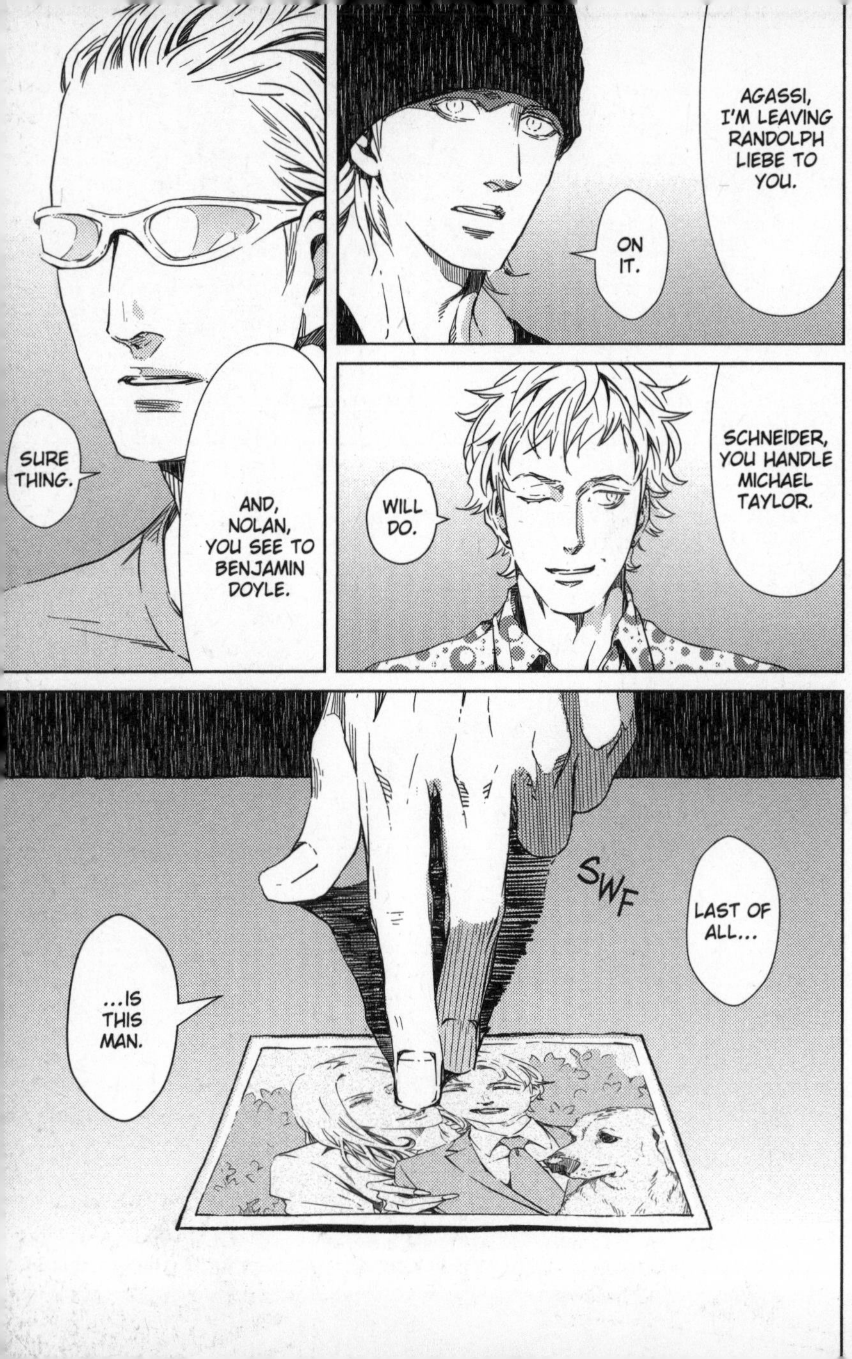
AGASSI, I'M LEAVING RANDOLPH LIEBE TO YOU.
ON IT.
SCHNEIDER, YOU HANDLE MICHAEL TAYLOR.
WILL DO.
AND, NOLAN, YOU SEE TO BENJAMIN DOYLE.
SURE THING.
LAST OF ALL...
SWF
...IS THIS MAN.

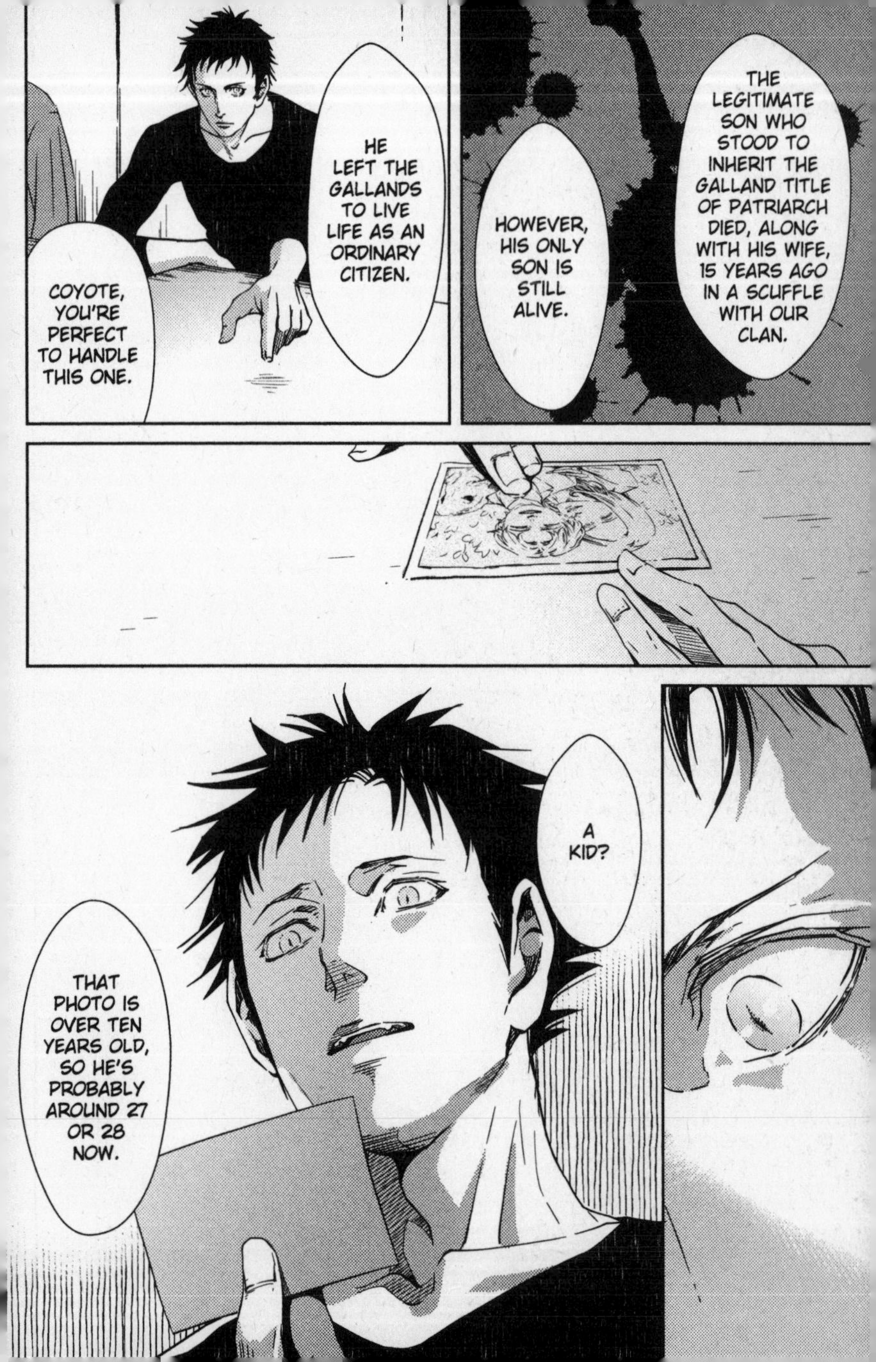
THE LEGITIMATE SON WHO STOOD TO INHERIT THE GALLAND TITLE OF PATRIARCH DIED, ALONG WITH HIS WIFE, 15 YEARS AGO IN A SCUFFLE WITH OUR CLAN.
HOWEVER, HIS ONLY SON IS STILL ALIVE.
HE LEFT THE GALLANDS TO LIVE LIFE AS AN ORDINARY CITIZEN.
COYOTE, YOU'RE PERFECT TO HANDLE THIS ONE.
A KID?
THAT PHOTO IS OVER TEN YEARS OLD, SO HE'S PROBABLY AROUND 27 OR 28 NOW.

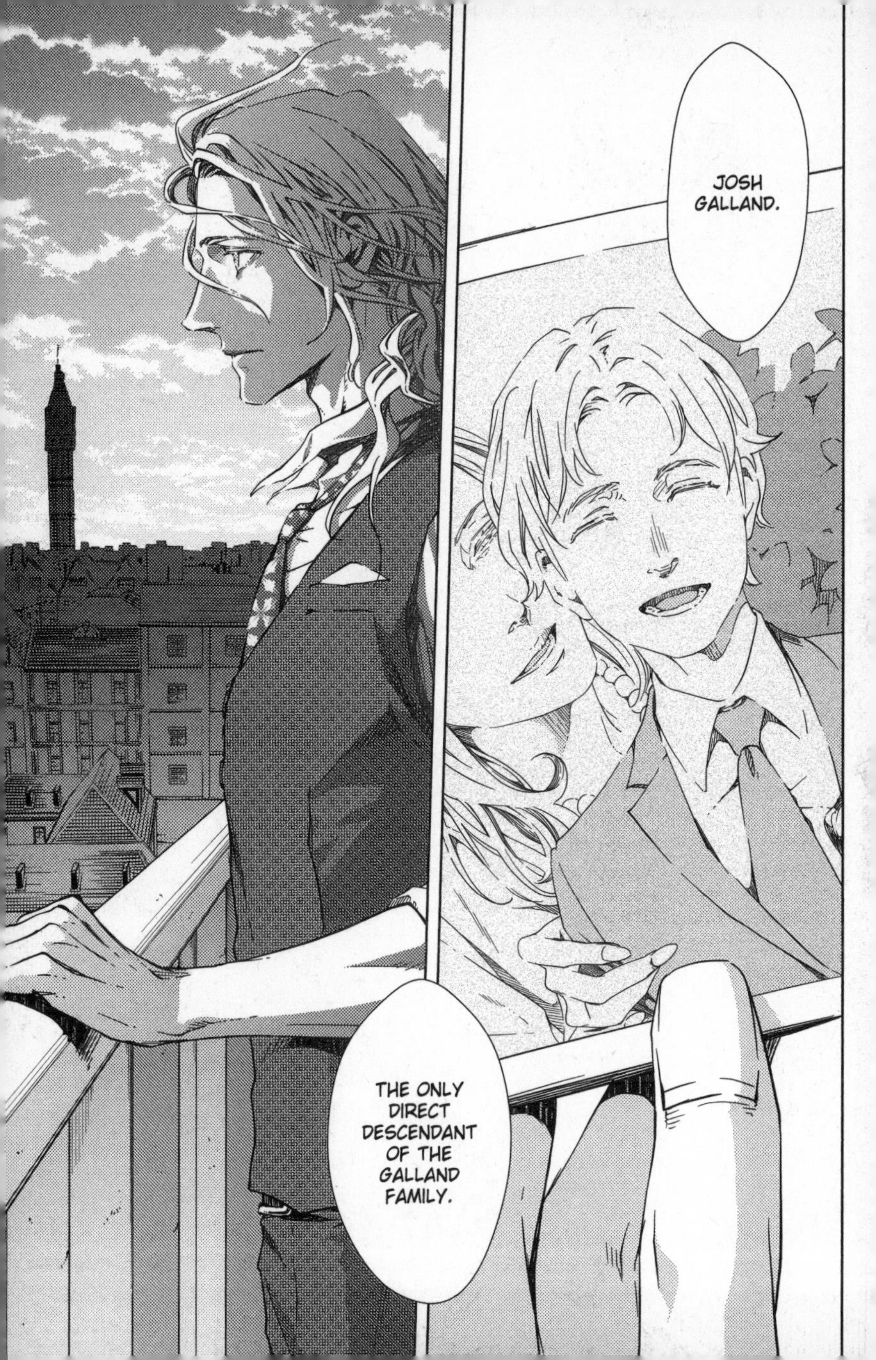
JOSH GALLAND.
THE ONLY DIRECT DESCENDANT OF THE GALLAND FAMILY.

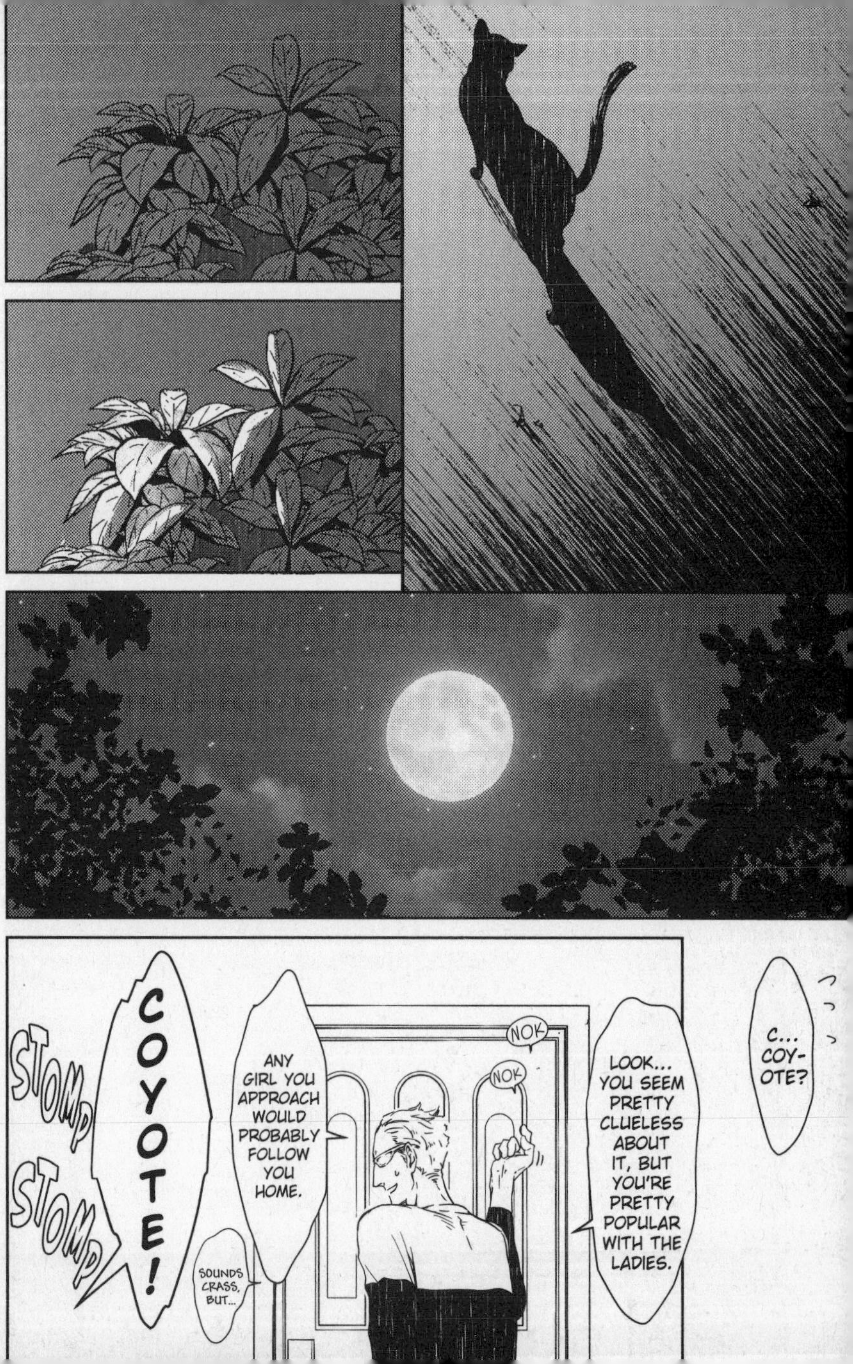
C... COY-OTE?
NOK
NOK
LOOK... YOU SEEM PRETTY CLUELESS ABOUT IT, BUT YOU'RE PRETTY POPULAR WITH THE LADIES.
SOUNDS CRASS, BUT...
ANY GIRL YOU APPROACH WOULD PROBABLY FOLLOW YOU HOME.
COYOTE!
STOMP STOMP

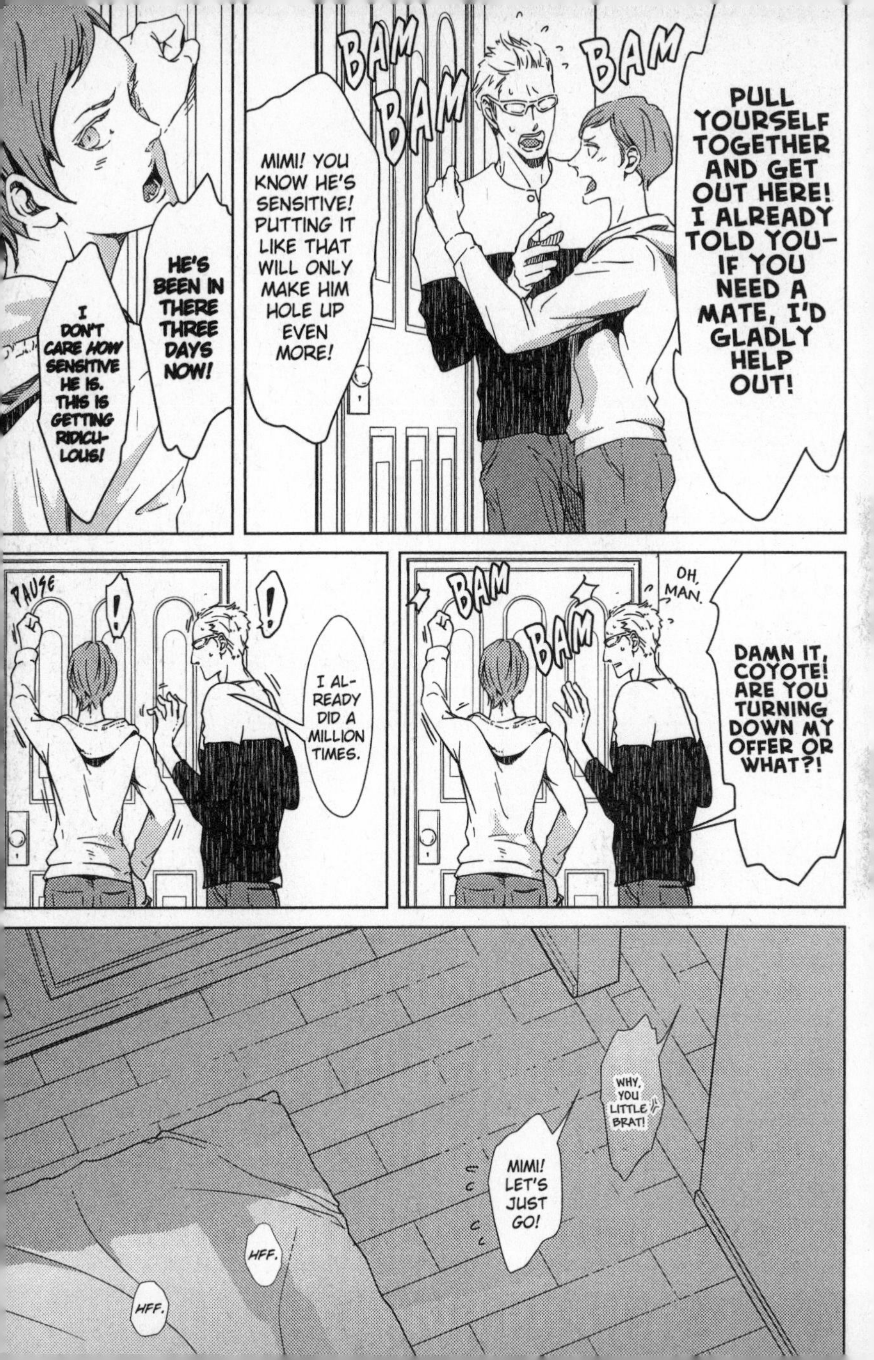
BAM
PULL YOURSELF TOGETHER AND GET OUT HERE! I ALREADY TOLD YOU– IF YOU NEED A MATE, I'D GLADLY HELP OUT!
BAM BAM
MIMI! YOU KNOW HE'S SENSITIVE! PUTTING IT LIKE THAT WILL ONLY MAKE HIM HOLE UP EVEN MORE!
HE'S BEEN IN THERE THREE DAYS NOW!
I DON'T CARE HOW SENSITIVE HE IS. THIS IS GETTING RIDICU-LOUS!
OH, MAN.
DAMN IT, COYOTE! ARE YOU TURNING DOWN MY OFFER OR WHAT?!
BAM
BAM
!
I AL-READY DID A MILLION TIMES.
!
PAUSE
WHY, YOU LITTLE BRAT!
MIMI! LET'S JUST GO!
HFF.
HFF.

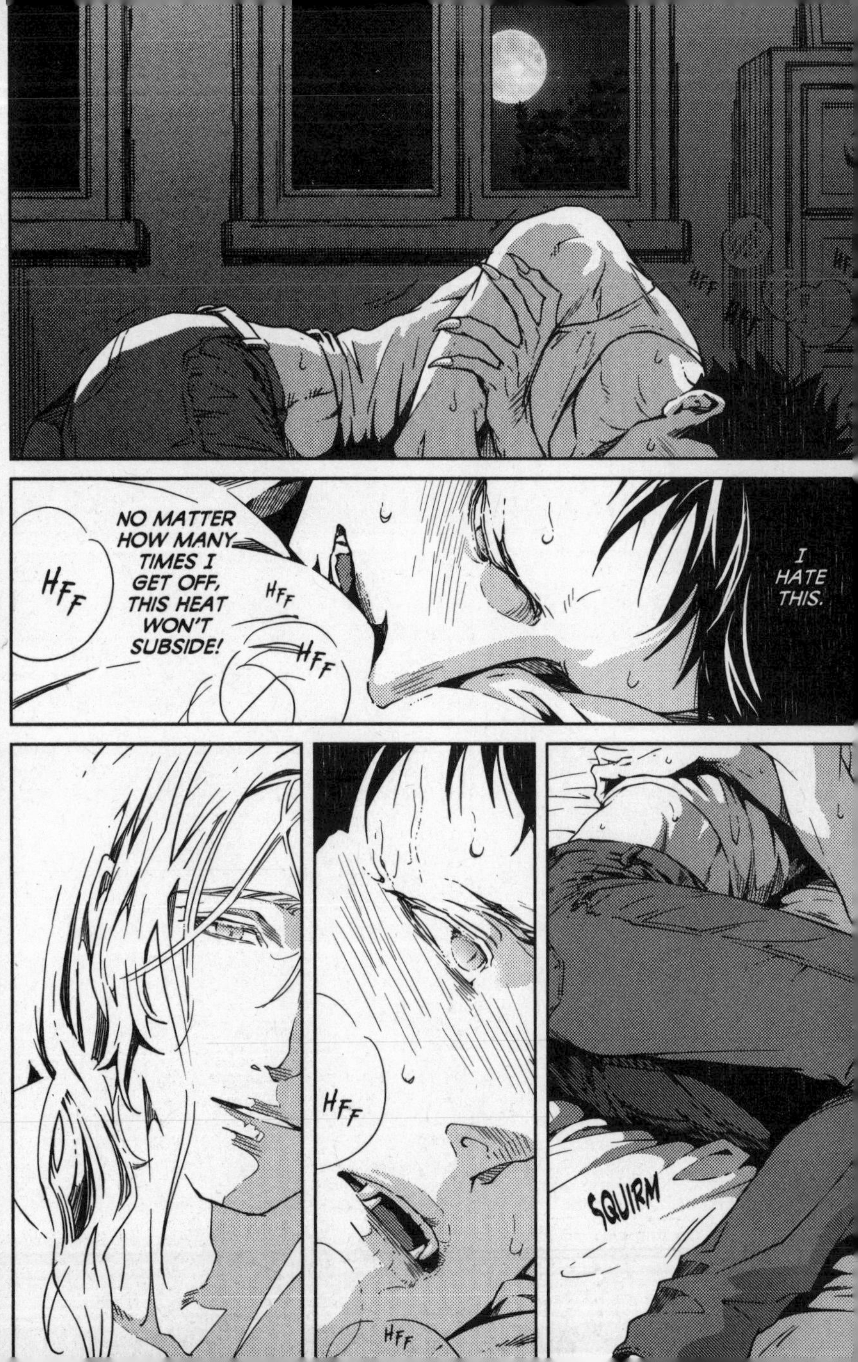
HFF
HFF
I HATE THIS.
HFF
NO MATTER HOW MANY TIMES I GET OFF, THIS HEAT WON'T SUBSIDE!
HFF
HFF
SQUIRM
HFF
HFF

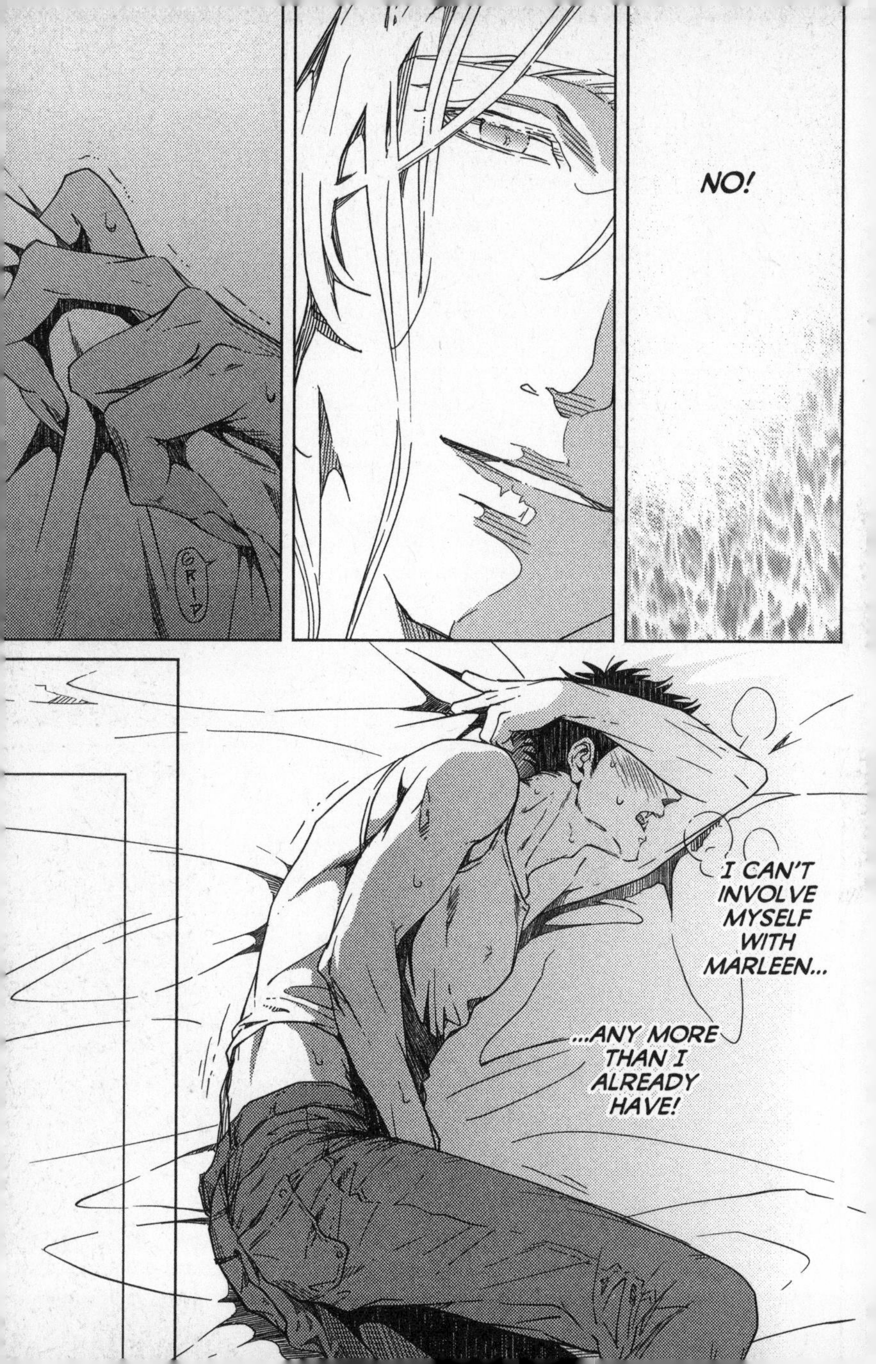
NO!
GRIP
I CAN'T INVOLVE MYSELF WITH MARLEEN...
...ANY MORE THAN I ALREADY HAVE!

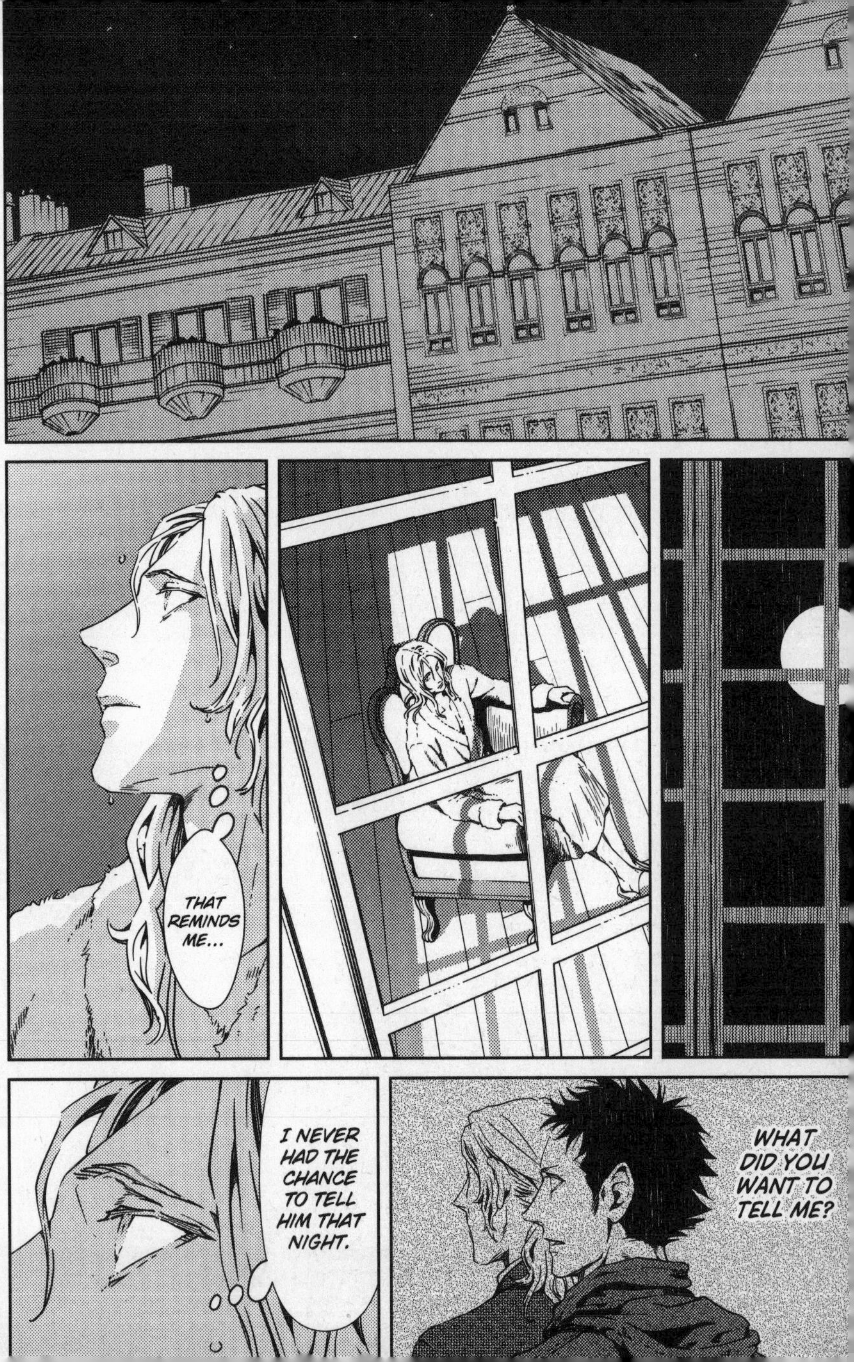
THAT REMINDS ME...
WHAT DID YOU WANT TO TELL ME?
I NEVER HAD THE CHANCE TO TELL HIM THAT NIGHT.

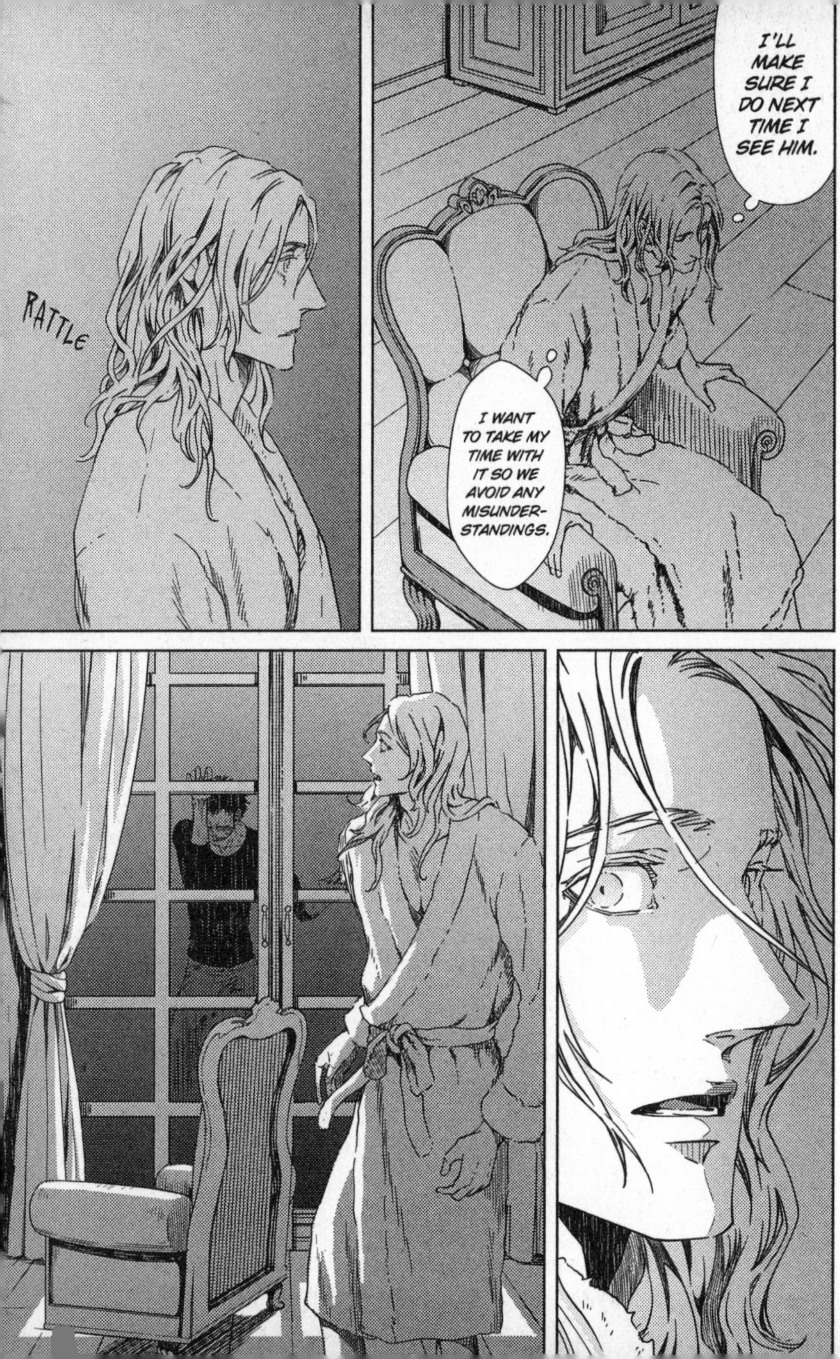
I'LL MAKE SURE I DO NEXT TIME I SEE HIM.
I WANT TO TAKE MY TIME WITH IT SO WE AVOID ANY MISUNDER-STANDINGS.
RATTLE

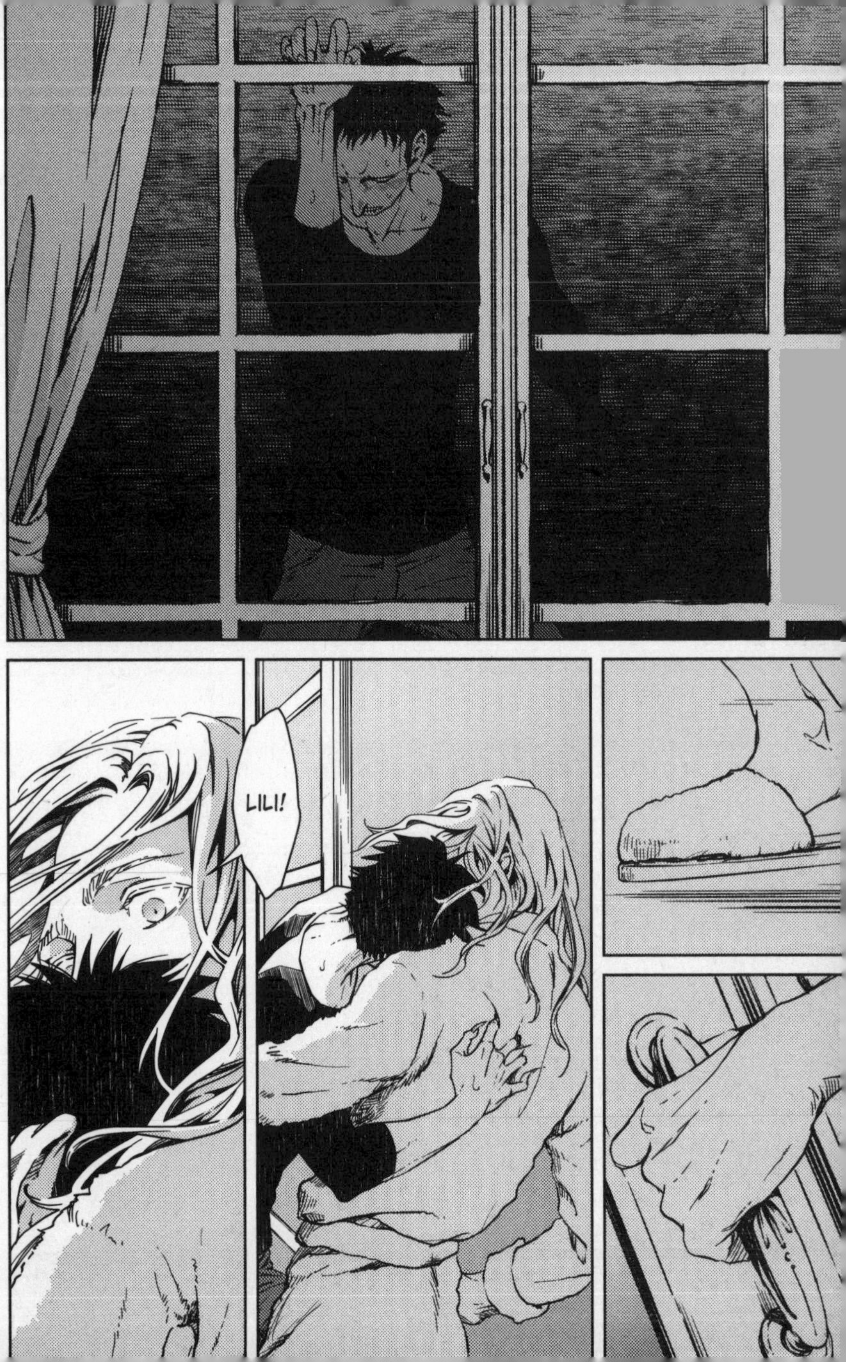
LILI!

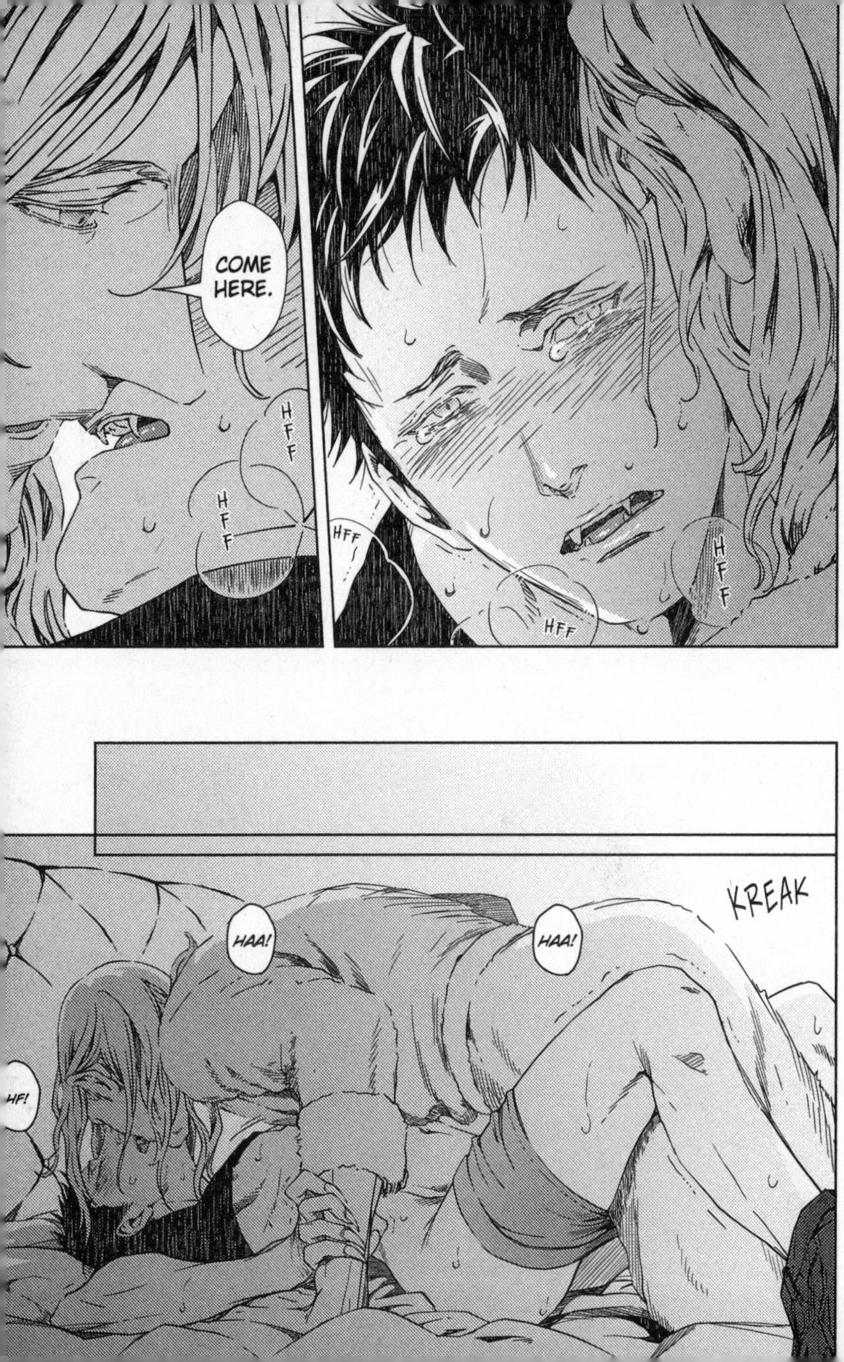
HFF
HFF
HFF
COME HERE.
HFF
HFF
KREAK
HAA!
HAA!
HF!

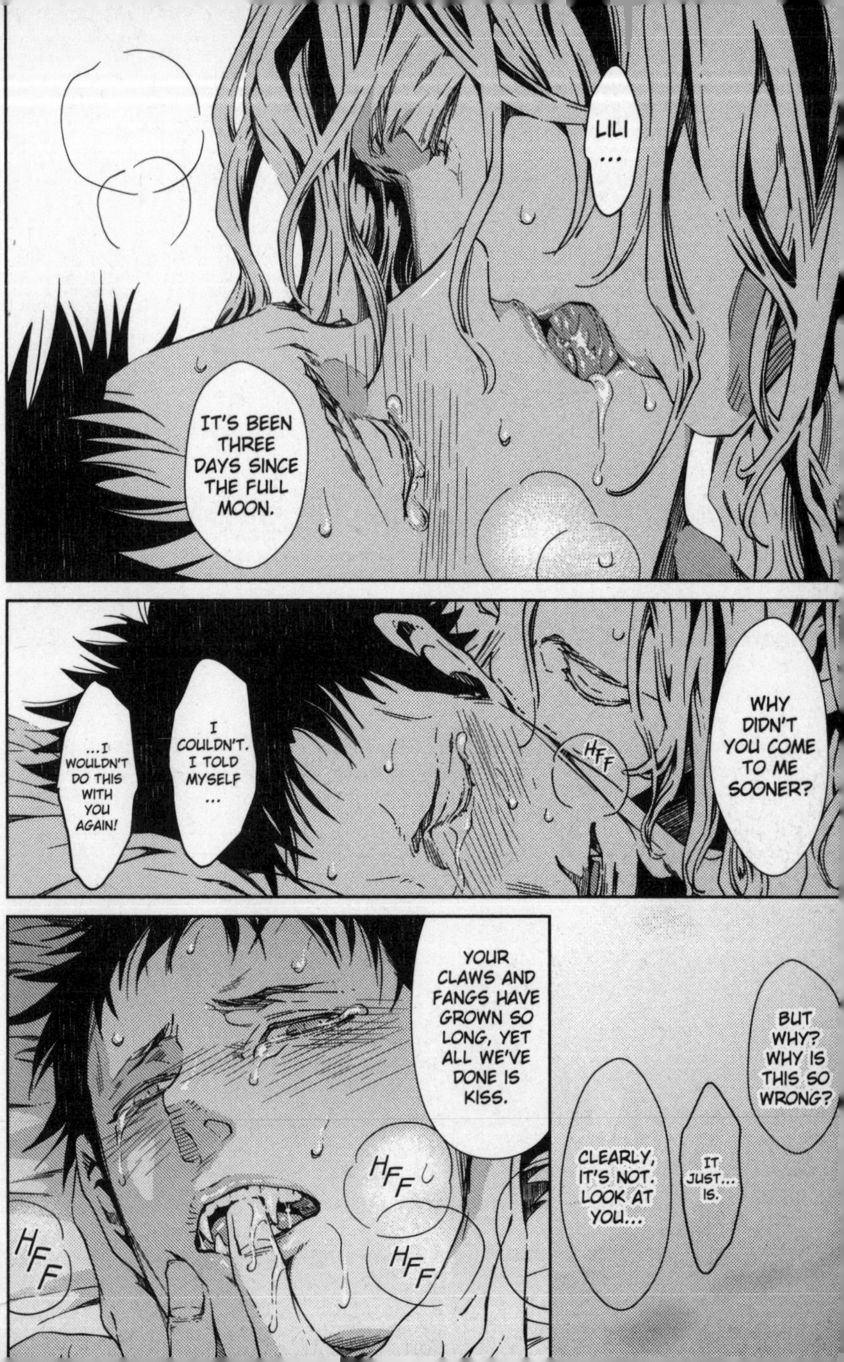
LILI...
IT'S BEEN THREE DAYS SINCE THE FULL MOON.
WHY DIDN'T YOU COME TO ME SOONER?
HFF
I COULDN'T. I TOLD MYSELF...
...I WOULDN'T DO THIS WITH YOU AGAIN!
BUT WHY? WHY IS THIS SO WRONG?
IT JUST... IS.
CLEARLY, IT'S NOT. LOOK AT YOU...
YOUR CLAWS AND FANGS HAVE GROWN SO LONG, YET ALL WE'VE DONE IS KISS.
HFF
HFF
HFF

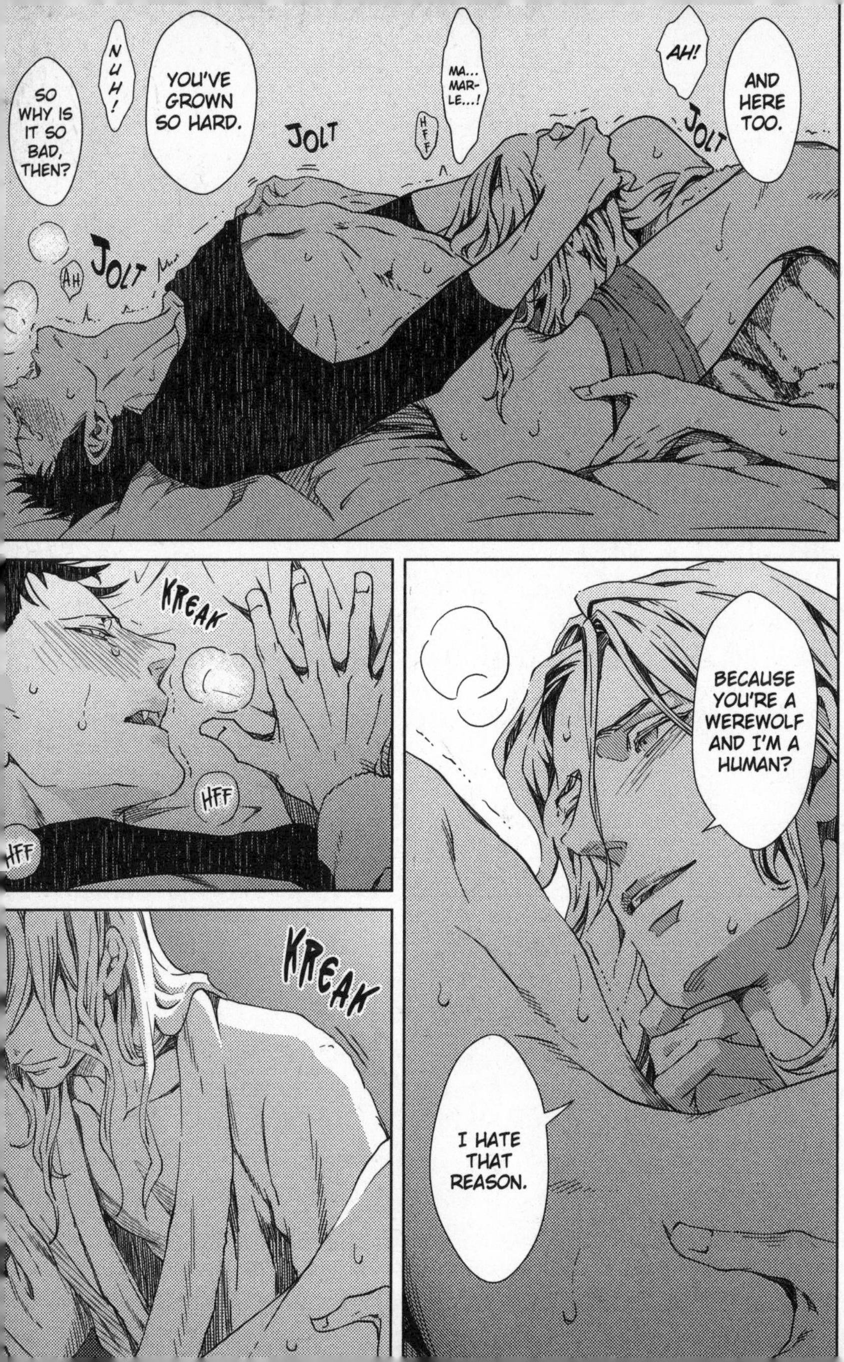
AND HERE TOO.
AH!
JOLT
MA... MARLE...!
HFF
JOLT
YOU'VE GROWN SO HARD.
NUH!
SO WHY IS IT SO BAD, THEN?
JOLT
AH
BECAUSE YOU'RE A WEREWOLF AND I'M A HUMAN?
I HATE THAT REASON.
KREAK
HFF
HFF
KREAK

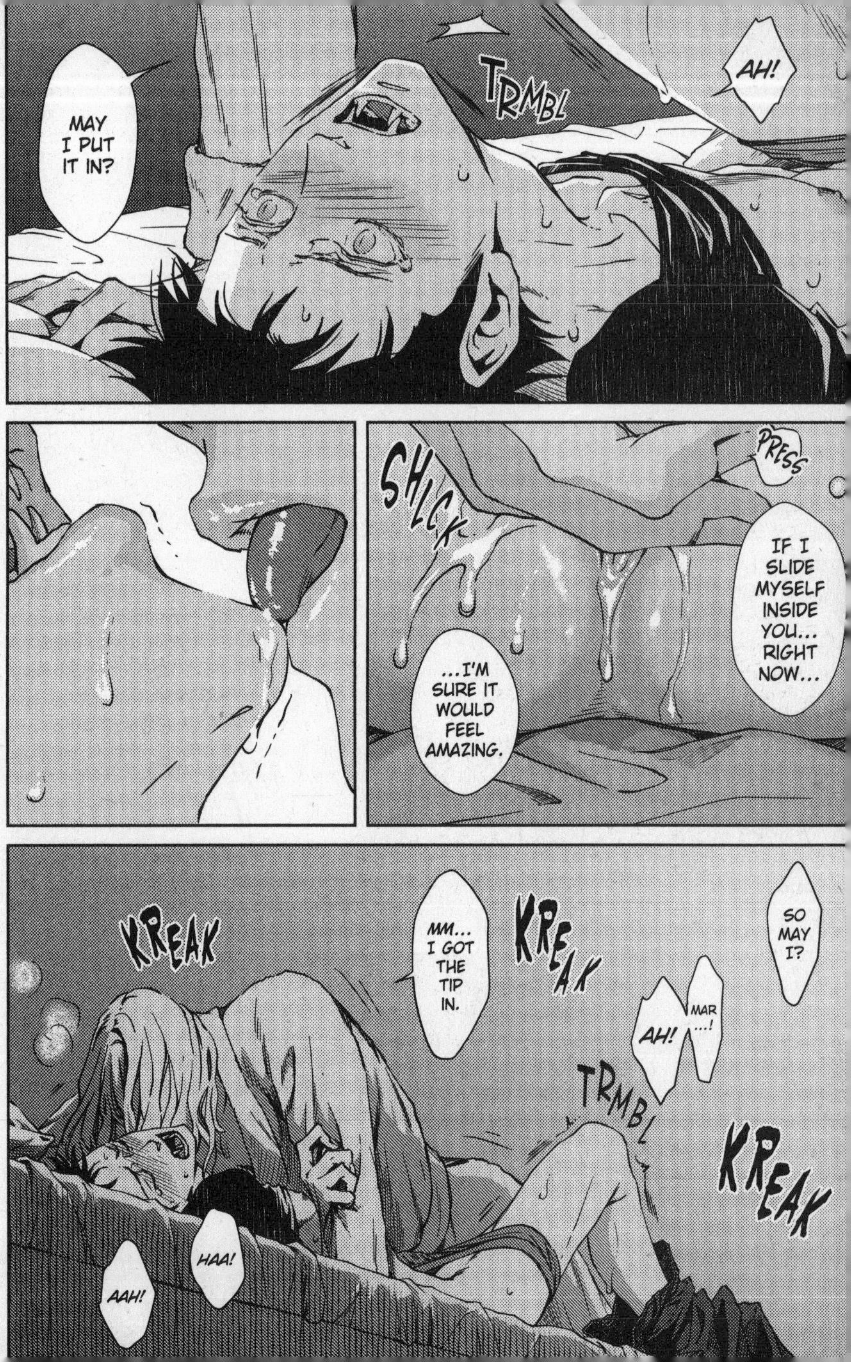
AH!
TRMBL
MAY I PUT IT IN?
PRESS
IF I SLIDE MYSELF INSIDE YOU... RIGHT NOW...
SHLICK
...I'M SURE IT WOULD FEEL AMAZING.
SO MAY I?
MAR ...!
AH!
KREAK
MM... I GOT THE TIP IN.
KREAK
TRMBL
KREAK
HAA!
AAH!
KREAK

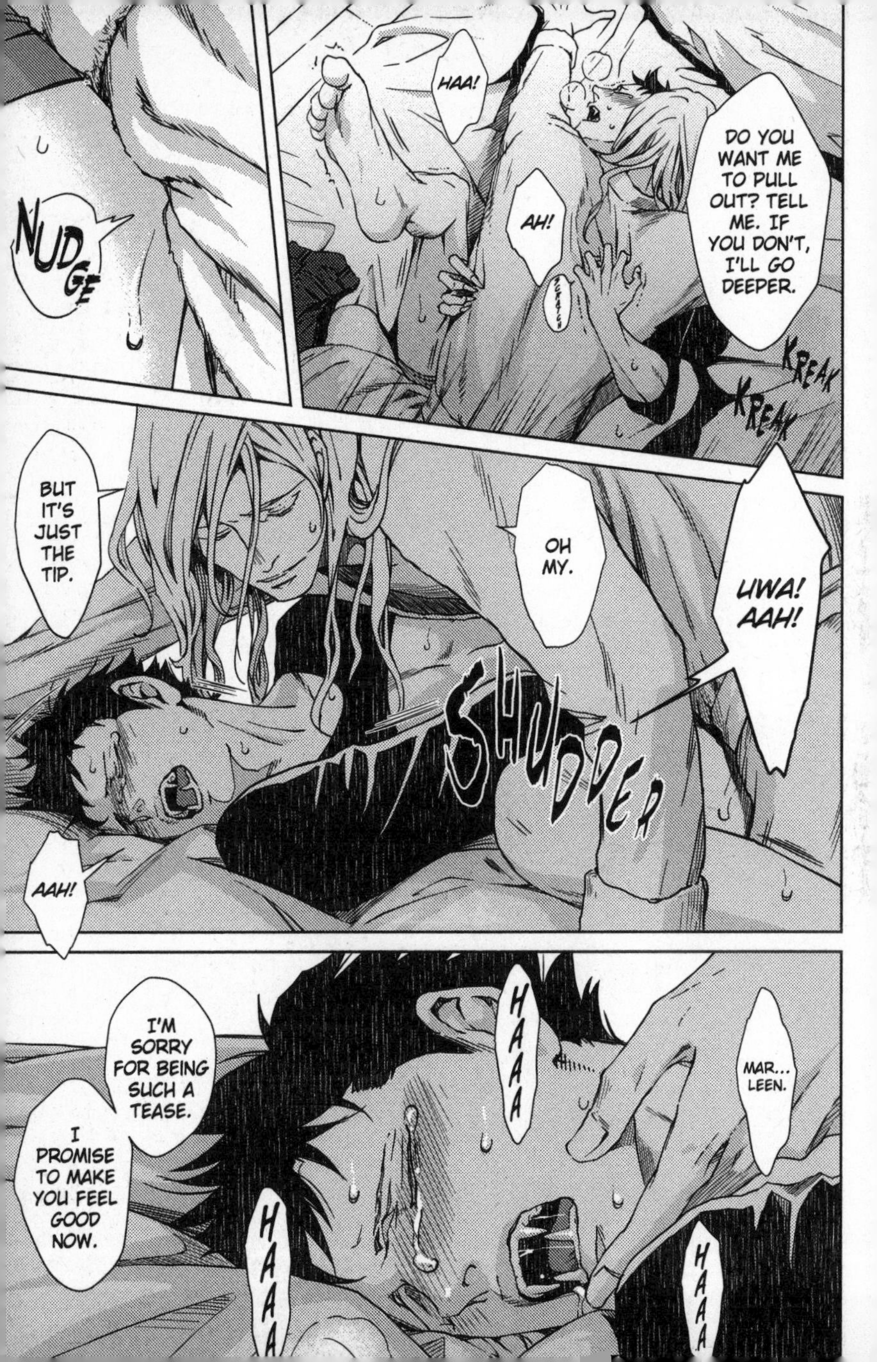
HAA!
DO YOU WANT ME TO PULL OUT? TELL ME. IF YOU DON'T, I'LL GO DEEPER.
AH!
KREAK
KREAK
NUDGE
UWA! AAH!
OH MY.
SHUDDER
BUT IT'S JUST THE TIP.
AAH!
MAR... LEEN.
HAAA
HAAA
I'M SORRY FOR BEING SUCH A TEASE.
I PROMISE TO MAKE YOU FEEL GOOD NOW.
HAAA

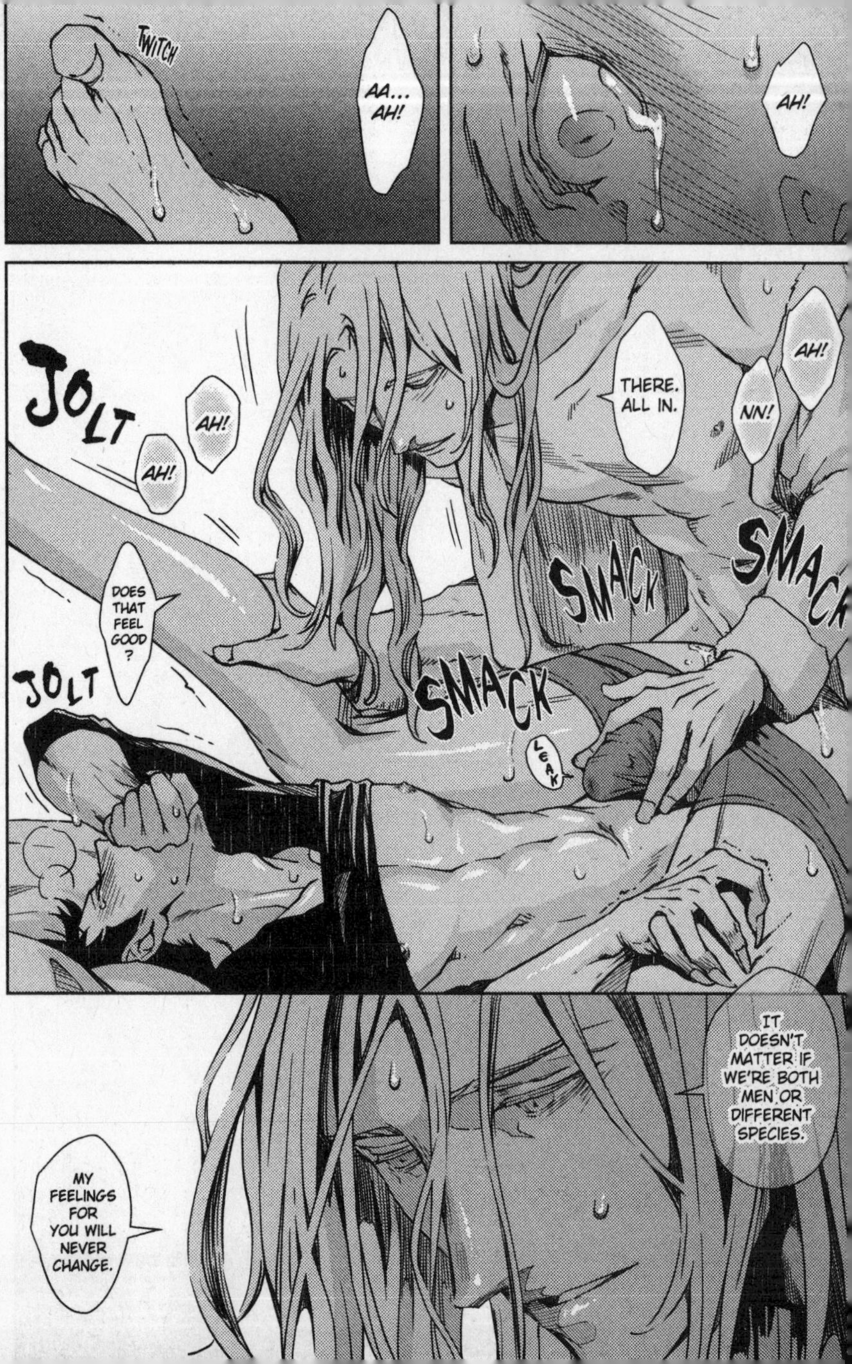
AH!
TWITCH
AA... AH!
AH!
NN!
THERE. ALL IN.
SMACK
SMACK
AH!
AH!
JOLT
SMACK
LEAK
DOES THAT FEEL GOOD?
JOLT
IT DOESN'T MATTER IF WE'RE BOTH MEN OR DIFFERENT SPECIES.
MY FEELINGS FOR YOU WILL NEVER CHANGE.

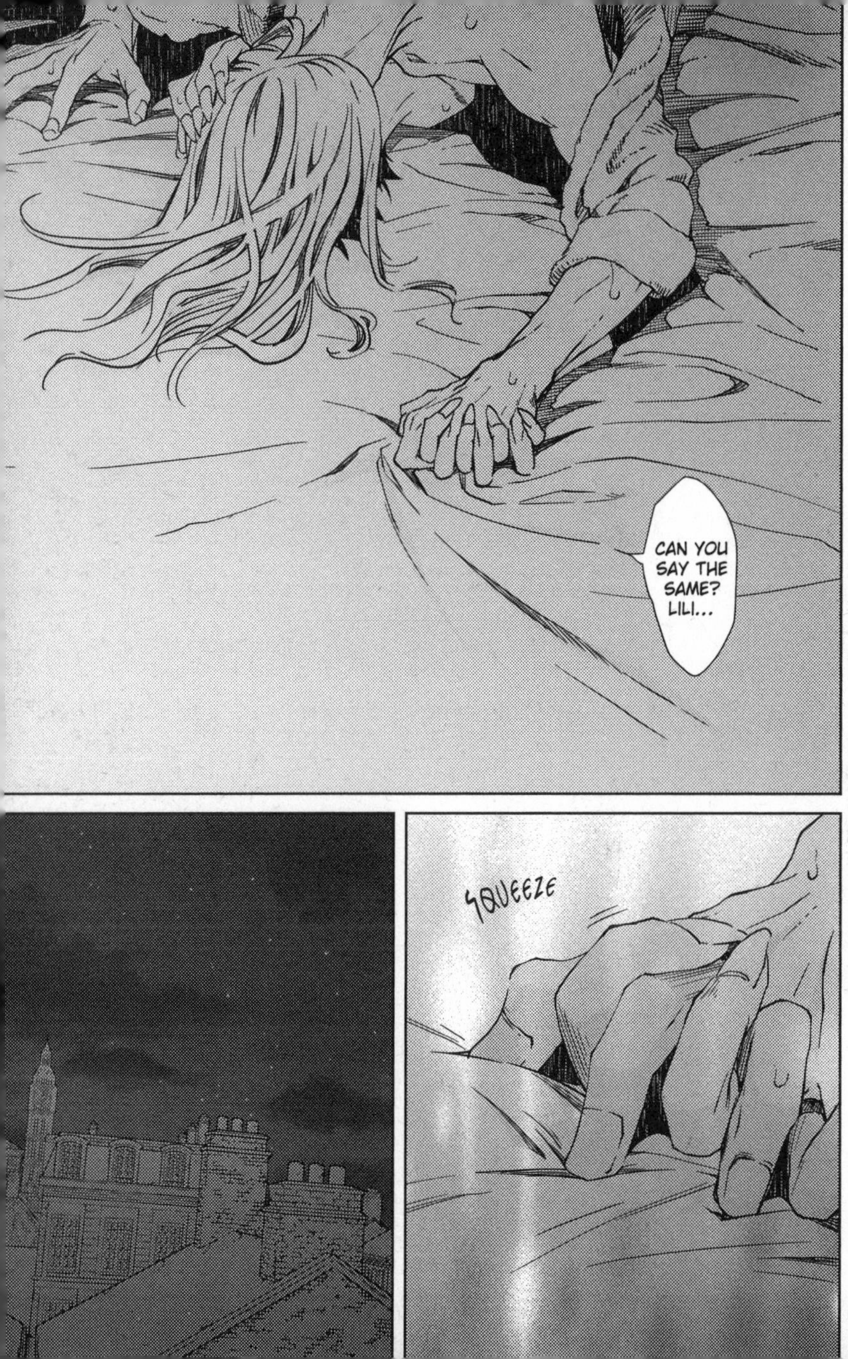
CAN YOU SAY THE SAME? LILI...
SQUEEZE

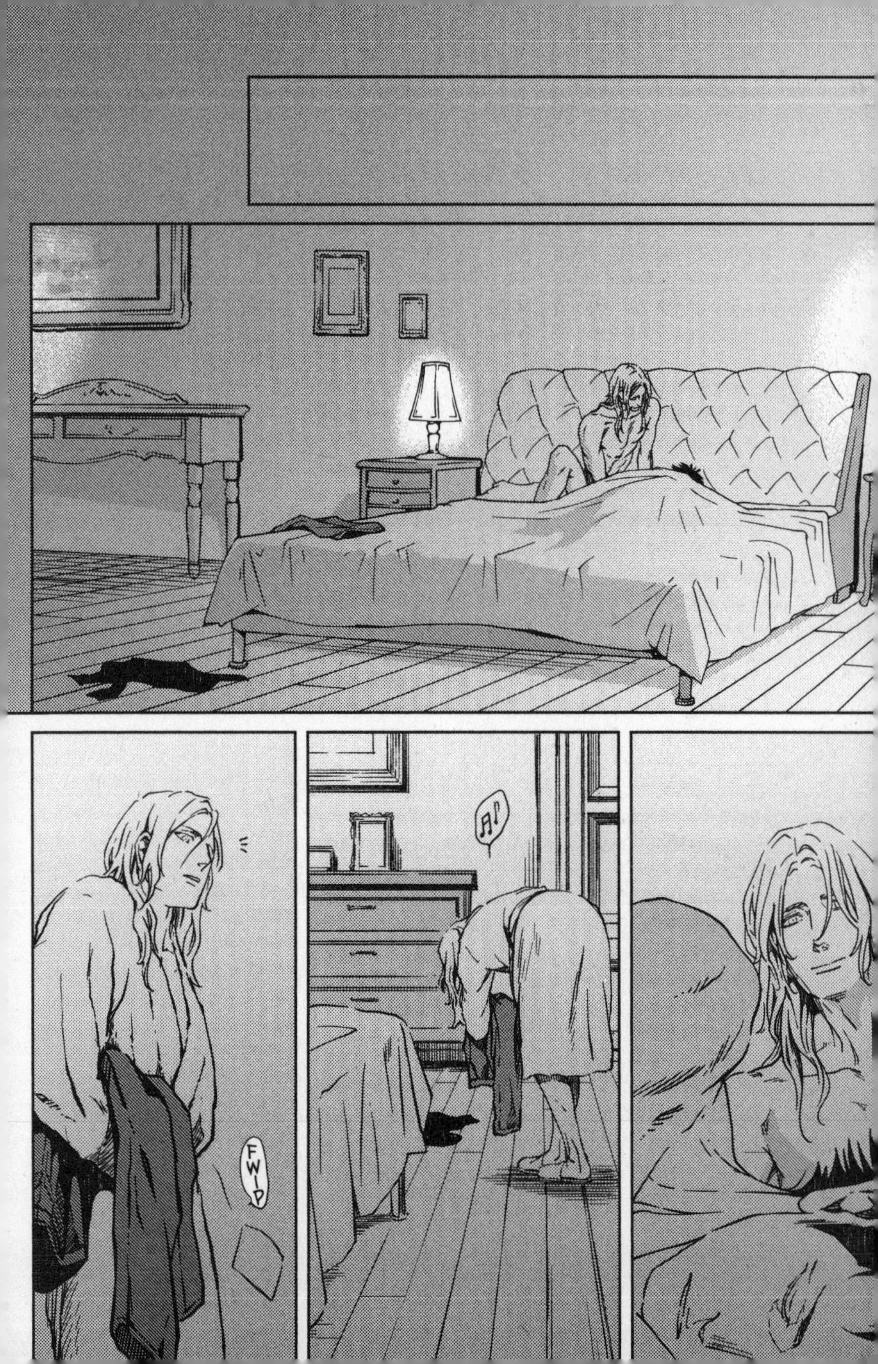
FWIP

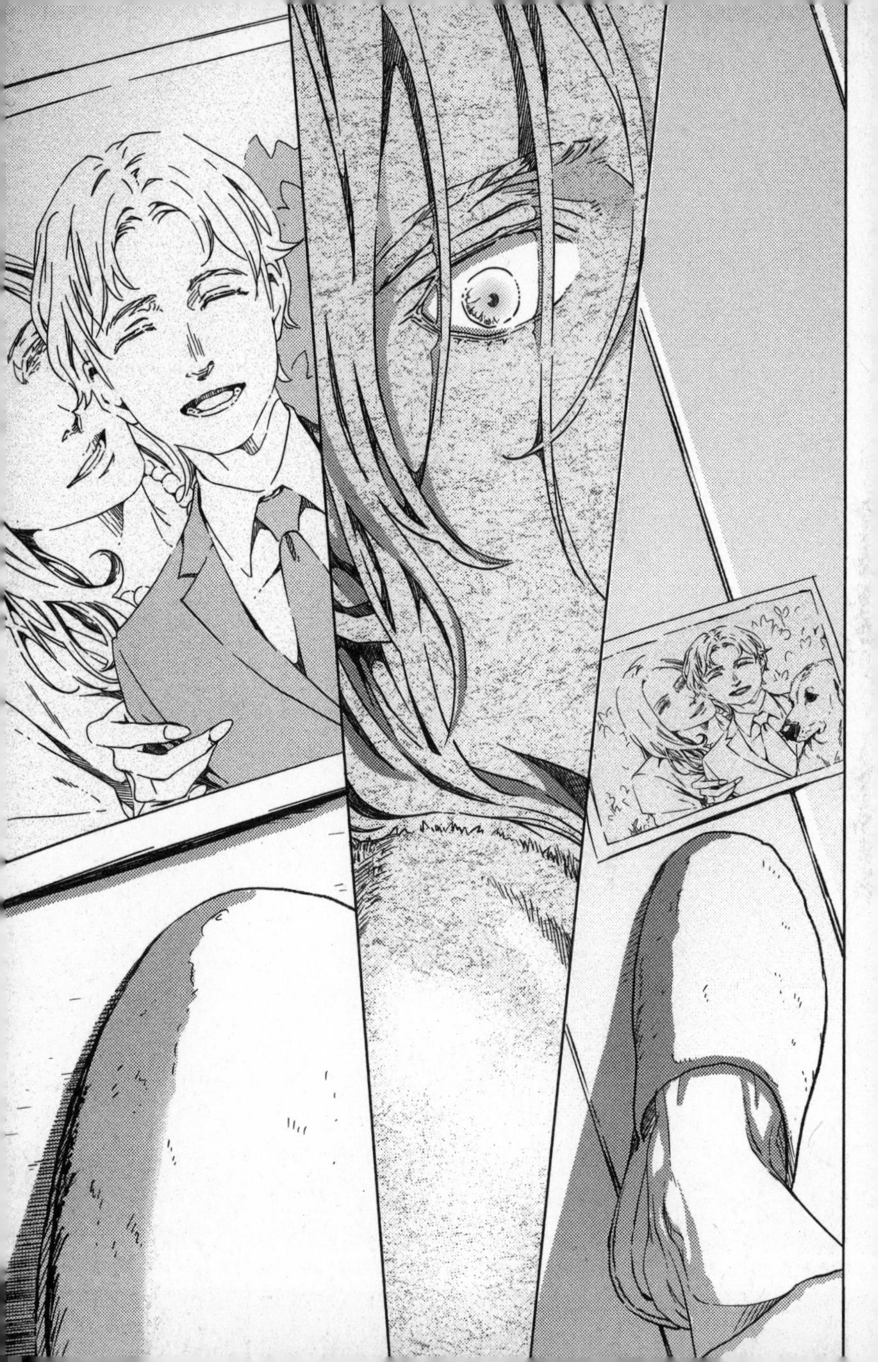

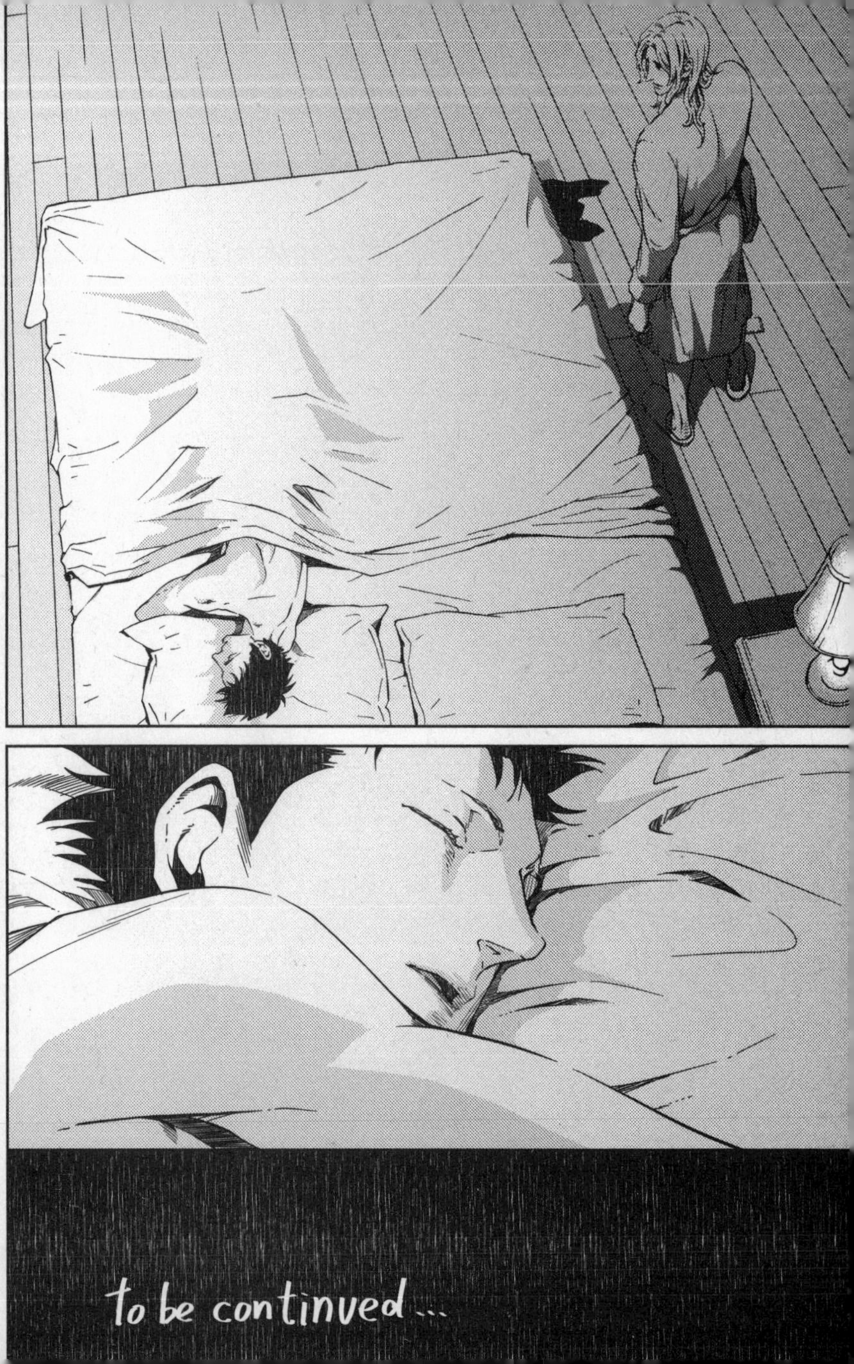
to be continued...

sweet days

Scene 2: A Week at Marleen's Place

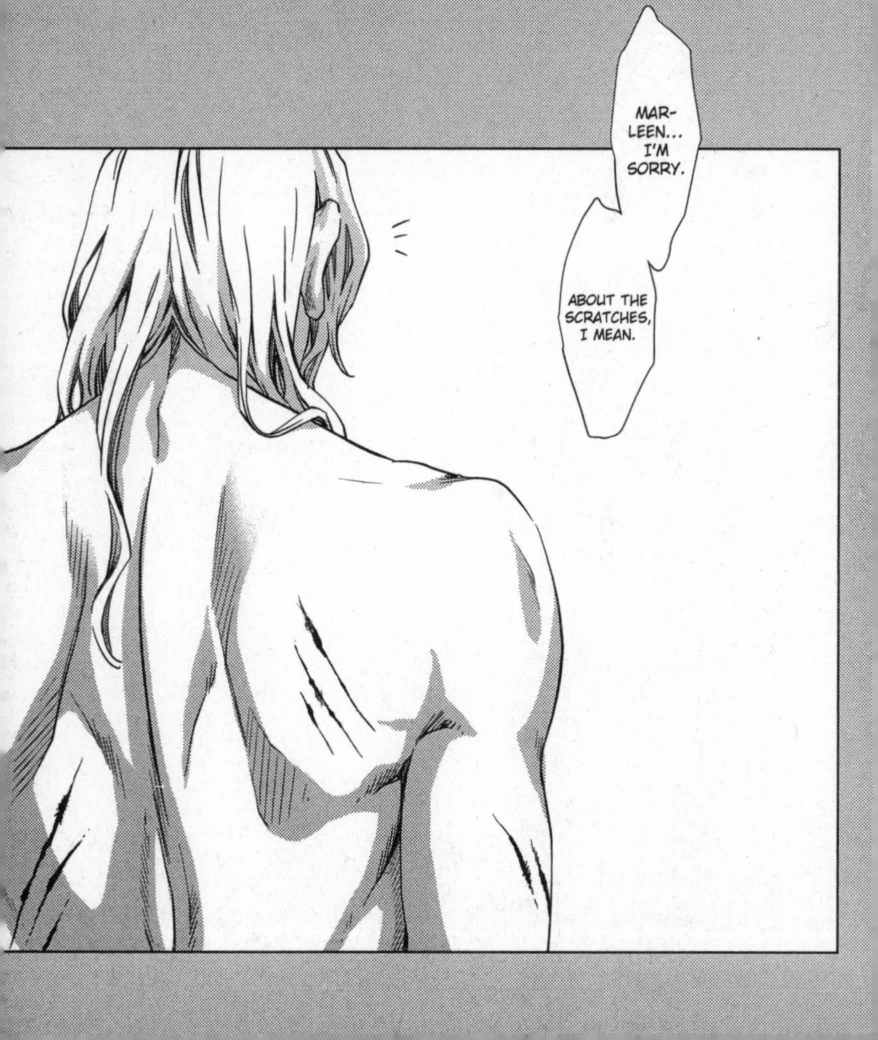
MAR-LEEN... I'M SORRY.
ABOUT THE SCRATCHES, I MEAN.

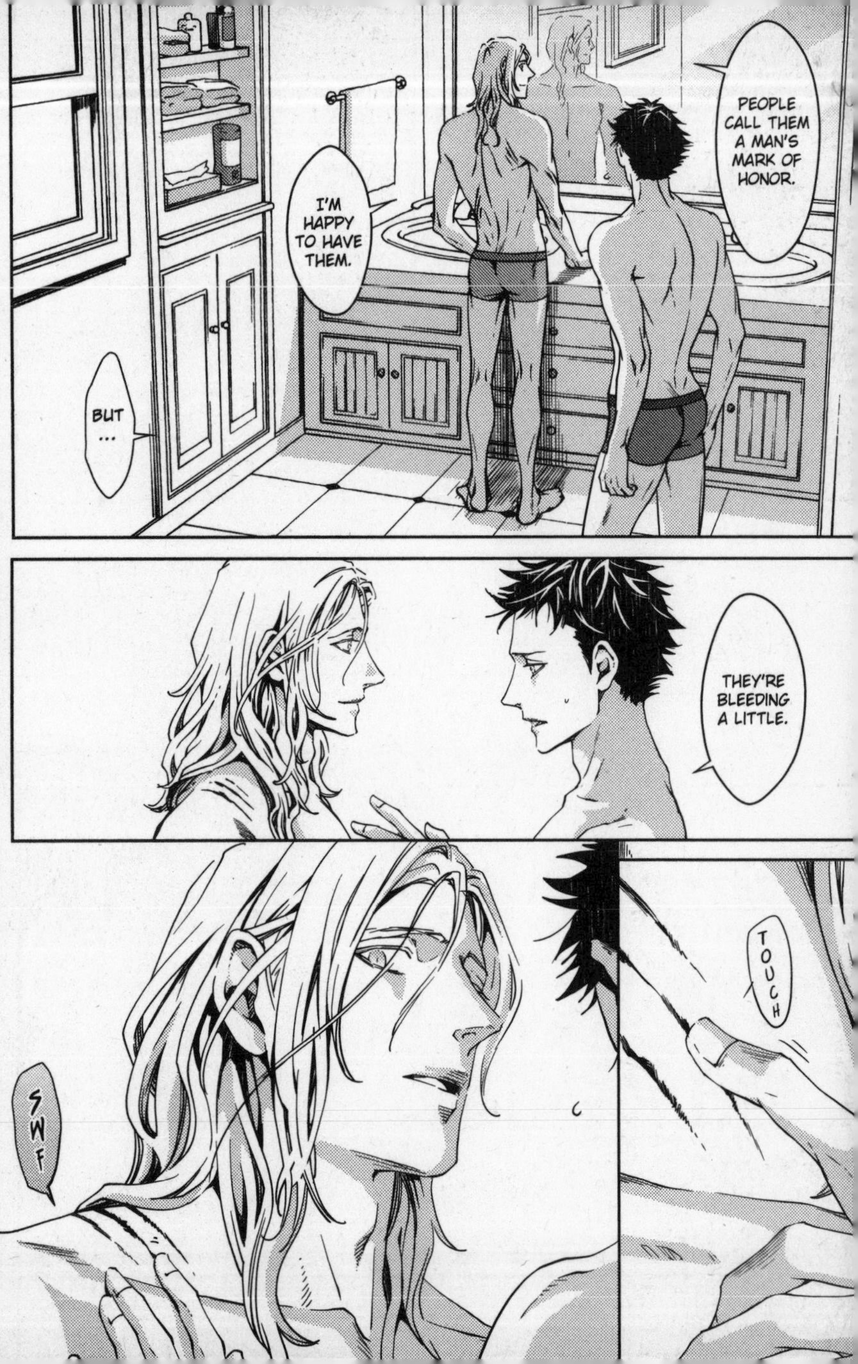
PEOPLE CALL THEM A MAN'S MARK OF HONOR.
I'M HAPPY TO HAVE THEM.
BUT ...
THEY'RE BLEEDING A LITTLE.
TOUCH
SWF

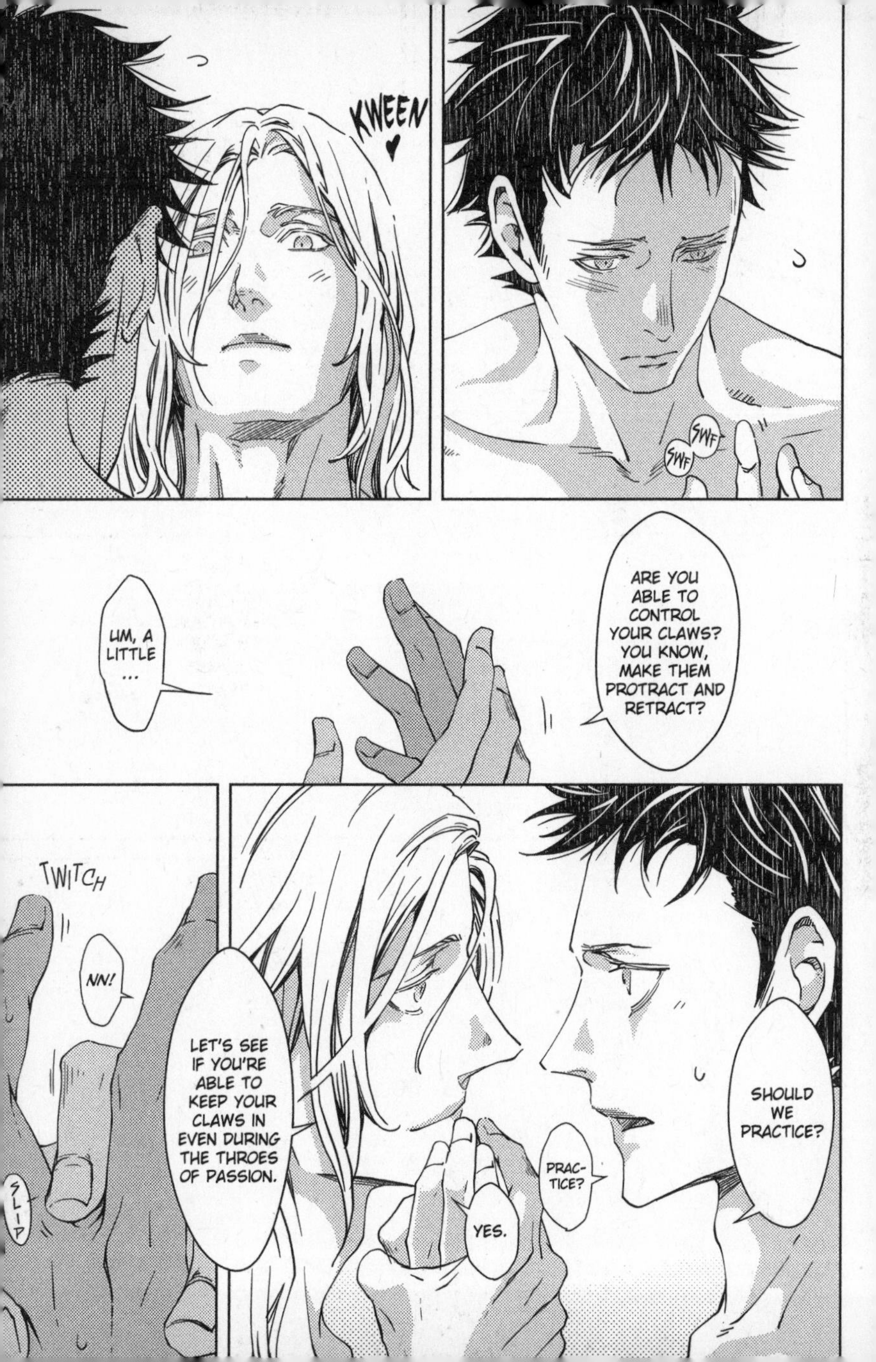
SWF
SWF
KWEEN ♥
ARE YOU ABLE TO CONTROL YOUR CLAWS? YOU KNOW, MAKE THEM PROTRACT AND RETRACT?
UM, A LITTLE ...
SHOULD WE PRACTICE?
PRAC-TICE?
YES.
LET'S SEE IF YOU'RE ABLE TO KEEP YOUR CLAWS IN EVEN DURING THE THROES OF PASSION.
TWITCH
NN!
SLIP

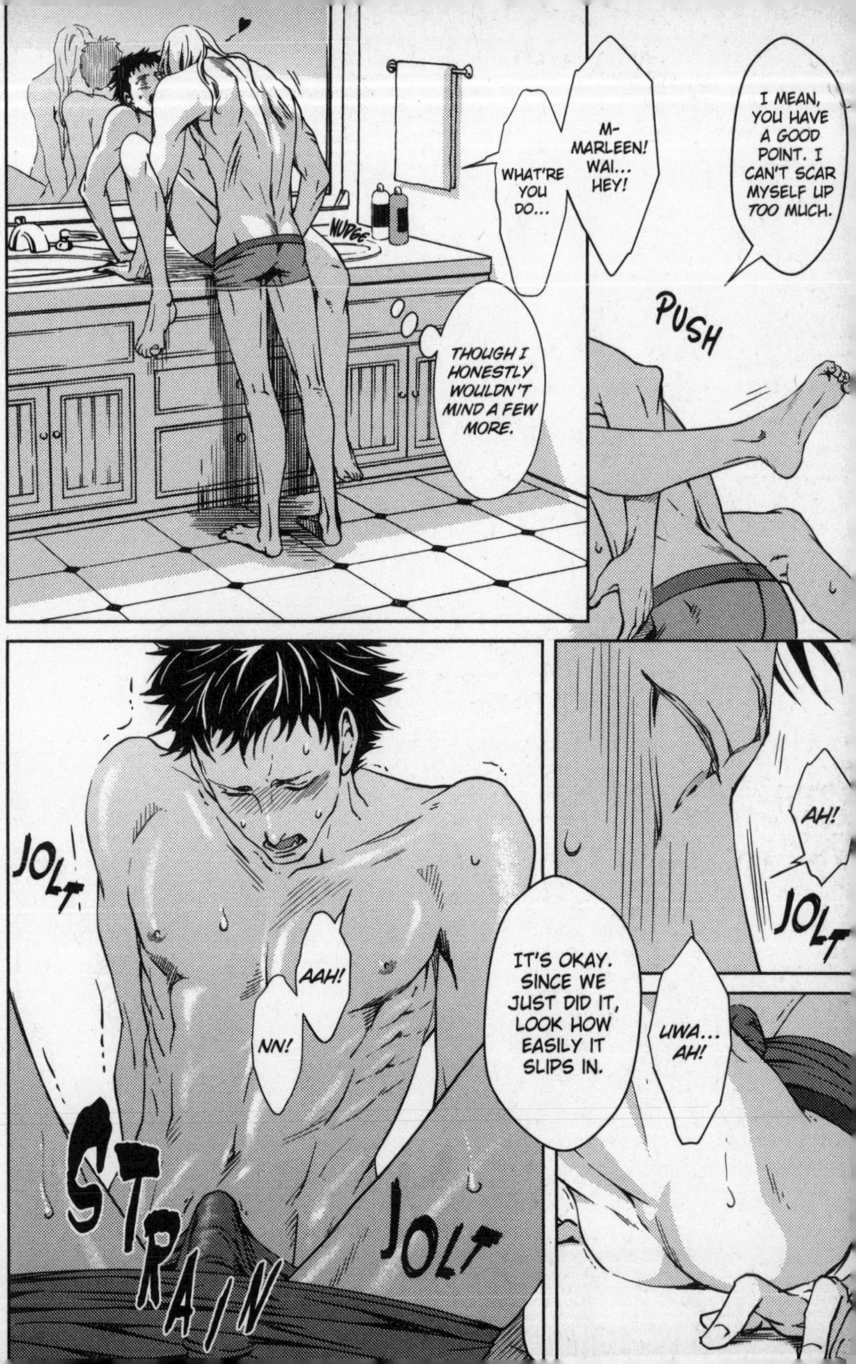
I MEAN, YOU HAVE A GOOD POINT. I CAN'T SCAR MYSELF UP TOO MUCH.
PUSH
M-MARLEEN! WAI... HEY!
WHAT'RE YOU DO...
NUDGE
THOUGH I HONESTLY WOULDN'T MIND A FEW MORE.
AH!
JOLT
UWA... AH!
IT'S OKAY. SINCE WE JUST DID IT, LOOK HOW EASILY IT SLIPS IN.
AAH!
NN!
JOLT
JOLT
STRAIN

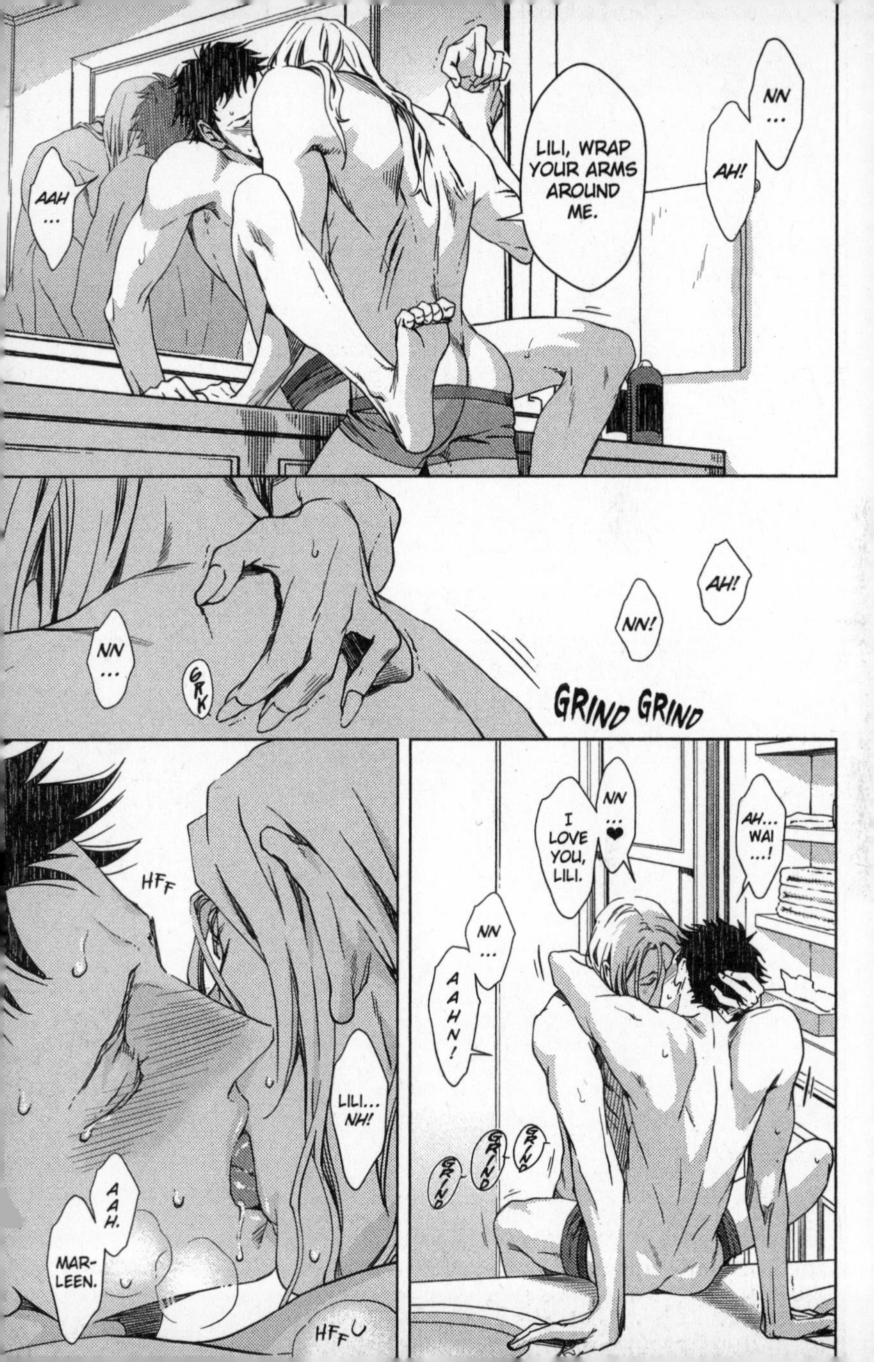
NN...
AH!
LILI, WRAP YOUR ARMS AROUND ME.
AAH...
AH!
NN!
GRIND GRIND
GRK
NN...
AH... WAI...!
NN... ❤
I LOVE YOU, LILI.
NN...
AAHN!
GRIND
GRIND
GRIND
LILI... NH!
HFF
AAH. MARLEEN.
HFF

DIG

...? MAR- LEEN?

AH?

PAUSE

HFF

HFF

NOW'S A GOOD TIME TO PRACTICE. TRY RETRACTING YOUR CLAWS. WHEN YOU DO... I'LL CONTINUE.

YOU CAN DO IT.

B... BUT...

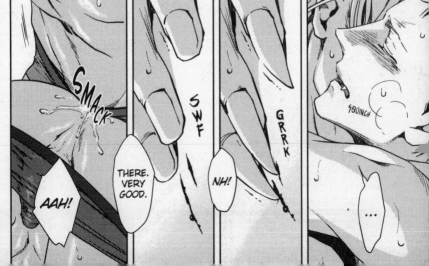

SMACK

SWF

GRRK

SQUINCH

AAH!

THERE. VERY GOOD.

NH!

...

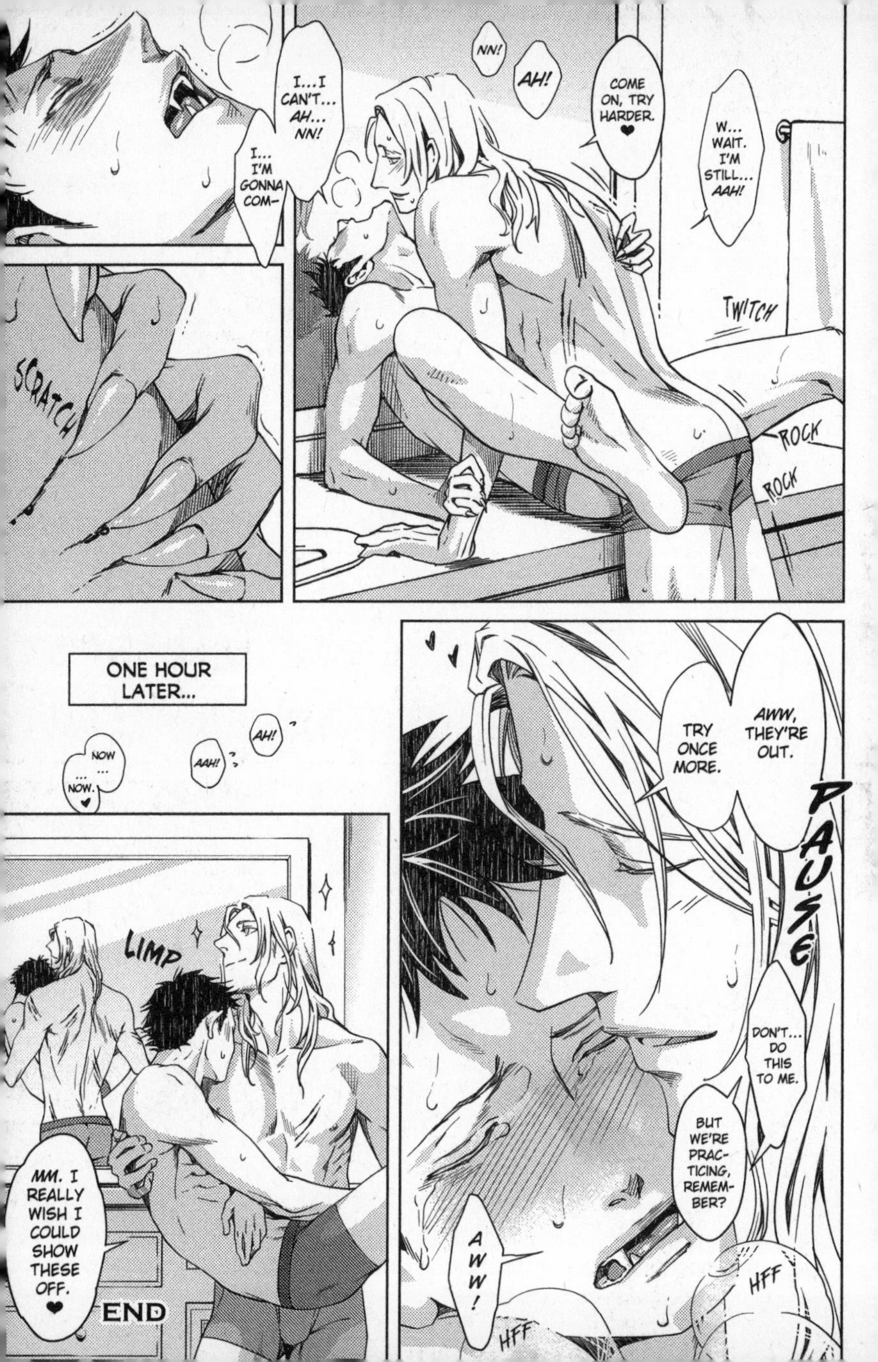

W... WAIT. I'M STILL... AAH!
COME ON, TRY HARDER. ❤
AH!
NN!
TWITCH
ROCK
ROCK
I...I CAN'T... AH... NN!
I... I'M GONNA COM-
SCRATCH
AWW, THEY'RE OUT.
TRY ONCE MORE.
PAUSE
DON'T... DO THIS TO ME.
BUT WE'RE PRAC-TICING, REMEM-BER?
AWW!
HFF
HFF
ONE HOUR LATER...
AH!
AAH!
NOW... NOW. ❤
LIMP
MM. I REALLY WISH I COULD SHOW THESE OFF. ❤
END

About the Author

Coyote is **RANMARU ZARIYA**'s second English-language release following *Void*. She also publishes *doujinshi* (independent comics) under the circle name "**ZARIA**." You can find out more about her on her Twitter page, **@zaria_ranmaru**.

Coyote
Volume 1
SuBLime Manga Edition

Story and Art by **RANMARU ZARIYA**

Additional Translation—**Christine Dashiell**
Touch-Up Art and Lettering—**Mara Coman**
Cover and Graphic Design—**Yukiko Whitley**
Editor—**Jennifer LeBlanc**

Originally published in Japan in 2016 by Frontier Works Inc., Tokyo Japan.

Printed in the U.S.A.

Published by SuBLime Manga
P.O. Box 77010
San Francisco, CA 94107

10 9 8 7 6 5 4 3 2 1
First printing, October 2018

M
MATURE
PARENTAL ADVISORY
COYOTE is rated M for Mature and is recommended for mature readers. This volume contains graphic imagery and mature themes.

SUBLIME
www.SuBLimeManga.com

For more information

on all our products, along with the most up-to-date news on releases, series announcements, and contests, please visit us at:

 SuBLimeManga.com

 twitter.com/**SuBLimeManga**

 facebook.com/**SuBLimeManga**

 instagram.com/**SuBLimeManga**

 SuBLimeManga.tumblr.com

Downloading is as easy as:

1

2

3

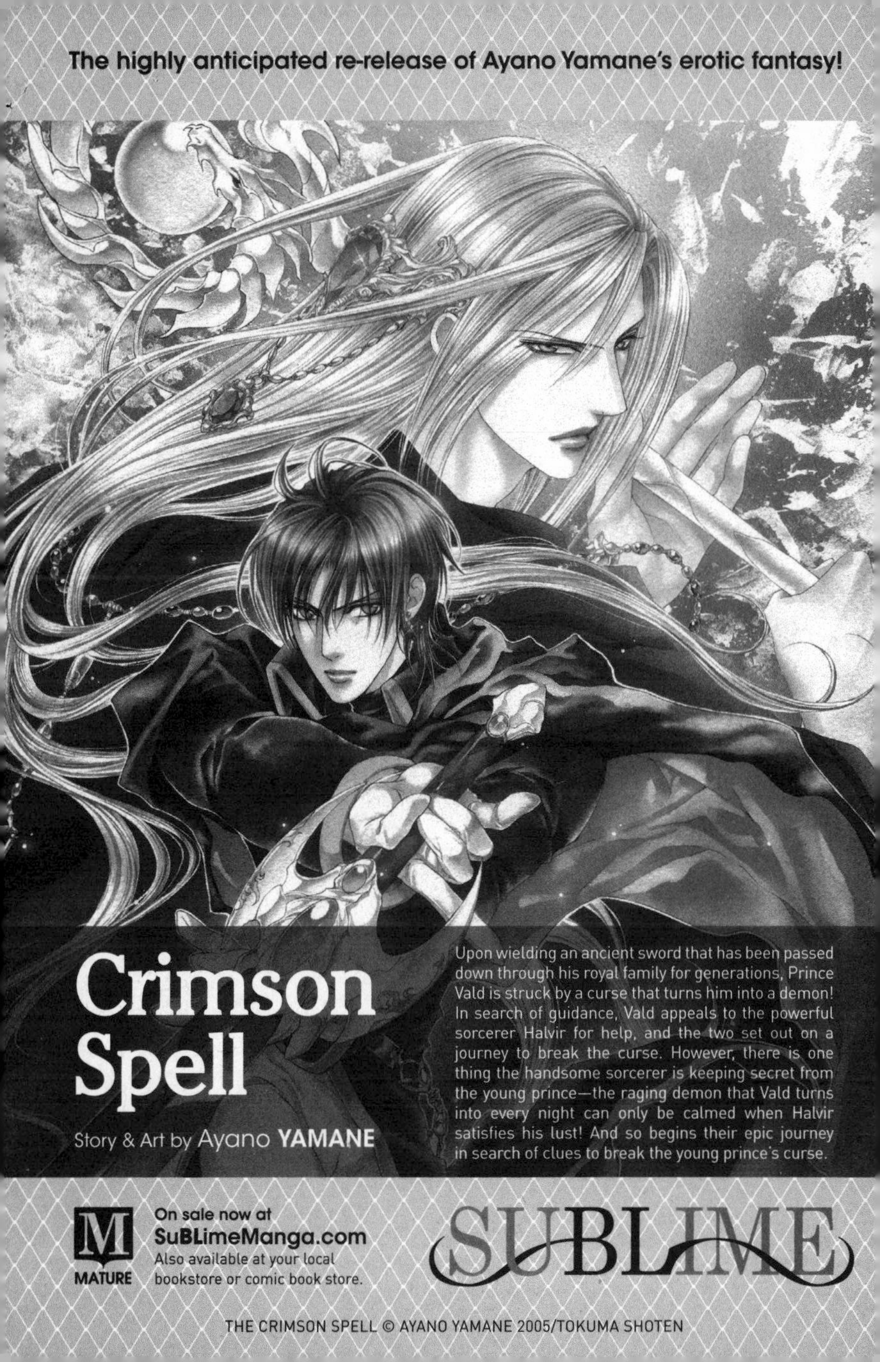

A collection of masterful, sensual stories by Kou Yoneda!

NightS

Story & Art by Kou YONEDA

In the title story, Masato Karashima is a "transporter," a man paid to smuggle anything from guns to drugs to people. When he's hired by yakuza gang member Masaki Hozumi, he finds himself attracted to the older man, and what starts out as a business transaction quickly spirals into a cat-and-mouse game of lust and deception. In "Emotion Spectrum," a high-school student tries to be a good wingman for a classmate, with an unexpected result, while "Reply" is told from the alternating perspectives of an emotionally reserved salesman and the shy mechanic who's in love with him.